OKLAHOMA

A History of Five Centuries

Second Edition

by Arrell Morgan Gibson

University of Oklahoma Press : *Norman and London*

By **Arrell Morgan Gibson**

The Kickapoos: Lords of the Middle Border (Norman, 1963)
The Life and Death of Colonel Albert Jennings Fountain (Norman, 1965)
Fort Smith: Little Gibraltar on the Arkansas (with Edwin C. Bearss) (Norman, 1969)
The Chickasaws (Norman, 1971)
The Canadian: Highway of History (New York, 1971)
Wilderness Bonanza: The Tri-State District of Missouri, Kansas, and Oklahoma (Norman, 1972)
(editor) *Frontier Historian: The Life and Work of Edward Everett Dale* (Norman, 1975)
The West in the Life of the Nation (Lexington, Mass., 1976)
America's Exiles: Indian Colonization in Oklahoma (Oklahoma City, 1976)
The Oklahoma Story (Norman, 1978)
Will Rogers: A Centennial Tribute (Oklahoma City, 1979)
The American Indian: Prehistory to the Present (Lexington, Mass., 1980)
Oklahoma: A History of Five Centuries (Norman, 1981)

Library of Congress Cataloging-in-Publication Data

Gibson, Arrell Morgan.
Oklahoma, a history of five centuries.

Bibliography: p. 289.
Includes index.
1. Oklahoma—History. I. Title.
F694.G49 1981 976.6 81–40284
AACR2

ISBN: 0–8061–1758–3

 First printing of the University of Oklahoma Press edition, 1981; second printing, 1985; third printing, 1988; fourth printing, 1991.

To
Samuel D. Gibson
Chickasaw Nation Pioneer

Contents

Illustrations

MAPS

Preface

The American West is probably the most popular single subject in history today, and all the fixtures of the American West—Indians, cavalry, frontier military posts, outlaws, lawmen, traders and trappers, ranching and trail drives, and the homesteaders—are basic in Oklahoma's past.

Writing this Oklahoma history has been one of my most delightful and challenging assignments. I found in the epic of Oklahoma a fascinating tone and a sustained drama that absorbed my interest from beginning to end. Yet it seemed presumptuous even to attempt to write the history of this state, for it is exceptionally long. The known Oklahoma story goes back fifteen or possibly twenty thousand years, and its chronicle is vast. As one of the last American frontiers, Oklahoma's historical dimension extends well beyond that of most American states.

Oklahoma history is diverse. Its components range from primitive Clovis man and the fabulous Spiro people of prehistory through a fascinating variety of Indian tribes. These blend with outlaws and lawmen, the cowboys, the Boomers, and the homesteaders. From all points of the compass came the hardy Eighty-Niners, bringing their politics and religion, their customs and lore. The frontier tradition for probing the unknown is carried forward by modern pioneers in the Frontiers of Science program in Oklahoma.

Oklahoma history is different, and it is dynamic. The frontier spirit still asserts itself in the energy, impulsiveness, irrepressible enthusiasm, and enduring optimism of modern Sooners.

Research resources on the Oklahoma epic are enormous and varied. Sources of prehistory include the writings of the Sooner State's archaeologists, notably Robert Bell, and artifact collections in Oklahoma museums. The National Archives, the Library of Congress, and the Bureau of American Ethnology, all in Washington, D.C., yielded significant information on the Oklahoma story. The Oklahoma State Historical Society in Oklahoma City contains extensive collections on Oklahoma's past. Society officers and staff members deserve praise for their interest and help.

Treasures of the Thomas Gilcrease Institute of American History and Art, in Tulsa, including the Catlin Journals, the John Ross Papers, and an outstanding collection of Boomer literature, supply vital information on Sooner State history. The University of Oklahoma Library, especially its Western History Collections, which contains vast resources on Indian, Oklahoma, and western history, has been a fundamental source in producing this story.

Unless otherwise noted, the illustrations in this book were reproduced from the collections of the University of Oklahoma Library.

Arrell Morgan Gibson

Norman, Oklahoma

OKLAHOMA
A History of Five Centuries

Chapter 1

The Natural Setting

A few decades ago Oklahoma was distinguished more for the migration of its people out to other, more economically promising states than for any of its distinctly different qualities. Then, in the 1950s, far-sighted and progressive Oklahoma leaders at the state and national government levels began to develop much-needed water resources and to actively campaign to attract new industries that would provide jobs to keep Oklahomans at home. Today Oklahoma is rapidly becoming much like other states in its political, economic, and social qualities.

Aside from features of the natural environment such as climate and land forms—and some of these are being changed by technology—one finds modern Oklahoma little different from Massachusetts, New York, Illinois, or California. Communications, the stirring about of people, and economic diversification are erasing those unique local characteristics that formerly made it easy to identify the geographic origin of an individual. World War II triggered a massive geographical circulation of people, and postwar industrial transfers and other movements have accelerated cultural integration to the point that provincial accents and viewpoints are fading. In addition, radio, television, interstate highway systems, and air travel are doing their share to replace state and local cultures with a national culture. Regional economic specialization is passing, too. For example, until recently, stock raising was largely restricted to the grasslands of the American West. Now it is practiced in almost every region of the United States, while other industries and associated economic activities once the exclusive specialty of the industrial East are being established in the West. Certainly the increasing activity of the national government in state and local affairs—through court decisions; entry into public education, research, conservation projects, and urban renewal; and increased control of business, communications, and transportation—has helped to destroy state and regional uniqueness and to nationalize culture.

This nationalizing process makes it likely that events in Oklahoma and other states for the remainder of this century will be so nearly alike that it will become difficult to justify individual modern state histories. Oklahoma's history to the middle of the twentieth century, however, has a depth, variety, and dramatic quality that very few states can surpass. Except for the original thirteen states and Texas, Hawaii, California, and Alaska, the states of the American Union, formed under the pattern of the old Northwest Ordinance, share stories so similar that one could create a common mold and stuff each history into it—probing entries by daring settlers, expulsion of the aborigines, the increase in population to achieve territorial status, and then statehood—a formula repeated time and again from the Appalachians to the Pacific.

Oklahoma's fascinating past is due in part to the abundant exceptions to the general pattern of state histories. "Anomaly" is the best single word to characterize Oklahoma history. Oklahoma has more anomalies—has deviated more from the general pattern of state evolution—than any other state.

Abundant evidence of anomaly is found in Oklahoma's natural environment. Even the state's geographical outline fits this theme. The Indian Territory was at the mercy of the federal government until Oklahoma entered the Union in 1907. The surrounding states and territories were permitted to cannibalize the once vast domains of the Indian nations until that which remained became Oklahoma. Oklahoma's geographical format is also the product of international diplomacy. The southern boundary and most of the western boundary of Oklahoma were established by the Adams-Onís Treaty with Spain in 1819. A geographical orphan, No Man's Land, a ribbon of public land running between 100° and 103° west longitude, was attached to Oklahoma Territory in 1890, providing the Sooner State with the most conspicuous "panhandle" of all the states with similar appendages.

An inland state bounded by Kansas and Colorado on the north, Missouri and Arkansas on the east, Texas on the south, and Texas and New Mexico on the west, Oklahoma has an area of about seventy thousand square miles, or 45 million acres. Among the states of the Union, Oklahoma ranks eighteenth in geographical size, larger than the six New England states combined or any single state east of the Mississippi River. The Sooner State is divided into seventy-seven counties, the largest being Osage County in the north and the smallest, Marshall County in the south.

While Oklahoma's format was not completed until 1896 with the famous Greer County decision, discussed in chapter 14, its internal form, based on the regular United States public-land survey system of townships, sections, and quarter sections, was begun in 1870. To provide the future Oklahoma (then the Indian Territory) with this gridwork of north–south and east–west lines, surveyors selected a bearing point situated one mile south of Fort Arbuckle and eight miles west of present Davis, in what was then the Chickasaw Nation. Designating this location the Initial Point and marking it with a conspicuous stone shaft, government workers surveyed the entire Indian Territory. First, they ran a true north–south line from Kansas to Texas, which shows on Oklahoma maps as the Indian Meridian. Parallel lines called range lines, spaced six miles apart, were surveyed east to Arkansas and west to Texas. These six-mile ribbons east of the Indian Meridian were numbered consecutively Range One East, Range Two East, and so on, and those west of the Indian Merid-

ian were numbered consecutively Range One West, Range Two West, and so on. Next, an intersecting base line, running east to Arkansas and west to Texas, was laid off from the Initial Point. Parallel lines to this base line, called township lines, were laid out north to Kansas and south to Texas at six-mile intervals.

Each six-mile square thus formed became a township; Oklahoma was divided into two thousand townships, each containing thirty-six square miles or thirty-six sections of land, each section containing 640 acres. Cornerstones were placed in the ground at each section corner and on the corner of each quarter section. The Oklahoma Panhandle was surveyed by range on the Cimarron Meridian (the western boundary of Oklahoma at 103° W), and the township lines were laid off from the Panhandle's southern boundary (36°30') as a base line.

In relief and landforms Oklahoma is a sort of crazy quilt that provides the state with a variety of environments. The state's drainage plane is from northwest to southeast, ranging from 5,000 feet above sea level at Black Mesa in the far-northwestern corner of the Panhandle to 325 feet in the southeastern corner on the Red River. Oklahoma's mean elevation is 1,300 feet above sea level. So scrambled are the landforms that some streams flow north and west before they enter the regular drainage pattern. The average slope for the entire region from the Rocky Mountains to the Mississippi is 6 to 8 feet per mile.

Four principal mountain systems are found in Oklahoma: the Ozark, Ouachita, Arbuckle, and Wichita formations. The Ozarks overflow into northeastern Oklahoma from southwestern Missouri and northwestern Arkansas. Several of Oklahoma's most beautiful streams form and drain on the western slopes of the colorful Ozarks. South of the Arkansas River in eastern Oklahoma is a series of local mountain chains, including the Kiamichi, San Bois, Winding Stair, and Jack Fork mountains, all of which are associated with the parent Ouachita formation in western Arkansas. South-central Oklahoma has the famous Arbuckle chain, an extensive mountain system covering 1,000 square miles, and of interest to the naturalist and geologist because of the surface exposure of the base materials of which mountains are

Glass Mountains, Major County.

made. On Oklahoma's southwestern margins are the Wichita Mountains, rich in history and a welcome relief to the Great Plains environment occurring on all sides of the formation. Several local systems, including the Quartz Mountains, are satellites of the greater Wichita formation.

Throughout Oklahoma the prairies and plains are interrupted by peculiar ancient formations, many now eroded into buttes, mesas, and low-lying hills. These include the Osage Hills of north-central Oklahoma; the Glass Mountains of northwestern Oklahoma; the Antelope Hills, far up the valley of the Canadian; and majestic Black Mesa, a lava cap that is Oklahoma's closest association with the towering Rocky Mountain system, in the far-northwestern corner of the state. Many classes of rocks and minerals (limestone, sandstone, granite, gypsum, and shale) are dispersed over the state, and the weathering, decomposing, and eroding of these primary rocks have produced a variety of soils.

Oklahoma is drained by two great regional river systems: the Arkansas River system, which carries about two-thirds of the state's runoff, and the Red River system, which car-ries the other third. The Arkansas forms a snow-fed, fast-running, clear mountain stream in the Colorado Rockies. After entering Oklahoma, the river gathers the Salt Fork; the Chikaskia; the Cimarron or Red Fork; the Verdigris; the Grand; and the Illinois, which flow from the northern margins of the state. The principal southern feeder of the Arkansas is the Canadian. This stream, which crosses the Texas Panhandle into Oklahoma, is often improperly called the South Canadian. The North Canadian, formed by the junction of Beaver River and Wolf Creek in the northwestern corner of the state, enters the Canadian at historic North Fork Town, near present Eufaula. Nearby a stream flowing from the south across Pittsburg County, in early times known as the South Canadian, but now called Gaines Creek, joins the parent stream. Gaines Creek is the true South Canadian.

The other major drainage stream for Oklahoma is Red River. Forming on the high plains of the Texas Panhandle, the Red forms Oklahoma's southern boundary from the 100th meridian east, picking up the North Fork, the Washita, the Boggy, the Blue, and the Kiamichi rivers.

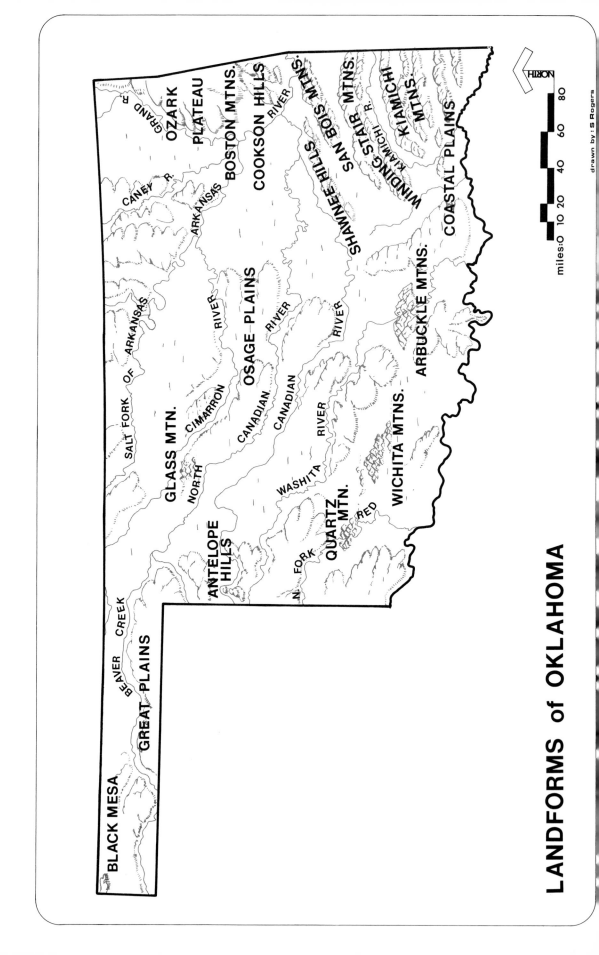

LANDFORMS of OKLAHOMA

miles: 0 10 20   40   60   80

drawn by : S Rogers

Geographers have labeled Oklahoma variously: as the most northerly of the southern states; as the most southerly of the northern states; as a part of the Southwest; as a middle-western state; and as a border state. In terms of natural as well as human factors, all designations apply to some degree—some more accurately than others. Oklahoma is a border land, a zone of transition climatically and politically, as well as in virtually every other respect. Oklahoma's climate is broadly classed as temperate but with variations caused by the blending of horizontal and vertical climatic zones. A humid belt in southern Oklahoma merges with a more variable and colder continental climatic belt on the northern margins of the state. The two vertical climatic zones in Oklahoma are the humid belt in the east and a dry western belt. The mixing of these climatic types produces generally pleasant, mild weather interspersed with widely variable seasonal fluctuations that include occasional hot summers and cold winters.

While Oklahoma's annual average temperature is about 60°F., the state's summers usually have several days above 100°F. Oklahoma winters frequently produce subzero temperatures, although the bitterly cold periods seldom last for extended periods. The highest recorded summer temperature in state history is 120°F. registered at Alva, Altus, Poteau, and Tishomingo in 1937; the lowest, a bitterly cold −27°F. registered at Vinita and Watts in 1917.

Rainfall distribution in Oklahoma varies more than temperature. Oklahoma City, near the center of the state, averages 32 inches a year, but in the southeast the average is 56 inches, and in the arid northwest the precipitation average is only 18 inches. In 1949 a record annual rainfall of 67 inches was recorded in the Kiamichi Mountains of southeastern Oklahoma. The least annual precipitation recorded in the state was 8½ inches in Boise City in the Panhandle in 1934.

Oklahoma is known throughout the nation and the world for many things, not the least of which are its climatic vagaries. Strategically situated on the continent, the state is a collision point for warm and cold air masses that produce abrupt weather changes—a sudden rise or fall in temperature, "northers" carrying destructive blizzards, and violent thunderstorms dispensing hail, lightning, and heavy rainfall. Throughout the year, but especially during the late-spring and early-summer months, these fronts spawn funnel-shaped, death-dealing tornadoes. The tornado that smashed Woodward in April, 1947, was one of the most destructive storms of this kind on record. Fatalities totaled 101 persons, nearly 1,000 persons were injured, and property losses amounted to approximately $10 million. While no part of Oklahoma is free of winds, the western half of the state, situated in the Great Plains weather focus, receives a steady airflow most of the year, predominantly from the south. The scattered trees in western Oklahoma are permanently bent toward the north.

Just as Oklahoma is a transition zone in terms of climate, the same is true for plant and animal life. Over 130 different kinds of trees have been identified as native to the state. Mixed-hardwood stands of maple, box elder, honey locust, sweet gum, oak, hickory, pecan, walnut, ash, beech, sycamore, dogwood, redbud, persimmon, and sassafras are found on the eastern margins of the state. Pine, cedar, cypress, holly, and magnolia grow in the east and southeast. Wild grape, Virginia creeper, poison ivy, the parasitic mistletoe, and sumac clumps add variety to the larger forest species.

Oklahoma's eastern forests gradually blend into the prairies and plains of the central and west, but even on the grasslands forest growths appear now and then, especially along the watercourses. These stands include cottonwood, elm, pecan, blackjack, post oak, willow, hackberry, cedar, and wild plum. West of the 98th meridian are the arid zone plants: shinnery oak, or shinoak; scraggly blackjack; mesquite; sage; and several species of cactus.

One of Oklahoma's most curious vegetation belts, important historically, is the Cross Timbers, a thickly packed stunted forest five to thirty miles wide, running almost diagonally from the southwest toward central Oklahoma. It includes blackjack, hickory, post oak, and shinnery oak, laced together with tightly woven, tangled undergrowth and briar. The Cross Timbers serve as a divide between the prairies of the east dominated by the bluestem and the shortgrass plains of western Oklahoma.

Buffalo herd grazing on the Great Plains of western Oklahoma.

Scattered through the eastern forests are grassy parks and glades that gradually blend with the prairies of central Oklahoma, where bluestem and goldentop grasses predominate. Farther west on the plains is the so-called shortgrass country—short curly grama, mesquite, and buffalo grasses that form a thick, absorbent sod.

Oklahoma's fauna is just as varied as its flora. Recent excavations along streambeds and in gravel pits reveal that in prehistoric times Oklahoma's prairies and plains were the range of creatures long extinct—the mammoth, the giant bison, and the diminutive camel and horse. In the historic period hunters and trappers found this region richly endowed with flocks of wild turkeys, prairie chickens, bobwhite quail, ducks, geese, and passenger pigeons so numerous that their flights darkened the sky (the last flock of this now extinct species was recorded in Osage County in 1890). Virtually every species of bird found in the area extending from the Mississippi Valley to the Rocky Mountains has been observed in Oklahoma, including the mockingbird, sparrow, cardinal, oriole, thrush, blackbird, bluejay, lark, warbler, robin, roadrunner, scissortailed flycatcher, and at times the now extinct Carolina paroquet. Elk, deer, antelope, rabbit, black bear, cinnamon bear, raccoon, opossum, timber wolf, coyote, fox, beaver, otter, muskrat, mink, squirrel, groundhog, prairie dog, badger, skunk, panther and wildcat, and big-

horn, or Rocky Mountain, sheep (in present upper Cimarron County) were common in earlier times. Alligators still sometimes ascend Red River as far as McCurtain County.

The American bison, or buffalo, was the most historically significant creature in Oklahoma's past. At one time an estimated 20 million bison were scattered in herds of varying size up and down the Great Plains. The annual migration of these huge, hairy beasts brought great numbers of them to Oklahoma.

Oklahoma's natural environment included the horned toad and other lizards; nonpoisonous snakes (garter, bull, green, ribbon, and black); and poisonous snakes (timber, prairie, and diamondback rattlers, the copperhead, and the vicious cottonmouth). At the time of discovery by Europeans, Oklahoma's streams abounded in bass, perch, channel and flathead catfish, and drum.

In terms of human occupation, Oklahoma is one of the oldest areas on the continent. Traces of human life possibly fifteen to twenty thousand years old have been found. Yet in terms of its age as a state, Oklahoma's population is of recent arrival because the Indian Territory was not officially opened to homesteading until 1889. Today, nearly 3 million persons reside in the state.

The era for separating the historic from the prehistoric in North America is the sixteenth century. The historian, basing his findings on recorded history, can go back for only a limited time. Then he has to rely on the archaeologist, who, by studying human signs, reconstructs early occupations and places time sequences. Through his research and interpretation, the archaeologist explains the prehistoric period. His findings show that some of the earliest human life in North America was present in Oklahoma.

As it is in modern times, prehistoric Oklahoma was strategically situated in the great concourse of human groups. During the Pleistocene Age, more than eight thousand years ago, Oklahoma's climate, moderated by the Ice Age, was considerably milder and wetter than it is today. The savannas, swamps, and water holes of central and western Oklahoma attracted Columbian mammoths, giant primordial bison, horses, camels, and other creatures. Oklahoma's terrain allowed easy access for the wandering bands of hunters who probably were members of America's first human family. The plains and prairies of the state's western half allowed easy entry from the southwest and north, and broad river valleys of northeastern Oklahoma permitted penetration from that direction.

The moderate climate of this region encouraged occupation by primitive human groups. Natural shelter was available in many parts of the state because of an abundance of projecting rock ledges and caves. Durable weapons fashioned from hard stone, generally flint, were important to the prehistoric hunters. Several exposed deposits of this material in Oklahoma, notably the flint quarries in present Ottawa County, were worked by early craftsmen.

Thus Oklahoma's earliest people were wandering families of big-game hunters who sought out the mammoth and other creatures for food and hides. Two kinds of early man have been identified in Oklahoma by the distinctive projectile points used by these primitive hunters: Clovis man, the earlier, and Folsom man, his successor. Near Stecker, Oklahoma, lies a major deposit of prehistoric material called the Domebo mammoth kill site. Archaeologists use the carbon-14 test to date culture sites. This test measures the amount of radioactive carbon in the site material and provides a measure of age with an error factor of about 200 years. Tests of

Weapon points used by Oklahoma's earliest settlers. Left to right—Clovis, Folsom, and Plainview.

Domebo mammoth kill-site material divulge an age of 10,243 to 11,061 years.

After the period of hunters of now extinct fauna, there was probably a span of several thousand years during which primitive Oklahomans hunted wild creatures that were still here when Spanish explorers first visited Oklahoma in early historic times. This interval of several thousand years was the second period of Oklahoma prehistory. Signs of human existence from this epoch have been found in Oklahoma in three broad locations: the caves and ledges of the Ozarks of northeastern Oklahoma, the caves of the Oklahoma Panhandle, and scattered creek and riverbed sites.

Although the early Oklahomans were wandering hunters, they traveled a circuit in search of subsistence, and habitually camped each season on the same creek and riverbank sites, usually near springs of fresh water. They undoubtedly used the caves and rock ledges during the winter periods. Continued use of these accustomed sites through the centuries caused accumulation of debris in layers. From time to time wind-driven soil or floodwaters distributed a protective mantle of earth over

Prehistoric cliff markings, Cimarron Canyon, Oklahoma Panhandle.

these ancient human sites and separated one culture from another. In some Oklahoma caves archaeologists have found camp-debris accumulations ten to twelve feet deep. Similar deposits have been excavated along the streams; one of the most revealing riparian sites is on Fourche Maline Creek near its junction with the Poteau River in southeast Oklahoma.

A painstaking examination of these culture sites reveals a time sequence, and in the cultural advance of Oklahoma's early peoples certain landmarks stand out. The bow and arrow, implements of agriculture (especially corn culture), pottery and elaborate mortuary, all absent from the lower layers of human sign, appear toward the tops of these prehistoric habitation sites. Such materials signal substantial human advancement. As archaeologists worked from bottom to top on the sites, a profile could be traced to reveal the evolution of early Oklahomans. They hunted for meat and supplemented their diets by fishing and gathering nuts, berries, and other products of nature. In the cave ruins for this period, probably five or six thousand years old, archaeologists have found charcoal, animal

bones, flints, wild seeds, and nuts. Flint objects include points, drills, scrapers, knives, and chopping tools.

The intermediate layers in these caves report the slow but steady advance of Oklahoma's prehistoric people. For example, food surplus and storage have always been important factors in man's advance. Though pottery vessels, so important before the use of metalware for carrying and storing food, water and other human essentials, are absent from the intermediate layers, this cultural horizon indicates remarkable improvisation during the period. Bark containers and fabric bags, lined with pitch for waterproofing and preservation, were in wide use. These pre–pottery-making people used cache pits, lined with leaves, grass, bark, and stone slabs, for storing sunflower seeds and other foods either gathered from nature or produced by an early premaize (precorn) agriculture. The hunter in this period was equipped with the atlatl, or spear thrower, and with cane-shafted darts. He tipped his projectiles with flint heads and used stone knives, stone scrapers, and hammer stones.

In the top layers of Ozark cave habitations are found arrows, indicating, of course, the adoption of the bow for hunting. Fragments of pottery, notched net sinkers, bone fishhooks, animal bones, horns, and antlers adapted for use as crude agricultural implements, document the advance of these people. Corn appears in materials collected from the Ozark caves.

The caves near Kenton in Oklahoma's Panhandle have yielded abundant material indicating human occupation in that area during the intermediate period of Oklahoma's prehistory, possibly four thousand years ago. Searchers have found human habitation sign that includes buffalo, deer, antelope, and rabbit bones; wild seeds; acorns; and round, flattened cakes made of ground acorns mixed with wild plums and berries. This primitive pastry was similar to the modern doughnut, for each cake had a center hole. The hole apparently was used to string the delicacies for drying and storing. Whole kernels of corn and corncobs have turned up in the household litter of these caves, indicating an advanced agriculture. The inventory of these early western Oklahoma homes includes stone scrapers, stone knives, stone chopping tools, and wood drills for kindling fires. While again no pottery has been found, these inventive Oklahomans contrived skin bags and elaborately coiled baskets. Their unique skill produced a wide range of household containers and fixtures including, in addition to baskets for carrying and storing human essentials, colorful mats, rugs, and cradles.

Though they lacked the bow and arrow, the Kenton cave dwellers were first in one aspect of Oklahoma's cultural advance: the fine arts got their start in Oklahoma among the early Panhandle cave dwellers, who decorated the walls of their households with red-painted figures.

Toward the close of the intermediate period of Oklahoma's prehistory, the people moved out of the caves and away from their ledge dwellings to make their homes in the valleys. From early times they camped in small hunting bands along the creeks and rivers, but until out of their inventiveness they devised a year-round shelter, they had to return each winter season to the relative warmth and protection of their cave and rock-ledge dwellings. Sites like the Fourche Maline not only confirm this general movement to adopt year-round dwellings in the lowlands but also reveal evidence of human use from earliest times. The lower levels indicate that the area was a favorite campground, the debris including animal bones, burned rocks, flint chips, charcoal, and fragments of mussel shells. Successive flooding and alluvial cover have separated one age of human use from another. So many locations have been discovered in the Fourche Maline area that archaeologists have named the prehistoric campsite and later village location the Fourche Maline Complex.

Signs of primordial hunting camps and their successors, the prehistoric villages, are scattered along creeks and rivers all over the state. Therefore, there must have been a general movement of Oklahoma's early dwellers from their caves and ledge homes to the riverbanks. On Red River alone archaeologists have identified fifteen prehistoric communities that have yielded the entire spectrum of early man's cultural evolution in Oklahoma, ranging from crude stone implements, animal bones,

and charcoal to pottery, arrows, and corn. The Cedar Creek site in Caddo County has produced Folsom points and animal bones of the same age, followed by evidence associated with the intermediate level of primitive man in Oklahoma. Toward the top of the site charred beans and corncob fragments tell of agricultural advance and adoption of a sedentary way of life, including a community of dwellings constructed of grass-and-clay wattlework.

In Oklahoma's late prehistoric age, from about 2000 B.C. to A.D. 1500, a number of significant developments occurred. One of these, mentioned above—the change in the late intermediate period from cave and ledge shelters to lowland village dwellings—continued with certain refinements.

As might be expected, it is from the dwelling sites of Oklahoma's late prehistoric period that most of the evidence of human activity is derived. This epoch could well be called the age of mound builders, for the man-made eminences scattered over the state are the most conspicuous remains of this period. The mounds are concentrated in eastern Oklahoma, though a few have been found in the northwestern portion of the state.

In the eastern Oklahoma mounds today's investigators have found the most communicative links with the prehistoric past. The mounds were constructed for several purposes. Some served as platforms for mud-and-wattle houses, the elevated location providing protection against floods. Many of the mounds, well over forty feet high, were erected as religious pyramids, some of them solid and probably serving as open-air shrines. Others, built over cedar-framed structures, were used as burial temples.

The famous Fourche Maline Complex is related to the mound-builder epoch. In the thirty or more known sites of this prehistoric settlement area, archaeologists have found that during the village-building epoch Oklahomans carried in soil and constructed mounds and levees to place their villages above the flood levels. Early-day workers raised the Williams Mound (situated about two miles from the junction of Fourche Maline Creek with the Poteau River) five feet above the valley floor and banked the site to a

Workmen excavating Spiro Mound in eastern Oklahoma.

width of 150 feet. Beneath the Williams Mound and other eminences in the Fourche Maline group, researchers have uncovered layer on layer of cultural profiles, each separated by alluvial silt. At the lowest levels are the primordial campsites with fire-cracked stones, bones, mussel shells, flint chips and projectile points, and crude hammer stones. They are followed in sequence by advanced stone tools and weapons and signs of an incipient agriculture, then by upper levels containing arrows, fishhooks, bone whistles, pottery, and corn.

Atop the Williams Mound and other eminences in the complex searchers have found evidence of frame shelters (mud-and-wattle coverings), food-cache pits, stone artifacts, and sign of an advanced agriculture. The presence of perforated animal teeth indicates some attention to personal adornment. Apparently the people produced crops of corn, beans, squash, pumpkins, and sunflower seeds on the rich river-bottom plots.

Significantly, the Fourche Maline mounds have yielded some of Oklahoma's earliest known human burials; a single mound was found to contain 122 human and three dog skeletons. Like weapons, tools, pottery, and certain other cultural products, prehistoric mortuary often is a revealing sign of human advance. An emerging religious system, including a concept of an afterlife in which the deceased would need certain items, can be traced through the kinds and quantities of grave goods. It is also of interest that interment in the Fourche Maline Complex was beneath the mud-and-wattle house sites, indicating a practice similar to that of ancient peoples in other parts of the world who buried their dead beneath their hearthstones to be near the spirits of their ancestors. In the earliest Oklahoma mound burials no grave goods were found. In later burials a few simple pieces appear. The posthumous adornment gradually increased, reaching a climax in the splendor-laden Spiro graves.

The fabled Spiro epoch, A.D. 500 to 1300, marks the golden age of Oklahoma prehistory. The Sooner State's archaeological chronicle, at best fragmentary and sometimes nearly mute, suddenly spoke loudly of its past through a discovery made in the Arkansas River valley in eastern Oklahoma during the late 1930s at a cluster of man-made hills called Spiro Mounds. The site proved to be an archaeological treasure trove. The mounds' dimensions and elaborate mazes of subterranean chambers were a tribute to the engineering skills of the Spiro people. Each of the ceremonial pyramids and burial temples was constructed of rot-resistant cedar logs, covered by thousands of tons of hand-transported earth. While the Spiro people left no written record of their brilliant achievement, the epic of their amazing cultural progress can be reconstructed from the elaborate mortuary recovered from the mounds.

A partial inventory of goods taken from the burial chambers includes ceremonial maces; delicately decorated pottery vessels, each finished in exquisite art form; cedar masks; human and animal effigies; human and animal heads sculptured from rock crystal; Madonna-like mother-and-child figures; clay and stone pipes; pearl and shell beads; baskets and other woven utensils; textile pieces, including vegetable-fiber cloth with advanced weave designs containing elaborate geometric figures; blankets and mantles of buffalo hair, rabbit fur, and feathers; cane combs; embossed gorgets; fine ground and polished stone implements and projectile points; conch shells struck with drawings depicting Spiro history and ceremonials, including the busk—or green-corn—observance, winged and plumed rattlesnakes, masked dancers, and snake dancers; and sheet copper, copper axes, and copper-covered ear spools.

The material remains of the Spiro people indicate an amazingly advanced culture of populous communities with a sedentary mode of life. The Spiro economy was sufficiently developed for village craftsmen to employ specialized talents. Their creative and aesthetic senses were keen and active, as evidenced by the exquisite pottery, textiles, sculpture, and metal goods they produced. Their complex economic life included wide ranging trade and communication with other peoples, as evidenced by the nonlocal shells and copper found in the sites. Curiously, while authorities classify this pre-Columbian period as Stone Age, it is significant that the Spiro people had begun the use of metal goods.

Some time after A.D. 1200 the high Spiro culture was vandalized by peoples from the western plains. Pressure from the invaders brought decline to Spiro brilliance, much as invasions by the Goths and other tribes brought decline to the ancient Romans. It was during this period, 1200 to 1500, that the human setting was created for the discovery of Oklahoma by the Europeans.

We have fairly certain knowledge of this human setting because of the intensive research on the Indian tribes of North America by archaeologists, historians, anthropologists, and other scholars. Their findings reveal that the tribes of North America moved around

Copper mask and ear spools excavated from Spiro Mound.

frequently after the various European powers established colonies in the New World. It is certain that most tribes moved several times after the American colonies became the United States, for the new nation almost from the beginning of its life maintained a vast Indian removal program to open up new lands for its citizens. Even before the coming of the Europeans and the rise of the United States, however, the Indian tribes had moved about. Drought was a common factor in the migrations of primitive people. If the Indians were hunters, extended dry periods drove out the game; if they were farmers, their crops withered. In either case a prolonged drought caused people to move to better-watered areas. Conquest was another factor that impelled tribes to migrate. A vigorous tribe, perhaps on the north or east, might make war on neighboring tribes; the oppressed communities often moved south or west to avoid conflict. In turn, to gain control of a desirable new range, the refugees might themselves resort to conquest to drive out the occupants. Over a period of time this process produced a chain reaction. Sometimes drought and initial con-

Polished stone effigy excavated from Spiro Mound.

quest in a given area might be related and set off wave after wave of migrations. In any event, these natural occurrences suggest the reason why tribes living on the Atlantic seaboard or in Canada in earlier times might have been discovered by the Europeans in the Mississippi Valley, in the Southwest, or in present Oklahoma.

Research in Indian languages which has produced better understanding of the tribes, also casts additional light on the period of Oklahoma's history on the eve of European penetration. Scholars have found that, while the more than two hundred separate tribes of North America had rather similar religious, economic, and social practices, they spoke widely differing languages, and in no case did a tribe have a written language. In 1816 the American Philosophical Society sponsored a project to study and classify the spoken languages of the Indian tribes of North America. The work progressed slowly, and it was not until 1836 that Albert Gallatin was able to produce linguistic tables and a map showing the geographic distribution of the Indian-language stocks, or families. His work was completed by J. W. Powell in 1885. Powell's

standard linguistic classification system identifies fifty-one independent families of Indian languages spoken by tribes in the United States. The principal language families, or stocks, in the Powell system, which would accommodate most of the leading tribes, are the Algonkian, Caddoan, Shoshonean, Muskhogean, Iroquoian, Siouian, and Athapascan. More recently, Edward Sapir, Morris Swadesh, D. F. Vogelin, F. M. Vogelin, Harold Driver, and other linguists and anthropologists have altered Powell's model and formulated the genetic system of classification, borrowing from biology the use of the concept of phylum and family for Indian-language categories. The genetic-system stocks that embrace the principal tribes are the Algonkian, Athapascan, Iroquoian, Muskhogean, Siouian, Uto-Aztecan, and Penutian.

From the Spiro period and at least as early as the time of Coronado's expedition, Oklahoma was the residence area of tribes possibly representing three of the basic language stocks. After the United States acquired the area included in present Oklahoma as a part of the vast Louisiana Purchase, the state for many years served the nation as the Indian Territory, a special settlement zone where Indian tribes from all sections of the United States were relocated. The result is that today Oklahoma includes a greater number of tribes—sixty-seven—than any other state in the United States. Approximately one-third of all United States citizens who claim Indian ancestry now live in Oklahoma. This great number of tribes exhibits a conspicuous variety of Indian cultures, including languages. The principal linguistic stocks and tribes at some time present in Oklahoma (members of most of them living in the state today) include Algonkian (Arapaho, Cheyenne, Delaware, Fox, Kickapoo, Miami, Potawatomi, Sac, and Shawnee); Iroquoian (Cherokee, Wyandot, Seneca, Cayuga, and Erie); Muskhogean (Choctaw, Chickasaw, Creek, and Seminole); Siouan (Osage, Quapaw, Kansa, Missouri, Ponca, and Iowa); Caddoan (Caddo, Pawnee, and Wichita); Uto-Aztecan (Comanche); Shahaptian (Nez Percé); Athapascan (Apache); Tanoan (Kiowa); and Tonkawan (Tonkawa).

Few of today's resident Oklahoma tribes are native or indigenous to the area. Most of them are immigrants, settled in the Indian Territory in the implementation of the relocation policy of the United States government during the nineteenth century. The linguistic divisions in Oklahoma at the time of discovery by Coronado were the Caddoan (Caddo, Wichita, and Pawnee); Siouan (Quapaw and Osage); and Athapascan (the so-called Apaches of the Plains). They were the successors to the brilliant Spiro civilization; very likely their ancestors were the raiders who vandalized the splendor of Spiro. The Caddoans, the Siouans, and the Athapascans were the Oklahomans who received the treasure-mad conquistadors in 1541.

Notes on Sources, Chapter 1

Information about the early-day Oklahoma environment—natural and human—is found in a variety of books and articles. The natural setting is lucidly portrayed in John W. Morris, ed., *Geography of Oklahoma* (Oklahoma City, 1977), and Charles N. Gould, *Travels Through Oklahoma* (Oklahoma City, 1928); the evolution of its geographic format is plotted in John W. Morris, Charles R. Gains, and Edwin C. McReynolds, *Historical Atlas of Oklahoma*, new ed. (Norman, 1976). Oklahoma as part of the larger natural region of the Southwest is explained in Carl F. Kraenzel, *The Great Plains in Transition* (Norman, 1955), and Walter Prescott Webb, *The Great Plains* (Boston, 1931).

Recent discoveries of prehistoric sites in Oklahoma by archaeologists and anthropologists have substantially enlarged the understanding of this intriguing epoch. Sources include Waldo R. Wedel, *Prehistoric Man on the Great Plains* (Norman, 1961); Henry W. Hamilton, "The Spiro Mound," *Missouri Archeologist* 44 (October, 1952); Robert E. Bell, *Oklahoma Archeology: An Annotated Bibliography* (Norman, 1969); Robert E. Bell, *Oklahoma Indian Artifacts* (Norman, 1980); and Arrell Morgan Gibson, "Prehistory in Oklahoma," *Chronicles of Oklahoma* 42 (Spring, 1965).

Oklahoma's Indian heritage has been the subject of extensive study and has generated hundreds of books and several thousand articles depicting the sixty-seven tribes residing in Oklahoma by 1885. These include Frederick W. Hodge, ed., *Handbook of American Indians North of Mexico*, 2 vols. (New York, 1959); Muriel H. Wright, *A Guide to the Indian Tribes of Oklahoma* (Norman, 1951); Angie Debo, *A History of the Indians of the United States* (Norman, 1970); and Arrell Morgan Gibson, *The American Indian: Prehistory to the Present* (Lexington, Mass., 1980).

Chapter 2

Europe Builds a Future in Oklahoma

Artist's sketch of Coronado, Spanish conquistador and commander of the first European exploration of Oklahoma.

Oklahoma, a primitive community for over ten thousand years, entered the stream of recorded history in 1541. During the sixteenth and seventeenth centuries several European nations carried out competitive exploring and colonizing efforts that resulted in vast overseas empires. In the New World, Spain was the most successful European power in the early years of empire building. From Caribbean bases, daring conquistadors moved to the mainland, and their discoveries of dazzling wealth and advanced Indian communities in Mexico and Peru set off a frenzied search for even richer kingdoms, reportedly situated on the trackless northern frontier.

Stories of rich kingdoms with provocative names like Cale, Gran Quivira, and the Seven Cities of Cíbola filtered through to Mexico and Cuba by way of Indians and survivors of Spanish expeditions who had attempted to penetrate the northern frontier by sea routes. One of these fabled centers of wealth was reported to be twice the size of Seville, Spain's largest city. Its outer wall was said to be constructed of solid gold, and the doors of the shops and houses were described as covered with turquoise, green like a forest. Another story told of a land toward the sunset where wealth was so abundant that the people wore hats of gold. In a neighboring kingdom, it was said, people slept underwater and wore golden bracelets. They were served from golden utensils and made their weapons of war from silver. Indian informants told of a community of unipeds, of another tribe with long ears trailing on the ground, and of yet another nation that lived on smells. A report that especially appealed to the explorers concerned a silver island inhabited by lusty Amazons.

Many expeditions were sent north in search of Cale, Quivira, and other fabled kingdoms. Two of these wide-ranging quests by Spanish conquistadors, which would prove of great importance to the history of the Mississippi Valley and the American Southwest, were the Coronado and De Soto expeditions.

In 1539, Francisco Vásquez de Coronado, governor of New Galicia, New Spain's northernmost province, was authorized to search for the Seven Cities of Cíbola. At Compostela, on the west coast of Mexico, the governor gathered men, livestock, supplies, and equipment for the expedition. In February, 1540, the Cíbola-bound column, consisting of 250 mounted men, seventy foot soldiers, more than a thousand Indians, a mule train laden with baggage and camp equipment, a remuda of a thousand horses, and a mobile commissary of herds of cattle, sheep, and hogs, began its historic northward march. Scouting parties from the main column ranged widely over portions of Arizona and New Mexico, tracking every rumor or hint of treasure-rich kingdoms. In each case the Spaniards were disappointed to find only humble Indian villages, instead of glittering centers of wealth.

At Tiguex, on the Río Grande in New Mexico, an Indian guide assured Coronado that in the east there was a land of splendor—the Gran Quivira—where women served their men from golden pitchers, tiny golden bells tinkled from the branches of shade trees, and even the children wore heavy gold bracelets on their arms and ankles. This report sounded no more fantastic to Coronado and his band of conquistadors than the undreamed-of treasure already looted from the Aztecs by Hernán Cortés, or Francisco Pizarro's plunder of the Incas. Coronado and his men readily took up the eastward march, driven by that magnificent obsession, promise of the riches of the Gran Quivira.

Coronado crossed the grassy plains of eastern New Mexico and western Texas, turned north in western Oklahoma, and in July, 1541, arrived at Quivira on the Arkansas River in central Kansas. Quivira was a community of dome-shaped grass dwellings inhabited by a sedentary people, conspicuous for their tattooed bodies and sustained by their fields of corn, beans, squash, and pumpkins, feasting in season on the fruits of nature (sand plums and fox grapes) and buffalo; they had no golden bells, bracelets, or utensils. In disgust the disillusioned Coronado had his Indian guide put to death. Later he wrote his king: "What I am sure of is that there is not any gold nor any other metal in all this country." The Spaniards returned to Tiguex and then to Mexico.

Although from the Spaniards' point of view the Quivira expedition failed, it was of greatest historical significance for the Southwest and Oklahoma. The Quivirans were Caddoan-

Artist's sketch of conquistadors from Coronado's column.

speaking Indians of the Wichita tribe, who lived in communities scattered between the Arkansas and the Red rivers. Within a century or so after Coronado's visit the entire nation was concentrated in Oklahoma. The Wichitas played a key role in Oklahoma history during the seventeenth and eighteenth centuries, and Spanish reports supply the first information about them. Coronado described the Quivirans as large. He measured them, finding them to be "ten palms" tall, and he noted that the women were well proportioned with features like Moorish women. Before departing from Quivira, Coronado met in council with the tribal leaders. Later he wrote his king that the chiefs took an oath of fealty pledging their "obedience to Your Majesty and placing themselves under your Royal Lordship." By virtue of his councils on the Arkansas, Coronado brought the western half of the Mississippi Valley under Spanish dominion.

During the journey to Quivira and the return to Tiguex, Coronado observed other tribes, notably the Plains Apaches, daring hunters who roamed the western margins of Oklahoma preying on the buffalo herds. He

Artist's sketch of Coronado's march to the Gran Quivira.

noted that the Apaches planted no crops but sustained themselves on what he called hump-backed cows. According to Coronado, the Apaches ate the flesh raw and drank the blood of the huge hairy beasts. Their women tanned the hides for garments and portable shelters, characterized by the conquistador as "little field tents." They were, of course, dwellings characteristic of most of the buffalo- hunting tribes. The Apaches were reported to use dogs hitched to poles for transporting their shelters and other camp equipment. Coronado also told his king that on the plains wood was scarce away from the gullies and rivers and that his men had to cook their rations of buffalo meat over cow-dung fires. Oklahoma home-steaders in later times, faced with the same problem of scarce fuel, warmed their dugout dwellings and cooked their food with buffalo-chip fires.

When Coronado reached Tiguex on the Río Grande, on the way back to Mexico, one of the expedition chaplains, Friar Juan de Padilla, decided to return to Quivira and establish a mission for the Wichitas. Padilla selected Lucas and Sebastián, two Mexican Indian *donados* (lay brothers who wore the habit of

friars), and a Portuguese soldier, Andres do Campo, to accompany him. Six Wichita warriors who had guided Coronado on a direct route from Quivira across the Oklahoma Panhandle to Tiguex led Padilla's party back to the villages on the Arkansas. After laboring among the Wichitas during the spring and summer of 1542, the padre decided to visit the "Guas" (Kaws), whose country was east of Quivira. En route the Spaniards fell into an ambush, and Padilla died of his wounds. Do Campo and the two Indian *donados* were held as captives for nearly a year. Finally they escaped and traveled south by a route that took them across central Oklahoma.

Coronado's itinerary to Quivira had taken him over the eastern edge of the Oklahoma Panhandle. His Wichita guides followed an oblique route across the Panhandle in leading the Spanish column back to Tiguex. Thus the Coronado expedition barely crossed the western margins of Oklahoma.

Of the Spanish parties in the Southwest before 1600, only one—Do Campo's—spanned the state proper and spent any appreciable time in Oklahoma. Do Campo, Lucas, and Sebastián, fleeing from the land of the fierce

Kaws into the future Oklahoma, must have been a strange sight. The two pentitent *donados*, grieving over the death of Padilla, constructed a heavy wooden cross, which they carried by turns on their backs. At some point in their wanderings the trio was joined by a dog. This faithful animal kept Do Campo and the Indians supplied with rabbits and other small game during the five years they were on the trail. When the hardy Portuguese soldier finally reached the Spanish settlements at Pánuco on the northeast coast of New Spain, his hair was shoulder length and his beard hung in braids.

Do Campo has not received the public notice accorded Coronado and the other famed conquistadors who ventured beyond the borders of New Spain to explore the northern frontiers. Because of the months and possibly years he spent in Oklahoma, however, he must be accorded a special place in the state's history. From the Spanish settlements to Quivira, crossing Oklahoma, he blazed a new trail that was less than half as long as Coronado's circuitous march. For many years officials at Mexico City recommended the Do Campo route as the best and most direct route to Spain's new northern province, Quivira.

At the same time that Coronado's column was probing the Southwest in search of the splendor of Cíbola and Quivira, another Spanish expedition was penetrating the Mississippi Valley. In 1539, Hernando de Soto sailed from Cuba with six hundred treasure-seeking followers. The expedition landed at Tampa Bay on the Florida coast and wandered for three years over mountains and through swamps and forests in search of the fabled Cale. In its peregrinations De Soto's column discovered the Father of Waters, the Mississippi. The restless conquistador had explored Arkansas as far west as present Little Rock when he died in June, 1542. The survivors of the Cale expedition then turned south and returned to the Spanish settlements in Mexico.

While De Soto's explorations did not extend as far west as Oklahoma, they influenced the state's history in many ways. By declaring dominion on behalf of his king over the people and lands he discovered, De Soto established Spain's claim to the Lower Mississippi Valley, and thus brought Oklahoma firmly into the

Spanish orbit. Moreover, in the course of his wanderings, De Soto came into contact with several tribes that would later be removed to Oklahoma. These tribes included the Choctaws and Chickasaws. De Soto and his men spent a season with the Chickasaws, took native wives, and formed the beginnings of a mixed-blood community within the tribe.

In succeeding years the Spaniards extended their settlements north into Texas and New Mexico. From these forward bases they continued their explorations of the northern frontier, a vast region extending above Red River, bounded on the east by the Mississippi and on the west by the Río Grande. One of the most notable of these post-Coronado entries into Oklahoma was made in 1601, by Juan de Oñate, who had begun the colonization of New Mexico in 1598. Oñate headed an expedition to Quivira that crossed the buffalo plains into the Canadian River valley of western Oklahoma before turning north to the Arkansas.

The Spanish, preoccupied and probably overextended with the problems of administering a vast empire in the New World, were unable to show more than token interest in the northern frontier. Thus Oklahoma in the early Spanish period, between 1540 and 1700, figured as little more than a territory for wide-ranging Spanish parties to cross.

Shortly before 1700, however, France entered the Mississippi Valley and challenged Spanish dominion by carving out the new province of Louisiana from the neglected northern frontier of New Spain. The Mississippi River exploration of Robert Cavalier, Sieur de La Salle in 1682 led the French to claim the vast region comprising all the land drained by the western watershed of the Mississippi.

Vigorous French colonial managers followed up La Salle's plan for developing the resources of Louisiana by establishing an extensive and far-flung commercial empire that tapped the fur trade of the future Oklahoma and its peripheral areas. In 1699, Pierre Lemoyne, Sieur d'Iberville, established a French colony at Biloxi to control the entrance to the Mississippi, and in 1718, his brother Jean Baptiste Lemoyne, Sieur de Bienville, founded New Orleans, the capital of the

Buffalo herd grazing on the course followed by Coronado across western Oklahoma.

new province. New Orleans soon became a base of operations from which French traders swarmed up the Red, Arkansas, Canadian, Grand, and Verdigris rivers to tap the riches of Louisiana.

In addition to developing an extensive fur trade with the Indian tribes of Louisiana, the French were eager to establish trade contact with the Spanish settlements on the Río Grande. Severe internal commercial restrictions imposed by the Spanish government had caused scarcities of certain items, and the people were starved for trade goods the French could supply. French explorers also hoped to find a water route through the continental land mass to the Pacific. Many expeditions were launched from French settlements in the Illinois country and the Gulf region to achieve these objectives.

Four years before the founding of New Orleans, Juchereau de St. Denis had explored western Louisiana by ascending Red River. He may have been the first Frenchman to see Oklahoma. It is reported that he wandered as far west as the Río Grande, where he was arrested by Spanish officials for unauthorized entry.

During 1719 two official French entries were made into Oklahoma. One expedition headed by Bernard de la Harpe explored from New Orleans to the Indian towns on the Canadian in eastern Oklahoma. The other, led by Claude du Tisne, an officer from Fort Chartres,

in the Illinois country, traveled southwest to the Osage villages in southeastern Kansas and then south into Oklahoma to the Wichita villages near the Arkansas on a site near present Newkirk.

One of the most daring and lucrative expeditions into Oklahoma occurred during the winter of 1739–40, when two brothers, Pierre and Paul Mallet, with four companions and a train of packhorses laden with trade goods, ascended the Missouri to the mouth of the Platte. From there they traveled to the Rocky Mountains and southward into the Spanish settlements. The Mallet party, sponsored by a temporarily indulgent Spanish commercial policy, traded as far south as Santa Fe and in the spring returned to the French settlements. Three members of the party traveled overland to the Missouri. The Mallet brothers and one companion followed the Arkansas through Oklahoma to the Mississippi.

The final French expedition to Oklahoma occurred in 1741, very soon after the successful Mallet venture. Fabry de la Bruyère, a French officer, with a company of soldiers and some Canadian traders ascended the Arkansas to map a direct route to Santa Fe. La Bruyère's party entered the St. André River (the Canadian River), regarded as the most favorable and direct water course to the Spanish settlements in New Mexico. Shallow water and sand bars delayed the group and they camped for the winter on the north bank of the Canadian near the present boundary between McIntosh and Hughes counties before returning to the French settlements in the Illinois country during the spring of 1742.

Of these French expeditions to Oklahoma, the La Harpe entry, because of the journal kept by the expedition commander, is the most instructive and revealing with regard to the state's appearance in the early eighteenth century. From La Harpe's day-by-day account of his journey from New Orleans to the Indian villages on the Canadian, one can trace his route across eastern Oklahoma, learn of the natural environment, tribes resident in that portion of the state in 1719, their customs and relations with more distant tribes, and the role he expected the land and people to play in the design of New France.

La Harpe received a grant of land on Red River in 1718. During December of that year he departed from New Orleans, stopping on Red River near the southeastern corner of Oklahoma, where he established a trading post complete with a small fort for defense against Indians and Spanish patrols. Several French families collected about La Harpe's town, opened fields for crops, and built a mill for producing flour and lumber.

While supervising the construction of his trading post, La Harpe dispatched an aide, Gaston du Rivage, to the upper Red River to seek out the Indian tribes of that region and to examine the possibilities of establishing trade with the Spanish settlements. In late June, 1719, Du Rivage returned to report that he had found the Wichita villages on Red River and had delivered La Harpe's presents to the tribal leaders. He told of councils with the chiefs and of assurances of good will toward French traders. The French called the Wichita and Caddo tribes Taovayas.

Du Rivage's report on the tribes of western Oklahoma included references to the Apaches, a tribe noticed by Coronado in the same region nearly two hundred years earlier. He also reported the presence of the Comanches, newcomers to the southern plains and a fierce war-making people. He noted that the tribes, mounted on horses stolen from the Spanish settlements or captured in battle from other tribes, ranged widely between the Red and the Arkansas, preying on the buffalo herds

and making war. Only the Wichitas were settled and agricultural. The Indian warriors of all tribes used only bows, arrows, hatchets, lances, and knives, for the Spaniards maintained an inviolable law against supplying firearms to Indians. Du Rivage observed that the eternal warfare among the tribes of the region he visited was an obstacle to the commerce La Harpe hoped to establish. La Harpe's agent learned from his Red River councils with the Wichitas that there were settlements of their people toward the northwest who had good contacts with the Comanches and thus were an important link for trade with the Plains tribes and the Spanish settlements.

La Harpe's expedition to Oklahoma, as reported by his journal, came as a result of his agreement with Du Rivage that this incessant warfare "was an obstacle to commerce that I had attempted to make with the Spaniards." He "thought it would be of interest to the king to go to discover the nations which they had spoken of ... and to make an alliance with them in order to shorten the way into New Mexico and the territory of the Padoucas [Comanches] from whom the Spanish obtained much riches."

On August 11, 1719, La Harpe, with two Keechi guides, Du Rivage, three enlisted soldiers, two blacks, and a twenty-two-horse train, set out from his Red River post on a northwesterly course that led him through the rough Kiamichi country. He entered Oklahoma near the southeastern corner of present McCurtain County; went north across present McCurtain, Pushmataha, Latimer, and Pittsburg counties; and crossed the Canadian near present Eufaula. La Harpe then moved north across present McIntosh County through western Muskogee County to a site near the Arkansas River about midway between present Muskogee and Tulsa.

The Frenchmen subsisted on buffalo, bear, and deer killed along the way. On August 21, La Harpe killed "a very large bear" in present upper Pushmataha County. On the same day they met a band of thirty Caddoes. In fifteen days of hunting, the Caddoes had killed forty-six buffalo (these were wood buffalo, found in the parks and meadows of the mountains and hill country in eastern Oklahoma, not as numerous as plains buffalo). Since it was summer, the only way the hunters could keep the meat from spoiling was to smoke it over fires. At the time of their meeting with La Harpe, the Caddoes were trying to slip back to their villages on Red River, fearful of an attack by their enemies the Osages, "whose fire they had noticed."

In blazing a trail through the wild, rough country from Red River to the Canadian villages, La Harpe found travel very difficult. On the eighteenth day out, his favorite dog wandered from camp on the south fork of the Canadian (Gaines Creek) and was lost. The Frenchman was much attached to his pet hunter and made every effort to recover the animal. On August 29, La Harpe reached the Canadian and made contact with a party of Taovayas who were curing elk meat. The Indians led him past present Eufaula on August 31 to the Deep Fork, where he met another band of Taovayas, who, mounted on beautiful horses "saddled and bridled in the style of the Spanish," formed an escort for the French column.

Between the Canadian and the Arkansas, La Harpe found nine villages of Caddoan people. The tribes were organized into a confederacy, with the Taovayas the most numerous. La Harpe spent two weeks in the confederated villages, conferring with the chiefs, dispensing gifts (guns, powder, shot, knives, hatchets, and paint), and forming alliances on behalf of the French king. Each village tried to outdo the others in entertaining the Frenchmen with feasts, dances, and gifts. La Harpe's most prized gifts were a crown of eagle plumes; two calumet pipes, one of war and one of peace; and a magnificent horse.

La Harpe asked many questions of the chiefs concerning the country toward the west, the tribes there, and the best routes to the Spanish settlements. He was impressed with the fields of corn, pumpkins, beans, and tobacco scattered about the villages on the fertile river bottom. He noted that the Taovayas cultivated prodigious quantities of tobacco, which they pressed into flat leaves and used for trade. In addition to crops the Indians raised fine horses, and native craftsmen turned out well-made saddles, bridles, and leather breastplates for the warriors. La Harpe was told that the people quit their villages in October to go

hunting and returned in March to plant their crops. Their dwellings were built of straw and reeds and covered with earth to form domes. Over each door there was a plaque of brown leather on which had been painted the arms of the warrior and his clan insignia.

To seal their fealty to France, the chiefs had La Harpe carried on a buffalo hide to the council fire, where a calumet was sung, his face was painted blue, and additional gifts were showered upon him, including thirty buffalo robes. La Harpe noted in his journal that the chiefs added as a gift an eight-year-old Apache captive, "of which they had eaten a finger from each hand, a mark that one was destined to serve one day as food to these cannibals." Then the chief of the Taovayas "told me that he was sorry to have only one slave to present to me, that if I had arrived sooner he would have given me the seventeen that they had eaten in a public feast. I thanked him for his good will, regretting that I had not arrived in time to save the lives of these poor unfortunates."

Just before departing the Wichita villages for his post on Red River, La Harpe made two perceptive entries in his journal. One provides an intimate glimpse of the nature of these early Oklahoma residents. Taovayas

> are people of good sense, cleverer than the nations of the Mississippi but the fertility of the country makes them lazy. They are always sitting around their chief and usually they think only of eating, smoking and playing. They are also libertines but generous in their love affairs, giving to their mistresses all that they have. The women are pretty enough, they have nothing to find fault with. ... They push gallantry farther than the men. During our sojourn in their villages they never quit carrying us plates of greens and maize, prepared with the marrow of beef [buffalo] and smoked meat. They exerted themselves to outdo each other as to which should carry the best meat. We could not eat all they brought us.

The other entry contained La Harpe's recommendation on how the colonial authorities should exert themselves to integrate this strategic community into the French design:

> There is not in the whole colony of Louisiana an establishment more useful to

Wichita village scene. These are descendants of the Taovayas of French times in Oklahoma.

make than on the branch of this river not only because of the mild climate, the fertility of the land, the richness of the minerals, but also because of the possibility of trade that one might introduce with Spain and New Mexico. If one could control the trade which the Spanish carry on with the Padoucas [Comanches] . . . one could become master of this region. It isn't necessary to add that one could handle a quantity of cow hides [buffalo] and other peltry that would be easily obtained from the Spanish.

Du Rivage carved the arms of the French king on a post near the principal council fire, together with the date La Harpe took possession of eastern Oklahoma in the name of the crown. Curiously, as the French column prepared to return to the Red River, a Chickasaw trader, an agent for the British, appeared in the Arkansas River villages with a packtrain of goods.

After La Harpe's visit to eastern Oklahoma, the French flag flew over the Wichita villages on the Canadian and the Arkansas, and colonial officials were quick to follow the recommendations he had made for reaping the riches of

this portion of Louisiana. The next spring restless, wide-ranging *coureurs de bois*, traders up from New Orleans or down from the Illinois settlements, swarmed over the waterways of Oklahoma and established trading posts among the tribes, especially the Wichitas. Because they were able to adapt to life in the wilderness, the French traders took up residence in the Indian villages and married native women. They generally were popular and well received by the tribes. By addicting the Indians to French trade goods, notably guns, ammunition, knives, beads, axes, hatchets, hoes, cloth, blankets, mirrors, and paint, the *coureurs de bois* caused the tribes to abandon their old ways and become commercial fur hunters. Each year the traders transported out of Oklahoma bales of beaver, otter, mink, and muskrat furs or beautifully tanned buffalo robes, all of which were in great demand in Europe.

The products of Oklahoma's first industry, the fur trade, were generally consigned to New Orleans by way of Arkansas Post or Natchitoches, in present Louisiana, by flatboats and pirogues. The remote traders used packtrains of horses to reach the river landings. The *coureurs de bois* returned in season with new supplies of trade goods to join their Indian families on the Canadian, Arkansas, and Red rivers. Tokens of French influence on this period of Oklahoma's history survive into these times. They include French bloodlines and names among Indian families, and in place-names. A few examples of the latter are river names: Poteau, San Bois, Fourche Maline, Cavanal, Sallisaw, Bayou Menard, Bayou Viande (Vian Creek), Verdigris, Salina, Grand, and Illinois.

Plunging raids by Osage war parties from the north finally disrupted the easy village life on the Canadian and Arkansas, and through the years the Taovayas followed the French traders to Red River, where they joined their kinsmen to form two famous Indian communities. The so-called Twin Villages, San Bernardo and San Teodoro, were situated adjacent to the riverbank, one in present Jefferson County, Oklahoma, the other across the Red River in what became Montague County, Texas.

Thus by 1749 only a single Taovaya village, Ferdinandina (at the site of today's Newkirk, Oklahoma), remained on the Arkansas. French traders called the people of this community Panipiquets because of their practice of decorating their faces and bodies with elaborate tattoos. Ferdinandina was strategically situated at the head of navigation on the Arkansas, on the eastern rim of the Comanche range. La Harpe had pointed out in 1719 that the eternal warfare among the tribes of the region was the greatest obstacle to developing the rich trade the area offered. French agents operating from their base at Ferdinandina sought to abate the conflict through councils with the Plains tribes, and during the 1740s they were able to establish a peace agreement and alliance with the Wichitas and Comanches. That agreement was never broken; it made possible the safe passage of French traders across the plains, although as a general rule the Comanches, too shy to come to the French posts, preferred to deal with the Panipiquets as middlemen for the French.

French traders from Ferdinandina, using the Panipiquets as their agents for trading with the Plains tribes, continued to try to open a route to Santa Fe. The success of the Mallet brothers

in reaching the Spanish settlements and trading there encouraged daring French merchants to make the attempt each season. Regularly, however, they were disappointed. Spanish officials either confiscated their goods and turned them back or, worse, arrested them and held them for trial at Santa Fe. The enduring Spanish hostility toward French traders stemmed from the Louisiana merchants' determination to sell firearms and ammunition to the Indian tribes.

Even Ferdinandina fell before the Osage assaults in 1757, and the Panipiquets and their French traders fled south to San Bernardo and San Teodoro. Through the following years the concentration of Wichita communities in southern Oklahoma came to exert a peculiar influence on the affairs of the Spanish borderlands. The Wichitas, still usually called Taovayas (though to the Spaniards in New Mexico they were Jumanos), prospered as middlemen for the French. With French assistance the warriors constructed elaborate fortifications around their villages to provide protection against Spanish and Apache raids. But their greatest strength lay in their enduring alliance with the most powerful Indian nation on the southern plains, the Comanches. During the 1790s, when the Kiowas entered the region, the Comanche peace pact with that fierce tribe was extended to include the Wichitas.

As the key group in the trading economy of the southern plains, the Wichitas continued to harvest furs for French traders. At the peak of the Taovayas' prosperity, as many as twelve traders operated in the Twin Villages. Moreover, the Taovayas were diversified. Some of them produced beans, corn, and pumpkins, which were much in demand as frontier trade items and were especially popular with the nonagricultural, buffalo-eating Comanches. They gathered salt and other products of nature. Each season Taovaya traders brought into San Bernardo and San Teodoro bales of furs, deerskins, tanned buffalo hides, and slaves for the plantations of Louisiana. Both Apache and Spanish slaves were sold, the latter swept up in Comanche raids on the New Mexico settlements. Each year at high water, flotillas of rafts and pirogues, laden with cargoes of salt, corn, bales of furs and hides, and shackled slaves, left the Red River landings at Twin Villages bound for Natchitoches and New Orleans.

Oklahoma's most colorful and influential people during the eighteenth century were the Wichitas. Their populous, advanced, and prosperous villages on the Red River comprised a sort of wealthy, well-managed city-state. Clever traders and shrewd diplomats, they used other tribes, especially the Comanches, to protect their special role in the French trading system on the Great Plains. Although they were primarily a mercantile people, the Taovayas could and did muster fighting forces on occasion. During the 1750s, French traders instigated attacks by the Wichitas and their Comanche allies on encroaching Spanish settlements in Texas that threatened the favored position of the French trading community on Red River.

Comanche raids on the Apaches' towns for slaves became so frequent during the 1750s that these unfortunates fled to mission settlements in south Texas, where Spanish padres tried to protect them. The principal Apache mission was at San Saba. In 1758 a combined Wichita-Comanche force attacked San Saba, drove off the defenders, sacked the buildings, and even threatened the nearby presidio of San Luis de las Amarillas.

Diego Ortiz Parilla, the presidio commander, was then directed to organize an expedition from the upper Mexico settlements to vindicate Spanish arms and punish the *norteños*, as the Wichitas and their Comanche allies were called. Parilla warned that it would be no easy task, for the Wichitas on Red River were "arrogant, . . . magnificient, and numerous, similar to the Moors in their manner of attack"—and, with their Comanche allies, almost invincible. During 1759, Parilla gathered a force of more than three hundred soldiers and marched north to Red River, arriving there in October. His Indian scouts found the Twin Villages. Parilla's report on the expedition revealed that the Wichita city-state was surrounded by a moat, which made assault charges on horseback dangerous if not impossible. On either side of the community were extensive fields of autumn-cured maize.

A well-constructed fort of palisade logs,

complete with a tall pole flying the French flag, protected the villagers, and an inner corral held the horses. The characteristic grass lodges of the Wichitas were between the fields and the fort. On a flat nearby, Parilla observed the buffalo-hide tipis of the Comanches. The Spanish column found it difficult to cross the river because the water was nearly five feet deep directly across from the villages. Just below the settlement was an ankle-deep ford, but it was heavily guarded.

While Parilla was placing his troops for an attack, he noticed small enemy parties slipping behind his lines to cut off retreat and place the attackers in a crossfire. Parilla's men charged the Indian positions time after time. The Wichitas had firearms and launched an effective, galling fire, hurling the Spaniards back on each assault. Parilla brought up his artillery and fired eleven volleys. The effect was so slight that the Indians laughed at the Spanish cannon. Warriors outside the palisade attacked Parilla's flanks and kept up a steady, punishing fire by working in relays. A line of Indian marksmen would move into range, fire, and rush back to the moat to exchange their weapons for loaded ones, while their place was taken by a new firing line. A warrior identified by Parilla as the commander of the Indian defenders was singled out for his leadership and daring, showing

in all his movements a well-ordered valor and a great dexterity in the management of his horse and arms. He had a jacket of white buckskin, a helmet of the same material with flesh-colored plumes, and was mounted on a well-kept horse that was suited to that kind of warfare. He had many men similarly equipped, but none of such spirit and conduct, and all were encouraged by his fighting.

Parilla's column was finally cut to pieces. Counterattacking Indians captured his artillery, and his men begged for mercy in retreat. The two padres serving as chaplains urged Parilla to abandon his attempt to take the Wichita city-state on Red River. All seemed hopeless, and Parilla gathered the remnants of his army and marched south. The battle at Twin Villages was the largest military engage-

Thomas Jefferson, the president responsible for bringing the Louisiana territory and thus Oklahoma into the Union. Painting by Rembrandt Peale.

ment in Oklahoma during the eighteenth century. A hundred years would pass before another military invasion occurred to match the extent and ambition of Parilla's ill-fated venture.

In four short years after Parilla's dismal failure, Spain received all of Louisiana, including the future Oklahoma, from France without firing a shot. By an agreement called the Family Compact between the ruling houses of France and Spain, each was bound to support the other in its regular wars against England. In the Seven Years' War (called the French and Indian War in North America), concluded by the Treaty of Paris of 1763, France and Spain were defeated. Spain demanded territorial indemnity from France for the loss of Florida to England, and France, under the terms of the Family Compact, ceded Louisiana, including the future Oklahoma, to Spain. Thus the Spanish flag returned to the country north of Red River.

For thirty-seven years Oklahoma was a frontier region in the Spanish province of Louisi-

ana, and the Spanish governor at New Orleans combined his efforts with those of the Spanish governor in Texas to control the Wichita city-state on Red River. The primary goal of the Spanish officials was to abolish the traffic in guns and ammunition for which the Twin Villages had long been a source. The Wichitas had enjoyed free trade under the French flag. To regulate frontier trade, their new masters established a restrictive government licensing system that included a careful scrutiny of the inventories of traders dealing with the Comanches and other "wild" tribes. When the Spanish administration abolished Indian slavery, its action ended an additional source of profit for the crafty Taovaya traders. The Indian middlemen continued to deal with their preferred French merchants, but Spanish surveillance of goods entering the country and restrictive commercial policies gradually dried up the long-enjoyed prosperity of the Wichita communities and brought a decline in their power and influence.

In 1786, Spanish engineers laid out a trade road between San Antonio and Santa Fe. The most important stop on the route was the Wichita city-state on Red River. This augured a revival of prosperity for the Twin Villages, but the continued restrictive commercial policy imposed by Spanish officials on the province, plus the lack of goods owing to the steady decline of Spanish power, assured the ultimate economic ruin of Oklahoma's native merchants. The once-proud, once-prosperous Wichitas were reduced to poverty and helplessness. Their guns were wearing out, no new weapons were coming in, and their misery was intensified by the rise of a new Indian power in Oklahoma. The Osages, patronized by traders from the northern Spanish post of St. Louis, were entering the old Wichita trading domain. In earlier times raids from their towns on the tributaries of the Grand had driven the Wichitas from the Canadian and Arkansas to Red River. Now, armed with new hatchets, knives, and guns, the northern intruders not only ranged throughout Oklahoma in search of furs but fell with vengeance upon all tribes they encountered. The vigor and power of their assaults were felt even in the Wichita villages on Red River.

Oklahoma as a frontier of Louisiana continued to figure in international affairs. The Spanish flag, which had returned to Oklahoma in 1763, was again replaced by the French banner after Napoleon Bonaparte, first consul of the French Republic, and the king of Spain signed the Treaty of San Ildefonso in 1800. The French, preoccupied with wars in Europe, were unable to follow up the territorial advantage gained by the Treaty of San Ildefonso.

Thus little change was noticeable in Oklahoma and other portions of Louisiana during the second period of French control. In 1803, American commissioners concluded negotiations with French officials that provided for the purchase of Louisiana by the United States. Thus by the Louisiana Purchase agreement Oklahoma became the most distant frontier of the United States in the Southwest.

Notes on Sources, Chapter 2

Much work remains to be done in the original sources to enable writers to present in satisfying detail the age of European dominion over Oklahoma. From the work done thus far, much of it peripheral to Oklahoma, some hints appear about this 300-year period. Coronado's estimate of the region is extracted from George P. Winship, ed., *The Coronado Expedition* (Washington, D.C., 1896). Additional information on early Spanish activity here is found in Herbert E. Bolton, *Spanish Borderlands* (New Haven, 1921); Herbert E. Bolton, *Coronado: Knight of Pueblos and Plains* (New York, 1949); Herbert E. Bolton, *Athanaze de Mézières and the Louisiana-Texas Frontier*, 2 vols. (Cleveland, 1914); Alfred B. Thomas, *Forgotten Frontiers: A Study of the Spanish Indian Policy of Don Juan Bautista de Anza, Governor of New Mexico 1777–1787* (Norman, 1932); and George P. Hammond and Agapito Rey, *Don Juan de Oñate: Colonizer of New Mexico, 1595–1628,* 2 vols. (Albuquerque, 1953).

Spanish activity along the Canadian River after 1763 is described in Noel H. Loomis and Abraham P. Nasatir, *Pedro Vial and the Roads to Santa Fe* (Norman, 1967). Elizabeth Ann Harper John has discussed French dominion over Oklahoma in *Storms Brewed in Other Men's Worlds* (College Station, Texas, 1975). Benjamin French, *Historical Collections of Louisiana*, 5 vols. (New York, 1846–53), presents the role of *coureurs de bois* in frontier commerce in Oklahoma. La Harpe's reconnaissance is detailed in Anna Lewis, "La Harpe's First Expedition in Oklahoma, 1718–1719," *Chronicles of Oklahoma* 2 (December, 1924): 331–49.

The account of the Battle of Twin Villages is drawn from Henry E. Allen, "The Parilla Expedition to the Red River in 1759," *Southwestern Historical Quarterly* 18 (July, 1939): 51–71.

Chapter 3

Long Knives on the Canadian

Artist's sketch of American explorers reconnoitering Oklahoma and the Southwest.

The American flag came to Oklahoma in 1803. The price the United States paid to France for Louisiana was very low; Oklahoma as a component of this vast territorial acquisition cost only about $1.5 million. Certain lead mines and oil wells in the state have individually produced more wealth than that.

Restless, daring Americans, sometimes called "Long Knives" on the international frontier, had entered the eastern margins of Louisiana even before 1803. With the United States' acquisition of this vast, uncharted province, American trappers and traders

flowed into Louisiana. Oklahoma was one of the most appealing portions of Louisiana because of the rich commerce in furs already developed by French traders among the Osage, Quapaw, and Wichita tribes. Oklahoma's waterways provided easy access to the Plains tribes for additional trade, especially traffic in the much-sought-after buffalo robes, and the land was a natural highway to the trade center at Santa Fe, in New Mexico.

The United States government quickly devised a system for administering Louisiana. It was expected that the trappers and traders in the new land would be but a vanguard for permanent agricultural settlements and that very soon several states would be carved out of the new acquisition. The region comprising present Oklahoma, situated on the southwestern frontier of Louisiana with easy access to the Spanish borderlands, bid fair to become one of the first states formed from Louisiana. It is a curious fact that Oklahoma was the last state created from the Louisiana Purchase; the Sooner State's arrested development is another of those anomalies in which Oklahoma history abounds.

In 1804, by an act of Congress, Louisiana (and thus Oklahoma) was placed under the jurisdiction of Indiana Territory, which at that time extended west of the Mississippi. The trans-Mississippi portion of Indiana Territory was called Upper Louisiana. The governor of Indiana Territory, William H. Harrison, was the chief executive for Upper Louisiana. Harrison later became a hero of the War of 1812 and the ninth president of the United States. In 1805, Congress created Louisiana Territory, with headquarters at Saint Louis. General James Wilkinson, whose son was one of the first official American explorers to visit Oklahoma, was appointed governor of the new territory. In 1812 the administration of the future states of the Louisiana Purchase, including Oklahoma, was changed by an act of Congress that established Missouri Territory. When Missouri was on the threshold of statehood in 1819, all of Oklahoma south of 36°30′N and present Arkansas were organized into the Territory of Arkansaw (hereafter spelled Arkansas). At different times between 1819 and 1829 the legislature of Arkansas Territory organized counties to accommodate the spread of American settlements across the eastern third of Oklahoma.

President Thomas Jefferson, whose vision and energy had brought about the acquisition of Louisiana, was eager to learn as much as possible about the new land. While he wanted to satisfy his personal curiosity concerning the rocks and minerals, the flora and fauna, and the native peoples of Louisiana, he was also eager to have the area explored and mapped. He was especially interested in specific places in the highlands and in the rivers descending to the Mississippi, which he believed would in time be accepted as the western and southern boundaries of Louisiana, and he ordered the secretary of war to use the army to explore Louisiana. Two government ventures were undertaken during 1806 to trace out the headwaters of the Arkansas and the Red as principal streams of the southern margins of Louisiana. These were the first official United States explorations of present Oklahoma.

The Spaniards in Texas and New Mexico were very sensitive about United States claims concerning the southern and western boundaries of Louisiana. When reports of the projected expeditions reached the Spanish colonial officials at Nacogdoches in east Texas and at Santa Fe, they issued warnings that no explorations should be undertaken until the boundaries of Louisiana had been positively set. For the United States "to send a party of soldiers to the sources of the rivers in the disputed territory would be an insult to Spain and would cause that power to retaliate by forcing it to return."

Despite these warnings, preparations proceeded. The Red River expedition was organized in the lower American settlements by Captain Richard Sparks. He planned to transport his twenty-four men, equipment, and supplies in two flat-bottomed boats and pirogues, all light craft, to Twin Villages on the Upper Red, where he hoped to trade for horses to carry his party to the "top of the mountains." The Red River expedition departed from Natchitoches (in present Louisiana) on June 2, 1806. Its progress was very slow because the channel was choked for many miles by a vast log accumulation called the "Raft." At various points along the river Sparks visited Caddo villages. Indian warriors recently returned from a hunt in Texas warned the American commander that the Spaniards had learned of his purpose and that a force of three hundred cavalry was scouring the riverbank to intercept him.

The American party had reached the southeastern corner of present Oklahoma and had beached the boats to prepare camp when a column under Don Francisco Viana from the garrison at Nacogdoches burst from the timber on the Texas side and rode through the shallow water at full speed into the American camp. Viana offered Sparks a choice: turn back to the American settlements or face arrest and detention at Nacogdoches. Vastly outnumbered by Viana's troops, Captain Sparks ordered his men downriver to Natchitoches. While Captain Sparks's Red River expedition must rate as a failure, it had two interesting aspects. One was that Captain Sparks—although his Red River camp was barely within the southeastern corner of the state—was the first United States official to visit Oklahoma. Second, Commander Viana's action indicates the interest of the Spaniards in thwarting American expeditions in the Southwest.

Another venture that suffered a similar fate, also launched in 1806, was the Arkansas River expedition to the Rocky Mountains, led by Captain Zebulon M. Pike. Captain Pike's party of twenty-three men departed Saint Louis during the summer of 1806, traveling by boat up the Missouri and Osage rivers to the head of navigation. At the Osage villages Pike obtained horses to transport his column across the plains. Before departing the Indian community, Lieutenant James Wilkinson, Pike's second-in-command, recorded that the expedition members were treated to a feast of

Zebulon M. Pike, commander of the expedition which brought Lt. James Wilkinson to Oklahoma.

"green corn, buffalo meat, and watermelons about the size of twenty-four pound shot, which, though small, were high flavored."

Pike's men rode northwest from the Osage villages to the Pawnee towns on the Republican River (in Northern Kansas), where Indian informants reported that a sizable Spanish force from Santa Fe had stopped only a few days before. Pike found the report to be true, for a Spanish flag flew over the lodge of the Pawnee chief. After persuading the chief to exchange the Spanish banner for a United States flag, Pike led his men south to the Great Bend of the Arkansas. There Lieutenant Wilkinson was ordered to take five men and descend the river to its mouth. For his mission Wilkinson constructed two boats, one a pirogue hewed from a cottonwood log, the other a light craft constructed of a pole frame covered with elk skin and buffalo hide. On October 28, 1806, the Arkansas River expedition divided. Lieutenant Wilkinson and his five men descended the Arkansas, bound for the Mississippi, while Captain Pike and his column rode west along the banks of the Arkansas to its source. Eventually Pike and his men were arrested by a Spanish patrol in the wilds of the Rocky Mountains and were subjected to a long detention, first at Santa Fe and then at Chihuahua in Mexico.

Lieutenant Wilkinson, in the meantime, soon had to abandon his boats because of shallow water, and he and his men marched along the riverbank. At the mouth of the Little Arkansas there was deeper water; Wilkinson constructed two pirogues and the party was water-borne for the remainder of the journey. The Wilkinson party spent November and December in Oklahoma. Winter came early in 1806 and was very severe. The Wilkinson party's boats capsized several times, dumping their meager supplies into the icy water. The little band subsisted by hunting and by exchanging personal effects for food among the Osages in their camps along the river. Ice, sometimes running from shore to shore, sometimes drifting in huge crunching floes along the Arkansas, slowed the party's descent.

On the morning of December 3, the river was completely frozen, and Wilkinson recorded that "this circumstance placed me in a situation truly distressing, as my men were almost naked; the tatters which covered them were comfortless, and my ammunition was nearly exhausted." Three days later the ice broke and began to drift, and Wilkinson pushed off with it. "But," he wrote,

> as my evil stars would have it, my boats again grounded, and being in the middle of the river, my only alternative was to get out and drag them along for several miles, when we halted to warm our benumbed feet and hands. The next day several large cakes of ice had blocked up the river, and we had to cut our way through them with axes; the boats as usual grounded, and the men, bare legged and bare footed, were obliged to leap into the water. This happened so frequently that two more of my men got badly frosted.

Finally, on December 31, the exploring party passed the mouth of the Poteau, and on New Year's Day, 1807, it left present Oklahoma for the Mississippi. Wilkinson's journal of his expedition down the Arkansas provides the first American account of northeastern Oklahoma. He reported passing several Osage villages and a number of encroaching Cherokee, Choctaw, and Creek camps. He referred to reports of rich lead mines northeast in the Osage country, and he observed American trappers on the Poteau and other streams.

The Sparks and Wilkinson ventures of 1806 were followed by the Sibley expedition of 1811. George C. Sibley, Indian agent at Fort Osage, Missouri, accompanied by a servant, two interpreters, and fifteen Osage warriors, traveled to the buffalo plains during May, 1811. Sibley's party was on this expedition for two months and ranged over present Kansas, Nebraska, and northern Oklahoma. They entered Oklahoma along the valley of the Arkansas River, visited its tributaries, including the Salt Fork (Nescatunga), the Cimarron (Nesuketonga) or Grand Saline, and found a band of Osages camped on the Chikaskia River near present Blackwell, Oklahoma.

Sibley was most impressed by the Salt Plains, "glistening like a brilliant field of snow in the summer sun" on the banks of the Salt Fork. The area, now about one-third covered by a man-made lake, was described by Sibley as a vast flat of salt crust, uniformly of the thickness of a wafer, on either side of the river. "This beautiful white dazzling surface (bordered by a fringe of verdant green)," he noted, "has the effect of looming, as the sailors call it, producing to the unpracticed eye much delusion."

Salt was an important item in frontier trade, not only for seasoning food but also for preserving meat, and Sibley was optimistic about the prospects of the Salt Plains region. He recommended building a wagon road from the Missouri settlements to the Salt Fork. Before returning to Fort Osage, Sibley visited other salt deposits in northern Oklahoma and reported that the area had an "inexhaustible store of ready made salt," waiting to enter "into channels of commerce." He observed that saline springs issued from the base of surrounding hills and spread slowly over the flat. The solution was converted into pure salt by the action of the sun:

> A long continuance of hot dry weather produces a solid mass of salt from five to fifteen inches thick, covering a hundred acres very much resembling a large pond of water covered with rough ice. . . . There are several springs which rise within the flat, around which the salt forms in solid masses.

George C. Sibley, explorer of northwestern Oklahoma.

> . . . At one of these springs I hewed out a piece of salt sixteen inches thick, then dug about a foot below the surface of the ground, and still found an almost solid mass of salt.

While, of course, no immediate commercial development of the rich salt deposits of northwestern Oklahoma occurred, the Salt Plains more and more became a supply point for the traders, trappers, overland expeditions, and Indian tribes of the southwestern frontier.

The most extensive United States reconnaissance of Oklahoma was made by the Stephen H. Long expedition. Major Long, of the United States Corps of Topographical Engineers, was well acquainted with eastern Oklahoma. For years the Osages had waged a devastating war on the Western Cherokees, Delawares, Shawnees, Caddoes, and Wichitas. In 1817 the warriors of these tribes confederated for the announced purpose of exterminating the predatory Osages. Settlers in Arkansas, fearful of becoming involved in this intertribal war, appealed to the federal government for protection, and the War Department ordered Major Long to visit the danger zone and

Stephen H. Long, explorer of eastern Oklahoma and the Canadian River Valley. From a painting by C. W. Peale.

select the site for a military post which, it was hoped, would maintain peace on this wild frontier. Long finally decided upon a location, called by the trappers Belle Point, high on the bluffs on the south bank of the Arkansas at the mouth of the Poteau. Major William Bradford and a company from the rifle regiment constructed a log palisade post called Fort Smith, named for General Thomas A. Smith, commander of the Ninth Military District. Fort Smith was the first United States military installation in the Southwest. Meanwhile, Major Long continued his explorations, which included a reconnaissance on the Poteau to its headwaters, across the divide to the Kiamichi, and down that stream to the Red River.

In 1819 the United States government sent Major Long west on another assignment. His mission was to search out the sources of the Arkansas and the Red, and to trace each stream back to the Mississippi valley settlements. Long transported his men and supplies by boat up the Missouri to the mouth of the Platte and thence overland on horseback, reaching the Rocky Mountains during July, 1820. At the

headwaters of the Arkansas River, Long directed his second-in-command, Captain John R. Bell, and twelve men to follow that stream to Fort Smith. One of the notables in the Bell column was Thomas Say, the acknowledged father of American zoology. Bell's men suffered great hardships on the Arkansas route, riding through the heat of a scorching August sun that daily produced temperatures in excess of 100°F. By the time Bell's party entered Oklahoma their provisions were exhausted, the intense heat had made game very scarce, and the men were reported to be casting longing eyes toward their puny horses and mules, calculating which animal they would slaughter. This drastic step was delayed when Julien, their French guide, killed a skunk. That night they feasted on skunk soup, enriched with a half-pint of bread crumbs salvaged from knapsacks. The food restored their strength for additional marches, and while the hunters ranged far and wide for game without success, they did bring in wild grapes "and some unripe persimmons, all of which were eaten." Bell's Arkansas expedition camped near the mouth of the Cimarron on August 31. During the night, Privates Nolan, Myers, and Bernard deserted with the three strongest horses. They took certain personal effects of the officers and men and, worst of all, the journals of Mr. Say, which contained his notes on the plants, animals, rocks, and minerals observed along the route, sketches and maps, and descriptions and vocabularies of the Indian tribes encountered. Bell's party searched for the fugitives for several days without success; grim and hungry, they then continued along the river to Fort Smith, arriving there on September 9, 1820.

After dispatching Captain Bell southward along the Arkansas, Major Long led his ten-man detachment, which included the eminent botanist and geologist Edwin James, in search of the headwaters of Red River. A daring five-day ride across eastern New Mexico, still a Spanish province, brought the Americans to a deep creek bed, now Major Long's Creek, which Long identified as a tributary of the Red. Unknown to him at the time, this watercourse was actually a tributary of the Canadian. As Long's party crossed the high plains the stream bed gradually widened until it was two miles wide in some places in the area where the group entered present Oklahoma. On August 17, Long's Red River expedition camped in the Antelope Hills of western Oklahoma. The "highway across the plains," the watercourse the expedition conceived to be the Red, was dry. Long's men gouged shallow pits in the riverbed, trying to find water. By the time the group arrived at the Antelope Hills the summer heat was so intense that no amount of digging produced water, but they found a substitute in wild fruit—grapes, "vines loaded with ripe fruit, and purple clusters crowded in such profusion" that they colored the landscape. Botanist James claimed the "fruit of these vines is incomparably finer than that of any other, either native or exotic, which we have met within the United States." Long's men were impressed with the abundance of wild game—bears, turkeys, antelope, bison, deer, and wild horses—which they had observed all across Oklahoma.

Both Long and James were convinced that the area comprising the present panhandle of Texas and western Oklahoma was properly labeled "the Great American Desert," which was "providentially placed to keep the American people from ruinous diffusion." They characterized the region as a wide sandy desert, stretching westward to the base of the Rocky Mountains:

> We have little apprehension of giving too unfavorable an account of this portion of the country. Though the soil is in some places fertile, the want of timber, of navigable streams, and of water for the necessities of life, render it an unfit residence for any but a nomad population. The traveller who shall at any time have traversed its desolate sands, will, we think, join us in the wish that this region may forever remain the unmolested haunt of the native hunter, the bison, and the jackall [coyote].

The great surprise and disappointment of Long's Red River expedition occurred on September 10, 1820. Dr. James recorded that on this day the party

> arrived at the confluence of our supposed Red River with another of much greater size, which we at once perceived to be the Arkansas. Our disappointment and chagrin at

discovering the mistake we had so long laboured under, was little alleviated by the consciousness that the season was so far advanced, our horses and our means so far exhausted as to place it beyond our power to return and attempt the discovery of the sources of Red River.

Three days later, Long's column arrived at Fort Smith to be welcomed by Captain Bell and the Arkansas River expedition party. The uncouth appearance of the members of Long's party was reported "a matter of astonishment both to dogs and men" of that place.

Through the abilities of Say and James, the Bell and Long expeditions produced an exhaustive and descriptive inventory of Oklahoma's geology, flora, fauna, and weather. However, their reports were not the first environmental surveys of the region. At about the time that Long's men were moving up the Platte toward the Rocky Mountains, another scientist, the world-famous English naturalist Thomas Nuttall, was ascending the Arkansas River bound for Fort Smith. Arriving at the post in early spring, 1819, he spent several months in eastern Oklahoma collecting botanical specimens.

In the course of his stay at Fort Smith, Nuttall was invited to accompany a military expedition to Red River. Major William Bradford and a company of riflemen had been ordered to expel white intruders from land the national government was preparing to assign to the Choctaws. On the march up the Poteau to the divide and back down the Kiamichi, Nuttall wrote:

> Our route was continued through prairies, occasionally divided by sombre belts of timber, which serve to mark the course of the rivulets. These vast plains, beautiful almost as the fancied Elysium, were now enamelled with enumerable flowers, among the most splendid of which were the azure larkspur. Serene and charming as the blissful regions of fancy, nothing here appeared to exist but what contributes to harmony.

Nuttall reported that near the mouth of the Kiamichi about twenty families had cleared "considerable farms," and that they were receiving heavy yields of corn and cotton from the fertile soil, the corn "producing eighty bushels to the acre, and settlers demanding three dollars a bushel for it." Nuttall observed that most of the settlers, in view of the improvements they had made, were resentful at being driven from the Kiamichi, but he excused Bradford's action by explaining that most of the people were fugitives from the States, "such as had forfeited the esteem of civilized society."

On one of his daily field trips into southern Oklahoma, Nuttall became lost. The troops searched for him in vain and returned to Fort Smith. The scientist wandered alone three weeks over the wild lower Kiamichi country. He noted that buffalo and wild horses ranged the deep valleys, while deer, bear, and other game flourished on the heavily wooded benches. Nuttall finally found his way back to Fort Smith, just in time to take passage on a trading boat bound for Three Forks. From there, two traders took Nuttall in a canoe fifty miles up Grand River to a commercial salt works. He observed that the saline springs and wells at this frontier manufacturing plant produced 180 bushels of salt each week, worth a dollar a bushel in the settlements. Eighty gallons of water from the wells and springs, evaporated in huge iron saucer-shaped vats over wood fires, yielded a bushel of salt.

Nuttall returned to Three Forks and spent some time studying the flora in the neighborhood of Joseph Bogy's post. He then explored far up the Cimarron with a trapper named Lee before returning to Fort Smith. Nuttall's journal of his explorations of eastern Oklahoma provides some of the most detailed descriptions available of the region's resources and its people.

These scientific and topographical explorations were of importance in making known to the world the wonders of the southwestern frontier, but the leaders and men of the expeditions were transients and personally had little or no direct effect on the settlement of Oklahoma. The Long Knives—the daring trappers and traders from the east—were Oklahoma's earliest American settlers. Even before the transfer of Louisiana to the United States in 1803, adventurers from Kentucky and Tennessee were mingling in the trade on the Upper Red and the Canadian, and the impact of their energy and initiative was felt in every French-Indian settlement in Oklahoma.

Some of these trade communities, dating back to the 1720s and well dispersed over the principal rivers of Oklahoma, contributed to the economies of Twin Villages on the Red River and to Arkansas Post near the mouth of the Arkansas. About 1800, Three Forks on the Arkansas became the focus of the fur trade in the Southwest. This change came about through the influence of the Chouteaus, merchant princes of Saint Louis, who became the proprietors of a vast fur-trade empire on the Missouri and its tributaries.

While Spain was in control of Louisiana, the Spanish governor at Saint Louis had annulled exclusive trading privileges held by the Chouteaus on the Missouri and its tributaries (primarily with the Osages), and had granted this monopoly to a countryman, Manuel Lisa. Pierre Chouteau, a resourceful man with great influence over the Osages, persuaded about three thousand members of this tribe to move from Lisa's territory to the Three Forks area. This placed about half of the Osages in the Arkansas trade orbit near the mouth of the Verdigris. Chouteau selected Cashesegra, or Big Track, as chief of this faction of the tribe, although Clermont, whose principal village was the famous Clermont's or Clermo's town (present-day Claremore), was the hereditary and accepted leader. Wilkinson had met hunting bands of Chouteau's Osages on his trip down the Arkansas in 1806.

The Chouteaus established a family line prominent in modern Oklahoma and formed several communities in the northeastern section of the state, including Salina, situated on the east bank of Grand River in Mayes County.

Another prominent early-day trader in the Three Forks area was Joseph Bogy from Kaskaskia. He settled at the old French town of Arkansas Post and gradually extended his trading operation up the river. Wilkinson met him on the Arkansas in 1806. A year later, while landing a boatload of goods near the mouth of the Verdigris, Bogy was attacked and the goods plundered by a wandering band of Choctaw hunters led by the famous Pushmataha. When called to task by the national government, the venerable Indian chief excused this raid on the grounds that Bogy was supplying goods and arms to the Choctaws' enemies, the Osages. Bogy prospered as a competitor with the Chouteaus for the rich Osage trade and constructed a post on the Verdigris at its rapids, several miles above the river's mouth. Nuttall visited Bogy in 1819 and the hospitable Frenchman invited the naturalist to use his settlement as headquarters for field trips in northeastern Oklahoma. Nuttall recorded, "I soon found him a gentleman though disguised at this time in the garb of a Canadian boatman," and accepted the invitation, spending several months at Bogy's settlement at the falls.

It is difficult to identify the pioneer American trappers on the Arkansas and the Red, for they were generally referred to only as Americans or Long Knives, but one name—Alexander McFarland—appeared early, even before Bogy and Chouteau. McFarland hunted along the Grand, Illinois, and Poteau rivers. In the summer of 1812 he organized a trading party at Cadron on the Arkansas to traffic for horses and mules with the tribes on Upper Red River. Near the Wichita villages in August, an Osage war party struck the Americans' camp, killed McFarland, and made off with the party's trade goods. John Lemmons survived the raid and later in the year, while on a trading expedition to the mouth of the Verdigris with William Ingles, Robert Kuyrkendall, and Benjamin Murphy, Lemmons identified several of McFarland's effects in the possession of Osage warriors who had gathered on the river bank to trade.

After the War of 1812 the number of American settlements in Oklahoma increased. They were primarily small commercial centers established in the vicinity of Three Forks and at other strategic locations to tap the rich Indian trade. Nathaniel Pryor, a daring and picturesque frontiersman from Kentucky and one of early Oklahoma's most distinguished citizens, set up a trading enterprise on the Six Bulls (Grand River) in 1815. Pryor was well qualified for a life on the rugged southwestern frontier. He had served as a sergeant in the Lewis and Clark expedition to the Pacific Northwest, followed by several years of army service in the West with the rank of lieutenant. Pryor was promoted to captain for gallantry in action during the War of 1812.

Shortly after his arrival on the Six Bulls,

Captain Pryor married an Osage girl. He introduced high-bred Kentucky horses into Oklahoma, established a following among the Indian tribes, and in due time became one of the most influential men on the frontier. As his business prospered, Pryor formed a partnership with Samuel B. Richards, and their success attracted several additional settlers to the Grand, Illinois, and Verdigris. These citizens included Robert French and Samuel Rutherford, traders on the Verdigris; Colonel Hugh Love, an agent for various fur companies; and Hugh Glenn, a merchant from Cincinnati and later a partner of Pryor. One of the largest settlements was established on the Verdigris by the firm of Barbour and Brand in 1819. Henry Barbour was a merchant from New Orleans. George W. Brand, a Tennessean, had married a Cherokee. Barbour and Brand's settlement consisted of twelve log houses, three warehouses, a general store, thirty acres of cleared land, and a ferry.

By 1820 hunters and trappers were bringing in their families or forming families among the Indian nations, raising log cabins, clearing farms, and introducing livestock. Tom Slover, an early-day Grand River hunter, brought in his family about this time and was reported to have developed "a good farm on a fine elevation on Grand River." During 1820, Mark Bean settled on the Illinois, and was reported to have a "neat farmhouse with considerable stock of cattle, hogs, and poultry, and several acres of corn."

The increasing settlement brought a change in the kinds of goods shipped by flatboat to markets on the Mississippi River and the Gulf of Mexico. The Indian trade continued; each season the tribes brought to Three Forks bales of beaver, bear, panther, wolf, and otter skins, buffalo robes, elk and deer hides, and containers of much-sought-after bear oil. The Indians exchanged these items for earrings, twists of tobacco, pipes, rope, vermillion, axes, knives, beads, bright-colored cloth, and guns and ammunition. Until approximately 1820 the cargoes launched on the Arkansas were almost altogether packs of furs and stacks of hides, but after this date they included grain, salt, bacon, lead, beeswax, leather, and pecans. Mark Bean was typical of the diversified settler, for, in addition to shipping furs and hides, he

Thomas James, merchant explorer of western Oklahoma. Courtesy Missouri Historical Society.

also collected cargoes of grain, bacon, and salt. On his farm was a saline spring that flowed at a volume sufficient to fill his salt kettles three days a week.

Oklahoma figured in international affairs again in 1819 when the disputed Louisiana boundary was finally settled by the Adams-Onís Treaty. By this agreement the southern and western boundaries separating the territory of the United States and Spain were established by a line that began in the Gulf of Mexico at the mouth of the Sabine River and extended up the west bank of this stream to the 32d parallel. From this point the boundary was set due north to the south bank of the Red River and along the south bank of that stream to the 100th meridian; north on that line to the south bank of the Arkansas and along that stream to its source; thence north to the 42d parallel and out that line to the Pacific. Thus it was by the Adams-Onís Treaty of 1819 that the principal southern and western limits of the future Oklahoma were established.

The year 1821 was important in the Southwest. At that time, Mexico became an independent nation and thereby acquired control of the former Spanish provinces of Texas and New Mexico. As long as these provinces were ruled by Spain, restrictive trade laws had the effect of banning American traders from Santa Fe and other potential markets in the Spanish Southwest. The sad fate of two attempts before 1821 to breach the Spanish embargo on trade with outsiders will illustrate the risks involved. In 1812, Robert McKnight of Saint Louis formed a company of associates to open trade with the Spanish towns of the Río Grande. Shortly after arriving in New Mexico, the intruders were arrested on the charge of entering the Spanish provinces without a passport. The company's goods were confiscated, and McKnight and his men were sent to prison in Chihuahua, Mexico, for nine years. Three years after the ill-fated McKnight expedition, Colonel August P. Chouteau, a leading proprietor in the fur trade at Three Forks, and Jules de Mun delivered a train of goods to Santa Fe. They, too, were arrested and their merchandise was seized by Spanish colonial officials.

American traders, made optimistic by reports that the Mexican government planned to repeal the old colonial commercial restrictions, prepared to establish trade relations with the goods-starved towns on the Río Grande. A fascinating double coincidence linked Oklahoma with the fulfillment of a dream that had intrigued adventurers from the earliest days of French travel up the Arkansas and the Canadian—trade with romantic Santa Fe. It began with the escape of one of McKnight's associates, Peter Baum, from his Spanish captors. After a desperate time of wandering over the Indian-infested Southwest, Baum found his way to the Canadian, crossed Oklahoma to the Arkansas, and arrived at Three Forks early in 1821. He stopped at Pryor's, related his adventures, and traveled on to Saint Louis, where he reported to John McKnight concerning his brother. McKnight joined with Thomas James, a seasoned trapper-trader with years of experience on the Upper Missouri, to form an expedition to New Mexico for the double purpose of trading in the Río Grande settlements and locating his brother.

The eleven-man party of Missourians, with James in charge, departed Saint Louis in May, 1821, their keelboat laden with flour, whiskey, lead, powder, biscuit, and cloth. They reached

Three Forks on the Arkansas in the late summer and met another party preparing to travel overland to Santa Fe.

Pryor and his partner Hugh Glenn, on the basis of Baum's glowing account of the reception Americans could expect at Santa Fe, had been gathering goods, packhorses, and men throughout the summer. Most of the twenty men in Pryor's column, Tom Slover among them, were recruited from the Grand River and Verdigris settlements. Jacob Fowler, a surveyor from Kentucky, joined the Pryor-Glenn party, and his journal of the expedition furnishes an intimate glimpse of the day-to-day adventures of the group. Both the James and Pryor-Glenn columns traveled on horseback, their pack trains laden with trade goods and beaver traps. Though the parties followed separate westerly routes, they were within sight of each other now and then all the way to Santa Fe.

Fowler's journal depicts the adventures of his party while crossing Oklahoma to the Rocky Mountains. One of the most dramatic and tragic episodes involved a contest with a huge grizzly bear, told in Fowler's primitive but moving style:

We maid eleven miles west this day. We stoped heare about one oclock and sent back for one hors that was not able to keep up. We heare found some grapes among the brush. While some were hunting and others cooking some picking grapes a gun was fyered off and the cry of a White Bare [grizzly] was raised. We were all armed in an instent and each man run his own cors [course] to look for the desperet anemel. The brush in which we camped contained from 10 to 20 acors [acres] into which the bare head [bear had] run for shelter finding him self surrounded on all sides.

Glenn and four other men searched the thick brush for the grizzly. Suddenly,

It sprung up and caught Lewis doson [Dawson] and pulled him down in an instent. Coln Glanns [Colonel Glenn's] gun mised fyer or he would have releved the man. But a large slut [Pryor's dog] which belongs to the party atacted the bare with such fury that it left the man and persued her

a few steps in which time the man got up and run a few steps but was overtaken by the bare. When the Coln made a second attempt to shoot but his gun mised fyer again and the slut as before releved the man who run as before but was son again in the grasp of the bare who semed intent on his distruction. The conl again run close up and as before his gun wold not go off the slut makeing an other atack and releveing the man. The conl now be came alarmed lest the bare wold pusue him and run up . . . tree and after him the wounded men and was followed by the bare and thus the[y] were all three up one tree. But a tree standing in rich [reach] the conl steped on that and let the man and bare pas till the bare caught him [Dawson] by one leg and drew him backwards down the tree,

Glenn desperately worked on his weapon, sharpening the flint; then, priming the chamber and taking careful aim, he fired. The bullet felled the bear, but he pulled Dawson

by the leg be fore any of one the party arived to releve him. But the bare soon rose again but was shot by several other [men] wo head [who had] got up to the place of action. It is to be remarked that the other three men with him run off. And the brush was so thick that those on the out sie [side] ware some time getting threw. I was my self down the crick below the brush and heard the dredfull screems of man in the clutches of the bare, the yelping of the slut and the hollowing of the men to Run in Run in, the man will be killed . . . Before I got to the place of action the bare was killed and I met the wounded man with Robert Fowler [the author's brother] and one or two more asisting him to camp where his wounds ware examined. It appeers his head was in the bares mouth at least twice and that when the monster give the crush that was to mash the mans head it being two large for the span of his mouth the head sliped out only the teeth cutting the skin to the bone where ever they tuched it, so that the skin of the head was cut from about the ears to the top in several directions. All of which wounds ware sewed up as well as cold be don by men in our situation haveing no surgen nor surgical instruments. The man still retained his understanding but said I am killed, that I heard my skull brake. But we ware willing to beleve he was mistaken as he spoke chearfully on the subgect till in the after noon of the second day when he began to be restless and some what delereous and on examening an hole in the upper part of his wright temple which we beleved only skin deep we found the brains workeing out. When [we] then sposed that he did hear his scull brake.

Dawson died three days after the grizzly attack. Fowler stated that his comrades

lay at camp and buried him as well as our meens wold admit. Emedetely after the fattal axcident and haveing done all we cold for the wounded man we turned our atention [to] the bare and found him a large fatt anemel we skined him but found the smell of a polcat so strong that we cold not eat the meat. On examening his mouth we found that three of his teeth ware broken off near the gums which we sopose was the cause of his not killing the man at the first bite, and the one not broke to be the caus of the hole in the right temple which killed the man at last.

The James party also had an exciting passage to Santa Fe. The men feasted on buffalo meat. Wood was scarce, and the Missourians, like Coronado's followers three hundred years earlier, used buffalo chips for cooking fuel. The column moved southwest from the bed of the Cimarron to the North Canadian. Water was very scarce and, according to James's account, they "drank large draughts of the blood of this animal [buffalo] which I recollect tasted like milk." James followed a route beyond the North Canadian to the Canadian and stayed with this stream course into New Mexico. In western Oklahoma he met a large Comanche band and gave gifts to the chiefs. In return he was given a Mexican captive who served him as guide and interpreter. Before James's departure, the Comanches invited him to return the next season and trade with them.

The Missouri company reached Santa Fe in December, 1821. While McKnight went to Chihuahua to locate his brother, James traded on the Río Grande. The American party, including the liberated Robert McKnight, took leave of New Mexico in the spring of 1822. The lure of the western country remained strong with James and the McKnight brothers, and remembering the invitation of the Comanche chiefs to return and trade with them, they organized a second expedition in the autumn of 1822.

Again they transported their goods from Saint Louis to the Arkansas and went up that stream past Three Forks on a keelboat. Their craft was frozen in the ice for several weeks, just above the mouth of the Canadian. They finally broke loose, navigated to the mouth of the North Canadian, and ascended that stream to its shoals. There they tied up the keelboat, loaded their goods on horses obtained in the settlements and into pirogues hewed from logs on the riverbank, and resumed their march. Game was plentiful; they killed twenty black bears in a matter of a few days. James was enthusiastic about central Oklahoma, describing it as "very fertile and beautiful country, which will in a few years teem with a dense population. The prairies are interspersed with valuable woodland, and will make as fine a farming country as any in the Union."

At a place that later would be called Spring Valley in Canadian County, James had his men erect a fort to serve as a trading headquarters and storage for their goods. Heavy rains on the headwaters caused such a rise on the North Canadian that James had to abandon his post and move upstream in search of a higher location. He stopped in present Blaine County where his party constructed a stockade, complete with a small cannon and flagpole. One of his men had become ill with pneumonia and nearly died. In addition, the trader became crippled by hip and back pains and had to be carried about on a blanket stretcher. Near the post a huge rattlesnake was killed; in its stomach were found two prairie dogs. James rendered oil from the dead snake and rubbed the preparation on the afflicted joints of the suffering man. He reported that in a very short time the man became "limber and supple."

James and his men traded for a season with the Comanches, realizing huge profits from the exchanges. By the time James was ready to return to the settlements, he had traded for nearly four hundred horses and mules and more packs of buffalo robes and beaver skins

Artist's sketch of Fort Smith, mother post for the Southwest.

than could be carried home. James himself admitted that a plug of tobacco, a knife, and a few strings of beads, "in all worth but little more than a dime, brought one of these valuable skins or robes, worth a least five dollars in any of the states."

Oklahoma was following a familiar pattern. In other frontier regions of the United States the traders and trappers were the vanguard of settlement and intensive development by farmers, artisans, and builders of towns. These changes culminated in territorial status and statehood in the Union. So it was in Oklahoma. McFarland, Slover, Pryor, and James blazed a broad trail in the wilderness, and settlements inched up the Arkansas and the Red into the fertile valleys of the Grand, the Illinois, and the Kiamichi. In 1823, Fort Smith was no longer a lonely outpost on the forward rim of the frontier. It had become a gateway to the West.

The new settlements west of Fort Smith were in need of protection from Osage reprisal, and in 1824 the stockade at Belle Point was temporarily abandoned and the garrison moved upriver to the Grand. Three miles above the mouth of the Grand on the east bank a new post was established, typical of frontier

forts, with log blockhouses, barracks, and log wall enclosures ten feet high, cannon, and parade ground. Colonel Matthew Arbuckle, post commandant, named the new outpost Fort Gibson in honor of General George Gibson of Revolutionary War fame. The same year, Arbuckle sent Major Bradford south to the Red River to construct a military post there. On Gates Creek near the mouth of the Kiamichi, Bradford supervised the erection of Fort Towson, named for General Nathan Towson, a heroic officer in the War of 1812.

It is significant that the first military posts established in Oklahoma created a new frontier line, running north and south from the mouth of the Grand to the mouth of the Kiamichi. They opened up a settlement zone west of Fort Smith and existed primarily to protect the settlers from the Indians. The functions of Forts Gibson and Towson was evident in 1824 when Congress located the western boundary of Arkansas Territory on a line from Fort Gibson south to Red River. The Arkansas territorial legislature organized Lovely County in the north, with the county seat situated on the west bank of Sallisaw Creek thirteen miles above its mouth. Almost overnight a town of log buildings grew up and was named Nicksville in honor of General John Nicks, a hero of the War of 1812. On the Red River a similar development occurred. An Arkansas county was organized there, Miller County, with its principal settlement named Miller Court House.

Oklahoma was well on its way to becoming a state, either piecemeal as an absorbed portion of Arkansas, or as a separate and distinct commonwealth. Then the national government devised a unique role for the future Oklahoma—it would serve the nation as the Indian Territory, a special settlement zone in which federal agents could consolidate the Indian tribes from east of the Mississippi. By this action, instead of becoming one of the first states created from the gigantic Louisiana Purchase, Oklahoma was destined to be the final one. It is ironic that Fort Gibson and Fort Towson, originally established to protect the settlers from the Indians, very soon thereafter were used to protect the Indians from the settlers.

Notes on Sources, Chapter 3

American occupation of the Oklahoma portion of the Louisiana Purchase area is derived from explorer accounts, scientific journals, and trapper-trader memoirs. Materials for the Sparks, Pike, and Long expeditions are found in William H. Goetzmann, *Army Exploration of the American West, 1803–1863* (New Haven, 1959); Joseph A. Stout, Jr., ed., *Frontier Adventurers: American Exploration in Oklahoma* (Oklahoma City, 1976); W. Eugene Hollon, *The Lost Pathfinder: Zebulon Montgomery Pike* (Norman, 1949); Donald M. Jackson, ed., *The Journals of Zebulon Montgomery Pike, with Letters and Related Documents*, 2 vols. (Norman, 1966); Edwin James, *Account of an Expedition from Pittsburgh to the Rocky Mountains, 1819–1820*, vols. 14–17 in *Early Western Travels, 1748–1865*, ed. Reuben G. Thwaites (Cleveland, 1905); and H. M. Fuller and Leroy R. Hafen, eds., *The Journal of Captain John R. Bell, Official Journalist for the Stephen H. Long Expedition* (Glendale, Calif., 1957).

The Sibley expedition across northern Oklahoma is the subject of "Major Sibley's Diary," *Chronicles of Oklahoma* 5 (June, 1927): 196–211.

The first scientific exploration of eastern Oklahoma is the subject of Thomas Nuttall, *A Journal of Travels into the Arkansas Territory during the Year 1819*, ed. Savoie Lottinville (Norman, 1980).

Three commercial classics detail early-day economic life here: Elliott Coues, ed., *The Journal of Jacob Fowler* (New York, 1898); Walter B. Douglas, ed., *Three Years Among the Mexicans and Indians* (Saint Louis, 1916), which chronicles the trading enterprises of General Thomas James in Oklahoma; and Max L. Moorhead, ed., *Commerce of the Prairies* (Norman, 1954), Josiah Gregg's account of the Santa Fe trade.

Chapter 4

The Indian Country

From earliest times Oklahoma has played a vital and often curious role in history. During the Spanish period the region was regarded as an important link connecting New Spain's southern provinces with Quivira and the mysterious lands of the north. Then, after 1700, the north-south Spanish concourse shifted to an east-west flow of men and goods when the French entered the region. Daring French explorers and traders not only tapped the rich fur resources of Oklahoma itself but also used the river valleys notably of the Red and the Arkansas rivers, as highways for commerce with the Plains Indians and the Spanish towns on the Río Grande.

After the United States acquired Louisiana, Oklahoma played a far more conspicuous and significant role in national affairs than was commonly the case for such remote frontiers. After the Adams-Onís Treaty of 1819, the nation's southwestern boundary (Oklahoma's present southwestern corner) was established on Red River and the 100th meridian, and for many years Oklahoma was the nation's foremost defense area on an unfriendly southwestern frontier. The fact that several military posts and cantonments (Forts Smith, Gibson, Towson, Coffee, Wayne, Arbuckle, Holmes, and Washita) were established in present Oklahoma to defend the nation against possible foreign intrigue and invasion from this quarter, as well as to keep peace among the Indian tribes, was an indication of the importance of this region to national security.

Moreover, although situated far beyond American settlements at the time of the Louisiana Purchase, Oklahoma very early became directly involved in the phenomenal expansion of the American people from the Atlantic seaboard to the Pacific shore. Wide-ranging, hardy, adaptable frontiersmen, fired by an insatiable thirst for new land and fresh opportunity, and a curious combination of historical coincidences involved Oklahoma on at least three counts.

First, the numbers of frontiersmen increased rapidly in the fertile valleys of eastern Oklahoma rather soon after the transfer of Louisiana. Second, the fast-developing Arkansas Territory, eager for statehood, was permitted to annex a forty-mile-wide strip along the entire eastern boundary of today's Oklahoma to bring the infant settlements on the Arkansas, the Red, and the Grand under its jurisdiction. It was only by a curious turn of events, again one that linked Oklahoma to national affairs, that the entire future Sooner State escaped this fate. A statement issued by Senator Thomas H. Benton of Missouri, as he waged a bitter struggle on behalf of Arkansas Territory to retain that portion of Oklahoma, epitomizes the third development that linked the future Oklahoma to national events.

In response to a growing demand by the citizens in the East that the Indians resident in their states be relocated west of the Mississippi so that the whites could have the vacated tribal lands, the national government decided to set aside the future Oklahoma as a settlement zone, reserved exclusively for Indian nations. To make the land transfer more attractive to Indian leaders, the national government in 1828 reclaimed the forty-mile-wide strip in eastern Oklahoma attached to Arkansas Territory in 1824, and divided it among the several tribes. Senator Benton attempted to thwart this "crippling and mutilating of Arkansas," claiming that it reduced the territory

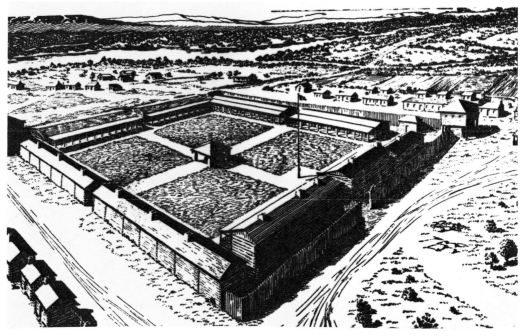

Sketch of Fort Gibson, established in 1824.

to the class of weak states . . . against all the reasons which had induced Congress, four years before, to add on twelve thousand square miles of her domain. . . . The reason for the southern members [of Congress] for promoting this amputation of Arkansas in favor of the [Indians] was simply to assist in inducing their removal by adding the best part of Arkansas with its salt springs, to the ample millions of acres west of that territory already granted to them.

Benton also explained that what happened to those pioneer settlers in eastern Oklahoma after the forty-mile-wide strip was assigned exclusively to the Indian tribes.

I have said that amputated part of Arkansas was an organized part of the territory, divided into counties, settled and cultivated. Now, what became of these inhabitants?—their property?—their possessions? They were bought out by the federal government! A simultaneous act was passed, making a donation of 320 acres of land [within the remaining part of Arkansas] to each head of a family who would retire from the amputated part; and subjecting all to military removal that did not retire. It was

done. They all withdrew. Three hundred and twenty acres of land in front to attract them, and regular troops in the rear to push them, presented a motive power adequate to its object; and twelve thousand square miles of slave territory was evacuated by its inhabitants, with their flocks and herds and slaves; and not a word was said about it; and the event has been forgotten.

Thus Oklahoma's natural development from a frontier wilderness into an emerging state, or at least into a satellite of Arkansas, was abruptly arrested with the creation of the Indian Territory. Various leaders in the federal government were sensitive to the destructive effect on the tribes of the successive waves of settlers across the frontier. For some time they had been considering the possibility of establishing a permanent Indian Territory to the west beyond the line of settlement where the tribes would never be bothered again. One of the uses President Jefferson hoped to make of the vast territory acquired by the Louisiana Purchase was to create an Indian colonization zone on its western margins beyond the pressure and influence of the American settlements. Of course, in 1803 no one could possibly foresee the occupation of the American West during the nineteenth century to such an extent that even the Indian Territory lands would be demanded by the citizens of the United States.

In the early days of tribal relocations the Indian colonization zone in Louisiana Territory was a vaguely defined area on the western margins of the United States, including present Oklahoma, shown on maps of the time as the "Indian Country." An act of Congress in 1804 authorized the president to begin removal negotiations, and by 1808 tribes from both north and south of the Ohio River began emigrating to the West.

The removal program was poorly coordinated. Settlers regarded it as their right to settle any place they chose and often they "squatted" on treaty-assigned Indian lands in such numbers that new territories and states were organized before the tribes assigned a given area could complete their removal. For example, the portion of Indian country that later became Missouri received many tribes from the Old Northwest. The area filled so quickly with settlers that the emigrant tribes in a short time had to be relocated farther west in what became Kansas. United States settlements had seriously reduced the Indian Country by 1830, though many populous tribes had yet to be evacuated from Georgia, Alabama, and Mississippi. As a consequence, Congress withdrew from settlement a strip of land west of Missouri and Arkansas, extending from the Platte to the Red River, identified it as the Indian Territory, and restricted its use to the colonization of eastern Indian tribes. As will be shown, even the northern portion of Indian Territory was opened to the settlers in 1854 when Kansas and Nebraska territories were organized, and subsequently the resident tribes were moved to the only remaining portion of Indian Territory, present Oklahoma.

All of Oklahoma except the Panhandle remained Indian Territory until 1889. Thereafter, successive areas in western Oklahoma were opened to the homesteader. By 1907 only the eastern half of Indian Territory remained. In that year the remnant of Indian Territory and the Oklahoma Territory were joined to form the state of Oklahoma. During the century that Oklahoma served as an Indian colonization zone, more than sixty tribes were

Washington Irving, popular American author and explorer of central Oklahoma.

settled within its borders. Because much of Oklahoma history is Indian history, a general knowledge of the Indian tribes is essential to understanding this unique and significant phase of the heritage of the Sooner State.

The United States government continued the British method of dealing with the tribes—that of recognizing each tribe as a sovereign entity. As autonomous communities, the tribes governed their members and conducted their internal affairs by traditional tribal methods. Whenever a change in relations between a tribe and the United States was required, such as making peace, altering trading privileges, or more important, the cession of tribal lands, a treaty was negotiated with tribal leaders by the president and ratified by the United States Senate, much like any of today's pacts between the United States and foreign powers. Because conflict was common between the United States and various tribes, Indian affairs were under the jurisdiction of the War Department.

The federal officer responsible for conducting Indian relations was called the Commissioner of Indian Affairs. In 1848 the Department of the Interior was established and the Commissioner of Indian Affairs was transferred to this new department. Each tribe maintained relations with the United States through delegations of chiefs that regularly visited Washington to call on the president, and the federal government assigned an agent, somewhat like a diplomatic officer, to each tribe. The agent's function was to hold the Indians' friendship, distribute gifts and annuities, and watch for British and other foreign intrigue. To discharge his duties, he was required to live with the tribe.

The removal story requires some emphasis on the diverse cultures of the tribes settled in Oklahoma. Between 1820 and 1880, the some sixty tribes colonized in Oklahoma joined the Wichitas, the Caddoes, the Kiowas, the Comanches, the Quapaws, and the Osages who were already there. While most of the immigrant tribes came from east of the Mississippi, others came from the South, the West, and from the North. These tribes were by no means alike. Several were sedentary, agricultural, and peaceful. Others were migratory hunters and extremely warlike. Each tribe was an independent and self-contained social unit with a system of government based in a few cases on written constitutions. For most of the tribes, however, a sort of unwritten common law and custom prevailed. Whatever the system, it seemed to control the members sufficiently for tribal needs.

Regardless of the cultural level, each tribe practiced a religion based on the concept of a Great Spirit, a pantheon of lesser spirits, good and evil, and a hereafter referred to as "the happy hunting ground." Tribal tradition explained such basic things as human origin, and often gave accounts of a flood and a migration in early times "from the land of the setting sun." Individual power of the warrior was derived from his medicine—an assortment of omens, creatures, and phenomena that produced good fortune in battle, the chase, and romance. The warrior crafts and hunting skills were emphasized for the men, and status in most tribes was based on success in these activities. The social system included recognition of the clan for marriage purposes and the practice of polygamy.

The more prominent language stocks and tribes settled in Oklahoma were the Iroquoian (Senecas, Wyandots, Mohawks, Tuscaroras, and Cherokees); Algonkian (Sacs, Foxes, Potawatomis, Shawnees, Delawares, Kickapoos, Cheyennes, and Arapahoes); Caddoan (Wichitas, Caddoes, Pawnees, Wacoes, and Tawakonis); Lutuamian (Modocs); Muskhogean (Choctaws, Chickasaws, Creeks, and Seminoles); Tanoan (Kiowas); Uto-Aztecan (Comanche); Athapascan (Apaches); and Tonkawan (Tonkawas). Perhaps the best known of the tribes relocated in Oklahoma were the so-called Five Civilized Tribes—the Cherokees, Choctaws, Chickasaws, Creeks, and Seminoles.

A voluntary removal to Oklahoma was under way long before Indian Territory was established. Bands of Kickapoos, Delawares, and Shawnees from north of the Ohio River, attracted by the abundant wild game and freedom from the contaminating influence of the American settlements, migrated to central Oklahoma and settled on the North Fork and other tributaries of the Canadian. Cherokee and Choctaw hunters crossed the Mississippi and hunted in Oklahoma during preremoval times, too.

The first substantial Indian colonization in the trans-Mississippi West occurred among the Cherokees. This tribe, possibly numbering twenty thousand, occupied an area extending over western North Carolina, eastern Tennessee and Kentucky, northern Georgia, and northeastern Alabama. Very early they came under the influence of traders from English settlements on the Atlantic Seaboard. Traders introduced firearms, trade goods, horses, cattle, hogs, and chickens, and they frequently took Cherokee wives. This gave rise to mixed-blood families with such notable names as Rogers, Ward, Adair, Vann, Chisholm, Ross, Lowry, Reese, and Hicks, who came to play significant roles in Cherokee affairs in the East and later in Oklahoma. The mixed bloods, more like their fathers than their mothers, came to adopt the European manner of living and undertook the development of farms, ranches, and businesses in the Cherokee Nation. Many of them became prominent slaveholders. The full bloods, however, continued to live in log cabins, cultivated only a subsistence patch of food crops, raised horses, excelled in the old tribal crafts of hunting and fishing, preferred a life close to nature, and now and then joined in a war party for a strike against the encroaching white settlements.

In 1794 a Cherokee band led by The Bowl, a war chief, ambushed an American party on the Tennessee. For this so-called Massacre of Mussel Shoals, The Bowl and his followers were ostracized by the Cherokee tribal council. To escape retribution by frontier militia as well as by their own people, The Bowl and his warriors with their families crossed the Mississippi into Spanish territory and settled on the Saint Francis River in what later became Arkansas Territory. This western community became the nucleus for additional Cherokee migrations.

Representatives of two factions of the Eastern Cherokee Nation met with President Thomas Jefferson in 1808. One group was known as the Lower Cherokees. Less advanced in the arts of Anglo-American civilization, they preferred to continue their old ways. Disturbed by the advancing American settlements and diminishing game, they believed removal to the West was desirable. The other group, known as the Upper Cherokees, had adopted the ways of their Anglo-American neighbors; many already were successful planters and stock raisers, and they desired to remain on the lands of their ancestors. They requested that the president define their nation's boundaries to protect them from being overrun by the settlers. Jefferson promised to respect the wishes of both factions.

Soon after the Washington council, a delegation of Lower Cherokees visited their kinsmen in Arkansas, found the country to their liking, and began moving their families west. Encroaching white settlements in eastern Arkansas caused the Cherokee migrants to establish their towns, which by 1815 had a cumulative population of 3,000, on the northwestern frontier of present Arkansas between the White and the Arkansas rivers. The Western Cherokees were permitted to occupy this new country by consent until 1817. In that year a delegation of their chiefs, headed by John Jolly, went east to meet with certain Eastern Cherokee chiefs and leading men, including George Lowry, Walter Adair, Going Snake, and Charles Hicks, at the Cherokee agency in Tennessee.

Charles J. Latrobe, British author and explorer of central Oklahoma.

In the presence of United States Commissioners Andrew Jackson, Tennessee Governor Joseph McMinn, and David Meriwether, Eastern and Western Cherokee chiefs signed a treaty. By ceding one-third of the tribal lands in the East (principally in Tennessee, Alabama, and Georgia), the Cherokee Nation received title to the tract already occupied by the Western Cherokees in northwestern Arkansas between the White and the Arkansas rivers. The treaty encouraged the Eastern Cherokees to migrate and settle with their kinsmen in the West by giving each emigrating warrior a "rifle gun and ammunition, one blanket and one brass kettle, or in lieu of the brass kettle, a beaver trap." The federal government pledged to compensate the emigrants for improvements on land left in the East, and to transport them at public expense. Under the terms of the 1817 agreement, more than three thousand Cherokees moved to Arkansas, with the result that by 1820 about six thousand Cherokees— nearly one-third of the tribe—had taken up residence in the West.

From their earliest days in Arkansas, Cherokees had hunted on the Grand and the Verdigris. The Osages, who claimed the land both north and south of the Arkansas as their range, regarded the hunting trips as intrusions and attacked Cherokee parties whenever they were encountered west of Fort Smith. Cherokee war parties found their revenge in attacks on Osage towns in northeastern Oklahoma. The Osages countered with raids on the Cherokee settlements. Incidents mounted, resulting in a long, bloody war that brought terror and destruction to the southwestern frontier.

William L. Lovely, United States agent for the Arkansas Cherokees, labored for years to arrange a truce between the Osages and Cherokees. Finally, in 1816, he persuaded Clermont and other Osage chiefs to meet with Cherokee leaders at the mouth of the Verdigris for the purpose of settling their differences. At the Verdigris council, Lovely, believing that the principal cause of the trouble was the Cherokees' hunting on lands claimed by the Osages, proposed that Clermont's people cede a 7-million-acre tract situated between the Cherokee towns and the Verdigris, north of the Arkansas, to the United States in return for the federal government's paying all depredation claims held by the Cherokees and whites against the Osages. The Osage chiefs accepted the proposal, and the surrenderd territory, known as Lovely's Purchase, was assigned to the Cherokees as a hunting outlet adjacent to their Arkansas lands.

The Cherokee Treaty of 1817 confirmed the Western Cherokee hunting outlet, but when Cherokee hunters attempted to assert their rights along the Grand and the Verdigris, they were laid upon as of old by Osage war parties. Osage raids on Cherokee towns in Arkansas also continued. During 1817, in a memorial addressed to the government, Talluntusky and other Cherokee chiefs claimed they had been trying to make friends with the Osages for nine years. They charged that Osage raiders had stolen their horses and that to raise crops for their families the Cherokees were reduced to working the land with bare hands. Because the "rivers were running with blood of Cherokees," the chiefs warned that they were determined to proceed against their oppressors.

One of the bloodiest Indian engagements in Oklahoma history, known as the battle of Claremore Mound, in October, 1817, fulfilled

Talluntusky's warning. A well-armed Cherokee force struck Clermont's village, the principal Osage town on the Verdigris, sacked and burned it, and carried off a pack train of plunder and fifty prisoners. Instead of cowing the Osages, the Claremore Mound defeat stirred them to greater fury. The bitter frontier war continued unabated, with the Osages raiding and killing indiscriminately.

Anglo-Americans suffered too. A fatal climax occurred late in 1824 when Major Curtis Wilburn, an officer from Fort Gibson, was slain by an Osage war party on Blue River in southern Oklahoma. Federal officials then summoned the Osage chiefs to council at Saint Louis and exacted from them a treaty by which the Osages ceded to the United States all lands in Oklahoma, agreed to vacate their villages along the Verdigris, and promised to move north into what later became southern Kansas.

With the Osage evacuation, government agents began to pressure the Western Cherokees to exchange their lands in northwestern Arkansas for a new home in the Indian Country, generally contained within their old hunting outlet as established by Lovely's Purchase. This was agreeable to the Western Cherokees because American settlements were pushing up the valleys of the White and the Arkansas. White hunters had begun to poach on the Cherokees' Arkansas domain, wantonly killing the game. The Long Knives slaughtered buffalo for tallow, and the stench from rotting carcasses carried even into the Cherokee towns. Bears were killed solely for oil.

The Western Cherokees were therefore ready for another move, and in 1828 a delegation of their chiefs journeyed to Washington and negotiated a treaty with the United States for an exchange of Cherokee lands in Arkansas for a new home on the Lovely Purchase in the Indian Territory. This placed the Cherokee Nation in present northeastern Oklahoma on a domain of 7 million acres, with a perpetual outlet fifty-seven miles wide that extended to the 100th meridian. This tract remained the home of the Cherokees until 1907 when Indian Territory and Oklahoma Territory were joined to form the state of Oklahoma.

By the 1828 treaty, the United States agreed to remove all white persons resident in the new Cherokee Nation; to compensate the

John Mix Stanley's painting depicting an Osage scalp dance. Courtesy Bureau of American Ethnology.

Cherokees for improvements made on their Arkansas lands; to pay the Indians a sum of $50,000 for the inconvenience the move caused them; to buy the nation a printing press and type; to grant the tribe an annual payment of $2,000 for ten years for the support of Cherokee schools; and to subsidize the removal of those Eastern Cherokees—more than two-thirds of whom remained in the East—who elected to join their kinsmen in the West, including the cost of removal and subsistence for one year. This treaty contained a promise to the Cherokees that, in view of what ultimately happened to their nation, became empty words, even though elegantly expressed:

> Under the most solemn guarantee of the United States, [this land shall] be and remain theirs forever—a home that shall never, in all future time, be embarrassed by having extended around it the lines, or placed over it the jurisdiction of a Territory or State, nor be pressed upon by the extension, in any way, of any of the limits of any existing Territory or State.

Most of the Western Cherokees moved to their new home within a year after the treaty was signed. On the Illinois River, Cherokee leaders established a new capital for the tribal government and the people went to work clearing fields, establishing settlements, and opening the wilderness. The eastern boundary of the Cherokee Nation (the present Oklahoma boundary north of the Arkansas River) was set by government surveyors on a line from the southwest corner of Missouri to a point a hundred paces east of Fort Smith.

Many notables joined the Western Cherokees in their new home. Among them was George Guess, or Sequoyah, the Cherokee genius, who, by reducing his native tongue to written form in an alphabet or syllabary of eighty-six characters, made his nation literate almost overnight. In June, 1829, Sam Houston, best known as the founder of the Texas Republic, who had abandoned his wife and his office as governor of Tennessee, arrived in Oklahoma. He lived with his friend Chief John Jolly for a period, then took a Cherokee wife named Tiana (Talihina) and settled three miles northwest of Fort Gibson. There he established Wigwam Neosho, a trading post and frontier saloon.

Although the Cherokees were the first of the Five Civilized Tribes to migrate to the trans-Mississippi West, they were not the first of these southern tribes to be assigned a homeland in Oklahoma. In 1818 government commissioners had negotiated a treaty with the Quapaws through which this tribe abandoned all claim to lands in Oklahoma south of the Arkansas. Subsequent treaties with the Osages cleared additional claims to the country between the Canadian and Red River, and in 1820 the Choctaws were assigned a grant of land in southern Oklahoma.

Thus the Choctaws were the first of the Five Civilized Tribes to be assigned a domain in Indian Territory. Their ancestral homeland extended from the Gulf shore inland into present Alabama and Mississippi. At the time of removal they numbered about 22,000 and were the most numerous of the Five Civilized Tribes. Of Muskhogean linguistic stock, these people had a rich traditional history, including the account of Nanih Waya, a sacred hill or mountain located near Noxapater, Winston County, Mississippi, which they believed was built up from the flooded plains by their all-powerful deity to serve his children as a refuge from the deluge. Another account explained the migration of the Choctaws from "the land of the setting sun." A sacred pole, carried by the principal chief, was the tribe's guide in its search for a new home. Each day the sacred pole bent eastward and the wanderers followed its mandate until one morning, soon after the Choctaws crossed the Mississippi, the guiding rod stood erect, indicating this was where the Choctaws were to build their villages.

At the time of discovery by Europeans, the Choctaws had developed a village life based on agriculture, although the warriors were skilled hunters. The Choctaw Nation was divided into three districts or provinces, each ruled by a principal chief. The relationships and powers of this triple leadership could be properly compared with the old Roman triumvirate. A national council composed of leading men and warriors also had a voice in the affairs of Choctaw government. The location of the Choctaws on the Gulf of Mexico brought them into more frequent contact with the Spaniards, French, and British than others of the Five Civilized Tribes. Undoubtedly this contact had the effect of increasing tribal skill in diplomacy, which showed itself time and time again in Choctaw dealings with the United States government. Their constant exposure to the representatives of the leading powers of Europe accelerated the acculturation of the Choctaws. The presence of French, Scottish, and English agents and traders shows up in the mixed-blood family names—LeFlore, McCurtain, Folsom, McKenney, Walker, Perry, Jones, and Locke—prominent in Choctaw affairs both in the East and in Indian Territory.

American missionaries went to work among the Choctaws quite early, and the results were indicated by the surprising number of schools functioning in the nation, the high literacy rate, and the enduring interest of Choctaws in education. Like other eastern tribes, the Choctaws were pressed by the American settlements, demands were made for their lands, and the federal government encouraged the tribe to move west.

The Choctaws were well acquainted with the West long before removal. Bands of Choctaws had lived on the west bank of the Mississippi in Louisiana since early French times, and as game became scarce in the East, Choctaw hunting parties ranged up the Red and the Arkansas into Oklahoma. Chief Pushmataha, the most prominent warrior in the tribe, often declared that his favorite hunting ground was on the western waters in the area that later became Indian Territory and Oklahoma.

For years government agents had encouraged the Choctaws to consider exchanging their eastern lands for a new domain west of Arkansas, and finally in 1820 the redoubtable Pushmataha and lesser Choctaw chiefs met with General Andrew Jackson at Doak's Stand on the Natchez Trace in Mississippi to discuss the removal proposition. From these negotiations came the famous Treaty of Doak's Stand, whereby the Choctaws, in return for ceding a portion of their eastern lands, received a vast tribal estate in the Indian Country. It was bounded on the north by the Arkansas and the Canadian, on the south by the Red River, and it extended into southwestern Arkansas. The treaty pledged the United States government to supply to each Choctaw warrior who would emigrate a rifle; a bullet mold; a camp kettle; a blanket; enough ammunition for hunting and defense for one year; and payment for any improvements he left in his ancestral home. Pushmataha insisted that a clause be written into the treaty providing that fifty-four sections of eastern Choctaw land were to be surveyed and sold at auction, the proceeds to go into a special fund to support schools for Choctaw youth in the new country.

While government officials were hopeful that the Choctaws would remove at once, and tribal leaders knew that total removal was inevitable, the treaty had made removal a voluntary matter. Therefore, only about one-fourth of the tribe moved west under the terms of the Doak's Stand Treaty; most of the tribe remained in Mississippi, since by the treaty the Choctaws had surrendered only about a third of their eastern lands.

The pioneer Choctaw immigrants found the Arkansas settlements as far west as the Kiamichi, occupying some of the best land assigned them by the Treaty of Doak's Stand. Their protests eventually resulted in the expulsion of the most westerly situated settlers by United States troops. A new treaty in 1825 set the Choctaw-Arkansas boundary to begin on the south bank of the Arkansas River at a point a hundred paces east of Fort Smith and extending due south to the Red River. Thus the eastern Choctaw Nation perimeter was established. The boundary then was extended west on that stream to the 100th meridian, north on that line to the Canadian, then on that river and the Arkansas downstream to Fort Smith. In effect, by the Doak's Stand Treaty and the Boundary Treaty of 1825, the Choctaws received what is now the southern half of Oklahoma. The Choctaw Boundary Treaty of 1825 and the Cherokee Treaty of 1828 established the eastern boundary of the future state of Oklahoma. Present Oklahoma, the southern half of the Indian Country, was almost completely absorbed by the Choctaw and Cherokee grants. As indicated, the Choctaws held the entire southern half, and the Cherokees, with their nation in northeastern Oklahoma and the vast outlet to the 100th meridian, filled the upper fourth. All that remained was a triangular center. This area was assigned to the Creeks.

The Creeks or Muskogees, another of the Five Civilized Tribes and a leader in the Muskhogean linguistic family, claimed a 25-million-acre domain in Georgia, Alabama, and Mississippi. The Creeks were numerous in removal times, possibly mustering twenty thousand tribal members, but they were a hospitable people and had absorbed into their powerful Muskogee Confederacy the remnants of other tribes—Alabamas, Koasatis, Euchees, Natchez, and at one time the Seminoles—so that as a confederacy they numbered as many as twenty-five thousand individuals.

The right of the Creeks to be classed as members of the Five Civilized Tribes group is shown in their remarkably advanced village life, productive agriculture, stable government, and sophistication in dealing with other tribes. The Creek Nation was divided into two broad communities—the Upper Creeks and the Lower Creeks. The Upper Creeks were conservative, the Lower Creeks progressive. The chief spokesman for the Upper Creeks at the time of removal was Opothleyaholo, while William McIntosh led the Lower Creeks. In the Creek system, each town was governed by a *micco*, or king. A bicameral national council consisting of the House of Kings (representatives from the towns) and the House of Warriors (one delegate for every two hundred persons) made the laws for the nation.

Traders from the English settlements came among the Creeks very early, especially the Scots, and the mixed-blood community in this tribe—McIntosh, Grayson, Stidham, and McGillivray—furnished important leadership. The arts of civilization flourished there, for the Creeks were generally eager to have missionary teachers and schools.

During 1811, Tecumseh, the great Shawnee-Creek orator, came among the Five Civilized Tribes to preach a doctrine of resistance to the intrusive whites. Only the Creeks listened, and one faction from the Upper Creeks, led by the warrior chief, William Weatherford, supported Tecumseh. Weatherford's followers were called Baton Rouges or Red Sticks, from the distinctive coloring of their war clubs. Support of Tecumseh's doctrine meant alliance with the British during the War of 1812, and the Red Sticks cut a swath of death and destruction through the southern settlements of the United States. The Fort Mims massacre was their most infamous raid. Weatherford's Creeks fell on this southern Alabama community during 1813 and slaughtered four hundred men, women, and children. Terrorized settlers fled from Alabama; territorial leaders appealed to the federal government for succor. General Andrew Jackson with his Tennessee troops, plus a Cherokee regiment under Major Ridge, a Choctaw regiment under Pushmataha, and General William McIntosh's loyal Creeks, made contact with the Red Sticks and finally trapped them on the Tallapoosa River in eastern Alabama at a place called Horseshoe Bend. There, Jackson's combined Tennessee-Indian army smashed Weatherford's Creeks. The entire Creek Nation was made to pay for the depredations of the renegades; the United States took as a sort of war reparation a large tract of Creek territory in southern Georgia.

The Creek retreat from south Georgia caused the settlers to push even harder, and in 1818 and 1821 additional Creek lands there were ceded. Tribal leaders became concerned over the reduction of their national domain, and in 1823, on the recommendation of William McIntosh, chief of the Lower Creeks, the Creek National Council adopted a law prescribing the death penalty for any citizen of the tribe who signed away Creek lands without approval of the national council.

Nevertheless, depredations by the white settlers increased at an alarming rate, and Chief McIntosh finally concluded that it would be in the best interests of his people to exchange their eastern lands for a new home in the Indian Country. Thus when United States Commissioners Duncan Campbell and James Meriwether came into the Creek Nation during 1825 and invited tribal leaders to discuss removal to the West, McIntosh called a tribal council at Indian Springs. In exchange for the remaining Creek lands in Georgia, the commissioners offered a new domain in the Indian Country situated between the Arkansas and Canadian rivers, a payment of $400,000, and compensation for abandoning improvements.

The Upper Creek chiefs refused to sign the treaty and walked out of the council after their spokesman, Opothleyaholo, warned, "We told you we had no land to sell. The chiefs here have no right to treat. General McIntosh knows our laws. We have no lands to sell." After the American commissioners promised McIntosh protection in return for his influence in continuing the council, the Lower Creek chief explained to the assembled headmen and warriors:

The white man is growing. He wants our lands; he will buy them now. By and by he will take them and the little band of our people, poor and despised, will be left to wander without homes and be beaten like dogs. We will go to a new home and learn, like the white man, to till the earth, grow cattle and depend on these for food and life. This knowledge makes the white men like the leaves; the want of it makes the red men few and weak. Let us learn to make books as the white man does and we shall grow and again become a great nation.

When William McIntosh, with twelve other chiefs and thirty-nine headmen, signed the Treaty of Indian Springs, he in effect signed his death warrant. Shortly thereafter, the Creek council met as a court of final judgment and tried William McIntosh on the charge of violating tribal law by signing the treaty without proper authority. An added charge against McIntosh was venality—the American commissioners had paid him $25,000, ostensibly for his improvements on land vacated by the treaty. The council pronounced him guilty and ordered his execution. On April 29, 1825, a party of one hundred Creek warriors traced McIntosh to a house near Milledgeville. The executioners set fire to the dwelling, and when the heat and flames flushed McIntosh into the dooryard, they shot him to death.

The Treaty of Indian Springs was ratified by the Senate, but before John Quincy Adams, the newly inaugurated president, could put the agreement into effect he was informed of the circumstances associated with its negotiation, including Chief McIntosh's execution. He decided to delay promulgating the Treaty of Indian Springs until he could discuss the matter with Creek leaders. A Creek delegation, headed by Opothleyaholo, journeyed to Washington. This delegation was vested with authority of the national council to negotiate with the president on Creek lands in Georgia, thereby exempting its members from the treatment McIntosh had received. The willingness of the Creek government to proceed with an action that had been unacceptable only a few months earlier undoubtedly was due to the threat of civil war in the Creek Nation. The McIntosh party, principally composed of Lower Creeks who were incensed at the execution of their leader by the conservative Upper Creeks, was threatening revenge. Opothleyaholo believed it would be better to allow the dissident group to move. The result was the Treaty of Washington of 1826, through which the Creeks ceded their lands in Georgia to the United States in exchange for a domain in the Indian Country, situated between the Arkansas and the Canadian rivers.

During the spring of 1827, a delegation of five Lower Creek leaders, headed by Arbeka Tustenuggee and accompanied by Creek agent Colonel David Brearley, ascended the Arkansas on the steamboat *Catawba*. The party obtained horses at Fort Gibson and rode over much of the land granted the Creeks by the recent Treaty of Washington. Their return to the Creek Nation with glowing reports of the new country caused the McIntosh party to make preparations to emigrate. Before the end of 1827, eight hundred Creeks were on their way west; within five years their number had increased to 2,500.

By 1830 all of Oklahoma except the Panhandle had been assigned to three of the Five Civilized Tribes, but much work remained to be done by the United States government before the total removal of these powerful and resistant barriers to white settlements in Georgia, Tennessee, Florida, Alabama, and Mississippi was completed.

First, of the three tribes assigned to Oklahoma by 1830 (Choctaws, Creeks, and Cherokees), only a fragment of each nation had come

Troops in dress uniform required at Fort Gibson during the 1830s. From a lithograph by H. A. Ogden in the Army of the United States, *Washington, 1888.*

west. Most of the population of each tribe remained on the ancestral domain. Second, two additional tribes, the Chickasaws and Seminoles, had yet to be dealt with, not only in the matter of finding them homes in the Indian Country, but also, once this was accomplished, of persuading them to move. The story of the determined attempt of the United States government to erase all sign of the Five Civilized Tribes in the Southeast in response to the demands of land-hungry settlers, is an epic of pain, bloodshed, and dishonor—a chronicle of man's inhumanity to man.

Notes on Sources, Chapter 4

Insights into federal Indian policy that led to Indian removal and the formation of the Indian Territory are provided by Reginald Horsman, *Expansion and American Indian Policy, 1783–1812* (East Lansing, Mich., 1967); Francis Paul Prucha, *American Indian Policy in the Formative Years: The Indian Trade and Intercourse Acts, 1790–1834* (Cambridge, Mass., 1962); Bernard W. Sheehan, *Seeds of Extinction: Jeffersonian Philanthropy and the American Indian* (New York, 1973);

George D. Harmon, *Sixty Years of Indian Affairs: Political, Economic, and Diplomatic, 1789–1850* (Chapel Hill, N.C., 1941); S. Lyman Tyler, *A History of Indian Policy* (Washington, D.C., 1973); and Wilcomb Washburn, *Red Man's Land, White Man's Law* (New York, 1971).

The following works, primarily biographies of Indian leaders, are especially instructive as studies in acculturation: John W. Caughey, *McGillivray of the Creeks* (Norman, 1939); Ralph Gabriel, *Elias Boudinot, Cherokee, and His America* (Norman, 1941); and Grant Foreman, *Sequoyah* (Norman, 1938).

Accounts of white-Indian relations that produced conflict and eventual removal to Indian Territory include Mary Elizabeth Young, *Redskins, Ruffleshirts, and Rednecks: Indian Allotments in Alabama and Mississippi, 1830–1860*, (Norman, 1961); and David H. Corkran, *The Cherokee Frontier: Conflict and Survival, 1740–62* (Norman, 1962).

Early removals of eastern tribes to Indian Territory are the subject of Grant Foreman, *Last Trek of the Indians* (Chicago, 1946); Grant Foreman, *Indian Removal: The Emigration of the Five Civilized Tribes* (Norman, 1942); Grant Foreman, *Indians and Pioneers* (New Haven, Conn., 1934); Grant Foreman, *The Five Civilized Tribes* (Norman, 1934); and Annie H. Abel, *Indian Consolidation West of the Mississippi, Report of the American Historical Association for 1906* (Washington, 1906).

Chapter 5

The Trail of Tears

The continued removal of the eastern Indian tribes to the West was profoundly affected by the election of Andrew Jackson as president in 1828. Jackson had spent much of his life on the Tennessee frontier, and he had the typical frontiersman's attitude toward any Indian tribe that presented a barrier to white settlement. His views appeared clearly in his first message to Congress in which he pointed to the progress already made in assigning western lands to the tribes. He cited the Indian colonization already accomplished, notably that of the populous Five Civilized Tribes, and he asked Congress for legislation that would remove completely all Indian tribes east of the Mississippi.

Jackson's wholesale removal plan was adopted in 1830. So obsessed was the president with driving the Indian tribes to the far frontiers of the United States that he gave his personal attention to the matter. It is significant that most of the Indian removals took place during his administration and that those not completed before he left office had been set in motion. The fulfillment of the Jackson removal program, with its ruthless uprooting and prodigal waste of Indian life and property to satisfy the president's desires and the demands of his constituency, has been aptly described by Indian leaders as the "Trail of Tears."

Meanwhile, those vanguards of the Five Civilized Tribes already in Oklahoma were making a remarkable adjustment. Choctaw, Cherokee, and Creek settlers on the Arkansas, Grand, and Verdigris rivers had developed herds of cattle, horses, and hogs, and flocks of sheep and poultry. They had opened fields, constructed log cabins, enclosed their farms with rail fences, and were raising bountiful crops. In 1831 these pioneer Indian farmers raised a surplus of fifty thousand bushels of corn, which they sold to government contractors. With all their early successes, however, they faced a number of serious problems, and government officials realized that these had to be settled before their Indian kinsmen east of the Mississippi could be persuaded to join them in Indian Territory.

One of the problems was that the Osages, who in 1825 had ceded all their Oklahoma lands in exchange for a new range in present Kansas, had only partially vacated their old homeland on the Grand and the Verdigris. Several Osage towns remained on Cherokee land. These towns served as bases for raids on the infant Cherokee and Creek settlements. The immigrant Indians threatened retaliation, and it appeared the southwestern frontier would again be bathed in blood. Another problem was that the lands in Indian Territory assigned to the Cherokees and Creeks were vaguely defined and poorly marked. Creek immigrants had settled on the Arkansas and the Verdigris near the protection of Fort Gibson, on lands belonging to the Cherokees. This situation created friction between the Cherokees and Creeks. Additional conflict was possible in that the tribes in western Oklahoma resented the colonization of eastern Indians so close to their hunting grounds, and they made dark threats of extermination. The government felt obliged to placate the indigenous tribes and to attempt to induce them to accept the immigrant Indians.

To deal with these problems and generally to expedite the removal of the eastern tribes, Congress passed an act in 1832 authorizing the

Cheyenne artist Dick West's painting of the Trail of Tears.

president to appoint a special three-member Indian commission. Jackson selected Montfort Stokes of North Carolina, Henry R. Ellsworth from Connecticut, and John F. Schermerhorn of New York. This commission was known as the Stokes Commission, taking its name from the chairman, a former governor of North Carolina. Fort Gibson was designated as headquarters for the Stokes Commission, and the War Department provided the commission with a military unit because its work would entail the use of force if peaceful means failed. Military action was thought possible, especially in dealing with the warlike Osages, Kiowas, and Comanches.

Major Henry Dodge had been ordered to recruit a battalion of heavily armed cavalry called mounted rangers for service in the Illinois-Wisconsin Black Hawk War of 1832. By the time this special force had been raised, its services were not required east of the Mississippi, and the secretary of war ordered three companies of mounted rangers, one headed by Captain Jesse Bean, another by Captain Nathan Boone, and the third by Captain Lemuel Ford, to Fort Gibson to assist the Stokes Commission by maintaining peace on the Indian Territory frontier and settling the immigrant tribes.

Ellsworth was the first commissioner to arrive at Fort Gibson, reaching Grand River on October 8, 1832. His party included three distinguished guests. On his way west, while on Lake Erie, he had met Washington Irving, then America's most prominent writer; Charles Latrobe, an English naturalist and author; and Count Albert de Pourtalès, a Swiss nobleman. Ellsworth invited the trio to accompany him as his guests on the trip to the Indian Territory, promising high adventure including a buffalo hunt, and they accepted. Upon arrival at Fort Gibson, Ellsworth and his guests learned that Captain Bean and his mounted-ranger company had preceded them by three weeks, and that Colonel Arbuckle had already sent the rangers on an assignment. The rangers' mission was to travel around the upper areas of the Cimarron, the Washita, and the Canadian rivers to locate bands of Kiowas and Comanches and invite them to Fort Gibson the next year for a peace council with the Stokes Commission.

Colonel Arbuckle sent two Indian scouts to intercept Bean's rangers with instructions to wait for Ellsworth and his guests. Accompanied by an escort from the Fort Gibson garrison, the Irving-Latrobe-de Pourtalès party caught up with Bean on the Arkansas above Three Forks on October 14. The combined force moved up the Cimarron, then turned south to the Canadian into central Oklahoma. Bean's frontier reconnaissance extended to October 24, and by the time he ordered his column back to Fort Gibson, Irving, Latrobe, and Pourtalès experienced all the adventure and excitement Commissioner Ellsworth had promised them and more—hunting buffalo, deer, and wild turkey, and capturing wild horses. Their experiences furnished material for three books that are colorful and dramatic descriptions of life in Oklahoma during the early 1830s: *The Rambler in North America,* by Latrobe; *On the Western Tour with Washington Irving,* by Pourtalès; and Irving's classic *A Tour on the Prairies.*

By early 1833 all three members of the Stokes Commission had reached their headquarters at Fort Gibson and were ready to carry out their assigned duties. Their first tasks were fairly simple.

The Seneca Indians needed a home. Remnants of this once-powerful tribe from New York, in common with others, had been pushed across the frontier by the settlers. Before 1833 a band of Senecas had resided near Sandusky, Ohio. In 1831 they had ceded this land to the United States; the Stokes Commission had the duty of finding a home in Indian Territory for the Senecas and for a band of Shawnees, reduced in numbers and power like the Senecas and recently affiliated with this tribe. The commissioners assigned the Senecas and Shawnees a 127,000-acre home north of the Cherokee Nation in present Ottawa County between the Missouri state line and Grand River.

The Stokes Commission had been instructed to look into reports that the Quapaws were destitute and needed help. In 1818 this tribe had ceded to the United States all claims to land south of the Arkansas and east of the Kiamichi. Commissioner Schermerhorn found the Quapaws, numbering 200, living among the Caddoes on the Red River. He negotiated a treaty with the Quapaw chiefs in which they agreed to locate on a 96,000-acre reserve north of the Senecas, between the western boundary of Missouri and the Grand River in present Ottawa County.

The Cherokee-Creek boundary controversy was settled in the same fashion. A council of chiefs headed by John Jolly of the Cherokees and Rolly McIntosh of the Creeks met with the commissioners at Fort Gibson and produced an amicable solution. A new line was drawn between the Cherokee and Creek nations. This line gave the Creeks some Cherokee land between the Verdigris and Arkansas rivers. The Cherokees were awarded a thirty-five-mile-wide strip running from the western boundary of Missouri—excluding the Seneca and Quapaw reserve—to the 100th meridian. Thereafter, the Cherokee north boundary ran along the 37th parallel, the present northern border of Oklahoma.

Dealing with the Osages was a different matter. The Stokes Commission members found harmony and conciliatory attitudes in their negotiations with the Cherokees, Creeks, Senecas, and Quapaws, but they met hostility and obstructionism from the Osages in their first council with the tribal leaders at Chouteau's Post on Grand River near Salina on February 23, 1833. The proceedings recessed briefly and resumed at Fort Gibson on March 11. For three weeks the Osage chiefs bitterly denied charges by the Cherokees and Creeks of horse stealing, burning cabins, and theft of immigrant Indian property. Repeatedly the commissioners attempted to get the Osage leaders to promise a time at which they would move their villages from the Cherokee Nation to their northern lands as assigned by the treaty of 1825.

Finally on April 2, Clermont and his Osages struck their lodges and departed Fort Gibson, with no treaty made, and headed west to hunt buffalo. They were next heard from in May. Reports came to Fort Gibson that the Osages were holding scalp dances on the Verdigris, celebrating the taking of more than a hundred trophies, and that they held five captives. Gradually the authorities pieced together a ghoulish drama. When Clermont's people arrived on the buffalo range they picked up a Kiowa trail that led them into the Wichita Mountains to a place later known as Cutthroat Gap. Finding an undefended Kiowa village, the Osage warriors terrorized the women, children, and few old men present; plundered the lodges; killed more than one hundred Kiowas; decapitated the bodies and placed the heads in brass camp kettles; burned the village; and returned to the Verdigris laden with plunder and captives.

The Kiowa captives provided the Stokes Commission a possible link with the Plains tribes with whom they still had to deal. Two unsuccessful attempts had been made to establish contact with the Kiowas and Comanches. The first was the reconnaissance by

Captain Bean in the autumn of 1832. In 1833, Colonel James B. Many, with two companies from the Seventh Infantry, of the Fort Gibson garrison, and three companies of mounted rangers, had been sent west to the Wichita Mountain area in search of Kiowa and Comanche camps in order to deliver an invitation from the Stokes Commission to attend a council at Fort Gibson.

Among the captives held by the Osages was a Kiowa girl named Gunpandama and a boy called Tunkahtohye. Hugh Love, a trader on the Verdigris, had purchased these two children from the Osages, paying seventy-five dollars for the boy and one hundred forty dollars for the girl. The commissioners suggested purchasing the prisoners from Love and using them as a means of approaching the elusive Kiowas and Comanches. Preparations centering on the captives were made for a third expedition to the buffalo country. The boy died before the commissioners could negotiate with Love, but they did manage to obtain Gunpandama for two hundred dollars.

Meanwhile, in Georgia, Alabama, Mississippi, and Tennessee settlers were urging the government to remove the Five Civilized Tribes to Indian Territory. Indian leaders were making excuses to delay removal, one being that their people were afraid to come west because of the threat of attack from the fierce Plains tribes that roamed the borders of Indian Territory. The government therefore insisted that the Stokes Commission remove this excuse by pacifying the Kiowas and Comanches. Probably the busiest time in the history of Fort Gibson was the first six months of 1834, when all energies were being directed toward establishing tranquility in the Indian Territory in order to assure the leaders of the Five Civilized Tribes that life and property were safe there.

In the first stages, General Henry Leavenworth succeeded Colonel Mathew Arbuckle in command at Fort Gibson. The new commander sent detachments into the field to establish a line of posts on the frontier west of Fort Gibson for the purpose of checking raids into the eastern settlements. Three cantonments were constructed: one at the mouth of the Cimarron named Camp Arbuckle; Camp Holmes at the junction of Little River and the Canadian; and at the mouth of the Washita, one

appropriately named Camp Washita. Each was connected to the command center at Fort Gibson by a system of military roads. Horsemen patrolled these roads, maintaining surveillance from the Cherokee Nation in the north, through the Creek Nation, and south into the Choctaw Nation to the Red River.

Next, the military force in Indian Territory was strengthened by the arrival of an entirely new type of unit called dragoons. The First Dragoon Regiment was organized late in 1833, commanded by Colonel Henry Dodge. The core of experienced men for the unit came from the disbanded mounted rangers. Captains Bean, Ford, and Boone, key officers in the new regiment because of their frontier experience, were joined by Lieutenant Jefferson Davis, who later became president of the Confederate States of America, and Lieutenant Colonel Stephen Watts Kearny, who would later become a hero of the Mexican War. Most of the recruits were from Boston, New York, Philadelphia, Baltimore, and Saint Louis.

After the briefest training, the newly formed dragoon regiment prepared for an expedition to the buffalo country. Its purpose was to intimidate the Plains tribes into a peace treaty with the United States. This regiment was undoubtedly the most colorful military force ever mustered on the southwestern frontier. The splendid dragoon trappings and accoutrements were calculated to produce a lasting impression on the Kiowas and Comanches. Each mounted trooper was dressed in

> a double-breasted dark blue cloth coat, with two rows of gilt buttons, ten to the row; cuffs and yellow collars, the latter framed with gold lace and the skirt ornamented with a star. Trousers of blue gray mixture, with two stripes of yellow cloth three-quarters of an inch wide up each outside seam. A cap like an infantryman's, ornamented with a silver eagle, gold cord, and with a gilt star to be worn in front with a drooping white horsehair pompon. Ankle boots and yellow spurs; sabre with steel scabbard and a half-basket hilt; sash of silk net, deep orange in color, to be tied on right hip and worn with full dress. Black patent leather belt, black silk stock, and white gloves.

Epaulets, a blue cape, and his weapon and ammunition completed each trooper's outfit.

General Leavenworth's sparkling column, with guidons flying, rode out of Fort Gibson on the morning of June 15, 1834. The wagon train contained commissary supplies; ammunition; gifts for the Indians; the Indian captives—Gunpandama and some Wichita prisoners the commissioners had liberated; and a guest of General Leavenworth's, George Catlin, the Philadelphia artist. The line of march was over the new military road to Camp Holmes and then south to Camp Washita.

Disaster stalked the expedition from its first day. Summer heat came early to Oklahoma in 1834 and the proud dragoons suffered in their heavy uniforms. By the time the regiment arrived at Camp Washita, nearly half the men were ailing, some from heat stroke and exhaustion, others from a gastrointestinal malady. By the time the expedition was a few miles west of Camp Washita, in present Marshall County, so many officers and men had been striken that a hospital called Camp Leavenworth was established on the prairie. Here General Leavenworth, suffering from injuries received in a fall from his horse while chasing a buffalo calf, went to his deathbed. Before he died he ordered Colonel Dodge to select 250 healthy men and proceed to the Wichita Mountains.

Dodge succeeded in drawing the Kiowas, Comanches, and Wichitas to council. His return of Gunpandama and the other captives established good relations with the chiefs, further enhanced by the gifts he lavished on the tribal leaders. By patient negotiation he obtained from them a promise to remain peaceful and to come to Fort Gibson for a treaty council. Catlin, the artist, although ailing, rode west with Dodge and visited in the villages while Dodge's councils were in progress. He sketched the people and camp scenes, and kept a daily journal. He later published both the journal and his sketches in a two-volume work titled *Letters and Notes on the Manners, Customs, and Condition of the North American Indians.*

The dragoon column straggled back to Fort Gibson during August, its line of march both to and from the buffalo country well-marked by gravestones. The Dodge-Leavenworth expedition paid a high price for its success in pacifying the tribes of Oklahoma's buffalo range. Of the 500 proud young troopers who rode west from Fort Gibson on that sunny June day in 1834, only about 350 returned.

In September, 1834, the chiefs of the Comanches and Wichitas came to Fort Gibson for a council with the leaders of the Cherokees, Creeks, Choctaws and other immigrant tribes, and the Osages. Unfortunately, by this time the authority of the Stokes Commission to negotiate treaties had expired, but Colonel Dodge and other United States officials praised the Indians for their interest and invited them to attend a grand council the following summer. Tribal leaders made declarations of good will and pledges of peace, and promised to be present at the council.

Colonel Arbuckle returned to Indian Territory late in 1834 and resumed his command at Fort Gibson. Early the next year he, Montfort Stokes, and Francis W. Armstrong, the superintendent of Indian affairs, were named commissioners to negotiate treaties with the Plains tribes. Arbuckle sent Major R. B. Mason with a Dragoon detachment to select a meeting site. He chose a location on the Canadian River in present McClain County and named it Camp Mason. His men cut a road to Camp Mason from Fort Gibson, constructed brush arbors to shade the delegates from the summer sun, and increased the comfort of the conferees by building puncheon benches. A commissary train brought supplies for feeding the Indian guests, who had begun gathering at the council grounds in late July. The commissioners, with a 150-man escort from Fort Gibson, arrived in early August and negotiated for several weeks with the Kiowa, Comanche, and Wichita chiefs.

The treaty signed at Camp Mason pledged the Plains tribes to live at peace with their new neighbors, the Five Civilized Tribes. Traffic to the Río Grande towns was increasing by way of the valleys of the Canadian and Red rivers, and the commissioners exacted from the signatory tribes the assurance of unmolested passage of traders through the buffalo range.

The Kiowas departed Camp Mason before the treaty was ready for signing. The cooperation of this powerful tribe was necessary to assure peace on the plains, and government

Greenwood LeFlore, Choctaw chief who signed the Treaty of Dancing Rabbit Creek, 1830, but elected to remain in Mississippi.

When tribal leaders protested this arbitrary action, which violated treaty assurances, President Jackson answered that the federal government could not protect the Choctaws from the laws of Mississippi. White settlers also made life miserable for the Choctaws by squatting on tribal lands, daring the Indians to evict them. Whites killed or stole Choctaw livestock and carried away other property with impunity. Law enforcement officers and the courts intervened only in cases in which white predators had to be protected from Choctaw wrath.

Reluctant as they were to leave the lands of their ancestors, Choctaw leaders finally saw the futility of attempting to thwart such a powerful combination of private citizens and state officials, especially when the president made it clear that the Indians could expect no protection from the federal government. Therefore, when President Jackson sent Secretary of War John Eaton and General John Coffee to Mississippi to negotiate a removal treaty, the three district chiefs, Greenwood LeFlore, Moshulatubbee, and Nitakechi, agreed to meet at the Dancing Rabbit Creek council ground. Reports indicate that more than six thousand Choctaw men, women, and children

agents continued to seek a treaty with Kiowa leaders. Finally they were successful in 1837 when a delegation of Kiowa chiefs came to Fort Gibson and signed a treaty with terms similar to the one negotiated the year before with the Comanches and Wichitas.

The Stokes Commission and the officers and men at Fort Gibson had pacified the Indian Territory. It appeared that life and property would be safe there in 1837, and the strongest excuse used by the leaders of the Five Civilized Tribes for not moving west no longer seemed to apply.

Moreover, the states of Mississippi, Alabama, and Georgia, where most of the Indian population was concentrated, were applying negative persuasion in their attempt to encourage the tribes to emigrate. The Mississippi legislature in 1829 and 1830 had already passed a series of laws providing for the abolition of the Choctaw tribal government, with the penalty of a prison term for those chiefs who exercised their tribal duties, and the Choctaws were made subject to state law.

came to the council grounds, and set up their camps. . . . The great gathering was not lacking in the picturesque, for Nitakechi and the leading captains could be distinguished from the crowd, dressed in Indian costumes of fringed hunting shirts and leggins, decorated with headwork and silver ornaments, and wearing bright colored turbans. Moshulatubbee appeared in a blue military uniform sent him by President Jackson. Colonel Greenwood LeFlore was noticeable in citizen's clothes, a circumstance that led some of the full-bloods to suspicion that he was in sympathy with, if not in collusion with, the United States commissioners.

Whites "were numerous, too—a great many of them being gamblers and whiskey peddlers who had made their camps along one side of the creek and who kept a demoralizing revelry going on, night and day, throughout the negotiations, near the treaty grounds."

By the Treaty of Dancing Rabbit Creek, as finally approved and signed on September 27, 1830, the Choctaw Nation ceded to the United States all lands east of the Mississippi River and agreed to emigrate to the Indian Territory within three years. During the three-year grace period, they were to have unmolested use of their Mississippi lands. In addition to special gifts for the chiefs and leading men, the government agreed to the following: to pay the Choctaws $20,000 annually for a period of twenty years; to pay for the cost of educating forty Choctaw youths each year for twenty years; to pay $50,000 to the Choctaw Nation for the purpose of establishing new schools in the West; and to allot to those Choctaws who elected to remain in Mississippi 640 acres of land for each head of a family, 320 acres for each child ten years of age and over, and 160 acres for each child under ten. It was understood that those who remained on their allotments in Mississippi would be subject to the laws of that state. About 4,500 Indians selected allotments and separated from the Choctaw Nation. Today, approximately 2,500 members of this tribe reside in Mississippi and are known as the Mississippi Choctaws.

The Treaty of Dancing Rabbit Creek committed the federal government to pay the cost of transporting and subsisting the emigrating Choctaws, and to provide subsistence for one year after removal to allow the Indians time to settle and adjust to the new country and to raise their first crop. Choctaw families were to be issued plows, axes, hoes, blankets, spinning wheels, and looms, and each emigrating warrior was to receive a new rifle, bullet mold, and ammunition. The treaty contained the promise that the Choctaw Nation in Indian Territory would never be included in the limits of any state or territory, and that the Indians would have the right to make their own laws and govern themselves.

Immediately after the treaty was signed, and long before it was ratified by the Senate (in February, 1831), impatient settlers increased their harassment of the Indians. Many Choctaws were driven from their homes, and their property was seized. Life became so unbearable, especially for the Choctaws in LeFlore's district, that scarcely a month after the treaty was signed a party of 800 set out for Indian

Moshulatubbee, a Choctaw chief who signed the Treaty of Dancing Rabbit Creek, 1830, and who removed to Indian Territory.

Territory without benefit of government assistance. They straggled into Fort Towson three months later.

In 1831 the federal government established the Western Choctaw Agency at old Fort Smith, situated on the northeast corner of the Choctaw Nation, and Major Francis W. Armstrong was appointed agent. His principal duty was to supervise the relocation of the Indians. He found the old military structures so dilapidated that he ordered the construction of a new agency building fifteen miles up the Arkansas at a place called Skullyville. Armstrong had some of the buildings at Fort Smith renovated, and the old post became a depot for distributing provisions and supplies to the Choctaws as they arrived from the East.

Most of the emigrating Choctaws assembled at Vicksburg, Mississippi, to be transported west aboard river steamers. There were two principal migration routes to Indian Territory, one following the Arkansas, and the other the Red. If the water was high enough for navigation, steamers carried the Indian passengers all the way to landings in the new Choctaw Nation; if the water was low, as it was for most of the departures, the immigrants on the Arkansas route came by steamer as far as Little Rock, then disembarked and traveled overland. On the Red they came as far upriver as Camden, then by an overland trail to Fort Towson. Most of the Choctaws had arrived in Indian Territory by 1835, though small parties continued to straggle in as late as 1848.

Intense suffering seemed the common lot of all immigrating Indian parties, usually because of poor planning by the government agents supervising the removal. Most of the immigrants were on the trail in midwinter when the temperature was freezing and several parties of Choctaw émigrés had to travel on foot through deep snow. At Little Rock and Camden the Indians loaded their baggage into wagons. Transportation was so limited that only the very young, the old and feeble, the sick, and the blind were able to ride. The dirt roads were muddy and the wagons mired and slowed travel to less than five miles a day. A cholera epidemic devastated the columns, and the death rate rose—possibly as many as one-fourth of the population of the Choctaw Nation died. There was much to justify calling this relocation the Trail of Tears.

The misery continued after their arrival in the new country. The Choctaws built cabins in the wilderness, opened fields, and good crops were in prospect. Then in June, 1833, a destructive flood washed out crops, destroyed homes, and carried away livestock.

The Creeks had a similar experience. President Jackson kept special representatives in the Creek Nation, ever ready to negotiate a removal treaty and promising the chiefs

> money, provisions, agricultural implements, domestic animals, schools, teachers, in short everything which can enable you to sit down with an assurance of permanent prosperity, and to sit down where no bad white men will trouble you, where no ardent spirits will tempt you, and where the land will be yours as long as the grass grows and the rivers run.

Land-hungry settlers aided the government agents in their persuasion by carrying on a merciless harassment campaign—squatting on Creek lands, stealing Indian livestock, and tormenting the Creeks to fight back, thereby creating incidents that were publicized as savage Indian reprisals. The Alabama legislature abolished the Creek tribal government and, as Georgia and Mississippi had done, made all Indians subject to state law. It was an unfair system of law, however, because it was applied in an unequal manner. It did not protect Indians from white aggression; it merely protected whites from Indian retaliation.

By 1832, the Creek chiefs were finally persuaded of the futility of attempting to live according to the pattern of their ancestors, and Opothleyaholo headed a tribal delegation to Washington to negotiate with the federal government. Under the terms of the so-called Treaty of Washington, the Creek Nation in Alabama was dissolved. Tribal members had the option of joining their kinsmen in Indian Territory at once, in which case the government would pay the removal expense, or they could remain in Alabama and receive allotments. Each chief was to be allotted 640 acres of land and heads of families were to receive 320 acres each. After a trial period of living under white man's law, the allottee could, if he wanted to, sell his land and move to Indian Territory. If the allottee remained on his land for a period of five years, he would receive a patent of title. By treaty pledge, the United States government was obligated to expel white intruders and protect the Indian allottee in the residence and use of his land. The Creek Nation was to receive an annuity of $12,000 for five years, followed by a $10,000 annual grant for fifteen years.

As noted above, Creeks accepting allotments had a five-year period to try living as private citizens of Alabama. Only 630 Indians prepared to emigrate to Indian Territory. Most Creeks elected to try the white man's way of living. It was a very different way, for like the other tribes the Creeks had held their lands in common. Few of the Creeks understood the intricacies of private land ownership, and the whites callously exploited this ignorance. There were widespread land frauds, such as seizure of land for false debt and dispossession ordered by courts friendly to the white land-seekers. The federal government utterly failed to protect the allotted Creeks in the peaceful use of their lands. Settlers continued to harass the Indians, even shooting them down in their fields in broad daylight. When individual Creeks attempted to defend their homes and drive off their oppressors they were arrested by state officers for assault and disorderly conduct. Finally, in 1836, unified resistance developed around a Creek chief named Eneah Emothla. The encroaching settlers became alarmed; they appealed for protection, and United States troops under General Winfield Scott came to Alabama to put down the so-called "Creek Rebellion."

The Creek war was regarded as justification for the wholesale removal of the nation from Alabama. Squads of soldiers swarmed over the countryside rounding up Indians, holding them in heavily guarded concentration camps until a thousand or so had been accumulated. The Indians then were marched overland under military guard to Indian Territory. Torn from their homes, forced to abandon improvements and most of their personal belongings, the Creek immigrants, caught up in a merciless and determined government removal program, suffered more than any other tribe on their Trail of Tears. The army captured 2,495 chiefs and warriors who were classed as hostiles and considered dangerous. Bound in shackles and chains, they were driven to Fort Gibson during the bitterly cold winter of 1836–37. One party of 300 Creeks was taken down the Alabama River to the Gulf, transported to the Mississippi, then placed on a river boat that had been condemned as unsafe. Upriver the rotting craft sank, and all passengers were lost.

Fifteen thousand Creeks had arrived at Fort Gibson by early spring of 1837. More than thirty-five hundred died in the winter cold on the way west. The severe weather, lack of food, and general suffering killed virtually all infants, small children, and old people. The Creek Nation was slow to recover from this disaster. There were large gaps in Creek Nation age groups long after the removal. Conservative estimates indicate that the nation suffered a 40 percent decline in population during removal and in the years immediately following, as they

adjusted to a new life in Indian Territory. Not until the 1850s was a balance once more reached in age-group ratios in the Creek Nation.

During the spring of 1837, the Creek immigrants moved from Fort Gibson to the mouth of the North Canadian where they established a settlement known as North Fork Town.

By 1837 the government tally on evacuating the rich eastern lands of the Five Civilized Tribes for the benefit of the white settlers showed that two tribes, the Choctaws and Creeks, had been removed, and that one-third of the Cherokees also had been settled in Indian Territory. There remained a populous segment of the Cherokee Nation in Georgia, the Seminoles in Florida, and the Chickasaws in northern Mississippi. The Chickasaws, of Muskhogean linguistic stock, were closely related to the Choctaws; possibly at one time they were one tribe. The Chickasaws—adaptable, capable, and fiercely independent—were much sought after as allies because of their reputation as brave and daring warriors. Their historic range was along the western frontiers of Mississippi, Tennessee, and Kentucky.

During 1541, Hernando de Soto and his men had spent a season with the Chickasaws. The Spaniards had imposed on Chickasaw hospitality for a time, resting from their travels. As they prepared to leave, De Soto demanded that the chiefs supply two hundred Indian porters and several Chickasaw women. Tribal leaders were insulted by these demands and sent their warriors to attack de Soto's camp. The Spaniards were driven out of the Chickasaw country by the ferocity of this strike, abandoning large quantities of equipment and most of their horses.

In the eighteenth-century European drive for control of the Ohio and Mississippi valleys, the Chickasaws were drawn into the British orbit. Chickasaw warriors regularly attacked French towns north of the Ohio and preyed like river pirates on French and Spanish commerce on the Mississippi. The Chickasaws served as agents for British traders, too. Their commercial activities took them throughout the Southwest. The extent of their trading operations is shown by the presence of a

Chickasaw trader in the Wichita villages on the Canadian when Bernard de la Harpe was there in 1719.

Like the other nations of the Five Civilized Tribes community, the Chickasaws had undergone great cultural change before the coming of the Europeans. Although they were skilled as hunters, they had developed a high-level village life based on agriculture. Politically, the Chickasaw Nation was divided into clans, each clan ruled by a minor chief. The nation was headed by a *micco* chosen for life from the clan of highest rank in the tribe. Ishtehotopa was the last Chickasaw *micco*.

Traders came to the Chickasaw Nation early in the period of European penetration of the Mississippi valley, and many took Chickasaw wives. Many of their mixed-blood descendants became leaders in tribal affairs, both in the East and later in Indian Territory. Some of the mixed-blood family names conspicuous in Chickasaw history were Colbert, Adair, Cheadle, Gunn, McGee, Allen, Harris, Pickens, McLaughlin, Love, and McGillivray.

Like the other tribes, the Chickasaws were soon surrounded by American settlements and the United States government sought to persuade tribal leaders to sign a removal treaty. Successive cession agreements with the United States drastically reduced Chickasaw territory. Finally, an 1818 treaty cut them off from their range in western Kentucky and Tennessee and restricted the Chickasaws to northern Mississippi. Through the years government commissioners encouraged the chiefs to cede this last vestige of their once vast domain. The Chickasaws suffered harassment much like the other tribes, and in the usual pattern the Mississippi legislature erased the tribal government and made all Chickasaws subject to state law. The Chickasaw chiefs were aware that removal was inevitable, but with shrewdness and cunning they rebuffed attempts at removal long enough to make it possible to wring from the government commissioners by far the best removal treaty negotiated with the Five Civilized Tribes.

During October, 1832, at the Chickasaw council house on Pontotoc Creek in northern Mississippi, tribal leaders signed a treaty with President Jackson's representatives providing for the cession of all Chickasaw lands east of the Mississippi as soon as a suitable home in the West could be found. By the terms of the Treaty of Pontotoc, the federal government was to survey the Chickasaw Nation, and then each Indian family would be assigned a homestead as a temporary residence until the nation's western home was decided upon. The remainder of the land was finally to be sold at public sale, the proceeds to go to the Chickasaws.

Chickasaw delegations visited Indian Territory from time to time searching for a national home, and the Choctaws encouraged them to settle on their domain between the Canadian and the Red. The federal and state governments urged the Chickasaws to make a decision, but the chiefs were not to be hurried. Finally, a delegation of Chickasaws and Choctaws met at Doaksville in the Choctaw Nation in January, 1837, and signed an agreement that has come to be known as the Treaty of Doaksville. By this pact the Chickasaws purchased an interest in the Choctaw Nation for $530,000. In their new home the Choctaws had followed their old governmental pattern of dividing the nation into three districts with a chief over each district; by the Treaty of Doaksville, a fourth district, west of the Choctaw settlements in central Oklahoma, was established as the Chickasaw District. The Chickasaws were to be governed by a leader of their choosing, but were to be an integral part of the Choctaw Nation and to have representation on the Choctaw National Council. While tribal funds and annuities were to be kept separate, the citizens of either tribe could settle and reside in any of the four districts.

Prodded by government officials, the Chickasaws began migrating west in the spring of 1837, and by 1840 most of them had arrived in Indian Territory. With a shorter distance to travel and the wise management of their removal by tribal leaders, the Chickasaw relocation was the most peaceful and orderly experienced by any of the Five Civilized Tribes. The Indian families were able to collect most of their personal possessions, slaves, and livestock for transfer to Indian Territory. One report told of seven thousand Chickasaw ponies gathered at Memphis, Tennessee, waiting for transportation to the west bank of the Mississippi. The migration flow for the Chicka-

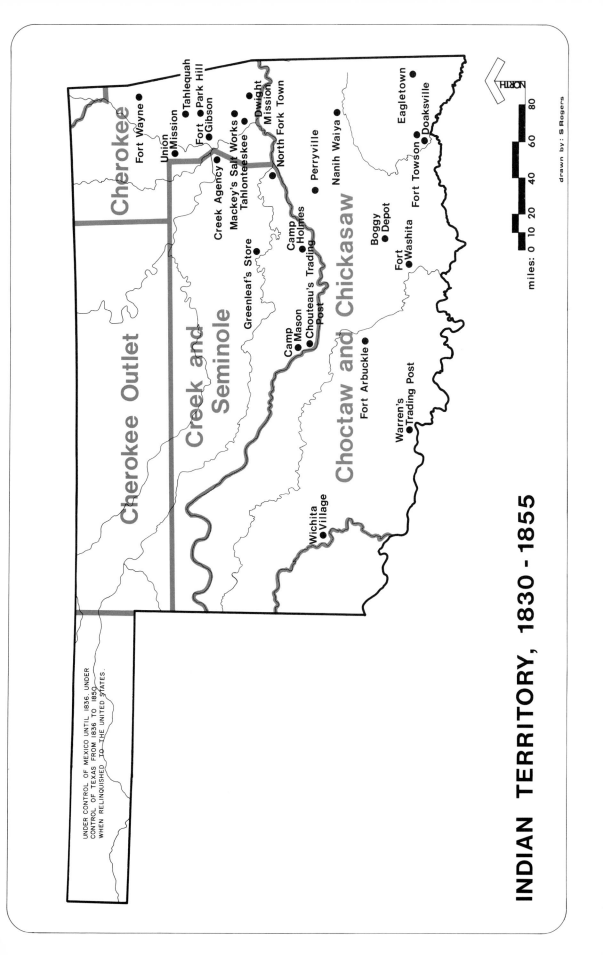

INDIAN TERRITORY, 1830 - 1855

drawn by : S Rogers

miles: 0 10 20   40   60   80

NORTH

UNDER CONTROL OF MEXICO UNTIL 1836. UNDER
CONTROL OF TEXAS FROM 1836 TO 1850,
WHEN RELINQUISHED TO THE UNITED STATES.

Cherokee

Cherokee Outlet

Creek and Seminole

Choctaw and Chickasaw

Fort Wayne
Union Mission
Tahlequah
Park Hill
Fort Gibson
Dwight Mission
North Fork Town
Creek Agency
Mackey's Salt Works
Tahlonteeskee
Perryville
Nanih Waiya
Eagletown
Doaksville
Fort Towson
Greenleaf's Store
Camp Holmes
Boggy Depot
Fort Washita
Chouteau's Trading Post
Camp Mason
Fort Arbuckle
Warren's Trading Post
Wichita Village

saws was principally by river steamer up the Arkansas to Fort Coffee, or up the Red to Fort Towson, but some Chickasaw families came overland by wagon. Even with their well-managed removal, however, they did not escape suffering and disease. Cholera struck some of their camps, and many suffered from spoiled meat and grain rations issued by unscrupulous government contractors.

Most of the Chickasaw immigrants settled in the western Choctaw Nation on Boggy Creek. Government contractors established an issue center there, and a frontier town grew up named Boggy Depot.

The Cherokee Trail of Tears was the most publicized removal in Indian history. By 1828 this tribe was divided into two nations—the Cherokees East, numbering about fifteen thousand, who lived in Georgia; and the Cherokees West, a self-governing Indian community of five thousand residing in northeastern Indian Territory. The federal government encouraged the Georgia Cherokees to join their Indian Territory kinsmen, but these people had made phenomenal progress. Most of them were prosperous, and they generally ignored the appeals to cede their eastern lands and move west. The cultural progress of the Cherokees East was primarily because of the influence of mixed-blood leadership, the contributions of missionaries and schools, and Sequoyah's Cherokee alphabet or syllabary.

The mixed bloods emulated their white neighbors, and many of them became prominent and wealthy as the result of being slave holders, or as operators of grain or lumber mills, plantations, stock farms, and other businesses in the Cherokee Nation. The estates of the Vann, Ross, Ridge, and other prominent Cherokee families were the envy of all. A northern visitor to the Cherokee Nation in Georgia in the 1820s observed:

> We saw many Indians . . . who live in comfort and abundance, in good houses of brick, stone, and wood. We saw several houses built of hewn stone, superior to any we had ever seen before. The people seemed to have more money than the whites in our own settlements; they were better clothed. The women were weaving, the men cultivating corn, and raising beef and pork in abundance; butter and milk everywhere. We were at an election for delegates among the Cherokees to form a constitution. They were orderly, and well behaved. No whiskey was allowed.

At the beginning of the nineteenth century, through the influence of Charles Hicks, a mixed-blood leader, the tribal council invited missionaries to establish schools and churches in the old Cherokee Nation. Their works bore marvelous fruit; by the time of removal, the mission schools had produced an informed and able leadership for the Cherokees. One of the earliest Cherokee schools was Spring Place in northern Georgia, founded by Moravian missionaries in 1801. Within two years the Presbyterians organized a school system for Cherokee youth. Shortly thereafter, this denomination joined with the Congregationalists and Dutch Reformed church in an organization known as the American Board of Commissioners for Foreign Missions, in order to strengthen the missionary effort among the Cherokees and other tribes. Brainerd School at Chickamauga Town, Tennessee, founded in 1817, was the best-known American Board institution of learning. Other religious groups active in organizing schools and churches among the Cherokees included the Methodists and Baptists.

The giant among Cherokee educators was Samuel A. Worcester, an American Board missionary from Vermont. He established several schools and churches in the Cherokee Nation and devoted his great energy and talents to enlightening the Cherokees about the advantages of formal education, at first in Georgia and later in Indian Territory. Worcester selected the most promising Cherokees for further education at Cornwall Academy in Connecticut, a school operated by the American Board. Two of his most brilliant students, Buck Watie, who took the name of Elias Boudinot, and John Ridge, both attended Cornwall and became prominent in Cherokee affairs.

Of all the factors that influenced the Cherokees' cultural progress, none was of greater importance than the creation of the Cherokee alphabet or syllabary by Sequoyah, whose name from his white father was George Guess. The Cherokee alphabet was the more remarkable because Sequoyah had never attended school; he was illiterate and could not speak English. A hunting accident in his youth left him crippled, and he became a skilled silversmith to support his family. Inactivity made Sequoyah reflective and contemplative. Impressed with learning, he admired the work of the missionaries in their schools and loved the books, which he called "talking leaves." He set himself the goal of developing a system that would provide a written language for Cherokee-speaking people. In twelve years of study he identified eighty-six consonant and vowel sounds in the Cherokee language. He refined and identified each of these with a symbol; thus the Cherokee alphabet or syllabary contains eighty-six characters.

There is a story that Sequoyah's Cherokee wife was suspicious of his work and regarded it as "bad medicine," and that one day while he was away, she set fire to the cabin and burned the notes accumulated over years of work. If the story is true, then Sequoyah patiently set about restoring his system, and finally succeeded.

He was reported to have tried the alphabet first on his young daughter and other children in the community. He gave a demonstration of the children's progress before the Cherokee National Council, and the tribal leaders were impressed. Sequoyah's syllabary was adopted by the council, and soon books were published in the Cherokee language. A tribal newspaper, the *Cherokee Phoenix*, edited by Elias Boudinot, appeared for the first time in 1828 with columns in Sequoyah's syllabary, and Samuel Worcester translated and published the Bible in Cherokee.

In 1822, Sequoyah went to live with the Cherokees West in Arkansas, and he introduced his written language in this portion of the nation. He moved to Oklahoma under the terms of the Cherokee Treaty of 1828. Through the development of this syllabary, the Cherokees very quickly became a literate people. They were the best-informed Indians in America, most of them better-read than the settlers who were competing with them for their land.

The Cherokee Nation abolished its tribal government in 1827 and formed a constitutional republic. Pathkiller, the last of the full-blood hereditary tribal chiefs, was replaced by Charles Hicks, a brilliant mixed blood, who led the way when the Cherokee constitution was written. This document contained an outline of the new government and defined the powers of officials, using Indian terms such as "principal chief" for "chief executive" and "council" for the "legislative body." In most respects, this constitution was similar to the United States Constitution.

Charles Hicks died in 1827, and William Hicks served as interim chief until an election was held under the constitution. John Ross was elected as principal chief. Although only one-eighth Cherokee, Ross was enduringly popular with the full bloods. Because full bloods outnumbered the mixed bloods by at least three to one, they could outvote the mixed bloods. Ross studiously adopted the full-blood point of view and thus assured his continuation as principal chief of the Cherokee Nation, winning every election until his death in 1866.

Georgia, in common with the other states of the Southeast, was anxious to have all Indians removed in order that tribal lands could be opened to white settlers. In 1802, Georgia had ceded western lands, later organized into Alabama and Mississippi, to the United States in exchange for a pledge that Indian title to lands in Georgia would be extinguished. From the time of Jefferson the federal government had encouraged the Cherokees to surrender their Georgia lands and migrate, but until 1835, only about one-third of the tribe had moved to Indian Territory. The reluctance of the Cherokees to vacate their lands irritated the Georgians, and the state government as well as private individuals took matters into their own hands, mounting a wrathful compaign of harassment directed at making life so miserable for the Cherokees that they would willingly leave Georgia to find peace.

Thus when the Cherokees organized a constitutional republic, in itself a remarkable advance, the state government attacked the change as subversive and claimed that it established a state within a state. During 1828 and 1829 the Georgia legislature passed a special code of laws abolishing the Cherokee government, declaring all Cherokees subject to state law, forbidding tribal officials to carry out their

Major Ridge, Cherokee leader who signed the Treaty of New Echota.

duties, and making it unlawful for the Cherokee council to meet except to discuss removal. Because of these special laws Indians could not be accepted as competent witnesses in Georgia courts, and all white persons residing in the Cherokee Nation were required to obtain permits from state authorities. This was aimed especially at the missionaries, who were suspected by the state officials of encouraging the Indians to oppose removal.

Cherokee troubles mounted. During 1829 gold was discovered in the mountains of northern Georgia within the Cherokee Nation. The state legislature passed a law forbidding Cherokees to prospect or mine gold on their own lands. The gold discovery set off a mad stampede. More than three thousand whites stormed across the Cherokee domain, wrecking fences, violating households, and creating general ruin and anarchy. When the Indians brought charges against the intruders for trespassing, stock theft, or violation of person, the Georgia courts refused to acknowledge the Cherokees' petition on the grounds that their testimony was incompetent and inadmissible.

In 1831, eleven missionaries were arrested for failure to obtain from state authorities permits authorizing them to teach and preach in the Cherokee Nation. Georgia courts gave the accused the choice of following the requirements of the law or going to prison for four years. Nine missionaries bowed to the state requirement; only Samuel A. Worcester and Elizar Butler refused. Their cause was appealed to the United States Supreme Court. In 1832, Chief Justice John Marshall issued the famous *Worcester* v. *Georgia* decision wherein he declared the state laws under which the two missionaries were imprisoned null and void and ordered the prisoners released. President Jackson refused to carry out the order, and Worcester and Butler remained in a Georgia prison.

During 1834 the Georgia legislature authorized the survey of Cherokee lands and the disposal of most of the choice locations in the nation by a state lottery. By this method, the estates of Chief John Ross and other leading Cherokees were confiscated and taken over by white settlers. Spring Place Mission, long a center of learning and culture in Cherokee history, was included in the lottery. The person who drew this ticket converted the mission into a frontier tavern.

In the year of the Cherokee land lottery, the Georgia militia marched to the Cherokee capital at New Echota and seized the printing press and type of the *Cherokee Phoenix*. The equipment was smashed and thrown into the river. Suppression of the *Phoenix* was excused because the state authorities charged that it had advocated resistance to removal.

The continued harassment caused a faction to emerge in the Cherokee Nation who saw removal to Indian Territory as the lesser of two evils. The leader of this faction was Major Ridge, who was one of the wealthiest slaveholders in the Cherokee Nation and speaker of the Cherokee National Council. His most prominent followers were his son, John Ridge, and Elias Boudinot and his younger brother, Stand Watie. Ridge's group came to be called the Treaty party and consisted largely of mixed bloods. The full bloods, who opposed removal, were more numerous. Since their leader was Chief John Ross, their faction was called the Ross party.

United States agents persisted in offering various and ever more favorable removal treaty terms to the Cherokees. The Ross party was adamant, Chief Ross declaring that his people would sell the nation and vacate for no less than $20 million, which was a sum beyond the power of the United States government to raise. It had the effect, as Chief Ross intended, of making negotiation impossible. In 1835, after repeated attempts to deal with Chief Ross, government commissioners, headed by John Schermerhorn, turned to the leaders of the Treaty party and at New Echota on December 29 negotiated a treaty of removal. The Ross party boycotted the council and the Ridge followers were warned by the Ross people that if they affixed their names to the Treaty of New Echota, they in effect signed their death warrants.

By the terms of the Treaty of New Echota, the Cherokees sold their eastern lands for $5 million. They were confirmed (with the Cherokees West) in joint ownership of the tribal land in Indian Territory to which the Cherokees East were obligated to remove within two years after ratification of the treaty (as it turned out, two years after May, 1836). The federal government was to pay the cost of removal and promised to subsist the immigrants for one year after arrival in the West. Also by the treaty, the Cherokees purchased a 600,000-acre strip of territory in present southeast Kansas to be known as the Cherokee Neutral Lands. However, the Ross party refused to recognize the treaty and declared that its members were not bound by it because the agreement was negotiated by a minority of the nation. Only 2,000 Cherokees, most of them members of the Ridge party, migrated peacefully under the terms of the Treaty of New Echota. When 1838 arrived and it was clear the Ross party Cherokees were determined not to migrate, United States troops under General Winfield Scott were ordered to the Cherokee Nation to round up the Indians and forcibly relocate them in Indian Territory. The Georgia militia assisted the federal troops.

The story of the Cherokee Trail of Tears is an epic of death and misery.

The troops were disposed at various points throughout the Cherokee country,

David Vann, Cherokee leader who supported removal to Indian Territory.

where stockade forts were erected for gathering in and holding the Indians preparatory to removal. From these, squads of troops were sent to search out with rifle and bayonet every small cabin hidden away in the coves or by the sides of mountain streams, to seize and bring in as prisoners all the occupants. . . . Families at dinner were startled by the sudden gleam of bayonets in the doorway and rose up to be driven with blows and oaths along the weary miles of trail that led to the stockade. Men were seized in their fields or going along the road, women were taken from their wheels and children from their play. In many cases, on turning for one last look as they crossed the ridge, they saw their homes in flames, fired by the lawless rabble that followed on the heels of the soldiers to loot and pillage. So keen were these outlaws on the scent that in some instances they were driving off the cattle and other stock of the Indians almost before the soldiers had fairly started their owners in the other direction.

After about five thousand Cherokees had

Spring Frog, Cherokee leader who opposed removal to Indian Territory.

been ruthlessly uprooted and marched to Indian Territory in this manner, Chief Ross appealed to General Scott to permit him and other Cherokee leaders to supervise the removal. With the army's permission, the Cherokees were organized into travel parties of 1,000 persons each, and the removal proceeded in a more orderly and humane fashion. By early 1839 most of the Cherokees had arrived in Indian Territory and were engaged in opening farms and plantations.

The last of the Five Civilized Tribes to be settled in Indian Territory was the Seminole nation. Of Muskhogean linguistic stock, these people were closely related to the Creeks, and probably in earlier times were a part of the Creek Nation. Indeed, "Seminole" is a Creek word meaning "runaway." The homeland of the Seminoles was Florida, southern Georgia, and Alabama. The Seminoles were the most nativistic of the Five Civilized Tribes, primarily because their principal European contact was with Spaniards, who, after 1650, were only slightly interested in Florida. Although the Seminoles were sedentary town dwellers,

their institutions were aboriginal. Their government consisted of a head chief and a council with moderate power. The nation was divided into bands, each named for the captain of the band. Some of the leading band chiefs at the time of removal were Osceola, Alligator, Emathla, Jumper, Coacoochee (Wildcat), and Micanopy.

In the early years of American history the Seminoles were famous for their terrorizing raids from Spanish Florida into the settlements of southern Georgia and Alabama. The Seminoles first came under the jurisdiction of the United States in 1819 when Spain ceded Florida to the fledgling American nation. Immediately thereafter, United States citizens moved into Florida Territory and began demanding that the federal government remove the Seminoles and open their rich coastal lands to settlement. In 1823 the Seminoles signed their first treaty with the United States. By the Treaty of Tampa, they agreed to move into the swampy land in the interior country east of Tampa Bay. This satisfied the whites only briefly, for soon they were demanding that the federal government remove the Seminoles altogether, claiming that the Indians stole their slaves and livestock and were a menace to the settlements.

In 1832, United States Commissioner James Gadsden met with the Seminole chiefs and negotiated the Treaty of Payne's Landing. By this agreement, the tribe was obliged to remove to the Indian Territory when a suitable home was found in the western country. The Indians had three years to make the move, and the United States government agreed to pay the cost of removal and subsistence for the Seminoles for one year after arrival in Indian Territory. The federal government was to pay the nation $15,400 for the land surrendered in Florida, plus a $3,000 annuity for fifteen years.

A delegation of seven Seminole chiefs, accompanied by agent John Phagan, traveled to the Indian Territory in search of a new home for the tribe. After examining various tracts west of Arkansas, the delegation stopped at Fort Gibson. The Creek leaders invited the Seminoles to make their home in the Creek Nation, and in February, 1833, the Seminole chiefs signed the Treaty of Fort Gibson, committing their people to move to the Creek Nation.

By the terms of the Treaty of Payne's Landing, the Seminole grace period of three years ended in 1835. A young dissident leader named Osceola headed a faction that refused to be bound by the removal treaties, but a portion of the nation did agree to move, and agent Wiley Thompson made preparations accordingly. In one of the councils held in connection with the preparations, Osceola killed Emathla, a signer of the Treaty of Fort Gibson. Agent Thompson had Osceola arrested and placed in irons. After a brief confinement, the chief was released. Shortly after this incident, Osceola and his warriors shot agent Thompson, an army officer, and several civilians near Fort King. The same day, Osceola surrounded Major Francis Dade and 110 soldiers on the road near the post. Only three men escaped the Seminole trap. The Fort King massacre set off the Seminole War, which lasted until 1842. No settlement was safe, and soldiers who went after the fierce Seminoles did so at great peril. Osceola promised that his warriors would fight "till the last drop of Seminole blood had moistened the dust of his homeland."

While peaceful Seminoles came forward every month or so to be outfitted for the relocation to Indian Territory (four hundred of them departed from Tampa in April, 1836), the resistance faction under Osceola carried on a fierce, unremitting war against the United States and the Florida settlements. General Thomas Jesup was placed in command of troops for what would be the final Seminole campaign. He was unable to bring the elusive followers of Osceola to bay, however, so he called a peace council and the warrior chiefs came in under a flag of truce. Osceola was taken prisoner in violation of the truce agreement and sent to military prison in Fort Moultrie at Charleston, South Carolina. The unconquerable war chief died there in chains in January, 1839, but his followers continued the war, with Wildcat and Billy Bowlegs becoming the leaders of the resistance. This was a costly war for the United States and the Seminole Nation. The hazards of flushing the Seminoles from their swamp hideouts caused the United States government finally to call off the strug-

Tukoseemothla, a Seminole chief who supported Osceola in his military resistance to removal from Florida to Indian Territory.

gle, and a community of Seminoles was allowed to remain in Florida.

A census of the Seminole camps near Fort Gibson in 1842 revealed that the federal government had managed to remove 3,000 Seminoles to Indian Territory; some came peacefully, most came by coercion. The cost was high: $20 million was spent in keeping an army in the field from 1835 to 1842, and fifteen hundred soldiers were killed, with countless others maimed for life. For each Seminole man, woman, and child removed to Indian Territory, it cost the government $6,500. Looking at these statistics another way, for every two Seminoles removed to the West, the army paid with the life of one soldier.

The Seminole removal brought to a close one of the blackest periods in American history. The Trail of Tears of the Five Civilized Tribes and other Indian groups, ruthlessly uprooted to make way for the white settlers, ranks with the tragedies of the ages.

Under the various removal treaties, all of present Oklahoma except the Panhandle was assigned to immigrant Indian tribes. As a consequence, from a few years after the Seminole removal until 1907, Oklahoma contained five semiautonomous Indian republics. How these tribes tamed the wilderness and made new beginnings in the Indian Territory is another of those anomalies that characterize the history of the Sooner State.

Notes on Sources, Chapter 5

Material used in this chapter is derived from a wide range of literature. The Jacksonian policy that led to the forced removal of the southern tribes to Indian Territory is explained in Ronald B. Satz, *American Indian Policy in the Jacksonian Era* (Lincoln, Nebr., 1975); Wilcomb Washburn, *Red Man's Land, White Man's Law* (New York, 1972); and Michael Paul Rogin, *Fathers and Children: Andrew Jackson and the Subjugation of the American Indian* (New York, 1975).

The conflict between Osage hunters and Plains tribesmen is found in John Joseph Mathews, *The Osages: Children of the Middle Waters* (Norman, 1962); Mildred Mayhall, *The Kiowas* (Norman, 1962; 2d ed., 1971); and Ernest Wallace and E. Adamson Hoebel, *The Comanches: Lords of the South Plains* (Norman, 1952).

Pacifying Indian Territory so as to remove one of the objections of the southern tribes to settling there is the subject of Edwin C. Bearss and Arrell M. Gibson, *Fort Smith: Little Gibraltar on the Arkansas* (Norman, 1969; 2d ed., 1979); and Brad Agnew, *Fort Gibson: Terminal on the Trail of Tears* (Norman, 1980).

The removal saga is derived from Gloria Jahoda, *The Trail of Tears* (New York, 1975); Arthur H. DeRosier, *The Removal of the Choctaw Indians* (Knoxville, Tenn., 1970); Arrell M. Gibson, *America's Exiles* (Norman, 1976); Grace Steele Woodward, *The Cherokees* (Norman, 1963); Edwin C. McReynolds, *The Seminoles* (Norman, 1957); Angie Debo, *The Rise and Fall of the Choctaw Republic* (Norman, 1934; 2d ed., 1961); Angie Debo, *The Road to Disappearance: A History of the Creek Indians* (Norman, 1941); Arrell Morgan Gibson, *The Chickasaws* (Norman, 1971); and Grant Foreman, *The Five Civilized Tribes* (Norman, 1934).

Chapter 6

Oklahoma's Five Republics

Oklahoma politics did not begin in 1907 with statehood, nor with the formation of Oklahoma Territory in 1890. Rather, this vital force in the Sooner State's history began during the 1820s when tribal governments were established in Indian Territory. Indeed, early Oklahoma politics were a factor in the agony of removal, the painful readjustment to a new land, and the turmoil, assassination, and civil strife that tormented the Five Civilized Tribes. All of the trappings of modern American political life—conventions, constitutions, political parties, elections, and the familiar governmental machinery—were present in Oklahoma nearly a century before statehood. About the only thing lacking was taxes, for the tribal governments levied none on their citizens. Expenses for the various functions of government, such as road building, education, and defense, were met from funds paid to the Five Civilized Tribes, generally on an installment basis, by the United States government for lands surrendered during the removal period.

Beginning in 1820, all of present Oklahoma, except the Panhandle and a fragment of land in the northeastern corner assigned to the Senecas, Shawnees, and Quapaws, was divided among the Five Civilizd Tribes. At first, three Indian nations—the Cherokees in the north, the Creeks in the center, and Choctaws in the south—had title to all of Oklahoma. Then, in 1833 the Seminoles agreed to join the Creeks in their territory, and four years later the Chickasaws accepted a new home in the Choctaw Nation. Five tribes occupied three national domains until 1855 when the Chickasaws received a separate territory in the center of the once-vast Choctaw Nation, and the next

year the Seminoles were granted an independent domain in the western Creek Nation, between the North Fork and Canadian rivers. Thus it was not until 1856 that the Indian Territory had five separate Indian republics.

By the time of removal to Indian Territory, a progressive cultural change had occurred among the Five Civilized Tribes. This was the result of (1) long exposure of the Cherokees and others to the white settlements on the peripheries of the Indian nations; (2) the rise of a substantial mixed-blood community in each tribe, the children culturally more like their white fathers than their Indian mothers, and (3) more than anything else, the influence of missionaries and their schools, which produced a corps of well-informed leaders for each tribe. In addition to imitating the white settlers in dress, speech, manners, and economic activity (including slaveholding), many of the educated Indians believed that as their customs and training became modernized, so should their governments be changed from the traditional aboriginal form to a modern republican constitutional system more compatible with their new life ways.

The Choctaws were the first of the Five Civilized Tribes to organize a constitutional government in Oklahoma. They had adopted a written code of laws before 1820 through which private action under the primitive *lex talionis*, or personal revenge code, was replaced by public law that treated crimes against persons and property as offenses against the nation. For several years squads of light-horsemen patrolled the Choctaw Nation in Mississippi to enforce the new tribal laws. In addition to arresting offenders, these mounted rangers conducted trials and administered

Choctaw council house, constructed near Tuskahoma in southeastern Oklahoma in 1834.

punishment. Gradually the Choctaws came to understand the necessity of justice for the accused, and a system of trial courts developed. In 1826 the Choctaws adopted a written constitution that was a curious blending of ancient tribal practice and modern thought.

From earliest times the Choctaw government had consisted of a council composed of warriors, leading men, and three principal chiefs. The office of chief had been hereditary, descent being traced through the females of the line under the clan system. Thus a son could not succeed his father as chief: only his father's sister's son was eligible. The Choctaw constitution of 1826 provided for election of the three district chiefs, but it seems that the candidate voted on in each province was the person who would have occupied the office by hereditary right under the old system. The constitution also provided for an elective council, a bill of rights, and a judicial system.

At the time of removal, the district chiefs were Nitakechi (Pushmataha's nephew) in the southeastern or southern district, Greenwood LeFlore in the western district, and Moshulatubbee in the northeast district. Before depart-

ing for the Indian Territory in 1831, the three chiefs met, studied a map of the western country, and assigned a district to each. LeFlore's constituency was in the country east of the Kiamichi river; Moshulatubbee's district was established on the Arkansas and the Canadian rivers; and Nitakechi selected a district west of the Kiamichi.

The constitutional history of the Choctaws in Oklahoma began in 1834 when tribal leaders gathered at a trading post on the Kiamichi, halfway between the Red and the Arkansas, to hold their first general council in the West. Their work resulted in the first constitution written in Oklahoma, and was similar to the organic law produced in 1826. It established executive, legislative, judicial, and military departments, with some provisions, though incomplete, for separation of powers. The triumvirate of principal chiefs continued. The settled portion of the Choctaw Nation was divided into the familiar three districts, each serving as a constituency for a particular chief executive: the Pushmataha District, the Moshulatubbee District, and the Okla Falaya or Red River (later Apuckshunnubbee) District.

The chiefs were elected and served four-year terms. No chief could serve more than two terms.

The Choctaw constitution of 1834—Oklahoma's first constitution—also contained a bill of rights, established an elective national council of twenty-seven members (nine from each district) chosen annually, and a national court system (elective judgeships). For defense, a militia was provided with a general, elected by the people, and thirty-two captains in each district, each responsible for mustering his quota of privates. Eighteen light-horsemen (six in each district) were to enforce the laws of the national council.

The bill of rights of the Choctaw constitution included the right to a jury trial, and eligible voters were defined as all male citizens twenty-one years of age and over.

The Choctaw National Council met annually for about two weeks, elected a speaker, and conducted the legislative business of the nation. The three chiefs occupied the seats of honor in the council house, which was a hewn log structure situated at a settlement designated as the Choctaw national capital and called Nanih Wayah (near Tuskahoma). Each of the chief executives reported to the national council on conditions in his district and made recommendations for legislation. The constitution vested the chiefs with veto power (two of the three were necessary to negate), and the council could override an executive veto with a two-thirds vote. In the first elections in Oklahoma under this constitution, Nitakechi carried the Pushmataha District, Joseph Kincaid was elected chief of the Moshulatubbee District, and since Chief Greenwood LeFlore had remained in Mississippi, his nephew, George Harkins, was elected to head the Okla Falaya (Apuckshunnubbee) District.

Following the 1837 Treaty of Doaksville, which absorbed the Chickasaws into the Choctaw Nation, a new constitution was written, providing for a fourth district to accommodate the Chickasaws. The national council membership was increased to forty, nine from each of the old districts, and thirteen from the new districts. In most particulars the provisions of the earlier Choctaw constitution continued in force. Light-horsemen were appointed by the district chiefs and the judicial system included a supreme court with appellate jurisdiction consisting of four judges from each district.

The Choctaw constitution was changed on a regular basis for several years. The Indians were clearly experimenting until they could develop an acceptable and workable system of government. Thus by 1860 the Choctaws had developed a body of organic law that served the nation with only minor revisions (such as a post–Civil War change concerning slaveholding) until tribal governments were abolished in 1906 and the Choctaw Nation prepared to be absorbed by the emerging state of Oklahoma. Throughout the period of experimentation some of the more significant changes included one in 1838 in which the council was apportioned on the basis of population. After a trial period it was found that under this system the populous Apuckshunnubbee District gained much additional power. This generated so much complaint in the other districts that in 1843 the Choctaw constitution was changed to provide for a bicameral national council. This new council was composed of a senate of four members from each district, each elected for a two-year term, and a house of representatives elected annually and apportioned among the four districts according to population.

An 1850 revision removed the national capital to Doaksville, and provided a basis for future statehood counties. The four districts of the Choctaw Nation were divided into nineteen counties. Skullyville, Sugar Loaf, Gaines, and Sans Bois counties were established in Moshulatubbee District; Red River, Eagle, Nashoba, Bok Tuklo, Towson, Cedar, and Wade counties comprised Apuckshunnubbee District; Kiamichi, Jacks Fork, Tiger Spring (in 1854 it became Blue County), and Shappaway (which became Atoka County in 1854) counties were organized in the Pushmataha District; and Panola, Wichita, Kulolachi, and Pali counties were established in the Chickasaw District. In 1855, Tobaksi County was organized in the western Moshulatubbee District. The 1850 constitutional revision also provided for a more elaborate judiciary with a national supreme court, four district courts, and nineteen county courts.

In 1855 the Chickasaws seceded from the Choctaw Nation and were given a national domain of their own west of the Choctaws where they established a separate independent government. This arrangement required revision of the Choctaw constitution, and a convention met at Skullyville in 1857 for this purpose. Instead of making routine revisions such as abolishing the Chickasaw National Council, the Skullyville delegates introduced revolutionary changes in the Choctaw political system. The old district system and district chiefs were replaced by a single constituency and a single chief executive called the governor. In addition to this drastic alteration, the national capital was changed from Doaksville to Boggy Depot and reaction immediately developed. The conservatives charged that the Skullyville constitution was illegally adopted and was unacceptable because it created a state government in place of the modified tribal government. They further argued that the Skullyville action was arbitrary, and that any changes in basic Choctaw law required a vote of the people. They added that the Skullyville constitution was largely drafted by designing lawyers who were promoting the organization of the Choctaw Nation as a regular territory under the laws of the United States, a change to which most of the Choctaws were violently opposed.

Opponents of the Skullyville constitution met at Doaksville in 1857, adopted a constitution that had most of the content of the earlier Choctaw constitution, and elected a rival set of officers for the nation. The attempt to operate two separate governments caused additional friction and strife, and civil war became imminent. The United States government threatened to send troops to maintain order, but before this occurred, the leaders of the Skullyville government proposed a compromise. This caused the Doaksville and Skullyville factions to meet in 1860 to frame a constitution acceptable to both groups. The result of their work was a combination of both points of view: the office of chief executive consisted of a principal chief assisted by three district chiefs, each officer elected for a two-year term and ineligible for more than two successive terms. There was a bicameral general council with a senate of four members from each of the three districts, who served two-year terms; a house of representatives elected to two-year terms and chosen from the counties in the ratio of 1,000 citizens per representative; and a judiciary, with a national supreme court of three members, a district judge for each of the three districts, and a county court and judge for each county. The compromise constitution had a bill of rights, provided for local government, and was similar to the constitutions of several states of the United States. It was this constitution that served the Choctaws, with only minor amendments, until the tribal governments were abolished in 1906. Meanwhile, the capital was moved from Doaksville to Armstrong Academy or Chahta Tamaha (Choctaw City) in 1863, and remained there until a new capital was built at Tuskahoma in 1884.

Until the outbreak of the Civil War in 1861, the Choctaw governmental system maintained an amazing degree of law and order. Various councils passed laws regulating marriage, wills, conditions under which whites could remain in the nation, and a special code forbidding the traffic and sale of whiskey. Life and property were safer in the Choctaw Nation than in the surrounding organized states of the United States. Choctaw agent William Armstrong claimed that, "in no country are the laws more respected or more certainly enforced when violated; an instance of robbery, or murder, by a Choctaw of an American citizen, while traveling through the nation, is not within my recollection." Laws were enforced by a troop of eighteen light-horsemen. "Punishment for the violation of laws in the Choctaw Nation consisted of fines, whipping [which ranged from nine to fifty lashes on the bare back—one hundred lashes inflicted in rare instances], and death by shooting." There were no jails in the Choctaw Nation until after 1860 for

It was a matter of honor on the part of an accused Choctaw to appear for his trial and to suffer the punishment that was meted out to him. The culprit would have been thought a coward—nothing being considered more degrading among the Choctaws —if he refused to receive or tried to escape his punishment, either of a whipping in public or of baring his breast to the ball of the rifle.

In addition, there were no habitual criminals because the district judges customarily handed down the death sentence for second offenses, even in cases involving lighter crimes such as theft.

Several other tribes, including the Chickasaws, followed the example of the Choctaws in establishing constitutional government. Under the Treaty of Doaksville, in 1837, the Chickasaws had agreed to move west and join the Choctaws. Presumably the Chickasaw government was dissolved by this pact, and the Chickasaws were expected to become an integral part of the Choctaw Nation. The Chickasaw District, situated in the center of the vast Choctaw Nation, was overrun by bands of Kickapoos and eastward-ranging Kiowa and Comanche war parties; life and property were unsafe there, so that the emigrants from northern Mississippi exercised their right to settle anywhere in the Choctaw Nation by scattering among the Choctaws in the safer eastern zone. After repeated urging, the United States government in 1842 established Fort Washita in the Chickasaw District for the purpose of taming this raw frontier, which was notorious up and down the middle border country as "scalp alley."

The Chickasaws, as a minority group in the Choctaw Nation, shared in the rights of the Choctaw constitution, including the right to participate in the Choctaw government. They were entitled to elect one of the four district chiefs and were allocated thirteen seats in the Choctaw National Council. The Chickasaws first participated in Choctaw Nation politics in the fall of 1841 by electing a district chief and their quota of council members. The Chickasaw chief, members of the council, and local officers were required to live in the Chickasaw District and the presence of troops at Fort Washita made it fairly safe for the Chickasaws to settle in their own area.

By 1845, however, the Chickasaws regarded their absorption into the Choctaw Nation with misgivings, and a secession movement got underway. The Chickasaws were a proud and independent people; they resented the inevitable domination by the more numerous Choctaws, and they preferred to handle their own affairs. Chickasaw leaders therefore began working for separation. This preference for a separate existence was purely political, for otherwise the citizens of the two tribes were on the friendliest of terms.

Despite the reluctance of Choctaw leaders to consider a dissolution of their union with the Chickasaws, Chickasaw nationalism grew stronger with each attempt of the Choctaws to discourage the separation. In 1846 at Boiling Springs, near Fort Washita, a Chickasaw convention met, adopted a constitution, and established a sort of de facto government, all of which seemed more of a demonstration or expression of intent than anything else.

The Chickasaws met again in convention in 1848 at Boiling Springs and wrote a second constitution that provided for a national council of thirty members and a chief executive with the title Chickasaw district chief to be appointed by the Chickasaw council. Edmund Pickens was elected chief under this constitution. Thus, the Chickasaws were in the curious position of living under two national governments, for they also continued to associate politically with the Choctaws, although grumbling all the while about the unpleasantness of their satellite role.

Apparently, Choctaw leaders grew weary of the constant complaints of their adopted community and in June, 1855, a Choctaw delegation consisting of Peter Pitchlynn, Israel Folsom, Samuel Garland, and Dickson W. Lewis met in Washington with a Chickasaw delegation that included Edmund Pickens and Sampson Folsom and negotiated a dissolution of the union formed by the Treaty of Doaksville in 1837. The United States government was an interested party, for settlements were continuing to expand into the West. In Texas, land-hungry farmers and ranchmen were pushing across the center of the state to the reserves and hunting grounds of certain Comanche bands and the remnants of the Tonkawa, Waco, and other Texas tribes. Also at this time, settlers were demanding that the federal government remove the tribes in the northern section of Indian Territory (present Kansas and part of Nebraska) so that this zone, currently off limits to settlers, could be opened under the land laws of the United States. The

Chickasaw capitol, Tishomingo, in southern Oklahoma.

federal government hoped to lease the western third of the Choctaw Nation, occupied by bands of Wichitas, Caddoes, Kiowas, Comanches, and wandering parties of Kickapoos and Delawares, as a general reserve for collecting and colonizing the Texas and northern tribes.

Thus the Choctaw-Chickasaw Treaty of 1855, negotiated by George W. Manypenny, commissioner of Indian affairs, provided for a three-way division of the old Choctaw Nation. The old area extended from the western border of Arkansas to the 100th meridian, bounded on the north by the Canadian and the Arkansas and on the south by the Red River. The Choctaws retained the eastern third of this vast domain as the new Choctaw Nation. The Chickasaws, for $150,000 paid to the Choctaws, received the center third of the old Choctaw Nation as their own independent, separate domain. The western third, that portion extending from the 98th to the 100th meridian, was leased on a perpetual basis to the United States government for $800,000, the Choctaws receiving three-fourths of this sum, the Chickasaws one-fourth.

Their political union with the Choctaws dissolved, the Chickasaws met in mass convention the following year at Good Spring on Pennington Creek, this time to write a constitution that would establish a de jure (by right under law) government to replace the de facto operation they had stubbornly maintained through the recent years. This organic law, produced by a convention headed by Jackson Kemp, provided for a chief executive, called governor, of the Chickasaw Nation, elected for a two-year term. It provided for a bicameral national council consisting of a house of representatives, with the members apportioned on the basis of population and elected annually, and a senate, with the members elected from four senatorial districts, which corresponded to the four counties of the nation (Panola, Pickens, Pontotoc, and Tishomingo). Each district was allocated three senators, with these officers elected for two-year terms, and a judiciary, consisting of a supreme court, a circuit court, and four county courts.

Local government provisions specified a sheriff and constables for each county, with each officer elected for a two-year term. A bill of rights was included, and eligible voters were defined as all male citizens nineteen years of age and older.

For many years the Chickasaws had been strong supporters of education; this support was reflected in their constitution. A superintendent of public instruction, elected to a four-year term by the national council, was assigned the duty of organizing a school system for the nation.

In the first election held under this constitution, Cyrus Harris was selected governor, and Holmes Colbert won the office of national secretary. The new Chickasaw government met in a hewn-log council house until 1858, when a brick capitol was constructed at Tishomingo City.

One of the most populous Indian communities to adopt constitutional government was the Creek Nation. The Lower Creeks, the followers of the late William McIntosh, had migrated to Indian Territory soon after the signing of the Treaty of Washington in 1826. Roley McIntosh, brother of the slain Lower Creek leader and successor to the headship of this division of the tribe, located his people on the Verdigris and Arkansas near the protection of Fort Gibson. The artist George Catlin visited the McIntosh Creeks in 1834, and observed that they were busily erecting good houses and opening immense fields of corn and wheat. He noted that it was a common thing to see a Creek planter with twenty or thirty slaves at work on the rich bottom-land plantations.

Opothleyaholo's Upper Creeks began arriving in Indian Territory during 1835 and 1836. Colonel Mathew Arbuckle, commander at Fort Gibson, aware of the ill will and trouble growing out of the assassination of Chief William McIntosh and fearing the newcomers would stir fresh turbulence, requested ten companies of volunteers from Arkansas to bolster his regular force. The leaders of the two divisions of the Creek Nation met at Fort Gibson shortly after Opothleyaholo's arrival. Chief Roley McIntosh extended a welcome to the recent arrivals, but pointed out that since his people had come voluntarily to the new country ten years earlier and had tamed the wilderness, established their own laws, and were living in comfort, the only terms under which they could accept the newcomers would be that they submit to the laws and government already established. The Upper Creek leaders accepted the conditions set by Chief McIntosh at the Fort Gibson council and settled peacefully, apart from the McIntosh Creeks, some forty miles west along the Deep Fork, the North Canadian, and the Canadian west to Little River.

By this pattern of settlement, the historic division of the Upper Creeks and Lower Creeks was preserved. Each segment maintained a separate government headed by a hereditary chief, with the political processes originating in the towns. Town living with common fields was more nearly the rule with the Upper Creeks, who were mostly full bloods, conservative, and bound to the old tribal customs. The town for the Lower Creeks, predominantly mixed bloods and progressive, served a function similar to that of the whites, more of a commercial and social center, with the families dispersed on farms, ranches, and plantations. In each group, however, the town government was headed by a chief and assistant chief, and the political function was shared by a town

Opothleyaholo, Chief of the Upper Creeks.

council of lesser chiefs and leading warriors.

The staff of each town government included an official known as the *heneha*, who was in charge of local tribal ceremonies and public works (such as construction and maintenance of public buildings and charity for the destitute). If the *heneha* was especially eloquent he served as the town chief's speaker before the town council. The town chiefs and leading warriors also served as members of the national council. On their return from the annual session, they informed the citizens of the new laws and other tribal business.

The Creek Nation functioned under this dual system of separate divisional chiefs and councils until after the Civil War. The Upper Creeks, while generally recognizing the McIntosh government as supreme, as attested by their agreement at the Fort Gibson council in 1836, were tolerated by the Lower Creeks in their determination to maintain a separate tribal establishment. Harmony and peace prevailed between the two factions until 1861, when they became divided over the issue of support for the Confederate States of America.

The principal landmark in the advance of the Creek constitutional government was a moderate union of the Upper and Lower Creeks through a pact negotiated in 1840 by the leaders of the two factions. By this agreement, the Upper and Lower Creeks continued their separate governments, each with a principal chief and council, but a national council was established that contained representatives from both groups. The executive branch of this unified Creek government was similar to the old Choctaw system, except that the Choctaws had three district chiefs and the Creeks two, one from each of the two divisions of the nation. Both the Upper and Lower Creek chiefs presided over the national council, but, in accordance with the pact of 1838, Roley McIntosh as head of the Lower Creeks was accorded precedence over the Upper Creek chief.

Following the union of 1840, a common council ground was established midway between the settlements of the two divisions at Council Hill, near present-day Muskogee, situated near a watering place called High Spring. A log council house was constructed, and each year the chiefs, national council members, and their families camped in the timber around High Spring to conduct the business of the Creek Nation. One of the national council's most significant actions was writing the Creek laws. Chief William McIntosh had begun this work in 1817. It was resumed by the Lower Creeks in 1828, and, shortly after the union of 1840, the national council adopted a uniform code of written laws.

In 1840 the understanding of the Creeks in regard to constitutional law had not advanced to the point of respect for the principle of separation of powers. While they made provisions for executive and legislative branches in their government, the judicial function, rather than being assigned to a third separate branch as in the Constitution of the United States, was given to the council, which served as the court. Violations of local and national laws were tried by the appropriate council, generally through an appointed committee of six council members.

An advance in Creek constitutional evolution occurred in 1859 when the two divisions of the tribe joined in convention to produce their first written constitution. This brief statement of Creek organic law included a bill of rights and a provision through which the chiefs—local, divisional, and national, heretofore hereditary—were made elective for four-year terms. The constitution of 1859 provided for a national council and five elected officials—a principal chief and assistant chief for each district and a national speaker to preside over the national council. Universal male suffrage was established, the two qualifications being citizenship in the Creek Nation and being at least eighteen years old. The electoral system was primitive and direct. At the national council meeting of 1859, the candidates were assigned special locations about the capitol grounds and their followers voted merely by lining up behind the candidate. In this election, Motey Kinnard and Jacob Derrisaw, both mixed bloods, were elected chief and assistant chief of the Lower Creeks, and Echo Harjo and Oktarharsars Harjo won these offices for the Upper Creeks. As in earlier arrangements, the chief of the Lower Creeks was to have precedence.

Enforcement by wide-ranging light-horse police kept the nation remarkably free of banditry, theft, and other crimes. The Creek criminal code included punishment for rape, set at fifty lashes on the bare back administered in public for the first offense. Abortion was punished by fifty lashes, as was incest. Homicide automatically called for the death penalty except that accidental killing and self-defense were recognized as mitigating factors. Whiskey runners were severely dealt with by the Creek system: heavy fines, confiscation of property, and expulsion from the nation. The Creeks pioneered in equal rights for women in Oklahoma; Creek women were given complete control and ownership of their property.

One of the most interesting features of Creek law was the slave code. If a slave killed an Indian, the death penalty was invoked; if an Indian killed a slave, he was required to pay the owner the value of the slave or suffer death. If a slave killed another slave, the killer received a hundred lashes, and his owner was required to pay half the value of the dead slave. Cohabitation between an Indian and a slave was punished by public whipping of both parties. If an Indian or a slave assisted a fugitive slave, the sentence was a fine and public whipping. A slaveholder could free his slaves if he took them out of the nation. An amendment to the slave code in 1856 indicates that the abolitionist crusade had reached Oklahoma; after 1856, Creek public school superintendents, in examining the qualifications of teachers, were forbidden to hire abolitionists.

By the terms of the 1833 Treaty of Fort Gibson, the Creek Nation agreed to receive the Seminoles, who were obligated by a removal treaty of the preceding year to relocate in the Indian Territory. The adoption of the Seminoles by the Creeks was fraught with trouble from the beginning. It created an additional burden for Creek leaders, who were having difficulty healing the breach between the upper and lower factions of the nation.

One of the reasons why this attempted adoption of the Seminoles by the Creeks did not work out was that most of the Seminoles, furiously resisting removal from Florida to Indian Territory, came to the West under military guard as prisoners of war. Having suffered heavy losses of family and property in the Seminole War, and persistently denying that they were obligated by the Treaty of Fort Gibson to join the Creeks, the transplanted Seminoles were conspicuously suspicious and belligerent or passively resistant. Another obstacle to harmonious relations with the Creeks was that the treaty of Fort Gibson obligated the Seminoles to submit to the Creek law. Like the Chickasaws in the Choctaw Nation, the Seminoles were a proud, independent people, and were averse to acknowledging the supremacy of the Creeks. Moreover, as if they did not already have enough cause for refusing to cooperate with the Creeks, the Seminoles charged that the land promised them by the treaty of 1833, situated between the North Fork and the Canadian, had been taken up by the settlements of the recently arrived Upper Creeks. Thus the Seminole emigrants squatted on Cherokee and Creek lands near Fort Gibson and flatly refused to be absorbed into the Creek Nation. An added source of controversy was the Creek charge that the Seminoles were harboring runaway Creek slaves. The Seminoles countered that their hosts were simply using this as a guise to appropriate slaves belonging to Seminoles. Still another source of complaint was the climate. The Seminoles were accustomed to the

John Jumper, Chief of the Seminole Nation.

mild weather of Florida and they found the winters of Indian Territory hard to bear.

The Creeks were friendly and, except for the runaway slave issue, were well disposed toward the Seminoles. The Florida emigrants were regarded as dangerous and the Creek government attempted to disperse them in small bands throughout the nation rather than allow them to settle in a compact group. The unhappy Seminoles declared they would never submit to the laws of the Creeks, and demanded a country they could call their own. Finally, in 1845, after years of sullen though passive resistance, the Seminoles persuaded the Creeks to allow them to settle on Little River in a body. The agreement gave the Seminoles some degree of autonomy; they could make their own laws, though in case of conflict they were required to acknowledge the supremacy of the Creek National Council.

Soon after the 1845 treaty, the Seminoles, including the bands led by the recalcitrant Wildcat and Alligator, began moving to their Little River domain. Farms, ranches, and plantations were opened in the new country, and a government similar to the old Seminole political system used in Florida was organized. The people settled in twenty-five communities called towns, each ruled by a local chief. He, with his council of warriors, conducted the business and passed and enforced laws for his jurisdiction. The general government of the Seminole Nation was headed by the warrior chief Micanopy. His head councilor was Wildcat (Coacoochee). The town chiefs and leading warriors of the nation met once each year in general council to conduct the business of the nation. As noted above, the laws passed by the Seminole town councils and general council were subject to review by the Creek government.

Although a satellite of the Creek Nation, the Seminole community refused to participate in Creek councils. Seminole leaders studiously shunned any activity that might acknowledge their submission to the Creek Nation. Once the Seminoles obtained a separate domain, they began to agitate for complete separation. Wildcat especially was irreconcilable, and, as a protest against what he regarded as the inferior status of his people in the Creek Nation, he led a group of Seminoles and their slaves to northern Mexico. At the invitation of the Mexican government, Wildcat's band settled in Coahuila. In a few years the chief and many of his followers returned to the Indian Territory, but several Seminoles remained in Mexico and their descendants, locally called Muskogees, reside there to this day.

In 1854 the Creeks began considering favorably the Seminole demand for complete separation. The esteemed Micanopy died in 1849, and was succeeded by his nephew Jim Jumper, who shortly was succeeded by John Jumper. Chief John Jumper, pointing to the favorable treatment accorded the Chickasaw demand for separation from the Choctaws in 1855, led a delegation of Seminoles to Washington in 1856 to meet with the Creek leaders Tuckabatchee Micco, Chilly McIntosh, and D. N. McIntosh.

The treaty that resulted from their negotiation provided for a Seminole domain, completely separate and independent from the Creek Nation, between the North Fork and the Canadian rivers, extending west from about the 97th meridian to the 100th meridian. The Seminoles moved to their new country and constructed a national capitol near present

Wanette in Pottawatomie County. They had hardly made a good beginning, however, when they were caught up in the Civil War. As will be seen, the participation of about half the tribe on the side of the Confederacy resulted in the Seminoles' loss of their national domain in 1866 as a kind of war reparation.

While not the first of the Five Civilized Tribes to adopt constitutional government, the Cherokees were probably the best known of the Five Civilized Tribes for their remarkable advancement in this field. It will be recalled that the Cherokees adopted their first written constitution in 1827, abolishing the old hereditary tribal system. Organization of the new government under this constitution included the election of John Ross as principal chief. At the time, the Cherokee Nation was divided: there were the Cherokees East, more or less concentrated in northern Georgia; and the Cherokees West, a growing community, first holding lands in northwestern Arkansas, and in 1828 exchanging this domain for a new home in Indian Territory. Each division of the tribe functioned separately with its own government and leaders. The Cherokees East split in the debate over removal, but in 1838 the Ross party followed the Treaty party to the West, under pressure by the United States Army.

The Cherokees West, or the Old Settlers as they came to be called, and the Treaty party members welcomed the Ross immigrants and assisted them in every way possible to reduce the pain and suffering of the overland trek and to make the newcomers comfortable. Soon after Chief John Ross arrived, he called a council of all Cherokees to meet at Tukattokah, situated about ten miles north of Fort Gibson. The Old Settlers, led by chiefs John Brown, John Looney, and John Rogers and backed up by the Treaty party members, regarded this action by Ross as presumptuous, since it was expected that the newcomers would simply be absorbed into the system already established by the Old Settlers. Thus there were two separate camps at the Tukattokah council ground, the Old Settlers and Treaty party in one camp and Ross's Cherokees in the other.

During the Tukattokah council proceedings, Ross advanced the view that the Western Cherokees were merely a part of the original tribe, that their government was temporary until the entire tribe was united, and he proposed a new constitution providing for the union of the two great divisions of the tribe. Aware that Ross's party could outvote them at least two to one, the Old Settler chiefs, supported by the Treaty party, refused, declaring that the Indian Territory domain had been granted to them alone and not to the whole tribe; that they had been forced to divide their tribal domain with the more numerous and powerful part of the tribe without their consultation or consent; that "the newcomers in coming into a territory which already had an organized government accepted that government; and accordingly, since the Western Cherokees had received and welcomed their brother emigrants, the two people were already united." The Old Settler chiefs argued that their people had been pioneers in the Western Cherokee Nation. They had tamed the wilderness by driving out the Osages and other enemies and had made the area safe. Their government was elective, and should continue in force; the Ross party could voice its choice in the regular elections in October.

The fact that the Treaty party leaders—Major Ridge, John Ridge, Elias Boudinot, and Stand Watie—stood behind the Old Settler chiefs in their response to John Ross's demand angered the Ross partisans. They held the Treaty party responsible for their suffering on the Trail of Tears, and they suspected that the Treaty party leaders were chiefly responsible for the Old Settler response. The Treaty party leaders were therefore an obstacle to Chief Ross's design.

This obstacle was removed a few days after the Tukattokah council. On the morning of June 22, 1839, three days after the council adjourned, at about the same hour in different parts of the nation, Major Ridge, his son John Ridge, and Elias Boudinot were slain by unknown parties. The timing and ghoulish certainty of the assassins' work indicated a plot of considerable planning and flawless execution. The slaying of Boudinot was especially treacherous. On the morning of his doom, he was assisting workmen in the construction of a new house. Three men called at his door for medicine. He went off with them to Worcester's house where the medicines were

John Ross, Principal Chief, Cherokee Nation. From a painting by John Neagle, Philbrook Art Center.

kept. On the way, two of the men seized him, the third stabbed him, then the three cut him to pieces with tomahawks. His murder occurred only two miles from Ross's house.

Stand Watie, also marked for assassination, arrived in Park Hill too late.

> He found the yard of his brother's house filled with armed men, who fell back and made way for him as he rode up to the porch, where the body of the slain brother lay. Lifting the cloth which covered the face of his brother, he gazed at it long and intently. Then, turning and facing the crowd of hostile spectators, he said: "I will give ten thousand dollars for the names of the men who did this." Not a word was spoken in reply, or did any one offer to molest him as he put spurs to his horse and rode away.

Any chance that Stand Watie might head an opposition to Ross was eliminated by the action of an Eastern Cherokee council that convened at Tahlequah (Illinois Camp Ground) on July 1, 1839. Ross had sent out a call for the council, indicating that the purpose was to discuss the formation of a union. The surviving leaders of the Old Settlers and Treaty party agreed to attend on condition that no Cherokees "be killed for their former political acts and opinions," that the council contain equal representation from both Western and Eastern Cherokees, and that the council convene at Fort Gibson. Chief Ross refused, insisting that the council meet at Tahlequah. Thus, of the 2,000 Cherokees in attendance, only five were from the Old Settler faction. The Ross council resolved that the signers of the New Echota Treaty "had forfeited their lives to the nation by their acts." They were declared outlaws, but an act of the council permitted them "to live if they would appear at the Council Ground to express their sorrow for having signed the treaty, and promise to live peacefully, but prohibiting them from holding office for five years." Another act granted pardon and complete amnesty to the slayers of the Ridges and Boudinot. On July 12, this same council adopted the act of union and ordered the convening of a constitutional convention in September.

One additional obstacle to the fulfillment of John Ross's design remained: the opposition of the three Old Settler chiefs. This was removed, according to Colonel Mathew Arbuckle, commander at Fort Gibson, in the following manner:

> Emissaries of Mr. Ross were passing through the Cherokee country with the object of collecting and bringing to the convention as many of the old settlers as possible, and since my return here, I am informed that John Looney, one of the principal chiefs of the old settlers, has joined the late emigrants. . . . I am of the opinion that Mr. Ross and his adherents have induced so many of the old settlers to join them that the chiefs Brown and Rogers and their friends will not attempt any resistance to the new government.

There suddenly developed in the Old Settler community a group demanding that Chief Brown and Chief Rogers be deposed. On August 23, 1839, a convention of Cherokees led by John Looney declared them removed from office. Thus a Machiavellian pattern in Oklahoma politics was set long before 1889 or 1907.

A national convention, held at Tahlequah on September 6, 1839, wrote and adopted a constitution for the united Cherokee Nation. With the addition of minor amendments concerning slavery adopted after the Civil War this constitution remained the organic law for the Cherokees until tribal governments were abolished in 1906. This constitution was similar to the 1827 document adopted by the Eastern Cherokees in Georgia. The executive power was vested in a principal chief and assistant chief elected every four years. An executive council (cabinet) of five members appointed by the legislative branch assisted the chief in directing the affairs of the nation. The legislative power was vested in a bicameral national council: an upper house called the national committee, composed of two delegates elected from each district for two-year terms, and a lower house, called the council, composed of three men from each district elected for two-year terms. All public officers were to be elected by voice vote, rather than by secret ballot. The judicial power was vested in a supreme court and inferior courts created by the legislative branch, and the judges also were appointed by that branch of the government. Other elective officers included a national treasurer and a superintendent of public instruction.

The constitution included a bill of rights; defined eligible voters as male Cherokee citizens at least eighteen years of age; and set qualifications for officers of the legislative, executive, and judicial branches must be Cherokee by blood. No one of African descent was eligible to hold office. The Cherokee national capital was designated as Tahlequah, tribal land was held in common, and any tribal citizen had the right to make improvements on the national domain.

The constitutionally defined districts, similar to counties, were identical to the Old Settler divisions dating from 1828. Until 1841, these were Neosho, Sallisaw, Illinois, and Lee's Creek. In that year, the nation was redistricted into eight units: Canadian, Illinois, Skin Bayou (in 1851 this was changed to Sequoyah), Flint, Delaware, Going-Snake, Tahlequah, and Saline. After 1842 a ninth district called Coowescoowee was added.

While the Cherokee Nation prospered and

grew under the benevolent despotism of Chief John Ross, the Watie-Ross vendetta continued with the partisans of each conducting a sort of private civil war until 1846, when a peace agreement was signed by the leaders of both parties. Thereafter until the outbreak of the American Civil War, the old differences were submerged. Ross was a perennial candidate for the office of principal chief and, with his more numerous and loyal full-blood followers, won every election until his death in 1866.

Notes on Sources, Chapter 6

Like the removal period, the adjustment of the southern tribes to the Indian Territory wilderness has been a popular subject for writers. The principal source explaining the territorial partitioning of Indian Territory by treaties with the Five Civilized Tribes assigning them national domains in the West is John W. Morris, Charles R. Goins, and Edwin C. McReynolds, *Historical Atlas of Oklahoma*, new ed. (Norman, 1976).

The constitutional experiences of the Five Civilized Tribes can be traced in Lester Hargrett, *Bibliography of the Constitution and Laws of the American Indian* (Cambridge, Mass., 1977); and Arrell Morgan Gibson, "Constitutional Experiences of the Five Civilized Tribes," *American Indian Law Review* 2 (Winter, 1974): 17–45.

Information on missionary and educational developments in pioneer Indian Territory is found in two books by Althea Bass, *Cherokee Messenger, (A Life of Samuel Austin Worcester)* (Norman, 1936), and *The Story of Tullahassee* (Oklahoma City, 1960).

Postremoval political disorders in the Cherokee, Creek, and Seminole nations are explained in Morris L. Wardell, *A Political History of the Cherokee Nation, 1838–1907* (Norman, 1938); Thurman Wilkins, *Cherokee Tragedy: The Story of the Ridge Family and of the Decimation of a People* (New York, 1970); and Grant Foreman, *The Five Civilized Tribes* (Norman, 1934).

Chapter 7

The Golden Years

Over all, the nineteenth century was a time of sorrow, travail, and disintegration for the Five Civilized Tribes. The one bright period in those dreadful hundred years was the interval between the conclusion of the removal, around 1835, and the outbreak of the Civil War in 1861. These were the "golden years" for the Five Civilized Tribes, a time of respite from the demands of settlers for their lands, when the Indians made remarkable progress in taming the Oklahoma wilderness. They organized constitutional governments and established towns, schools, farms, ranches, and plantations. They published newspapers, magazines, and books.

During these golden years, an extensive educational system, sustained by the tribal governments and certain missionary societies, provided noteworthy educational opportunities for the Indian youth. In most of the Indian nations, it was possible for every child to attend school from kindergarten through the academy level (the equivalent of high school), and in some cases, to complete the first two years of college. From the academies, many bright young men were sent to the eastern colleges to complete their studies. Many of the more sophisticated Indian families sent their children to private boarding schools and academies in the East. After 1850, many business, social, and political leaders of the tribes were college graduates. William P. Ross, nephew of Chief John Ross, for example, was a Princeton graduate. He returned to Indian Territory to edit the *Cherokee Advocate* and later became principle chief of the Cherokee Nation.

The curricula of Indian Territory schools were diversified. Students were taught voca-tional subjects in addition to the traditional subjects such as spelling, biology, history, astronomy, Latin, Greek, English, arithmetic, philosophy, and, in the mission schools, Bible studies. The boys were trained in animal husbandry, agriculture, the mechanical arts, and carpentry, while the girls were instructed in child care, cooking, sewing, and other domestic arts. So-called special education is not new in Oklahoma: the Indian Territory educational systems included schools for orphans, the deaf, blind, and mentally ill.

Support came from various sources for the schools of the Indian Territory. Congress appropriated an annual sum of $10,000 for the Indian Civilization Fund, which was administered by the missionary groups working among the tribes. There were many tribes to be served, however, and there was much competition for this money. Missionary societies of the various religious denominations raised money from private sources to build schools and churches in the Indian Territory and furnished teachers, ministers, physicians, and instructors in farming and the mechanical and domestic arts. The tribes appropriated funds through their tribal councils for the support of public school systems in their nations and to subsidize schools established by the missionary societies. Tribal revenues came from several sources but in no case from taxes on Indian citizens, for there were no taxes in Oklahoma in those times. Land, which is the usual source of tax revenue, was held in common by each tribe, and thus could produce no revenue. Income from fees, licenses, franchises, and fines collected by the Indian governments were reserved for the support of the schools. Most of the money the

Five Civilized Tribes poured into their educational systems came from the annuities earned on the invested proceeds of the sale of their eastern lands.

Educational and missionary work among the Five Civilized Tribes started long before removal. Even before 1800, local congregations, synods, presbyteries, conferences, and missionary associations situated on the periphery of the Indian nations in the Southeast organized schools and churches for the tribes. Emphasis on education was necessary to the missionary effort: to evangelize effectively and to win knowledgeable Indian converts, it was necessary to teach the white man's ways to the Indians. There were secular implications of the missionary programs, for an Indian who had been trained in a mission school to read and write the Scriptures could use the same skills in worldly matters, such as business and politics. As the missionary societies organized on more ambitious bases after 1800, their leaders developed a basic philosophy for Indian missions. Stated in simple terms the object of mission education was to educate the head, heart, and hands of each Indian. Missionary educators of all faiths achieved remarkable success in educating Indian children.

The earliest organized missionary effort among the Five Civilized Tribes was undertaken by the Moravians. In 1801 the brethren of this faith established a school and mission for the Cherokees at Spring Place, Georgia. Moravian teachers accompanied the Cherokees over the Trail of Tears and continued their work in Indian Territory.

In 1817 the United Foreign Missionary Society, formed from the Presbyterian Associate Reformed and Dutch Reformed congregations, was organized in New York City. Missionaries from this organization established schools and missions in Indian Territory. In 1826 the United Foreign Missionary Society was absorbed by the American Board of Commissioners for Foreign Missions.

The American Board, a missionary effort supported by the Congregationalists and Presbyterians, was established in 1810. Principally a New England organization, more than half of its teachers and missionaries came from Massachusetts, Vermont, New Hampshire, Con-

Cyrus Byington, ABCFM missionary teacher to the Choctaws. Courtesy Oklahoma Historical Society.

necticut, and Maine. The American Board began its Indian educational and missionary work among the Five Civilized Tribes in 1817 when these nations were still situated in the eastern United States. Teachers and missionaries from the American Board accompanied the tribes to the Indian Territory and in the Oklahoma wilderness redoubled their efforts to educate as many Indians as possible. When the American Board closed its work in Indian Territory in 1860, its record of service showed that more than five hundred of its teachers and missionaries had served the Five Civilized Tribes. A large proportion of American Board missionaries in Indian Territory were Congregationalists, including that man of great courage, Samuel Austin Worcester. The American Board missions followed the Presbyterian form and eventually all work passed under the control of the Presbyterian church.

The Baptists worked among the Five Civilized Tribes before removal, and several missionaries accompanied the Indians to Oklahoma, where they established schools and churches. The Methodists also evangelized among the Five Civilized Tribes before removal. Their work was conducted through Methodist conferences adjacent to the nations rather than through a missionary board. John Ross, principal chief of the Cherokee nation, and Greenwood LeFlore, a Choctaw chief, were among the early Methodist converts. When the Five Civilized Tribes first arrived in Oklahoma, the Missouri Methodist Conference and later the Arkansas Methodist Conference served the Indians. Then in 1844, leaders of this denomination organized the Methodist Indian Mission Conference at Riley's Mill, near Tahlequah in the Cherokee Nation, and appointed J. C. Berryman superintendent. This new conference contained three districts—Kansas River, Cherokee, and Choctaw—with seventeen stations, eleven of them in Oklahoma. Each station was a circuit presided over by an itinerant evangelist with six to twelve places for worship. At its formation, the conference had a combined membership of 2,992 Indians, 85 whites, and 133 blacks.

There was an interesting contrast between the approach of the sedate American Board missionary program that used fixed religious centers and schools in Indian Territory and the approach of the Methodists with their house-to-house visitations and circuit rider preachers. The Methodist station organization and camp meetings appealed to the Indians. However, the Methodists gave little attention to schools among the Five Civilized Tribes until the 1840s.

In addition to introducing their denominations to Oklahoma and spreading the gospel, the missionaries developed political, social, and business leaders among the Indians, trained Indian teachers for both the public and private schools in Indian Territory, and produced several native preachers. The sacrifice, devotion, and consecrated service demonstrated by these spiritual pioneers did much to ameliorate the suffering and sorrow of removal. Unquestionably the courage and energy of the missionaries inspired the Five Civilized Tribes to an early adjustment to life in Indian Territory. The missionaries' stress on temperance and education mitigated the hate and recrimination that surged in the hearts of the transplanted tribesmen.

In the 1840s, as the sectional crisis deepened in the eastern United States, religious denominations serving the Indian Territory divided into northern and southern factions. Many missionaries among the Five Civilized Tribes were zealous advocates of abolition, while others championed the cause of the South. Certain missionaries were influential in involving the Indian Territory in the Civil War on the side of the Confederacy. The cleavage in at least three of the Indian nations into Confederate and Union factions was on denominational lines.

The first missions and schools in Oklahoma were established among the Osages by the United Foreign Missionary Society of New York City. During May, 1819, Epaphras Chapman and Job Vinal, representatives of the United Society, came west with the intention of organizing a school among the Western Cherokees in northwestern Arkansas. When they learned that the American Board of Commissioners for Foreign Missions had already gained permission to work among the Western Cherokees, Chapman and Vinal traveled on to Grand River and examined the possibilities of establishing a mission among the Osages. Through the influence of Nathaniel Pryor, the frontier trader, the United Society received permission to organize a school and church.

Unfortunately, the rigors of frontier travel led to Vinal's early death, and he was buried at Fort Smith. Chapman, however, returned to the East and organized his staff for the western missionary venture. His group included his wife; the Reverend and Mrs. W. F. Vaill; Dr. Marcus Palmer and his wife, Clarissa Johnson Palmer; six farmers and mechanics; and six young women teachers. These missionaries came west by water from Pittsburgh. Chapman's party traveled during the summer heat of 1820, and all members were stricken with illnesses. Two of the young women died. Chapman selected a site for his school near Mazie in present Wagoner County. In 1821, a crude log settlement was completed, which Chapman named Union Mission. This mission was the first Indian School in Oklahoma. Over a period of twelve years, seventy-one Osages, twenty-nine Cherokees, and fifty-four Creeks attended Union Mission. To reach the full bloods among the Osages, a second mission named Hopefield was established five miles north of Union, more conveniently situated with respect to the Osage villages. The missionaries at this new station were William Montgomery and W. D. Requa. Hopefield was best known as an agricultural school. Both Union and Hopefield missions became American Board installations when that organization absorbed the United Society in 1826. When Western Cherokees came to Oklahoma in 1828, the Osages were moved north to present Kansas, and Union and Hopefield missions then served the Cherokees until both were abandoned in 1836.

No tribe responded more favorably to the missionaries than the Cherokees. The Moravians were among the first to evangelize this tribe. Their first school for Cherokees at Spring Place, Georgia, established in 1801, became a famous center of learning on the frontier. When the Moravians came west with their Cherokee followers in the removal, they constructed a mission center called New Spring Place near present Oaks in Delaware County. The Moravian effort among the Cherokees was never as extensive and ambitious as that of the Baptists and Presbyterians, but the brethren did important work. Of the many facets that compose Oklahoma's spiritual heritage, the familiar church house is one; and it is significant that the Moravians carried over the Cherokee Trail of Tears the first church bell hung in the belfry at New Spring Place Mission.

As indicated, Methodist circuit riders also ministered to the Cherokees before removal. One of the famous Methodist camp meeting revivals won John Ross, principle chief of the Cherokees, to this faith. John Fletcher Boot, a Methodist missionary, accompanied the Cherokees to Indian Territory following the Treaty of New Echota. Methodist missionary efforts continued after relocation in Oklahoma through the Missouri and Arkansas conferences. In 1844 the strength of Methodism among the Cherokees was shown by the organization of the Indian Mission Conference at Riley's Mill near Tahlequah. Because of the preeminence of Baptist and American Board education work among the Cherokees, the Methodists spent most of their time and energy on maintaining circuit rider preachers for Cherokee meeting houses, spicing this activity

from time to time with a lusty camp meeting revival.

As early as 1803, long before removal, Presbyterian congregations adjacent to the Cherokee Nation began establishing missions and schools for the Indians. Presbyterian efforts were combined with the Congregationalists by the organization of the American Board in 1810, and in 1817 this missionary society established Brainerd Mission, its first school among the Cherokees. Early Cherokee migrants bound for the West had no formal missionary attention until 1821. Western Cherokee Chief Tahlonteeskee appealed to the American Board on several occasions for schools for his people in northwestern Arkansas. Finally, in 1821, Cephas Washburn and Alfred Finney arrived in Arkansas and supervised the construction of a school and church in present Pope County. This mission was named Dwight Mission in honor of Timothy Dwight, president of Yale College and one of the charter members of the American Board. The Western Cherokee response to the new school was enthusiastic. Soon it was crowded, and the American Board directed the construction of a second church and school near Dwight, which was named Mulberry Mission.

In 1828, when the Western Cherokees exchanged their Arkansas lands for a new home in northeastern Indian Territory, preparations were made to have Dwight and Mulberry Missions follow the tribes, and the move was accomplished in the year following the signing of the treaty. American Board missionaries selected as a site for New Dwight Mission the settlement of Nicksville on Sallisaw Creek in Sequoyah County. Superintendent Washburn purchased a complex of log buildings from Colonel Walter Webber, and by the spring of 1830 facilities for sixty-five pupils were ready. In 1838, Dr. Elizur Butler, one of the principals in *Worcester* v. *Georgia*, became superintendent at New Dwight Mission. Dwight's satellite mission, Mulberry, was moved from Arkansas in 1829 and reestablished on a site fifteen miles north of New Dwight near present Stilwell ; following this transfer, Mulberry Mission was renamed Fairfield Mission. Dr. Marcus Palmer and his wife, Clarissa Johnson Palmer, were in charge of Fairfield Mission. In 1830 the American Board

Sequoyah (George Guess), creator of the Cherokee syllabary.

Cherokee Alphabet.

Sequoyah's Cherokee syllabary of eighty-six characters.

established a third school for the Cherokees, known as the Mission at the Forks of the Illinois, with Samuel Newton serving as superintendent.

Through its richly varied activities, emphasis on learning, and general enlightenment effort, Park Hill Mission could well qualify for the title of "Athens of the American Southwest." This mission was the creation of Samuel Austin Worcester. Following his release from the Georgia state prison in 1834, Worcester and his wife came to Indian Territory. Disasters on their journey slowed them so much that they did not arrive in Oklahoma until 1835. The great teacher had worked long and hard in eastern cities raising money to purchase a printing press, but the steamer carrying their personal effects, supplies, and the press sank in the Arkansas River. All seemed lost to the swirling muddy waters, but Worcester persevered, and finally recovered the press. This single piece of equipment became one of the most important devices ever brought to Oklahoma.

Worcester settled temporarily at Union Mission and looked about for a site to establish a permanent station. He set up his press at Union and published several pieces that bear the Union Mission Press imprint. Two merit special notice, for they are the first books published in Oklahoma—an eight-page Cherokee primer and a hundred-page translation of portions of the Scriptures in Creek.

In 1837, Worcester selected a site five miles south of Tahlequah for his Park Hill Mission. Under his vigorous and creative leadership, Park Hill became the most important learning center in Indian Territory. In addition to a complex of buildings (at first built of logs, and later of neat frame construction) for classrooms, a church, and dwellings for the missionaries and teachers, the station included a boarding hall and dormitory for students, a gristmill, shops, stables, and barns. Extensive fields were cleared near the station, for Worcester's goal was to make this community self-sufficient. The Indian students were to spend several hours each day learning the best-known methods of plant and animal husbandry and producing their own food.

Park Hill became famous for its press. The missionary compound finally included a two-story publishing house complete with bindery. The famous Park Hill Press imprint appeared on the annual *Cherokee Almanac*, the *Cherokee Primer*, and other textbooks, religious tracts, and various missionary and secular publications, both in Cherokee and English. The Park Hill publishing establishment did a massive volume of work for the Cherokees, numbering more than 14 million pages. Additional work came to Worcester from the Creeks, Chickasaws, and Choctaws; for the Choctaws alone Park Hill Press published more than 11 million pages of various materials.

Worcester's greatest work was translating most of the Old Testament and New Testament from English to Cherokee. A classical scholar, Worcester collated the English versions with Greek, Latin, and Hebrew texts to produce a Bible in Cherokee. Elias Boudinot, a mixed-blood Cherokee intellectual, for years editor of the *Cherokee Phoenix*, collaborated with Worcester as translator. When Boudinot was butchered by political enemies on that fateful June day in 1839, the grief-stricken Worcester is reported to have said: "I have lost my right arm." A well-educated Cherokee named David Foreman was Boudinot's replacement as translator.

Worcester's many additional activities included organizing the Cherokee Bible Society. This organization raised more than $2,500 for the distribution of 5,225 volumes of the Scriptures in the Cherokee language. He established the Cherokee Temperance Society to discourage the consumption of whiskey by the Indians. Worcester's great energy began to wane in 1859, and he called Charles C. Torrey from Fairfield Mission to Park Hill to succeed him. A few months later in the same year, the Cherokees' greatest teacher died.

Baptist activity among the Cherokees began in 1817 while the nation was still in the East and developed a curious one-sided following among the Indians. Two important names among Cherokee Baptists were Evan Jones and one of his Cherokee protégés, Jesse Bushyhead. Their appeal from the beginning was almost exclusively to the full bloods. The first Cherokee Baptists in Oklahoma arrived during 1832, when eighty families led by Duncan O'Briant established a settlement seventy

Evan Jones, Baptist missionary teacher to the Cherokees.

miles north of Fort Smith in present Delaware County. A thriving community developed there, complete with a water-driven sawmill and gristmill, a church, and a school. O'Briant died in 1834 and was succeeded by Samuel Aldrich, a missionary from Cincinnati. The hardships of the wild Oklahoma frontier killed Aldrich within a year, and Chandler Curtiss became the next missionary to serve this pioneer Cherokee Baptist community. Depredations by white renegades from Arkansas caused Curtiss to abandon this mission in 1836. Two years later the Cherokee Baptists fused with large numbers of their brethren arriving in Oklahoma from Georgia under the terms of the Treaty of New Echota.

Jones and Bushyhead reached Oklahoma in 1839, each serving on the overland trek as a detachment leader responsible for about a thousand immigrants. These Baptist leaders settled their followers at a place called Baptist, later Old Baptist Mission, near present Westville. The newcomers constructed a missionary compound that included a school, church, shops, stables, and barns, plus fields, orchards, and pasture, much like Park Hill. In addition to

Samuel Austin Worcester, ABCFM missionary teacher to the Cherokees.

its regular coeducational school for the primary grades, Baptist Mission included a special school known as the Cherokee Female Seminary.

In 1843 the Baptist Mission Board in Boston furnished Jones with a press and type. Henry Upham, a printer, was then engaged to establish the Baptist Mission Press. Through this agency, Jones supplied his followers with religious tracts, hymn books, and Baptist news published in the *Cherokee Messenger*. The *Messenger* was a sixteen-page periodical, the first magazine published in Oklahoma. Its initial issue appeared August, 1844. The material from Baptist Mission Press was printed both in Cherokee and in English, for Jones and Bushyhead had begun translating the Bible into Cherokee even before they came west. They continued their work and distributed copies of translated books of the Bible through the Baptist Mission Press.

Most of Jones's followers were full bloods, and he appealed to them in their own language, largely through Cherokee preachers he had trained. Bushyhead, who also served as a justice on the Cherokee Supreme Court, was

one of Jones's most famous trainees. Lewis Downing, a Union Officer during the Civil War, and later a principal chief of the nation, was another Jones trainee. In 1855, Jones was joined by his son, John B. Jones, a graduate of Rochester University, who became his principal assistant. Both father and son were ardent abolitionists and their propagation of this viewpoint among their parishioners had a great effect in committing Cherokee full bloods to the Union cause during the Civil War.

There was a curious link between Evan Jones, the Baptist, and John Ross, the Methodist, in political matters. One Cherokee observer claimed of Jones and his son:

"No man or men were ever able to sway the minds and politics of the full-blood Cherokees as did this father and son. They were the real dictators of the Cherokee Nation, from 1839 to 1867, through the numerically dominant full-bloods, who, as a body, were always swayed by impulse rather than reason. As ministers of the Gospel they were apparently meek and humble, but the sentiments which they powerfully and insidiously engendered among the full-bloods were perforce . . . the governmental policies of Chief Ross."

Despite the extensive educational activities begun by the various missionary societies for the Cherokees, far more Indian children were involved in the Cherokee Nation's public schools than in the missionary schools. The Cherokee constitution made a provision for a superintendent of public instruction whose function it was to organize a national school system. Stephen Foreman, a well-educated, mixed-blood Cherokee, was the first to be named to this position. Foreman appointed a three-member school board in each of the districts of the nation. Operating under the Cherokee Educational Law, passed by the national council in 1841, he directed the local boards to supervise the construction of schoolhouses in each district. Foreman established standards for certification of teachers and developed a curriculum for the district schools, which offered work through the first eight grades. The Cherokee public schools opened in 1842. By 1859 the number had increased from eleven schools to thirty, with a total enrollment of fifteen hundred. In 1859, only two teachers in the Cherokee public school system were non-Cherokee.

The Cherokee public school system was expanded in 1846 when the national council authorized the construction of two seminaries for advanced students. The Cherokee Female Seminary, situated at Park Hill, and the Cherokee Male Seminary at Tahlequah were completed and opened for enrollment in 1850. These two structures, each three stories high, were constructed of brick. A party of Mormons en route to Utah had stopped for a season at Tahlequah about the time the two giant structures were begun, and Mormon craftsmen taught the Cherokees brickmaking. Each of the structures contained dormitory rooms for students, dining room, kitchen, chapel, and classrooms. The seminaries enrolled both boarding and day students. Most of the teachers in these two institutions were college graduates from the East.

The Creek Indians have a different intellectual-spiritual history from the Cherokees. For one thing, the Creeks had no public school system during the golden years. However, the Creek council often appropriated funds to match those raised by church groups to support mission schools in the Creek Nation. The Creeks also experienced an anti-Christian period during which Indian Christians were persecuted and missionaries were driven from the Creek country. Finally, the number and quality of Creek Schools did not approach those of the Cherokee educational establishment and they were not served by the variety of religious faiths that patronized the latter.

American Board workers visited among the Creeks before removal but made no substantial impact on the tribe while it was in the East. Representatives from this missionary society came among the Creeks in Indian Territory during 1832. Dr. George S. Weed, a medical missionary, and his wife were the first American Board workers. In 1833, John Fleming joined them and a regular mission station was established for Creek children at a location seven miles west of Fort Gibson. Three years after he arrived among the Creeks, Dr. Weed became ill and was replaced by Roderick L.

Dodge, another medical missionary. Spectacular work for the Creeks was done by John Fleming. He gave careful study to the Creek language and was the first person to reduce this Muskhogean tongue to writing. In 1835, at Union Mission in the Cherokee Nation, Worcester's press published a book of one hundred pages containing portions of the Scriptures in the Creek language. As noted earlier, Fleming's book, of which 500 copies were printed, and Worcester's *Cherokee Primer* were the first books written and published in Oklahoma.

The Baptists had evangelized among the Creeks before this nation migrated to Indian Territory. A Creek Baptist convert, John Davis, accompanied a party of immigrant Creeks to Oklahoma in 1831. The previous year he had been licensed by the Baptist Mission Board. During 1832 he was joined by David Lewis, a Baptist missionary from New York. Together they established a mission station called Ebenezer, about fifteen miles west of Fort Gibson and three miles north of the Arkansas River.

In 1834, David B. Rollin of Cincinnati was sent to the Creek country to succeed Lewis, but the new missionary had hardly made a beginning when Opothleyaholo's Upper Creeks began arriving from the East. The new immigrants carried hate in their hearts for all white men. Missionaries were charged with meddling in their affairs, and it appeared that both Baptist and American Board missionaries in the Creek country were in grave danger. Consequently, the superintendent of Indian affairs ordered all missionaries from the Creek country.

In 1842 the Creek council reconsidered the missionary issue. Members investigated the old charges that the missionaries had meddled in removal politics and determined the charges to be unfounded. The missionaries were invited to return, and gradually they won acceptance. During 1842, Evan Jones, the Cherokee Baptist divine, visited the Creek Nation with Charles R. Kellam. In the same year, a group of Baptists at Louisville, Kentucky, organized the American Indian Mission Association and selected Isaac McCoy as executive secretary. This association ordained a Creek native preacher named Joseph Island, who through his own study of the Bible and independent preaching had already made a

Tullahassee Mission, Creek Nation near Muskogee.

name for himself among the Creeks. The association sent Sidney Dyer to work with Island.

H. F. Buckner came to the Creeks in 1847 and Joseph S. Murrow joined Buckner in 1857. The Baptist faith was so well established and so widely spread among the Creeks by 1851 that the Muskogee Baptist Association, one of the oldest in Oklahoma, was organized.

The Creek council invited the Presbyterians to return, and they did so, not under the American Board, but as workers for the Presbyterian Board of Foreign Missions. Their first school was established at Kowetah Mission in 1842 with Robert M. Loughridge and his wife in charge. Seven years later, the Creek council agreed to subsidize the construction of a new school to be known as Tullahassee. Situated near present Muskogee, this mission became the principal center of learning for the Creeks. William S. Robertson, who had married Worcester's daughter, Ann Eliza, vigorously pushed an ambitious learning program for the Creek youths. He imported a printing press and published books, hymns, religious tracts, and the Scriptures in the Creek language, benefiting from the earlier work of John Fleming. Tullahassee became widely known

through its publication called *Our Monthly*. With the assistance of a well-educated Creek named David Winsett, Robertson wrote the *Creek First Reader*, "which it is said did more than any other agency to aid the Creeks and Seminoles to read and write in their own language."

The Methodists began work among the Creeks rather late, but with their characteristic energy and drive they soon made a strong showing through circuit rider evangelism and camp meetings. For years the Creek nation was a part of the Cherokee District in the Indian Methodist Conference, South. So many converts had been won by 1857 that a separate district, with Thomas B. Ruble as presiding elder, was established with three mission stations. With a subsidy from the Creek council, the Methodists established Asbury Manual Labor School near North Fork Town in 1850 with Ruble as superintendent.

Just before the beginning of the Civil War, the Creek council authorized an ambitious neighborhood public school program. Before the program could be fully implemented, however, the Creeks became hopelessly divided over the issue of which to support—the

Union or the Confederacy—and their school plan had to wait until after the war for fulfillment.

The Seminoles belatedly developed an educational program for their young people. The tribe was obligated by the Treaty of Fort Gibson to settle in the Creek Nation. The Seminoles arrived in Oklahoma at the peak of the Creek anti-Christian campaign, and it was not until 1844 that an effort was made to establish mission schools for the Florida exiles.

The initiative in establishing Seminole mission schools was taken during 1844 by John Bemo, recently arrived in the Creek Nation from Philadelphia. Bemo was a Seminole, a nephew of the great war chief Osceola. Bemo, while a youth, was kidnapped on the Florida coast by a sea captain. After eight years on the high seas, he made his way to Philadelphia. There he came under the patronage of the Presbyterians, was educated and trained as a missionary, and was finally sent to Indian Territory to minister to his countrymen. He began teaching and preaching in the Seminole camps during 1844. Four years later he was joined by the Presbyterian missionary John Lilley. The team established a mission school for the Seminoles at Oak Ridge, near present Holdenville. They were joined in 1856 by James R. Ramsey, formerly a teacher at Tullahassee. Ramsey, an ardent abolitionist, won the Seminole assistant chief, John Chupco, to his faith and point of view. When the Civil War broke out in 1861, Ramsey, with Chupco's Seminole faction, fled north into Kansas and later returned to Indian Territory to fight for the Union.

Joseph S. Murrow, a Baptist missionary, arrived in the Seminole Nation in 1857. From Georgia and with southern beliefs, he won John Jumper, the principal chief of the Seminoles, to the Baptist faith and the Confederate cause. When the Civil War broke out, Jumper's Baptist followers fought for the Confederacy. As reward for his support, the Confederate government appointed Murrow to the office of Seminole agent.

In the mid-nineteenth century, the Choctaws were among the most enlightened of the Indian tribes, due largely to their excellent educational system and their intense enthusiasm for learning. No Indian community in America had better educational opportunities than the Choctaws. These were provided by tribal leaders, who, though under extreme pressure by United States offiicials to surrender their Mississippi lands and move west, were aware of the political implications of opening vast new tracts to the land-hungry settlers. Realizing their favorable bargaining position, they shrewdly exploited the situation to gain amazing concessions in the removal treaties, especially regarding tribal education. The Choctaws had substantial sums flowing from the federal government each year from the sale of their eastern land. The Choctaw national council appropriated most of this money for schools in order to assure the best possible education for their youth. The Choctaw talent for gaining concessions from the federal government was reflected in their dealings with private groups, too. When various mission groups attempted to evangelize the Choctaws, tribal leaders allowed them entry only if each society furnished qualified teachers equal to the number of preachers. Historians therefore find it difficult to distinguish between public and private schools in the Choctaw Nation. All Choctaw schools were public in the sense that the institutions were generally constructed from tribal funds. The schools were regularly inspected, graded, and accredited by Choctaw government officials, and substantial sums were appropriated each year by the Choctaw national council to support these institutions. In exchange for the privilege of spreading the Gospel, the churches were required to furnish teachers for each school.

American Board missionaries arrived in the Choctaw Nation in Mississippi in 1817. There, Cyrus Kingsbury established Elliot Mission, the first Choctaw school, in 1818. Itinerant Baptist and Methodist workers also labored among the Choctaws before removal, but the first big concession for Choctaw education came in the 1820 Treaty of Doak's Stand. At that time Chief Pushmataha shrewdly persuaded government commissioners to include in the treaty a proviso that fifty-four sections of Choctaw land in Mississippi be sold and the proceeds set aside for educating Choctaw children. A portion of this money was used to

Cherokee Female Seminary, Park Hill, near present Tahlequah.

establish the Choctaw Academy at Blue Springs, Kentucky, in 1824, under the auspices of the Baptist Mission Association, with Richard M. Johnson as superintendent. The Choctaw Treaty of 1825 included a provision for increasing the educational benefits for tribal youths at this school. At first, only twenty-five Choctaw youths could be enrolled at the Kentucky school each year at government expense; by the 1830 treaty, the number was increased to forty. The Choctaw Academy produced a corps of informed, well-trained leaders for the Choctaw Nation, including Principal Chief Peter P. Pitchlynn. While Choctaw students were the most numerous, other tribes represented at the Choctaw Academy included Cherokees, Chickasaws, Creeks, Seminoles, and Potawatomis. The Choctaw Nation continued to support the academy in Kentucky by sending its young people there and providing a large annual subsidy until 1843, when funds were withdrawn to support national academies and schools developing within the Choctaw Nation in Oklahoma.

American Board missionaries were actively organizing schools in the nation immediately after removal. Beginning in 1833, there were log schoolhouses in the three Choctaw districts, each staffed with a missionary-teacher and offering an elementary curriculum of reading, writing, spelling, arithmetic, and Bible study. These schools were financed jointly by tribal funds and missionary grants. A breakthrough in Choctaw learning occurred from the efforts of American Board teacher Cyrus Byington, who, after years of study, was able to reduce the Choctaw spoken language to a written form by using the English alphabet. He published the first Choctaw grammar in 1834. His coworkers, Cyrus Kingsbury, Loring S. Williams, and Alfred Wright, translated English text into Choctaw and produced a Choctaw-English dictionary. Wright translated portions of the Scriptures into Choctaw, including the books of Joshua, Judges, and Ruth.

By 1838, American Board mission schools in the Choctaw Nation had increased from three to ten. These were Bethabara, Clear Creek, Bethel, Bok Tuklo, Wheelock, Pine Ridge (Chuala Female Seminary), Greenfield (also known as Lukfata and White Clay), Mountain Fork, Goodwater, and Bennington. Later, Ebenezer Hotchkin established Living Land and Mayhew stations, and at Eagletown,

Byington organized a mission that he named for his native town of Stockbridge, Massachusetts.

In addition to maintaining regular school and mission programs through the week, American Board workers attracted parents of the students with a pioneer effort in adult education through Sabbath schools and weekend camps. These weekly gatherings, which offered elementary instruction in reading, writing, spelling, and arithmetic, helped to eliminate illiteracy in the Choctaw Nation. The Choctaw national council gave sustained and enthusiastic support to these early-day educators. In 1842 the council appropriated $26,000, a substantial sum for the time, for Choctaw education.

As the Choctaws advanced in learning, the neighborhood schools were found to supply only the foundation for an education. The demand for advanced learing was met during the 1840s by the construction of academies at key locations in the Choctaw Nation. In 1841 the Choctaw national council enacted legislation providing for the erection of an institution for advanced study for boys, near Doaksville. The school was named Spencer Academy, in honor of Secretary of War John C. Spencer, who had given sustained encouragement and support to the Choctaws in their efforts to improve education. Spencer Academy opened in 1844 under the leadership of Edward McKinney and functioned for nearly two years as an institution of the Choctaw Nation. The new academy failed to develop as rapidly as expected, so the national council placed it under the direction of the Presbyterian Board of Foreign Missions, supported by tribal funds, with James B. Ramsey as superintendent.

The development of an academy system in the Choctaw Nation involved religious groups other than the Presbyterians and Congregationalists. Methodist missionaries had worked among the Choctaws before removal, and two representatives of this faith, Alexander Talley and Moses Perry, accompanied the Choctaws over the Trail of Tears to the Indian Territory. During the 1840s, the Methodists enlarged their Indian mission program, then primarily circuit rider preaching and camp meetings, to include assistance in operating Choctaw schools. In 1840, Methodist officials and tribal leaders signed a contract to operate a school for Choctaw boys at old Fort Coffee, thereafter known as Fort Coffee Academy. Willian H. Goode was this institution's first superintendent and Henry C. Benson served as principal teacher. Each later published his recollections of life among the Choctaws.

During the 1840s the Methodists in the Choctaw Nation sided with the Methodist Episcopal Church, South, when the ecclesiastical split occurred. In 1844 the Southern Methodists assisted the Choctaw council in establishing New Hope Academy for girls near Fort Coffee Academy, and eight years later this faith organized the Choctaw Academy. John Harrel, a leading Methodist missionary in Indian Territory in the 1850s, served for a time as superintendent at Fort Coffee Academy; during the Civil War he held an appointment as chaplain for Confederate General Stand Watie's Cherokee Mounted Rifle Brigade.

The Baptists also were attentive to Choctaw spiritual and educational needs. Charles Wilson of Philadelphia was the first Baptist missionary who served the Choctaws after removal. He was based near Skullyville at a community known as Pleasant Bluff Springs. Joseph Smedley, Eben Tucker, and Alanson Allen also worked there. Other Baptist missionaries working with the Choctaws included Isaac McCoy, Joseph S. Murrow, and Ramsey D. Potts. Reverend Potts concentrated on the Choctaw settlements on Red River; one of his mission schools was situated at Providence, twelve miles west of Fort Towson. This work was managed by the American Indian Baptist Association based at Nashville, Tennessee. During 1844, Armstrong Academy, located in the southwestern portion of the nation, was opened, and the association named Ramsey Potts superintendent, with P. B. Brown and H. W. Jones as teachers. In 1854, A. G. Moffatt became superintendent at Armstrong Academy under an appointment of the Baptist Home Mission Board, but four years later the Choctaw national council assigned this school to the Cumberland Presbyterian Church Board.

Beginning in 1847, the outstanding graduates of these academies were granted scholarships by the Choctaw national council, enabling them to complete their educations in

Bloomfield School for Chickasaw girls, near Tishomingo. Courtesy Oklahoma Historical Society.

colleges and universities in the East. Before the Civil War, the Choctaw Nation counted among it citizens graduates of Dartmouth, Union (New York City), and Yale.

By joining the Choctaws in 1837 under the Treaty of Doaksville, the Chickasaws shared the excellent Choctaw educational system. Not only did the Chickasaws long for separate status, they also looked forward to the time that their children would have schools of their own in a separate and independent Chickasaw Nation. Before removal to Oklahoma, the Chickasaws received the attention of missionary teachers. In 1817, Robert Bell, from Elk Creek Presbytery of the Cumberland Presbyterian Church Board, began work among these people, and ten years later American Board teachers arrived in their Mississippi settlements.

In 1842, after it became safe for the Chickasaws to move west into their district, Methodist missionaries followed. In 1843, W. A. Duncan, of the Indian Methodist Conference, established a school and church at Pleasant grove near Emet. The Chickasaws used a large part of their Mississippi land sale money to establish a system of elementary schools in their district, and Methodist and Presbyterian missionaries assisted the Chickasaws by serving as teachers in the neighborhood schools. The Chickasaws provided for higher education beginning in 1844 by raising $12,000 to construct an academy two miles east of Tishomingo. Wesley Browning, a prominent Methodist teacher and missionary figure, supervised the construction of this institution, and John C. Robinson served as superintendent for several years. This coeducational school, with facilities for 120 students, was called McKendree Academy. In 1852 it enrolled young men only and was called the Chickasaw Manual Labor Academy. After the Civil War, its name was changed a third time to Harley Institute.

In 1852 the Methodists directed the Reverend John H. Carr to erect an academy, named Bloomfield, for Chickasaw girls. As the number of elementary school graduates increased, additional academies were constructed with Chickasaw subsidies during the 1850s. These included Wapanucka Institute, Collins Institute (later called Colbert Academy), and Burney Institute—this last named school under the Cumberland Presbyterian Church

Board until after the Civil War, when the Methodists took over its operation.

Acculturation had made progress among the Five Civilized Tribes before removal. After their arrival in Oklahoma, a massive educational program sponsored by various missionary groups and tribal governments accelerated this process. Education, especially among the mixed bloods of each of the five tribes, was a solvent of old customs and tribal ways, and became a vehicle for the economic and social advancement of the mixed-blood segment of each tribe. For certain of the full bloods, education, as provided by the missionary schools, was primarily a means of learning to read the Bible as translated into the native tongues, and of developing a simple Christian faith.

Notes on Sources, Chapter 7

Leaders of the Five Civilized Tribes encouraged education of their young people for several reasons. A principal reason was tactical—to produce a corps of leaders trained in law and business and able to understand and thereby better cope with the Anglo-Americans who were eternally pressing for tribal lands. Education would prepare all of them for the new age that was aborning for Indians. Since missionaries were about the only teachers available at the time, they were permitted to establish churches and preach the Gospel in the Indian nations if they also established schools and instructed Indian children in the essentials of learning. Material used in this chapter for the development of schools among the Five Civilized Tribes in Oklahoma was taken from the following books: Carolyn Foreman, *Park Hill* (Muskogee, Okla., 1948); Ralph Gabriel, *Elias Boudinot, Cherokee, and His America* (Norman, 1941); Carolyn T. Foreman, *Oklahoma Imprints, 1835–1907: A History of Printing in Oklahoma Before Statehood* (Norman, 1936); Grant Foreman, *Advancing The Frontier, 1830–1860* (Norman, 1933); Grant Foreman, *The Five Civilized Tribes* (Norman, 1934); Althea Bass, *Cherokee Messenger (A Life of Samuel Austin Worcester)* (Norman, 1936); Henry C. Benson, *Life Among the Choctaw Indians* (Cincinnati, 1860); E. B. Chusman, *History of the Choctaw, Chickasaw, and Natchez Indians* (Greenville, Texas, 1899); O. B. Campbell, *Mission to the Cherokees* (Oklahoma City, 1973); Grace Steele Woodward, *The Cherokees* (Norman, 1963); Angie Debo, *The Rise and Fall of the Choctaw Republic* (Norman, 1934; 2d ed., 1961); Angie Debo, *The Road to Disappearance: A History of the Creek Indians* (Norman, 1941); Edwin C. McReynolds, *The Seminoles* (Norman, 1957); and Arrell Morgan Gibson, *The Chickasaws* (Norman, 1971).

Chapter 8

Antebellum Oklahoma

A curious dichotomy was apparent in each of Oklahoma's five Indian republics. The elements of this dichotomy provided the Indian Territory frontier before the Civil War with a variety and color no other primitive area in America could match. The contrasts were based on distinct and often opposed communities within each tribe—the full bloods and the mixed bloods; the very wealthy and the extremely poor; the well-educated and the barely literate; and variant religionists, some Christian, others following the traditional tribal religions.

Even in family forms these dichotomies were apparent. While monogamy was becoming more common through the influence of missionaries, the tribes continued the practice of polygamy. Cherokee law forbade it, but polygamy was so extensive in that nation that the law was not enforced. The Choctaws openly tolerated polygamy, as did the other tribes. A missionary among the Choctaws during the golden years has provided a glimpse of this condition:

> "If a man should separate from, or abandon his wife, his property was liable to be seized by the light-horsemen and appropriated to the benefit of the divorced woman. I remember one man in our district who had two wives, and they resided fifteen or twenty miles distant from each other, and each had one or two servants to serve as housekeeper. One of these wives united with the church, after which she did not live with her man. She felt justified in her course as she was the one last taken, hence, could not be his lawful wife."

The ambition and energy of the mixed bloods and their zeal for imitating the white man were not shared by the full bloods. Rather, withdrawal was the full-blood response. Usually, they asserted themselves only to support certain candidates for election, as they did for Cherokee Chief John Ross; to protest mixed-blood domination, as during the Civil War; or when an ingrained tribal practice such as common ownership of land was endangered by the federal government's proposal of allotment in severalty.

Generally the full bloods kept to themselves, living in crude little cabins on ridges in the timber, away from the exposed and heavily traveled river valleys. They followed a subsistence kind of life, hunting, fishing, and raising small patches of corn and other food crops. They came to the settlements to trade furs, hides, and other products of nature for powder, shot, a few trinkets, and cloth, following the old ways except, sometimes, in religion. Occasionally missionaries like Evan Jones succeeded in overthowing the old tribal gods for Christianity.

The mixed bloods predominated in the fertile river valleys, where they developed farms, plantations, and ranches. Slavery was widely practiced by this group. Before the Civil War, the number of bondage laborers owned by these energetic developers of Oklahoma's natural bounty varied from one slave family to several hundred blacks. One Choctaw planter owned more than five hundred slaves. Each of Oklahoma's five Indian republics found it necessary to adopt a special slave code to control its black chattels. The Cherokee, Choctaw, Chickasaw, and Creek slave laws were very severe, especially regarding runaway slaves and the teaching of abolitionism.

Spencer Academy, Choctaw Nation.

The Seminoles, however, had a peculiar relationship with their slaves. The blacks had considerable influence over their Seminole owners, for many of the slaves were literate and served the Indians as clerks and interpreters. As a general rule Seminole slaves lived in separate villages and were free to come and go. Their only obligation was to furnish an annual tribute of grain, meat, and other products or services to their owners.

The typical Oklahoma antebellum plantation consisted of the owner's house, a log dwelling of two sections connected by an open gallery or passage called the "dog trot," with spacious porches in front. Behind the house were the slave cabins, barns, corral, smokehouse, stable, and a kennel for hunting dogs. Later, the more successful planters replaced their log houses with pretentious mansions furnished with carpets, music rooms and libraries, and other elegant fixtures found in many antebellum white homes.

The mixed-blood taste for white culture extended to dress. Many adopted the typical white man's attire of heavy boots, homespun shirt, and slouch hat. As their enterprises flourished and they became wealthy, the mixed bloods adopted the dress of southern planters and adorned their women in silks, imported shawls, and parasols. Such opulence was typified by Peter Folsom, a Choctaw district chief:

He was a dignified man, evidently regarding himself as a ruler of the people, and not unwilling to receive the attention and homage which are due to one who had been promoted by the people to a post of influence and power. Folsom's reputation was good; he was a man of wealth and character, but uneducated. He was the most aristocratic lord I saw in the Choctaw tribe, and the most ostentatious in all respects. He made a visit across the territory to the agency, bringing all his family; he had an elegant barouche in which his family traveled; a black coachman sat out in front and a well-dressed servant sat in the boot, while the lady within had one or two maids to give her attention; the old chief rode in front upon the back of a splendid saddle horse. Folsom was a friend to the schools, and did not fail to use his influence, personal and official, to advance the interests of his people and to promote their prosperity in all things.

National House Hotel, Tahlequah.

The full bloods mixed their attire. Their women, proficient in spinning and weaving, produced brightly dyed homespun for clothing their families. The men wore moccasins, fringed buckskin leggings, a hunting shirt, and a brightly colored turban. In winter, blankets were a feature of the full blood's dress.

It is interesting that the mixed bloods so willingly adopted the ways of the white man in almost every respect except landholding. The Indian custom of holding lands in common was one tribal practice they defended, largely because it was advantageous to their interests. All members had equal rights to share in the tribal domain. A tribal citizen could hunt, fish, and cut timber in all places not occupied by towns, farms, and plantations. In raising cattle, the Five Civilized Tribes followed the open-range practice. Livestock, carrying the owner's brand or mark, grazed at large on the unfenced public domain. Cultivated land was enclosed with rail fence. The population density of Oklahoma during the tribes' golden years was low. With a land area of nearly 70,000 square miles and a population of less than 100,000, there were fewer than two persons per square mile. Since all land was public, there were no real estate taxes. An Indian citizen could clear, improve, and cultivate as much land as he wished, provided he did not encroach on his neighbor. Tribal law permitted a citizen to sell his improvements or pass them on to his heirs. While the full bloods' subsistence patches might only cover from three to ten acres, the mixed-blood developments generally were considerably larger. The most extensive plantations in Oklahoma were in the Red River valley, where Choctaw and Chickasaw mixed-blood planters often maintained single fields for cotton and corn of fifty acres or more.

Robert Love, a Chickasaw, operated two large plantations on the Red and owned two hundred slaves. Each autumn he traveled to New Orleans and chartered a steamer to transport his cotton to market. Robert M. Jones, a Choctaw planter, and one of the wealthiest men in the American West, worked five Red River plantations with five hundred slaves, and owned a fleet of river steamers that operated between Kiamichi Landing and New Orleans.

The economies of the Cherokee, Creek, and Seminole nations were more diversified. Their farms, plantations, and mines produced meat, hides, grain, salt, lead, and associated products. While the holdings of Cherokee planter Stand Watie on Spavinaw Creek, Creek planter Benjamin Perryman on the Verdigris, and others were extensive, they did not match the vast estates of their Choctaw and Chickasaw neighbors.

The markets for Indian Territory producers were varied. The many military posts in Indian Territory were heavy consumers of local produce. The Fort Washita garrison alone purchased seven thousand bushels of corn and great quantities of eggs, butter, meat, and vegetables each year from Chickasaw farmers.

Additional markets were found in the towns of Indian Territory. Before removal, towns for the Five Civilized Tribes had been communal centers with common fields adjacent. Everyone lived in the towns, and tribal life revolved around the group. In Indian Territory, except for the more conservative element among the Creeks and Seminoles, the traditional Indian town declined as old tribal forms were altered and Indians came to follow the familiar American rural pattern—dispersing and settling on detached, separate family farms and plantations. The towns thereby became trade, political, and educational centers. The ordinary components of these early Oklahoma towns were a blacksmith shop, a cotton gin, a gristmill, a sawmill, stores, warehouses for traders, schools and churches, a post office, often a hotel, tribal government buildings, and a stage office.

The leading towns in the Cherokee Nation were Tahlequah, Beatty's Prairie, and Fort Gibson; in the Choctaw Nation they were Miller Courthouse, Perryville, Skullyville, Boggy Depot, Doaksville, and Eagletown. Tishomingo and Oak Grove were the Chickasaws' important towns; and leading centers for the Creeks and Seminoles were North Fork Town, Micco, Edwards' Post, Shieldsville, and Honey Springs. Mail, stage, and steamboat service and such newspapers as the *Cherokee Advocate, Choctaw Intelligencer, Choctaw Telegraph,* and *Chickasaw Intelligencer* kept the townspeople and country dwellers well informed on local, national, and world events.

During the golden years, the major outlets for Indian Territory products were the Gulf markets, especially New Orleans, by way of Oklahoma's water network. From earliest Spanish and French times, Sooner State waterways had been important arteries for trade and communication. After the Louisiana purchase in 1803, river traffic on the Arkansas and Red rivers and tributary streams increased. Pioneer traders and trappers used a variety of boats for transporting goods. There were canoes; pirogues (generally fashioned from huge cottonwood logs cut along the Canadian); clumsy flat-bottomed bateaux propelled by poles; flatboats; keelboats; and a western adaptation known as the bullboat, a small river craft constructed of a sapling frame covered with tough buffalo or elk hide. Canoes, pirogues, and bullboats could be used for both upstream and downstream travel. The flatboat, a huge, barge-like craft used only for downstream, with-the-current travel until the advent of the river steamers, was generally constructed at a river landing near the collection point for pigs of lead, baskets of salt, hides, and other cargo. Once all cargo was loaded, it was launched into the Grand or other Indian Territory stream bound for New Orleans. Upon reaching its destination and being unloaded, the crude barge was dismantled and the lumber sold as salvage in the Gulf ports. After the development of steam navigation, flatboats sometimes were towed back upstream to the tributary landings for reuse.

The head of navigation for larger craft lay in the eastern third of Oklahoma. Beyond that point, as the streambeds widened and the water became shallower, only pirogues and bullboats could ascend, except during periods of high water. Several prominent Indian Territory traders maintained shipyards at the head of navigation; Chouteau's works at the mouth of the Verdigris was the best known. An 1824 manifest covering 38,000 pounds of cargo originating on the Verdigris reports a typical early-day shipment of furs and skins: 387 packs of bearskins, 400 packs of beaver, 67 of otter, and 720 bales of wildcat and panther hides, plus 364 packages of deerskins, all stowed on Chouteau-constructed flatboats bound for New Orleans.

By the early 1820s the keelboat was a common craft on the upper waters of the Arkansas and the Red. In 1821, General Thomas James of Saint Louis brought the first keelboat to Oklahoma. He attempted to ascend the Cimarron,

Murrell House, Park Hill, one of the few extant antebellum houses in Oklahoma.

but the water was too shallow. He beached his craft, traded for horses among the Osages, and proceeded to the trading grounds with a pack-train. James returned to Oklahoma in 1823 with a keelboat laden with trade goods from Saint Louis. He found the water high enough to ascend the North Canadian as far as Keokuk Falls in central Oklahoma. At that point, his crewmen constructed pirogues to transport his trade goods to the Kiowa and Comanche country in western Oklahoma.

General James's pioneering on Oklahoma waterways popularized the keelboat, and during the 1820s it was the most common commercial craft found on the Arkansas and the Red and their feeders. These hardy vessels ascended Grand River seventy miles above Three Forks. Federal officials used keelboats to transport troops and supplies to Fort Smith, Fort Gibson, Fort Towson, and other Indian Territory posts. Government contractors brought in the first Indian immigrants on keelboats.

With wide use, the keelboat developed a lore of its own. These vessels varied between ten and twenty tons of load capacity. They had neat lines; there was a sharp bow and stern, and

the gunwales curved amidships to a width of twenty feet. Their length was about seventy-five feet. They had a thirty-inch draft, and cost $2,000 to $3,000 to construct. Amidships, extending five feet above the hull of this tough, almost unsinkable craft, was the cargo hold and cabin. Rising above the cabin was a heavy mast.

The advantage of the keelboat, in addition to its strength and cargo space, was its versatility of propulsion. Downstream passage, of course, was no problem. The current did the work with only a steersman required to guide the craft with the rudder. Upstream travel was another matter. Fifteen miles a day against the current was regarded as average. When there were favorable winds, a canvas sail would be raised from the mast. In a calm, however, several other methods could be employed to achieve the fifteen miles a day. Cordelling was one method. The cordelle, a rawhide line sometimes three hundred feet long, was secured to the mast, and twenty to thirty crewmen waded in the shallow water or walked on the bank, cordeling, or pulling, the vessel against the current. When an obstacle prevented the men from cordelling on the shoreline, the cordelle was secured to a tree or rock upstream and the vessel was advanced by crewmen on the deck who pulled on the line, moving the boat forward. Poling was a method used in shallow water to propel the keelboat. On each side of the cabin was a narrow walkway, the *passeavant*, along which the boatmen walked while pushing the craft along with poles. Crewmen on both sides of the bow thrust their poles to the river bottom and pushed against it as they walked toward the stern in a crude rhythm. At other times, oars were used.

Travel on the frontier waters was fraught with danger, and every keelboat was armed with a small cannon, called a swivel, placed in the bow. The keelboat master, called the patron, did the steering. His assistant, called the "*bosse*-man," was stationed in the bow, pole in hand, bellowing directions to the cordelle crew. This craft could accommodate as many as a hundred passengers and crew, if closely packed. Many of Oklahoma's pioneer settlers, the members of the Five Civilized Tribes, began their removal to Indian Territory by taking passage on keelboats plying the western waters.

The tough, slow-moving keelboat was gradually replaced as a principal carrier of the Indian Territory commerce by the sleek, faster river steamer. The first steamboat on the Arkansas was the *Comet*. It served the lower river towns during early 1820, and before that year was finished, this steam-powered craft reached Fort Smith. Regular steamer service was established for Fort Smith in 1822 when the *Robert Thompson* reached this frontier post with a keelboat in tow. For years, no steamboat could reach Fort Gibson because of the deep draft of the early river vessels. Then, in February, 1828, a boat of lighter draft at seventy-five tons—the *Facility*, under Captain Philip Pennywit—arrived at Fort Gibson Landing on Grand River. The *Facility* had two keelboats in tow that were carrying three hundred emigrating Creeks. Thereafter, Fort Gibson was the acknowledged head of steam navigation, although on certain occasions of high water, daring river captains operated their boats above the mouth of the Verdigris.

The *Facility*'s success wrought great changes in river transportation on the western

waters. The keelboats, barges, and flatboats were relegated to auxiliary craft, for a steamboat could pull as many as five of these. Of course, the chief advantage of the river steamer was that it could go upstream and downstream with almost equal facility.

In spite of the advantages of steam navigation, this new mode of travel on Oklahoma's waterways was not free of hazard. Low water from July to December made steam travel seasonal. Snags and submerged rocks smashed hulls and flooded the holds of many vessels. Explosions from overpressured steam boilers were common. River pilots had more obstacles to watch for on Oklahoma's two great drainage systems than on any other navigable streams in the Southwest.

The development of steam navigation on the Red was delayed for years because of the "Great Raft," a huge accumulation of closely packed trees, roots, and river debris extending from Fort Towson downriver for 150 miles. After eight years of work, United States Army engineers finally removed this vast obstruction from the stream-bed in 1838. Thereafter, steam transportation flourished on the Red. While the principal river ports were at Kiamichi Landing and Jones's Plantation at the mouth of the Boggy in the Choctaw Nation, during periods of high water, captains often ventured farther upriver. The record was set in 1843 when Captain J. B. Earhart took his vessel up the Washita to a mile below Fort Washita. When the Red was too low for upriver steamboating, Choctaw and Chickasaw planters hauled their cotton by wagon to Jefferson, Texas.

When the rivers were full all went well upstream, but when the Arkansas or the Red was low, ingenuity was required to get the steamers over the shoals. One of the most dreaded runs was at Webbers Falls on the Arkansas. Smaller vessels or craft with reduced power were towed over the riffle by a rawhide line stretched to the riverbank and pulled by several yoke of oxen. In the river lore of Oklahoma, there is a story that Captain Houston of the *Trident*, a prime carrier in the river trade between Pittsburgh, Cincinnati, and Fort Gibson,

could run his powerful stern-wheeler to Fort Gibson on less water than any other boat. If he struck a sand bar or other obstacle in the water, he would back his boat and repeatedly attempt to "jump over." In the meantime the women in the cabin screamed with fright, and the stewards held the swaying lamps to keep them from smashing on the walls.

Travel on the river steamer was more glamorous and comfortable than in the smelly, crowded hold of a keelboat. River gamblers, prostitutes from New Orleans, and the rough and tumble crewmen on the steamboats added color to the Oklahoma frontier. Once the steamboat was established as a means of moving people and goods, it functioned as the principal transportation source for Oklahoma until the coming of the railroads in the 1870s. Steamboat landings served as nuclei for early Oklahoma towns. The Arkansas River landings for Indian Territory, shown on old travel brochures published in New Orleans, indicate the proliferation of communities, small and large, growing up from the riverboat traffic: Fort Smith, Le Flore, Wilson's Rock, Fort Coffee, Skullyville, French Jack's, Black Rock, San Bois, Sallisaw, Vian, Pleasant Bluff, Canadian Shoals, Webbers Falls, Spaniard Creek, Bayou Menard, and Fort Gibson.

An early-day Oklahoma visitor has preserved the public excitement aroused by the arrival of a river steamer at the Frozen Rock or Fort Gibson landing:

> At the sound of the boat's whistle, or possibly the firing of the swivel gun at its bow, many of the inhabitants would gather at the landing which would soon be lined by a throng of welcoming spectators. . . . A crowd would rush aboard to the bar to get a drink of ice water or fresh lemonade [stronger drinks were forbidden above the line at Fort Smith]. The deck hands and roustabouts were busy and soon the landing was covered with piles of freight for the traders and stores for the government military post and the Indian agencies. . . . When all the cargo was discharged another was taken on for the downstream voyage. Thousands of beef hides, bales of buffalo robes, deer skins, and furs were taken aboard, and also barrels and sugar hogsheads filled with pecans. When the freight was aboard the

passengers appeared. These might include army officers on extended furloughs or soldiers who had been discharged by reason of expiration of enlistment. Besides these and the passengers for local points, there were almost sure to be one or two merchants or traders who had been awaiting the arrival of a "good boat" to take them to New Orleans, Memphis, St. Louis, or even faraway Cincinnati or Pittsburgh to buy goods to replenish their depleted stocks. When one of these came aboard he was generally followed by guards and servants carrying powder kegs or boxes filled with Mexican silver coin, a principal medium of exchange in the Indian country. Then, when the gangplank was raised the boat's bell clanged and the paddle wheels began to turn, the big craft would slip out into the channel while the deck hands gave voice to the wild chant of "Far' yo' well, Miss Lucy" and soon the steamboat disappeared around the bend of the river, leaving the little outpost to its wonted isolation and loneliness.

Although water transportation was widely used for moving people and goods in frontier Oklahoma, not all Indian Territory communities were situated at the river landings. The ancestor of the Sooner State's modern interstate highway and toll road system was the early-day network of wagon roads cut through the wilderness to connect the towns and military posts with the river ports.

Oklahoma was a maze of Indian trails and frontier traces long before the road-building era began, but the first road constructed in Oklahoma was a fifty-eight-mile wagon road laid out in 1825 to connect Fort Smith and Fort Gibson. A military road between Fort Gibson and Fort Towson was completed in 1827, and a road from Fort Smith to Fort Towson was cut through the Kiamichi wilderness in 1832. Additional road building took place in 1834, when Camp Arbuckle, Camp Holmes, and Camp Washita were constructed across the center of Indian Territory. These new posts were connected with Fort Gibson by roads. A military road ran from Fort Towson west to Camp Washita. By 1845 eastern and central Oklahoma were laced with roads, traces, and trails linking towns, military posts, missions,

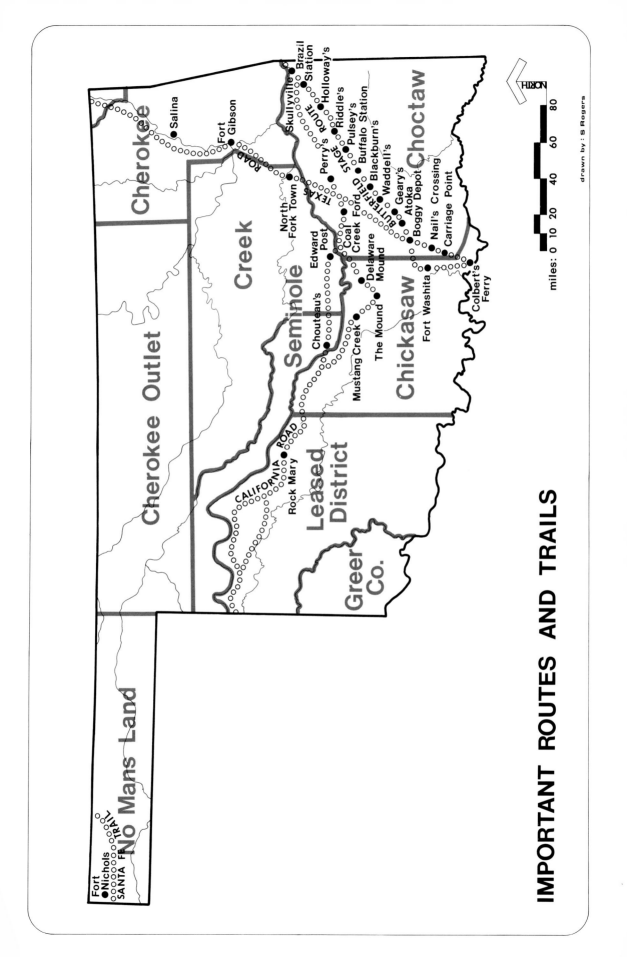

IMPORTANT ROUTES AND TRAILS

Shonion, a typical full-blood citizen of the Chickasaw Nation.

Annie Guy, a typical mixed-blood citizen of the Chickasaw Nation.

A typical Chickasaw Nation mixed blood, Palmer Mosley.

and schools situated in the domains of the Five Civilized Tribes.

Four of the most famous highways in the American West were built across Oklahoma before the Civil War. An early trail to Santa Fe followed the Canadian River. This course was used during the 1820s and 1830s by traders bound for the Mexican settlements on the Río Grande. Between 1825 and 1827 a new road to Santa Fe was surveyed, connecting the Missouri River settlements on the western border of Missouri with the Río Grande towns. This road, the most heavily used of the pre–Civil War wagon roads in the West, crossed Oklahoma's Panhandle through Cimarron County from north to south. Until 1880, when the Río Grande towns finally were connected by railroad, long lines of of canvas-covered freight wagons pulled by straining spans of oxen, mules, or horses, crossed Kansas and Oklahoma on the rutted Santa Fe Trail, bound for the frontier towns on the Río Grande.

Another famous early Oklahoma highway was the Texas Road. Laterals of this popular travel artery extended above the headwaters of Grand River into Kansas and Missouri. The road proper followed the valley of the Grand, crossed the Arkansas at Three Forks, then turned southwesterly to North Fork Town. From this point, the Texas Road angled across the Choctaw Nation and crossed Red River east of the mouth of the Washita. This was the principal north–south concourse for settlers bound for Texas.

The Butterfield Road, at least that portion south of the Canadian, bore a relation to the Texas Road. In 1858, a transcontinental stage line, the Butterfield Overland Mail, began service originating at Tipton, Missouri. The line ran southwest to Fort Smith, El Paso, and on to the Pacific shore. Nearly two hundred miles of the Butterfield route was in Oklahoma, from Fort Smith to Colbert's Ferry on the Red River through the Choctaw and Chickasaw nations. The Butterfield Overland Mail maintained twelve stage stations, spaced about fifteen miles apart, between Fort Smith and the crossing on the Red River.

Two kinds of vehicles were used on the Indian Territory leg of the mail route. One was the four-passenger Concord Celerity spring wagon, with a capacity of forty pounds of baggage per passenger and six hundred pounds of mail. The Celerity was equipped with canvas top and side curtains and seats with backs that reclined into beds for night travel. The other kind of vehicle used on the Indian Territory run was the elaborate Concord Coach. Both the Celerity and the Coach were pulled by four horses. Relays of drivers maintained continuous travel over the 2,795-mile Butterfield route. One-way fare was $200, and travelers paid for their meals at the stage stops. Passengers on the Butterfield Line were advised to include the following in their baggage:

> One Sharp's rifle and a hundred cartridges; a Colts navy revolver and two pounds of balls; a knife and sheath; a pair of thick boots and woolen pants, a half dozen pairs of thick woolen socks; six undershirts, three woolen overshirts; a wide-awake hat; a cheap sack coat; a soldier's overcoat; one pair of blankets in summer and two in winter; a piece of Indian rubber cloth for blankets [plus toilet articles].

The fourth great early-day Oklahoma highway was the California Road. The discovery of gold in California set off a feverish rush of goldseekers from the eastern states. It was expected that many of the overland travelers would follow a southerly course to the west coast diggings, and to accommodate them, in 1849 the secretary of war ordered Lieutenant J. H. Simpson to survey a route for a road from Fort Smith to the west along the valley of the Canadian. Simpson's route, which became the California Road, soon was a heavily traveled concourse. Before the gold fever ebbed, perhaps 5,000 persons passed over the California Road in Oklahoma on their way to the camps on the Sacramento River. Indian Territory towns became prosperous trade centers, as merchants and traders profited from the business of outfitting emigrant trains with wagons, mules, horses, and oxen, camp equipment, and provisions for the crossing. The gold fever hit the Five Civilized Tribes too, especially the Cherokees, and several hundred Indians made the trip to the gold fields.

Notes on Sources, Chapter 8

Indian pioneers in Oklahoma opened the Indian Territory wilderness much as Anglo-American settlers did in the surrounding states of Missouri, Arkansas, and Texas. Information about their experiences as slaveholders and frontier entrepreneurs is found in Annie H. Abel, *The American Indian as a Slave Holder and Secessionist* (Cleveland, 1915); J. B. Davis, "Slavery in the Cherokee Nation," *Chronicles of Oklahoma* 11 (December, 1933): 1056–72; Joseph H. Thoburn and Muriel H. Wright, *Oklahoma: A History of the State and Its People*, vols. 1 and 2 (New York, 1929); Grant Foreman, *Down the Texas Road* (Norman, 1936); Grant Foreman, *Marcy and the Gold Seekers: The Journal of Captain R. B. Marcy, with an Account of the Gold Rush on the Southern Route* (Norman, 1939); Grant Foreman, "The California Overland Mail Route Through Oklahoma," *Chronicles of*

Oklahoma 9 (September, 1931): 300–17; Muriel H. Wright, "Early Navigation and Commerce Along the Arkansas and Red Rivers of Oklahoma," *Chronicles of Oklahoma* 8 (March, 1930): 65–88; Roscoe Conkling, *The Butterfield Overland Mail* (Glendale, Calif., 1947); Waterman L. Ormsby, *The Butterfield Overland Mail* (San Marino, Calif., 1955); Josiah Gregg, *Commerce of the Prairies*, ed. Max L. Moorhead (Norman, 1954); Neil R. Johnson, *The Chickasaw Rancher*, ed. Arrell Morgan Gibson (Stillwater, Okla., 1961); Roy M. Johnson, *Oklahoma History South of the Canadian*, vol. 1 (Chicago, 1925); Norman A. Graebner, "Cattle Ranching in Eastern Oklahoma," *Chronicles of Oklahoma* 21 (September, 1943): 300–11; Norman A. Graebner, "Pioneer Indian Agriculture in Oklahoma," *Chronicles of Oklahoma* 23 (Autumn, 1945): 232–48; Norman A. Graebner, "The Public Land Policy of the Five Civilized Tribes," *Chronicles of Oklahoma* 23 (Summer, 1945): 107–18.

Chapter 9

The Federal Government in Oklahoma

Another of the anomalous features of Oklahoma history is the extended period of United States government control over Oklahoma's land and people. The territory that became Oklahoma was a satellite of the United States for much longer than it has been a state. In the period called the golden years of the Five Civilized Tribes, the tribes had much more freedom and independence from United States intervention and pressure than they had after the Civil War. During the pre–Civil War period, their governmental relationships were defined by treaties, and the United States was pledged to protect the Five Civilized Tribes in their title to lands in Oklahoma. Specific Indian nation boundaries were run by government surveyors. One of the well-known surveyors of Indian Territory boundaries was Isaac McCoy, the Baptist missionary. Soon after the Cherokees and Creeks received their lands in Oklahoma, he set the boundaries separating these nations, and his son John C. McCoy surveyed the Cherokee Outlet in 1837.

The United States government owed each tribe substantial sums of money as proceeds from the sale of their eastern lands. These sums were held in trust and paid to the tribal governments for schools and other public purposes and to individual Indians in yearly installments called annuities. The individual payments, varying from two dollars to twenty dollars, made in the form of specie, added to the prosperity of the Indian Territory. The United States currency increased the variety of money in circulation in each of the Indian nations. The local system of exchange included, in addition to barter and United States coins, pesos and other Spanish silver coins from Mexico and the West Indies, currency issued by the Indian governments, and trader's scrip.

Relations between the tribes and the United States were maintained by a resident commissioner assigned to each of the tribes. Before the Civil War, when the Five Civilized Tribes enjoyed a high degree of autonomy, the agent's role was much like that of a diplomat. Each United States agent in Indian Territory looked after the interests of his government, supervised the payment of annuities, and enforced various treaty stipulations. The Cherokee Agency, headquarters for the agent, was near Fort Gibson; the Creek Agency was forty miles northwest of Fort Gibson; the Choctaw Agency was situated at Skullyville; the Chickasaw Agency was established at Fort Washita after 1842; and the Seminole Agency was near Wewoka. Administratively, the Indian Territory was under the Southern Superintendency before 1861. Each of the Five Civilized Tribes maintained delegations in Washington to watch over and protect their interests in Congress and before the general government.

Another extended influence the United States government had over the Indian Territory lay in the chain of military posts the army had constructed across Oklahoma. These forts were important for several reasons. They represented a link in the nation's defenses against foreign attack. Several of these posts served as the beginnings of early Oklahoma towns because civilian communities grew up around them. These small settlements had stores, saloons, an inn or hotel, perhaps a race track, and other establishments to provide entertainment for the troops. The personnel stationed at these posts were important, too, not only for keeping peace on the frontier but also be-

General Zachary Taylor, commander of military posts in Oklahoma and later a U.S. president.

cause, after their enlistments expired, many took Indian wives and became pioneer settlers. Oklahoma's military posts furnished training and experience for many distinguished officers who fought in the Mexican War and the Civil War, in both Union and Confederate armies. These included Zachary Taylor, Jefferson Davis, Ulysses S. Grant, Robert E. Lee, George B. McClellan, John B. Hood, and Earl Van Dorn.

The first of the military posts in Indian Territory was Fort Smith, established in 1817. This station was activated from time to time until 1861, when it was abandoned to the Confederates. Recaptured by the Union Forces in 1863, Fort Smith was permanently abandoned as a military post in 1871, but it continued to play an important role in Oklahoma affairs. The old fort became the headquarters for Federal Judge Isaac Parker, the famous "Hanging Judge," who became famous for his stern campaign to eradicate lawlessness from Oklahoma after the Civil War.

In 1824, Fort Gibson was established three miles above the mouth of Grand River on the east bank. At first it was only a log palisade enclosure, three hundred feet square, with log blockhouses on the southeast and northeast corners. Through the years, permanent barracks, a commissary, and equipment buildings were erected of stone.

At the close of the Seminole War, all United States cavalry regiments were assigned to Fort Gibson. During the Mexican War, most of these troopers were ordered south of the Río Grande, but were reassigned to the Grand River post after the war. In 1857, the United States government, in an economy move, abandoned Fort Gibson and ceded the military reservation to the Cherokees. Tribal leaders laid out a townsite around the post, sold lots for a total amount of $20,000, and named the community Catoowah. In 1858, the Cherokee council proposed that the Cherokee national capital be relocated at Catoowah, but Principal Chief John Ross vetoed the bill.

Beginning in 1861, Fort Gibson served as a Confederate stronghold until Union forces captured it two years later, and Union officers renamed the old post Fort Blunt in honor of their commanding general. The United States government continued to occupy Fort Gibson until 1890, when it was permanently abandoned.

Fort Towson, a stockade of log walls, was established in 1824 by Major William Bradford near the mouth of the Kiamichi. After four years of guarding the United States-Mexican boundary on the Red River, the Towson garrison was reassigned to Fort Jesup in Louisiana. Shortly after this evacuation, all the Towson buildings except for a few cabins were destroyed by fire.

During the Choctaw removal, a post called Camp Phoenix was constructed of stone six miles northeast of old Fort Towson. Soon after completion, the name of this post was changed to Fort Towson. The new Fort Towson was occupied until 1854 when the garrison was reassigned to Fort Arbuckle.

The year 1834 was a busy one on the Oklahoma military frontier. Camp Arbuckle was established at the mouth of the Cimarron, Camp Holmes at the mouth of the Little River, and Camp Washita at the mouth of the Washita.

Also in 1834 army officers supervised the construction of Fort Coffee, on the south bank

Fort Coffee, contraband checkpoint on the Arkansas River. Courtesy Oklahoma Historical Society.

of the Arkansas twenty-five miles upriver from Fort Smith. This fort was situated on a high bluff and was constructed of hewn logs that formed a hollow enclosure a hundred feet square. Its purpose was to provide surveillance of the river for runners of contraband. Fort Coffee was abandoned after five years' service, but Methodist missionaries took over the post and established the Fort Coffee Choctaw Male Academy. This famous training institution was occupied by Confederate troops during the Civil War. A Union raid south of the Arkansas during 1863 resulted in the destruction of Fort Coffee. Troops from Fort Smith and Fort Gibson founded Fort Mason on the Canadian near present Lexington in 1835 to provide a point of contact with the tribes on Oklahoma's western border.

A new post—Fort Wayne—was established in the Cherokee Nation in 1838. Cherokee immigrants recently arrived from Georgia were making threats against Removal party members, and the government decided that federal troops stationed close to the Cherokee settlements would be essential to maintain order. Fort Wayne was first situated on the Illinois River in Sequoyah County, but the post was moved to Spavinaw Creek on Beatty's Prairie in 1839. Among the notables assigned to duty at Fort Wayne was Captain Nathan Boone, commander of a dragoon company, and son of the famous frontiersman. Fort Wayne was abandoned by the United States

government in 1842, and the garrison was moved to Fort Scott. However, the old post continued to play a prominent role in Cherokee affairs. Stand Watie used it as a stronghold during his trouble with Chief John Ross, and during the Civil War he mustered his First Cherokee Mounted Rifles there.

As the settlements of the Five Civilized Tribes pushed westward up the Canadian and Red rivers, and as transcontinental travel across Indian Territory increased, the United States government found it necessary to increase its control over the fierce tribes on Oklahoma's western boarders. Camp Washita, established in 1834, was abandoned in 1842, and the garrison was moved upriver to a new post constructed of stone, called Fort Washita. This station was evacuated by federal forces in 1861 and was subsequently occupied by Confederate troops. The Fort Washita military reservation was abandoned by the United States government in 1870.

The name of Colonel Mathew Arbuckle was given to a number of military locations in Oklahoma, first in 1834 with the establishment of Camp Arbuckle at the mouth of the Cimarron. In 1850, Captain Randolph B. Marcy, with a company of the Fifth Infantry, selected a site on the south bank of the Canadian in present McClain County for a new Camp Arbuckle. The following year, Marcy moved his troops to Wild Horse Creek in the Arbuckle Mountains of south-central Oklahoma and established Fort Arbuckle. At the outbreak of the Civil War, federal forces evacuated Arbuckle and the post remained in Confederate hands until 1865. United States forces returned to Arbuckle after the war and occupied the post until 1870, when it finally was abandoned.

Two additional military posts were built in Oklahoma before the Civil War. In order to establish a reservation for the Plains tribes, in 1855 the federal government leased from the Choctaws and Chickasaws the area between the 98th and 100th meridians south of the Canadian. This area was known as the "Leased District." Because the tribes used this zone as a sanctuary for raids into Texas, in 1858 Major Earl Van Dorn established a military base on Otter Creek for policing the Leased District. Van Dorn named the new station Camp Radziminski for Charles Radziminski, a Polish cavalry officer. The following year Major William H. Emory directed the construction of a second post in the Leased District—Fort Cobb on Cobb Creek near the Washita. Fort Cobb was abandoned to Confederate forces in 1861 but was reoccupied after the Civil War and was used by federal troops until 1869 when Fort Sill was established.

A bizarre phase of relations between the Indian Territory and the United States government appears in the Hitchcock Investigation. The removal treaties contained clauses obligating the government to pay for the cost of removal, including subsisting the Indians during the emigration from the East to Oklahoma, and to supply provisions for one year after the Indians' arrival in Indian Territory. The government, for the most part, leased out to private contractors the business of feeding and transporting the Indians, and the Indians who survived the Trail of Tears contended that much of their suffering and the high death rate was caused by the callousness of contractors who enriched themselves at the Indians' expense. Critics claimed that "at so much per head it was entirely a business proposition with the contractors." In their hands, "the removal of the Indians was not a great philanthropy, but was carried out with the same business considerations that would characterize the transportation of commodities of commerce from one point to another."

Vast sums of public money were paid to contracting firms that were newly formed to render this service for the government. As was later revealed, most of the contractors were friends and relatives of officials high in the government. The contracts customarily called for the following:

the ration of bread shall be one pound of wheat flour, Indian meal, or hard bread, or three quarters of a quart of corn; the meat ration shall be one pound of fresh meat, or three quarters of a pound of salt meat or bacon; and with fresh meat, two quarts of salt to every one hundred rations. The transportation shall be one six-horse wagon and fifteen hundred pounds of baggage to from 50 to 80 persons. The provisions and transportation shall be of the best of their kind. The average daily travel shall not exceed twelve miles.

Many of the able-bodied came west on foot. It was a long, straggling line of march for men, women, and children, through mud, dust, snow, and rain. The contracts provided that "the sick, those enfeebled from age or other cause, and young children, shall be transported by wagons or on horseback." The government allowed twenty dollars a head for transportation. For emigrant Indians who died along the way, the contractor was paid an amount proportionate to the distance traveled before death occurred. Each removal party was accompanied by a military escort and a surgeon. The surgeon's duties, in addition to rendering medical aid, were to see that the contracts were fulfilled. The lack of proper treatment lead to many deaths.

Angry protests by tribal leaders and charges of profiteering and fraud caused the federal government to investigate the removal contractors. Major Ethan Allen Hitchcock was ordered to Indian Territory to look into the complaints. Concerning his appointment, John R. Swanton has said: "Since ... the national administration was willing to look the other way while this criminal operation [the removal] was in progress, it made a curious blunder in permitting the injection into such a situation of an investigator as little disposed to whitewash iniquity as was Ethan Allen Hitchcock."

Jesse Chisholm, Cherokee mixed-blood trader who maintained several posts in central and western Oklahoma.

Black Beaver, Delaware Indian guide for army expeditions in western Oklahoma.

Major Hitchcock arrived in Indian Territory during November, 1841. A highly perceptive investigator, he confided to his journal that news of his coming had preceded him and there was much curiosity about his business in the Indian country. He added that one of the contractors who had settled on the border "came here so poor that a man with a $400 claim against him was glad to settle for $100. Now he owns a considerable number of Negroes and has offered $17,500 for a plantation." Hitchcock made little headway in collecting information in the border settlements, so he proceeded to the various towns of the Five Civilized Tribes. His exhaustive investigation yielded evidence of "bribery, perjury and forgery, short weights, issues of spoiled meat and grain, and every conceivable subterfuge was employed by designing white men on ignorant Indians."

Hitchcock took his findings to Washington where he prepared a report with one hundred exhibits attached, and filed this heavy document with the secretary of war. "Committees of Congress tried vainly to have it submitted to

them so that appropriate action could be taken; but it was stated that too many friends of the administration were involved to permit the report to become public. It disappeared from the files and no trace of it is to be found." Swanton's comment on the fate of the Hitchcock report was: "The fact that it did not allow the report to be made public and its mysterious disappearance from all official files proves at one and the same time the honesty of the report and the dishonesty of the national administration of the period."

Still another curious phase of Indian Territory-United States relations before the Civil War concerned the Plains tribes, notably the Kiowas and Comanches. At the time of the establishment of the Leased District, about the only regular contact with these tribes was through traders. Since mixed-blood merchants of the Five Civilized Tribes dominated the trade in their nations, the old Chouteau style trading posts disappeared from eastern Oklahoma and gradually moved west among the Plains tribes. Commerce in western Oklahoma was conducted in two ways. Daring,

Southwestern Oklahoma terrain explored by army expeditions guided by Black Beaver.

independent traders with small stocks of goods carried in wagons or on pack animals went each season to the Kiowa and Comanche villages. In addition, several prominent traders maintained permanent posts on the rim of the Kiowa-Comanche range. During the pre–Civil War period, the most successful traders operating in western Oklahoma were Abel Warren from Massachusetts; Jesse Chisholm, who was a mixed-blood Cherokee; Charles McIntosh, another mixed-blood Cherokee; and Black Beaver, the famous Delaware scout. Chisholm was the most prosperous of these frontier merchants. He operated a chain of trading stations that included one at old Camp Holmes, another near Camp Mason, a post in Council Grove, west of present Oklahoma City, and another near Asher.

Warren's post was on Red River in present Love County. A visitor at Warren's place had described this frontier merchant's method of dealing with the Comanches.

We were aroused one morning by whoops and yells and the tramping of horses around the enclosure. Several hundred Comanches had arrived and many were setting up their buffalo skin lodges close by the fort. . . . Presently the Indians came in crowds to the fort to trade, with bundles on their backs. . . . They were admitted, three or four at a time, each being required to leave his belt knife, hatchet and other weapons outside. . . . The trading lasted for several days. . . . Their stock in trade consisted of furs of all kinds, dressed buffalo robes, dressed and raw deer skins, dried buffalo tongues and beeswax. Some of them had Mexican silver dollars. They bartered for red and blue blankets, strips of blue cloth, bright colored gingham handkerchiefs, hoop-iron [for arrow and lance points], glass beads, heavy brass wire [which they wound into bracelets for the left wrist to protect it from the recoil of the bowstring], bright hued calicoes and wampum beads, which they wound around their necks in great quantities. These beads were from two to four inches long, pure white, and resembled clay pipe-stems in size. [These beads] were highly esteemed and served the part of currency in their dealings with one another. They wanted guns but the government forbade the selling of fire-arms to the wild Indians at that time. Much of the trading was done by means of signs. One finger was one dollar; five fingers, five dollars; crossed forefinger, half a dollar, etc.

The Kiowas and Comanches were inveterate raiders. Their depredations extended into lower Coahuila in Mexico and west to the Río Grande settlements in New Mexico. Their sweeping raids on Texas ranches and Mexican towns netted horses, mules, and captives, especially women and children. The raiders

Chimney Rock, landmark for army expeditions mapping northwestern Oklahoma. Photograph by Paul E. Lefebvre.

brought their plunder and captives into their villages in the Leased District, and a curious traffic in human beings developed. The usual price per captive was about two hundred dollars. Officials at Fort Gibson or Fort Washita provided the money to recover the captives and Leased District traders served as middlemen in the transactions.

At least two retaliatory campaigns were carried out against the wild tribes in the Leased District before the Civil War. One strike was made by a Texas Ranger force under Captain John S. Ford, and the other was a United States Army cavalry campaign led by Major Earl Van Dorn. In the late spring of 1858, Ford's men attacked a Comanche village near the Wichita Mountains and killed seventy-six Indians. Then during September, 1858, a cavalry patrol operating from Camp Radziminski scoured the Leased District for hostile bands. On October 1, Van Dorn's Tonkawa scouts found a Comanche camp near Rush Springs. The cavalry commander struck during the night while the Comanches were asleep; the surprise attack killed sixty Indians.

For the time being the Leased District seemed pacified, and during the summer of 1859, Wichita Agency was established on the Washita by Bureau of Indian Affairs officials. Its function was to receive and administer the affairs of 1,500 Texas Indians—the Waco, Tonkawa, Anadarko, Tawakoni, Ioni, Keechi, and Caddo tribes, and some Comanche bands. For several years these tribes had lived on the Brazos Reserve. By 1859, however, the line of settlement had reached the rim of this reservation, and the Texans were demanding that the Indians be removed or face extermination. Hurriedly, Agent Robert S. Neighbors collected the Brazos Reserve tribes, and, escorted by a United States Army force commanded by Major George H. Thomas, he conducted the Texas Indians to a new home in the Leased District near Wichita Agency.

Another event in the long relationship between the United States government and Indian Territory concerned attempts to organize a unified territorial government in the land of the Five Civilized Tribes as a preliminary to statehood. This matter came up during 1854 in connection with the dissolution of the northern half of Indian Territory, which set

Oklahoma's present boundary, at 37°N, and the organization of the Kansas and Nebraska territories. In that year, Senator Robert W. Johnson of Arkansas introduced a bill in Congress to organize three territories among the Five Civilized Tribes. These would be Cherokee (capital at Tahlequah), Muscogee (capital at Creek Agency), and Chatah (capital at Doaksville). The land of each Indian republic would be surveyed and allotment in severalty assignments made to each tribal citizen, i.e., each would receive a privately owned homestead of 80 to 160 acres. Surplus land would then be sold to settlers. The three territories

would later be fused into the "state of Neosho." The bill failed at final adoption, largely because of the opposition of tribal leaders, but the Johnson proposal was significant in that it was the beginning of a series of attempts to open Indian Territory to the homeseeker.

The federal government needed a strong excuse to pressure the Five Civilized Tribes into accepting the dissolution of their republics, and this excuse came conveniently between 1861 and 1865 as a result of the commitment of the tribal governments to alliances with the Confederacy.

Notes on Sources, Chapter 9

Accounts of relations between the people of Indian Territory and the national government are found in Katherine C. Turner, *Red Men Calling on the Great White Father* (Norman, 1951); Morris L. Wardell, *A Political History of the Cherokee Nation, 1838–1907* (Norman, 1938); W. David Baird, *Peter Pitchlynn: Chief of the Choctaws* (Norman, 1972); Arrell Morgan Gibson, *The Chickasaws* (Norman, 1971); Edwin C. McReynolds, *The Seminoles* (Norman, 1957); Angie Debo, *The Road to Disappearance: A History of the Creek Indians* (Norman, 1941); and Cheryl Haun Morris, "Choctaw and Chickasaw Indian Agents, 1831–1874," *Chronicles of Oklahoma* 50 (Winter, 1972): 415–36.

The continuing military influence in Indian Territory is traced in Grant Foreman, *Fort Gibson* (Norman, 1936); Brad Agnew, *Fort Gibson: Terminal on the Trail of Tears* (Norman, 1980); Ethan Allen Hitchcock, *A Traveler in Indian Territory*, ed. Grant Foreman (Cedar Rapids, Iowa, 1930); Edwin C. Bearss and Arrell M. Gibson, *Fort Smith: Little Gibraltar on the Arkansas* (Norman, 1969; 2d ed., 1979); and William B. Morrison, *Military Posts and Camps in Oklahoma* (Oklahoma City, 1936).

Pacification of the Leased District is discussed in Walter P. Webb, *The Texas Rangers* (Cambridge, Mass., 1935); Muriel H. Wright, "A History of Fort Cobb," *Chronicles of Oklahoma* 34 (Spring, 1956): 53–71; and Wilbur S. Nye, "The Battle of Wichita Village," *Chronicles of Oklahoma* 15 (June, 1937): 226–28.

The Civil War in Oklahoma

If the involvement of Oklahoma in the Civil War is a curious circumstance of history, stranger still seems the alignment of the people of the future Sooner State on the side of the Confederacy. There is a paradox in the action the Five Civilized Tribes took by signing treaties of alliance with the Confederate States of America. Had it been forgotten that the leading states of this secession-born political community—Georgia, Alabama, and Mississippi—had heaped insult, harassment, and untold suffering on the Indians during the removal period?

Possibly time had healed old wounds and dimmed painful memories. Another factor may have been that the United States government and President Andrew Jackson, rather than the southern states, had formally shared the blame for the agony of the Trail of Tears. Through the years, animosity toward the federal government had developed among the Indians, especially because of the government's slowness in making annuity settlements and general neglect of treaty obligations. During the spring of 1861, the administration in Washington had ordered the abandonment of all Indian Territory posts, an action that created anxiety among tribal leaders. Not only did it violate treaty pledges but it left the region exposed to possible invasion from Confederate Texas and Arkansas.

Meanwhile, tribal leaders had worried over the election of 1860, which had brought Abraham Lincoln to the presidency. In order to appeal to Free Soil voters, Lincoln's campaign workers, notably William H. Seward, had recommended appropriating the land of the Five Civilized Tribes and opening it to white settlers. Moreover, Lincoln's administration was committed to abolish slavery. Many Indian slaveholders faced substantial loss of investment.

Southern influence was strong. The mixed bloods in Indian Territory had emulated southern culture and their life-style was a replica of antebellum elegance based on slave labor. Because of the river transport system, the market orientation of Indian planters was to the South. Most of the tribal annuity funds from the proceeds of land sales were invested in enterprises in southern states. The Indian agents assigned to the Five Civilized Tribes, men of considerable influence in tribal affairs, were all southerners. Many of the prominent Indian families had blood ties with the South. And, at a time when the Union appeared to be abandoning the Indian Territory, the Confederacy was showing a strong interest in it.

The South's traditional agrarian economy had placed emphasis on growing and exporting cotton, sugar, and tobacco. Before the war substantial quantities of foodstuffs had been imported from north of the Ohio River. The war closed this source, and foreign markets were cut off by the Union blockade of southern ports. Of necessity the Confederacy turned to the West and imaginative Confederate planners developed a grand design for western expansion and the satisfaction of economic needs for their new nation. The Indian Territory played a key role in this Confederate plan for absorbing the American West. First, as a life-line for the Confederacy, the Indian Territory with its abundant cattle and horse herds could furnish beef, hides, and mounts for troops. Grain from Indian farms figured in Confederate planning, too. In northeastern Indian Territory, according to one Confed-

Albert Pike, Confederate emissary to Indian Territory and later commander of Confederate Indian troops.

erate report, lead deposits, linked with the thriving mines in southwest Missouri, were estimated as capable of providing enough refined lead to supply the total small arms needs for all Confederate troops in the field. Not to be overlooked was the abundant supply of salt available from Indian Territory sources.

The Indian Territory was important as a land bridge connecting the Confederacy with the far West. Across a friendly territory, Confederate agents could conspire to bring New Mexico, Arizona, and California into the Confederate orbit. The Indian Territory was basic to Confederate military strategy in the West, first as a buffer for Confederate Texas to protect it against invasion from Union Kansas, and second, as a base for launching armies into Union states and territories west of the Mississippi.

The first Confederate representatives who visited Indian Territory arrived from Texas in February, 1861. The Texas commissioners called on the Chickasaws, Choctaws, Creeks, Seminoles, and Cherokees. In their talks before the councils of these tribes, the Texans denounced the United States and encouraged the leaders of each tribe to join Texas in separating from the Union. The Texans reported to their government that "the Choctaws and Chickasaws are entirely Southern and determined to adhere to the fortunes of the South." They added that the councils of these two tribes authorized the raising of troops.

After being well received by the Creeks, the visitors from south of the Red River went among the Cherokees. They noted that Principal Chief John Ross received them "with courtesy, but not with cordiality.... He was very diplomatic and cautious. His position is the same as that held by Mr. Lincoln in his inaugural; he declares the Union not dissolved and ignores the Southern government." On their way home, the Texas commissioners stopped in the Creek Nation to attend an intertribal council called for the purpose of discussing secession. Cherokee, Seminole, Creek, and Quapaw delegates met on April 8. Heavy rains kept the Choctaws and Chickasaws away. The visitors observed that the Indian delegates "declare themselves Southern by geographic position, by a common interest, by their social system, and by blood, for they are rapidly becoming a nation of whites."

Soon after the commissioners reported to their government, a Texas Confederate army crossed the Red River to occupy United States military posts in southern Indian Territory. Simultaneously, Arkansas authorities seized federal arsenals in that state, and closed the Arkansas River to federal steamers carrying supplies for Fort Smith and other posts across Indian Territory. The federal garrison at Fort Smith, finding retreat closed to the east, abandoned that post and marched west to join federal troops at Forts Washita, Arbuckle, and Cobb. Texas troops closing in on these posts caused Colonel W. H. Emory, federal commander in Indian Territory, to unite the garrisons from Washita, Arbuckle, and Cobb, After linking with the force from Fort Smith, he made a northward retreat to Fort Leavenworth in Kansas. The famous Delaware scout Black Beaver guided Emory's column to safety. The invading Texas army occupied Forts Arbuckle, Washita, and Cobb until Choctaw and Chickasaw troops arrived to garrison these posts. A substantial quantity of military supplies fell to the Confederacy by this prompt action by Texas and Indian troops.

In the fast moving series of events that drew Oklahoma into the Civil War on the side of the Confederacy, the new secession government at Richmond organized the Indian Territory into a military district with General Ben McCulloch of Texas in command. His force included one regiment each from Louisiana, Texas, and Arkansas, and he was authorized to recruit three Indian regiments—one from among the Cherokees, and two joint units—one from the Choctaws and Chickasaws and one from the Creeks and Seminoles. Before the military organization of Oklahoma could properly occur, the Five Civilized Tribes had to be incorporated into the Confederacy, and to achieve this the Confederate government followed the same treaty practice as that used by the United States in dealing with Indian tribes. The Confederate government appointed Albert Pike of Arkansas as special commissioner to negotiate with Oklahoma's Five Civilized Tribes. A native New Englander, Pike was well known on the frontier for his explorations, writings, oratory, newspaper work, and law practice. He was prominent among the Five Civilized Tribes and enjoyed their respect.

Pike called first on the Cherokees, arriving at Tahlequah on June 1, 1861. There he received about the same reception as the Texas commissioners. Chief John Ross was still adamant that the Union was intact. Stand Watie, the mixed-blood leader, agitated for an immediate compact with the Confederacy, and he went about the nation recruiting troops for service in the southern army.

The more numerous full bloods, under the powerful influence of Evan Jones, the Baptist missionary and avowed abolitionist, were opposed to Pike's blandishments. Their opposition could have been predicted, if for no other reason than that the mixed bloods, led by Watie, wanted a Confederate alliance; it will be remembered that from earliest removal times it had been a consistent line of action by the full bloods deliberately and studiously to take an opposite position to that of the mixed bloods. Much of the full-blood tribal action through the years, such as the assassinations of Major

Ridge, John Ridge, and Elias Boudinot, had been taken through their ancient secret society, the Keetoowah (night hawks) or Pin Indians, as they were called from the badge of their organization—crossed pins worn on the shirt or coat. In the period just before the Civil War, as the disputes between the North and South coalesced around the slavery issue and became more intense, the Keetoowah, through Evan Jones's influence, had added abolition to its program.

Although Chief Ross was a mixed blood, very wealthy, and a slaveholder, he was also an astute politician. The source of his political power through the years had been the loyal support, including votes at election time, of the more numerous full bloods. Thus as the Civil War developed in Indian Territory, it provided a means for reasserting old differences. Before 1865 the Cherokees were again split and waging their own civil war. The two established factions used the national struggle to resume their bloody vendetta.

While at Tahlequah attempting to persuade the Cherokees to join the Confederate cause, Pike sent runners to the Choctaws, Chickasaws, Creeks, and Seminoles to announce his purpose and his plan to visit each of them. In the Creek Nation, at North Fork Town, Choctaw, Chickasaw, and Creek delegates met with him. By July 10 he had signed a faction of the Creeks to a Confederate alliance. Principal Chief Motey Kinnaird and Chilly McIntosh were the most prominent Creek signers. Two days later Pike obtained a joint treaty with the Choctaws and the Chickasaws. Robert M. Jones, Sampson Folsom, Forbis Leflore, George W. Harkins, and Allen Wright were the principal Choctaw signers. Edmund Pickens, Holmes Colbert, James Gamble, Joel Kemp, and Christopher Columbus were among the Chickasaw signatories. Traveling to the Seminole Nation, Pike met with leaders of this tribe and on August 1, he succeeded in negotiating a treaty, signed by Chief John Jumper.

It is significant that while the Choctaws and the Chickasaws were united in supporting the Confederacy, the Creeks and the Seminoles, like the Cherokees, were divided. Their differences were similar to those of the Cherokees and featured a split between mixed bloods and full bloods. Opothleyaholo, the old Upper

Creek chief who had differed with the McIntosh faction over removal, refused to meet with Pike and showed his disdain for the Confederate cause by calling a general council of all tribes of Indian Territory to meet near the Antelope Hills in far western Oklahoma. At this gathering he strongly recommended neutrality and advised the delegates to shun "this white man's war."

From the Seminole Nation, Pike went on to the Leased District, where, at Wichita Agency during early August, he met with representatives of the Caddoes and Wichitas and with several Comanche bands. The Pike treaties with these bands brought them under Confederate dominion. Immediately after each treaty was signed, Pike issued gifts and rations and pledged arms and supplies throughout the war. The signatory chiefs promised to stay out of Texas and to turn their raids on the Union settlements in Kansas.

While Pike was in western Indian Territory, a Confederate army under General Sterling Price smashed a powerful Union force at Wilson's Creek in southwest Missouri. It appeared from this victory that Confederate arms would reign supreme in the West. As a result, Chief John Ross decided to abandon his neutral position and to cast Cherokee fortunes with the Confederacy. Thus when Pike returned to Tahlequah in early October, he found the Cherokee government ready to sign a treaty of alliance. The principal Cherokee negotiators were John Ross, Joseph Verner, John Drew, William P. Ross, Thomas Pegg, and Richard Fields.

Pike's treaties with the Five Civilized Tribes were similar. The Confederate States of America accepted the role of protector of each nation. All land in Indian Territory was annexed to the Confederacy, but each of the Five Civilized Tribes was guaranteed title to its tribal domain forever. The Confederate government reserved the right to construct and garrison military posts, to lay out roads in each nation, and to establish a postal system for Indian Territory. Rights-of-way for telegraph and railroad construction were specified. Each of the Indian Nations promised to raise its quota of troops—from the Cherokees, one regiment; from the Creeks and the Seminoles, one regiment; and from the Choctaws and the

Chickasaws, one regiment. The Confederacy pledged to arm, equip, and pay these Indian troops, which were not to serve beyond the borders of Indian Territory without the consent of their respective tribal governments. Reciprocal handling of fugitive slaves was agreed upon, and it was stated that the "institution of slavery in the said nations is legal and has existed from time immemorial; that slaves are taken and deemed to be personal property." Finally, the Confederate States of America promised to protect each nation from invasion, and it assumed all annuity obligations due the tribes from the United States.

The Five Civilized Tribes responded quickly to meet the military obligation of their Confederate treaties. By August, 1861, the Choctaw-Chickasaw Regiment of Mounted Rifles had been recruited and was being trained by Colonel Douglas Cooper, a longtime Choctaw agent. His second in command was a Choctaw, Tandy Walker. Colonel Dan McIntosh, aided by Lieutenant Colonel Chilly McIntosh and Major John Jumper, raised a regiment of Creek and Seminole troops. Immediately after John Ross signed with Pike he called on the Cherokees to raise their quota of troops for the Confederacy. The officers of the Cherokee regiment were John Drew, colonel; William P. Ross, lieutenant colonel; and Thomas Pegg, major. Most of the men in the ranks were full bloods.

As early as July 2, Stand Watie had mustered a force of mixed bloods that he designated the First Cherokee Mounted Rifles. His troops elected him colonel and commander of the regiment, and Elias C. Boudinot was named major. Ross reluctantly recognized Watie's command, and although this exceeded the force authorized for Indian Territory, Pike welcomed Watie and his troops into the Confederate military establishment. The four regiments thus mustered numbered more than five thousand men.

Although Civil War hostilities broke out in the eastern United States in April, 1861, the first blood shed in Indian Territory during this struggle occurred in November, and it came from an attempt to force Opothleyaholo into the Confederacy. The Creek leader established a camp on the Deep Fork soon after Pike came to Indian Territory. Opothleyaholo invited all tribesmen who opposed the Confederate alliance and wished to remain neutral to join him.

Nearly seven thousand Indians—men, women, and children—most of them Creeks and Seminoles, collected at the Deep Fork camp. This neutral community became a motley array of people intermingled with cattle, horses, chickens, wagons laden with personal belongings and household effects, and every sort of temporary shelter. Confederate leaders in Indian Territory became apprehensive over the effect of this mass gathering, and in early November, 1861, Colonel Cooper led fourteen hundred Confederates (Choctaw and Seminole units under Colonel McIntosh, six companies of Choctaws and Chickasaws, and a Texas cavalry company) toward the Deep Fork neutral camp. Opothleyaholo learned of this movement soon enough to lead his followers to temporary safety, but Cooper's tenacious scouts found the neutral Indians camped at Round Mountain.

The main Confederate force moved up on November 19 and made several charges into Opothleyaholo's camp. Each assault was turned back by the brisk and valiant defense mounted by the neutral warriors, with the result that the first Civil War military engagement in Oklahoma, known as the Battle of Round Mountain, ended in defeat for the Confederate forces. Determined to gain a victory over the neutrals, Cooper regrouped his force and, reinforced by Colonel John Drew's full-blood Cherokee regiment, went after Opothleyaholo's column again.

By December 9 the old Creek chief had moved his people to a natural fortification of Bird Creek known as Chusto Talasah, or Caving Banks. Cooper eventually found the refugee camp but failed to dislodge the defenders. In the heat of battle a substantial portion of his fighting strength was lost when Drew's full-blood Cherokees deserted. Thus the second Civil War engagement in Oklahoma, the Battle of Chusto Talasah, fought on December 9, 1861, also ended in Confederate defeat.

Cooper fell back to Fort Gibson for supplies and reinforcements and Opothleyaholo sought a new hiding place for his people. By December 20 the determined Confederate commander was ready to move against the neutral Indians again. His scouts discovered their camp on the eastern edge of the Cherokee Outlet at a place called Chustenalah. On the day after Christmas, 1861, Confederate troops ringed Opothleyaholo's camp and swept like a tide over the battlements. The neutral Indians fought bravely as before, but with no sources of supply and their ammunition stores severely depleted by the two earlier battles, they were unable to defend their positions. The Confederate troops stormed through the camp, capturing most of the wagons, equipment, and livestock, and Opothleyaholo's people scattered and hid in the heavily timbered hills.

A fierce snowstorm swept over the countryside on the night after the battle, adding to the suffering of the survivors of Chustenalah, but eventually they reached safety in Union Kansas. A census taken by federal army officers who issued supplies to the refugee Indians in their south Kansas camps reported that 5,600 Creeks, 1,000 Seminoles, 140 Chickasaws, 315 Quapaws, 197 Delawares, and a scattering from other tribes numbering 300, had survived Chustenalah and the dreadful northward march. Soon thereafter, warriors from Opothleyaholo's neutral community, in federal uniform as troops of the First and Second Union Indian Brigades, returned to Indian Territory, determined to wreak vengeance on their Confederate tormentors.

The Confederate victory at Chustenalah brought to a close the first phase of the Civil War in Oklahoma. The attempted Union reconquest of the area, so vital to the fortunes and interests of the Confederacy, comprised the war's second phase for Oklahoma. When Albert Pike reported to the Confederate government at Richmond on the success of his mission to the Indian tribes west of Arkansas, he was rewarded with a commission of brigadier general and assigned to command the Indian regiments raised under authority of the Confederate treaties. General Pike returned at once to Indian Territory and directed the construction of a military post near present Muskogee. He named the post Fort Davis in honor of Jefferson Davis, president of the Confederacy. Pike planned to use Fort Davis as a command post and depot for supplying his Indian army.

In early March, 1862, a Union army commanded by General Samuel Curtis from the Department of Missouri moved south to confront Confederate forces and attempt to avenge the shameful defeat at Wilson's Creek. Confederate General Sterling Price fell back across southern Missouri in the face of this powerful Union thrust, eventually linking with General Ben McCulloch's troops in northern Arkansas at a place known as Elkhorn Tavern, on Pea Ridge. General Earl Van Dorn ordered General Pike to join McCulloch and Price at Pea Ridge with his Indian regiments. While this action violated Confederate treaty pledges that troops of the Five Civilized Tribes were not to fight outside Indian Territory without the consent of the Indian governments, for no such permission was solicited or received, Pike answered Van Dorn's order by rushing to the Confederate positions at Pea Ridge with the Indian troops most readily available—the two Cherokee regiments.

Fighting began when the Union force reached Elkhorn Tavern on March 6 and lasted two days. The Union forces were victorious, inflicting massive casualties upon their adversaries and capturing large amounts of arms and supplies. Colonel Stand Watie's Cherokee Mounted Rifles won one of the few minor victories attributed to the Confederates in this fiercely fought battle by capturing a strategically positioned Union artillery battery that had rained death and destruction on the Confederate ranks until the Cherokees silenced it. Watie's men held their position on the broad Confederate line; they were among the last to retreat and helped cover the general Confederate withdrawal. Colonel Cooper's Choctaw-Chickasaw regiment and Colonel McIntosh's Creek regiment arrived on the border in time to cover Pike's retreat to Fort Davis.

The Confederate defeat at Pea Ridge had far-reaching effects on the southern cause in the West, especially in Indian Territory. First, the disaster at Pea Ridge resulted in such a dreadful loss of Confederate fighting power, artillery, and supplies that thereafter it lacked the means to protect the Indian Territory as guaranteed by the treaties of 1861. The Five Civilized Tribes were required to use their local means and energies to maintain the necessary protection.

Second, the Confederate defeat set off a flurry of command changes in the Trans-Mississippi Department, as the Confederacy sought repeatedly to find a commander who could win victories for the South. General Van Dorn was replaced by General T. G. Hindman. Pike became involved in this command change; he resented the slighting by Van Dorn of the contribution the Indian troops made at Pea Ridge, and he charged that his Indian Territory command was being robbed of provisions, medical supplies, weapons, and ammunition by commanders in Arkansas. Disappointed and disillusioned, General Pike left Colonel Cooper in command at Fort Davis with a small garrison force, and took the Choctaw and Chickasaw troops to Blue River, deep in the western Choctaw Nation. There he established Fort McCulloch. He ordered the Creeks and the Seminoles to patrol and protect their own country. Watie's and Drew's Cherokee regiments were to guard the northern approaches to Indian Territory and watch for any attempted invasion from Union Kansas. Pike's sharp criticism of Confederate generals in Arkansas finally cost him his command. Cooper succeeded him as the officer in charge of the Confederate Indian regiments.

After the Pea Ridge victory, Union leaders, well aware of the weakened Confederate position in the West, at once undertook to regain Indian Territory. During the spring of 1862, Union commanders formed a force known as the Indian Expedition. Two brigades mustered from Wisconsin, Ohio, and Kansas troops, an artillery battery from Indiana, and two Indian regiments recruited from the refugee camps of Opothleyaholo's followers comprised this force. Colonel William Weer of Kansas had overall command.

The Indian Expedition marched into Confederate territory from the Union supply depot at Baxter Springs, Kansas, on June 1, 1862. The invaders followed the Grand River valley into the heart of the Cherokee Nation. Colonel Watie's cavalry harassed the Union column throughout its march, finally presenting the enemy with a frontal stand at Locust Grove on July 3. The Confederate Indian troops held up very well and completely checked the Union advance until the Union artillery battery was brought up. Bursting shells broke the Confederate ranks and Weer's men won the battle. The Confederate defeat at Locust Grove opened the approaches to Tahlequah and Fort Gibson to the Union invaders.

At this point Weer divided his forces. One column moved on Fort Gibson and captured this Confederate post, while the other surrounded Tahlequah, capital of the Cherokee Nation. Colonel Drew's full-blooded Cherokee regiment comprised the defense for this key town. Upon the approach of the Union army, Drew's men deserted en masse. On July 12, Tahlequah fell to the enemy without a shot having been fired. Principal Chief John Ross was taken into protective custody, and with his family, retainers, and official papers and treasury of the Cherokee Nation, he traveled to Philadelphia where he established residence for the remainder of the war. Shortly thereafter, through his agents, he organized a strong Union movement among the Cherokees.

It appeared that with the momentum it had mounted, the Indian Expedition would drive through Indian Territory to the Red River, but a curious thing happened. After the capture of Tahlequah, Weer's officers held a conference and debated whether to continue the offensive or return to Kansas. Many of the officers, led by Colonel Frederick Saloman of the Wisconsin Volunteers, were anxious about Colonel Watie's raids and feared he might cut off the Union column completely from contact with headquarters and supplies in Kansas. Finally, Saloman led a revolt against Weer, arrested him on charges of disloyalty and insanity, and ordered the Indian Expedition troops back to Kansas.

On the heels of the Union withdrawal, Confederate Indian troops reoccupied Fort Gibson, Tahlequah, and other key points in the Cherokee Nation. With Ross working for the Union, the Cherokee council added to Colonel Watie's duties by electing him chief of the Cherokees. From his bases on upper Grand River, Watie struck fear into the border settlements of Kansas and Missouri, his bold thrusts extending north to Fort Scott in Kansas and Neosho in Missouri.

During September, 1862, General J. M. Schofield directed his field commanders in the Southwest to revive Union attempts to drive

General James G. Blunt, commander of Union troops in Indian Territory.

the Confederates out of Arkansas and Indian Territory. In response to Schofield's order, General James G. Blunt, at the head of a Union force, struck west out of Arkansas in late October and caught Colonel Cooper's troops at Fort Wayne in the upper Cherokee Nation. Cooper escaped Blunt's trap but suffered an irreparable loss when the Union invaders captured his artillery. Sustained Union sorties into the Cherokee Nation during the remainder of 1862 made Watie's hold uncertain. Thousands of Ross's followers fled from the nation. The men of millitary age were mustered into Union companies and fought with federal troops. On Blunt's order, Colonel William A. Phillips organized the defecting Cherokees, most of them full-blooded followers of John Ross, into the Indian Home Guard. It consisted of three Indian regiments, a battalion of Kansas cavalry, and an artillery battery.

Encouraged by Colonel Phillips, the Union Cherokees gathered during February, 1863 at Cowskin Prairie in the northeastern corner of the Cherokee Nation. Guarded by a protective cordon of Union troops, the Ross Cherokees convened the now famous Cowskin Prairie

Colonel William A. Phillips, Union officer who convened the Cowskin Prairie Council.

Council. After electing Thomas Pegg acting chief, the Union Cherokees repudiated the Confederate alliance and declared John Ross chief of the Cherokee Nation. They denounced the Confederate Cherokee government headed by Colonel Stand Watie and declared his followers outlaws, their property to be confiscated. They abolished slavery in the Cherokee Nation. Provision was made by the Cowskin Prairie Council for a caretaker Union government to function for the Cherokees until Chief Ross's return.

In effect, the Cherokee Nation had two governments after the Cowskin Prairie Council. For the new Union Cherokee government to function completely, it had to have a territory over which its will could be asserted. Colonel Phillips sought to provide such a territory by undertaking an offensive to drive Stand Watie and the Confederate Cherokees south of the Arkansas and the Canadian. With superior forces and equipment he was able to accomplish the task, and by April he was in control of Tahlequah and Fort Gibson. He changed Fort Gibson's name to Fort Blunt and used it as his headquarters for the remainder of the war.

During July the Confederate cause in Indian Territory was further weakened by the crushing of an attempted Confederate movement to drive Union forces back to Kansas. Douglas Cooper, now a Confederate general, had penetrated north on the Texas Road to a place known as Honey Springs, twenty miles southwest of Fort Gibson. General Blunt rushed from Fort Gibson with three thousand troops to intercept Cooper's force. The famous Battle of Honey Springs, on July 17, resulted. Union superiority in artillery and faulty Confederate gunpowder turned the tide in favor of the Union army.

A month later, General Blunt learned of a Confederate buildup near Perryville in the Choctaw Nation. He crossed into the Confederate sector from his base at Fort Gibson on August 22, with forty-five hundred men. Cooper and Watie led their units south toward Boggy Depot. A small Southern force was left at Perryville to guard the vast supplies gathered there. Blunt's men dispersed the defenders and burned the depot in an engagement known as the Battle of Perryville.

The Confederate retreat southwest of Perryville opened the approaches to Fort Smith. Blunt marched east and easily took this historic post on September 1. The fall of Fort Smith to Union forces ended the major engagements in Indian Territory. However, Colonel Phillips with 450 mounted troops and one fieldpiece made a daring thrust into the Choctaw country during February, 1864, penetrating as far south as Middle Boggy and west to within twenty miles of Fort Washita. He confiscated corn and other forage, but his operation had little effect on the region. Since the Union held Fort Gibson and Fort Smith, the Arkansas River was closed to the Confederacy. Union forces held the country north of the Arkansas and the Canadian, while the Confederates dominated the southern half of Indian Territory.

From the fall of Fort Smith in September, 1863, to Confederate Indian surrenders in the early summer of 1865, the Civil War in Indian Territory took on all the barbarous aspects of internecine strife at its worst. Three types of guerrilla bands developed: the Quantrill guerrillas, the free companies, and Stand Watie's raiders.

Artist's sketch of the Battle of Honey Springs.

Colonel William Quantrill, who held a Confederate commission, built a dreadful reputation on the Missouri-Kansas border. He was most infamous for his sacking of Lawrence, Kansas, but he was indiscriminate in his raiding habits, attacking both Union and Confederate communities with satanic fury. From time to time the Quantrill gang roamed into the Indian Territory and spread their destruction and slaughter among the Five Civilized Tribes.

The free companies were gangs of local renegades, outcasts from the Five Civilized Tribes, who stole cattle and horses and plundered and burned both Union and Confederate Indian communities. Their depredations added to the general disorders plaguing Oklahoma during the last two years of the Civil War.

Stand Watie's activities were distinguished from those of the Quantrill gang and the free companies by his policy of raiding only military objectives. His men destroyed dwellings or barns only if they were used by the enemy for headquarters, billeting troops, or storing supplies. His favorite target was the Union supply line between Fort Scott and Fort Gibson. Watie preyed on this lifeline not only because of the military aspects of such an operation, but because the plunder he swept up in his raids could be collected and distributed among Confederate Cherokee refugees scattered in camps along the Red River in the Choctaw Nation and in north Texas.

Watie became cynical toward the Confederacy in general for what he regarded as its neglect of the Indian Territory, but this in no way affected the vigor of his defense of the Confederate cause in Oklahoma. The daring Cherokee raider charged that "the Indian troops who had been true to the South from the very first had been treated in many instances at though it were immaterial whether or not they were paid as promptly and equipped as thoroughly as other soldiers." He claimed that "no vigorous efforts had been made on the part of the southern troops to dislodge" the enemy from Indian Territory. Union troops in the Cherokee Nation, he charged,

have desolated the land and robbed the people, until scarcely a southern family is left east and north of the Arkansas River. . . . The promised protection of the Confederate government, owing, I am compelled to say, to the glaring inefficiency of its subordinate agents, has accomplished nothing; it has been a useless and expensive pageant; an object for the success of our enemies and the shame of our friends. I fear that we can reasonably look for no change for the better, but that the Indians will have at last to rely upon themselves alone in the defense of their country. I believe it is in the power of the Indians unassisted, but united and determined, to hold their country. We cannot

Stand Watie, Confederate Cherokee and only Indian to achieve the rank of general in the Civil War.

expect to do this without serious losses and many trials and privations; but if we possess the spirit of our fathers, and are resolved never to be enslaved by an inferior race, and trodden under the feet of an ignorant and insolent foe, we, the Creeks, Choctaws, Chickasaws, Seminoles, and Cherokees, never can be conquered by the Kansas jayhawkers, renegade Indians, and runaway Negroes.

During the spring of 1864 the Confederate War Department reorganized its Indian units. The First Indian Cavalry Brigade had as its components the First and Second Cherokee regiments, the Cherokee Battalion, the First and Second Creek regiments, the Creek Squadron, the Osage Battalion, and the Seminole Battalion. Stand Watie was placed in command of this unit and promoted to brigadier general, the only Indian to achieve this rank in either the Union or the Confederate army. The Second Indian Cavalry Brigade, commanded by Colonel Tandy Walker, was composed of Choctaw and Chickasaw companies and the Caddo Battalion. Walker's troops were held on

a stand-by basis, guarding the Canadian River frontier. Many were furloughed home to open fields and raise food for their families and Confederate refugees.

Watie's troops were active to the end of the war. From his base south of the Canadian he sent squads into Union territory to harass and raid. Federal details sent out to cut hay for the thousands of cavalry mounts at Fort Gibson were always in peril. Finally, to feed the starving animals, Union officers sent, under guard, great horse and mule herds out to graze on the prairie flats about the post. Watie's raiders regularly swooped down to drive the animals across the river, with the result that cavalry units at Fort Gibson became foot soldiers. Feeding the garrison, along with the sixteen thousand Cherokee, Creek, and Seminole refugees who had collected at the post, was a difficult task for Union officials. Watie tormented the garrison and refugees with the prospect of mass starvation by harassing and at times cutting the post's lifeline—the military road that ran from Fort Scott to Fort Gibson. Union officers attempted to provision the post by sending supply steamers up the Arkansas. During June, 1864, Watie's scouts discovered the slow-moving *J. R. Williams* toiling upstream toward Fort Gibson Landing on Grand River. At Pleasant Bluff, just below the mouth of the Canadian in the shallows, the colorful Watie swept from ambush and captured the ship with a cavalry charge. Great quantities of provisions, uniforms, and medical supplies fell to the Confederates by this feat.

Watie's greatest strike of the war occurred during September, 1864, at Cabin Creek crossing in the Cherokee Nation. A supply train of three hundred wagons and heavy military guard, en route from Fort Scott to Fort Gibson, was attacked and captured by the Cherokee general. By a skillful decoy he eluded a Union relief column from Fort Gibson and drove his prize into Confederate territory where the stores of food, medical supplies, clothing, and blankets were distributed among the Confederate Indian refugee camps.

Despite these valiant efforts to keep Confederate hopes alive, Union arms, east and west, triumphed. General Robert E. Lee surrendered to General Ulysses Grant at Appomattox Court House on April 9, 1865. General

E. Kirby Smith, commander of Confederate troops west of the Mississippi capitulated on May 20. Preparations for surrendering Confederate Indian forces began on May 15, 1865, when Israel G. Vore, Confederate Indian agent for the Creeks, invited belligerent tribes to meet at Council Grove on the North Canadian River. When Union forces threatened to disperse this meeting, delegates from the Five Civilized Tribes and Plains tribes met at Camp Napoleon near present Verden on the Washita River. Representatives at the Camp Napoleon Council adopted a compact of peace among all Indian tribes and in effect prepared themselves to present a united front against the United States in the forthcoming diplomatic negotiations.

The Camp Napoleon Council paved the way for additional surrenders. On June 19 the Choctaws surrendered at Doaksville. General Stand Watie signed a capitulation agreement for the Confederate Cherokees at Doaksville on June 23, and on July 14, Governor Winchester Colbert surrendered Confederate Chickasaw and Caddo troops.

Since 1862 the Union government, anticipating eventual victory, had been working out a system, known in history as Reconstruction, for dealing with the Confederate States of America. Inasmuch as the Confederacy and its satellite, the Indian Territory, had seceded from the American Union, government leaders regarded this separation as treason, and their Reconstruction program had many elements of punishment. Broadly, this system devised by Congress to enable the Confederate components to resume their place in the Union was based on the theory that the Confederacy was a conquered province and that its people must submit to the terms set by the conqueror. The Reconstruction plan devised for Indian Territory was not the same in every regard as that for the states of the Confederacy but was similar to it. The Territory's Reconstruction plan was worked out by the two senators from the new state of Kansas—James Lane and Samuel Pomeroy. Their scheme for reconstructing Indian Territory reflected the bitterness and vindictiveness Kansans generally held toward the Five Civilized Tribes for joining the Confederacy. At the same time, action by the Five Civilized Tribes gave the

Tandy Walker, commander of the Confederate Choctaw-Chickasaw regiment.

Kansans an excuse to carry out a long-hoped-for plan. Some of the best land in Kansas was held by Indian tribes; Kansas until 1854 had been the northern half of Indian Territory, and a score of tribes from east of the Mississippi had been colonized there. Kansas settlers coveted these Indian lands and demanded the removal of the tribes to Oklahoma so that the Kansas reservations could be opened to settlement. Thus, the association of the Five Civilized Tribes with the Confederacy provided a convenient excuse for taking land from the Indians, as a penalty for seccession, and for relocating the Kansas tribes thereon.

Beginning in 1862, Senators Lane and Pomeroy began introducing bills in the Congress to achieve this purpose, and in February, 1863, they gained passage of the legislation that became the Reconstruction program for Indian Territory. Basically the Lane-Pomeroy plan authorized the President to suspend treaties with the Five Civilized Tribes, appropriate certain portions of their domain, and direct the removal of the tribes from Kansas to Indian Territory.

During the summer of 1865, summonses

went out to the leaders of the tribes to meet with United States commissioners at Fort Smith in early September. The United States delegation to the Fort Smith Council consisted of D. N. Cooley, commissioner of Indian affairs; Elijah Sells, superintendent of the Southern Superintendency; Thomas Wistar, leading member of the Society of Friends; General William S. Harney; and Colonel Ely S. Parker, a mixed-blood Seneca Indian on the staff of General Grant. Although the council was primarily concerned with the Five Civilized Tribes, representatives from other tribes were in attendance. Tribal delegates included representatives from the Creeks, Choctaws, Chickasaws, Cherokees, and Seminoles, and spokesmen for the Osages, Wichitas, Caddoes, Senecas, Shawnees, Quapaws, Wyandots, and Comanches.

The Fort Smith Council convened on September 8 and lasted thirteen days. The United States commissioners opened the council with the statement that the Five Civilized Tribes had violated their treaties with the United States and had thereby forfeited all rights under those treaties, and that each tribe must consider itself at the mercy of the United States. The conditions for resuming relations with the United States were set forth: (1) each tribe must enter into a treaty for permanent peace and amity among themselves, and with the United States; (2) slavery must be abolished and steps taken to incorporate the freedmen into the tribes as citizens, with rights guaranteed; and (3) each tribe must agree to surrender a portion of its lands to the United States for colonizing tribes from Kansas and elsewhere, and the tribes must agree to the policy of uniting all tribes of the Indian Territory into a single, consolidated government.

As expected, the leaders of the Five Civilized Tribes dominated the council proceedings. The Cherokees, the Creeks, and the Seminoles were represented by northern and southern delegations. The most energetic delegations spoke for the Cherokees; the Union viewpoint was presented by John Ross, who had recently arrived from Philadelphia, while the Confederate viewpoint was urged by Stand Watie and Elias C. Boudinot.

The Confederate Cherokees objected to the Union Cherokee law that confiscated all Confederate Cherokee property. As a solution to the apparent irreconcilable differences and bitterness between the two factions, Stand Watie proposed that the United States government divide the Cherokee Nation into two separate jurisdictions—one to be a place of residence for the Union Cherokees, the other for the Confederate Cherokees. Ross and the Union Cherokees objected to this proposal, and finally the Confederate Cherokees were placated by the promise of the United States commissioners that the treaty would include a provision annulling the confiscation law.

The tribal delegations generally were shocked at the extreme demands of the federal government and deliberately delayed the proceedings. Each delegation of the Five Civilized Tribes claimed it lacked authority from its government to negotiate a final settlement. When it became apparent they would be unable to conclude Reconstruction treaties at Fort Smith, the commissioners recessed the council, calling for a resumption of negotiations at Washington the following year. The reasoning of the commissioners was that the tribal delegations could be more easily managed at a place far removed from the influences and pressures of their fellow tribesmen. Before the Fort Smith Council closed, however, the commissioners did negotiate a simple treaty of peace with the tribes through which allegiance to the United States was restored and the Confederate treaties were repudiated.

During 1866 the Five Civilized Tribes, through their delegations, reluctantly submitted to the Reconstruction treaties in Washington. Since the Choctaws and the Chickasaws signed a joint treaty, only four agreements were negotiated. In most respects the treaties were similar. A common provision established peace with the United States and other tribes; each treaty contained a clause abolishing slavery and granting tribal citizenship to freedmen with all the rights of Indians, making a provision for them in land and other benefits. Each tribe agreed to grant railroad rights-of-way to enable chartered companies to construct north–south and east–west lines across Indian Territory. Each tribe subscribed in principle to the development of a unified government for the Indian Territory, and the delegates pledged to begin this movement by participating in an annual intertribal council. The Choctaw-Chickasaw Reconstruction Treaty provided that the name of this unified Indian community would be "The Territory of Oklahoma." Allen Wright, a Choctaw delegate, was credited with proposing this name. Through the Reconstruction treaties the United States could establish courts in Indian Territory to handle cases involving non-Indians, and provision was made to compensate Union Indians for property losses due to war.

Each of the four treaties also contained clauses providing for the cession of tribal lands, in keeping with the Lane-Pomeroy Reconstruction plan. The Seminoles surrendered their entire domain (2.17 million acres) to the United States for fifteen cents per acre. The federal government took the western half of the Creek Nation, paying the tribe thirty cents per acre for the 3.25 million acres appropriated. The Choctaw-Chickasaw Treaty provided for the cession of the Leased District for $300,000, divided on the historic formula of three-fourths to the Choctaws and one-fourth to the Chickasaws. The Cherokees ceded the Neutral Lands, situated in southeastern Kansas and granted to them by the Treaty of New Echota in 1835, and the Cherokee Strip. This ribbon of territory in southern Kansas, two and one-half miles wide, extending west from the Cherokee Neutral Lands to the 100th meridian, was the result of an error in early boundary surveys. The federal government was to auction these lands and turn the proceeds over to the Cherokees. The federal government also in effect took an option on the Cherokee Outlet by asserting a right to settle tribes from other parts of the United States there. Until final decision, however, title to the Outlet remained with the Cherokees. In addition, the Cherokees agreed to permit the federal government to colonize certain tribes on land east of 96° longitude in the Cherokee Nation proper.

The seed for the destruction of Oklahoma's five Indian republics was sown by the Reconstruction treaties. The agony of war was augmented by the ordeal of Reconstruction and by necessary adjustment to new ways of life brought to Oklahoma by the railroads and the increasing stream of settlers. In fewer than twenty-five years a network of railroad lines laced the Indian nations. This improved transportation brought the cattleman, the Boomer, and the homesteader. By 1907, with Oklahoma statehood, the process of tribal dissolution begun in the 1830s was completed.

Notes on Sources, Chapter 10

Material explaining the anomaly of Oklahoma's involvement in the Civil War is found in two books by Annie H. Abel, *The American Indian as a Slaveholder and Secessionist* (Cleveland, 1915); and *The American Indian as a Participant in the Civil War* (Cleveland, 1919). Additional information on this intriguing subject is contained in Wiley Britton, *The Civil War on the Border* (New York, 1899); Wiley Britton, *The Union Brigade in the Civil War* (Kansas City, Mo., 1922); Rachel C. Eaton, *John Ross and the Cherokee Indians* (Menasha, Wis., 1914); Gary E. Moulton, *John Ross, Cherokee Chief* (Athens, Ga., 1978); Kenny A. Franks, *Stand Watie and the Agony of the Cherokee Nation* (Memphis, Tenn., 1979); Edwin C. Bearss and Arrell M. Gibson, *Fort Smith: Little Gibraltar on the Arkansas* (Norman, 1969); 2d ed., 1979); Edward E. Dale and Gaston Litton, eds., *Cherokee Cavaliers: Forty Years of Cherokee History as Told in the Correspondence of the Ridge-Watie-Boudinot Family* (Norman, 1939); Roy A. Clifford, "Indian Regiments in the Battle of Pea Ridge," *Chronicles of Oklahoma* 25 (Winter, 1947–48): 314–22; Annie R. Cubage, "Engagement at Cabin Creek, Indian Territory," *Chronicles of Oklahoma* 10 (March, 1932): 44–51; Edward E. Dale, "The Cherokees in the Confederacy," *Journal of Southern History* 13 (May, 1947): 160–85; Angie Debo, "Southern Refugees of the Cherokee Nation," *Southwestern Historical Quarterly* 35 (April, 1932): 255–66; Charles R. Freeman, "The Battle of Honey Springs," *Chronicles of Oklahoma* 11 (June, 1935): 154–68; and Kenneth McNeal, "Confederate Treaties with the Tribes of Indian Territory," *Chronicles of Oklahoma* 42 (Winter, 1964–65): 115–16.

Guerrilla warfare in the Indian Territory is described in Jay Monaghan, *Civil War on the Western Border* (Boston, 1955); and William E. Connelley, *Quantrill and the Border Wars* (Cedar Rapids, Iowa, 1910).

Chapter 11

Reconstruction of the Five Civilized Tribes

No period in Sooner State history can match the quarter century between 1865 and 1889 for drastic social, economic, and political change. Oklahoma became a dumping ground for American Indians as the federal government colonized tribes from all sections of the United States on lands taken from the Five Civilized Tribes by the Reconstruction treaties. The Indian Territory became a kaleidoscope of tribal cultures. The Five Civilized Tribes were joined by the Caddoes, the Wichitas, the Delawares, the Shawnees, the Kickapoos, the Poncas, the Pawnees, the Osages, the Modocs, and others.

The interval between 1865 and 1889 was also a time of rapid economic development for the future Oklahoma. The construction of railroads created a revolution in the transporting of men and goods and nourished new enterprises. Mining, lumbering, ranching, expanded farming, and the related service activities brought about startling changes in the resistant Indian nations.

It was during this postbellum epoch that the stamp of the West was indelibly imprinted upon Oklahoma. Everything that reinforces the modern image of the American West was observable on the Oklahoma scene during this period. There were Indians and cavalry—General Custer's raid on Black Kettle's camp on the Washita, to mention only one incident; and there were cowboys—Oklahoma was a great cattle highway with the East Shawnee Trail, the West Shawnee Trail, and the Chisholm and Dodge City trails connecting Texas ranches and Kansas cow towns. It was the cattlemen's last frontier, epitomized in Old Greer County and the extensive Cherokee

Strip Live Stock Association holdings. There were outlaws—Indian Territory produced a bumper crop of "owl hoot" travelers, and the James boys, the Youngers, the Daltons, Belle Starr, and Ned Christie introduce a long list of desperadoes who found sanctuary in the Indian nations; and there were lawmen—Bill Tilghman, Chris Madsen, Jim Rhodes, and Charlie Colcord to name only a few of the dedicated United States deputy marshals who tamed the Indian Territory and the West. The chilling justice meted out by "Hanging Judge" Isaac Parker in his Indian Territory Court at Fort Smith is a part of the lawman's image; and there were the pioneers whose plows did more to tame the West than all the posses. They made a last stand here, too, through the Run of 1889.

This quarter century was a time of attempted rehabilitation by the Five Civilized Tribes. Leaders of Oklahoma's Indian republics labored to retrieve from the ruin of war the internal strength, order, and progress their nations had enjoyed before 1861. There was futility in their noble efforts and waste in their unremitting energy, however, because the inevitable forces of disintegration of the Indian nations had begun to be felt.

When hostilities ceased in Indian Territory during the early summer of 1865, the people of the Five Civilized Tribes were scattered. Most of the men of military age were in eastern Oklahoma serving in Union or Confederate units. The civilian population was widely dispersed. Union refugees, most of them Creek, Seminole, and Cherokee, were in camps in Kansas or near Fort Gibson. The Confederate refugees were dispersed along Red River in the

Choctaw and Chickasaw nations and in northern Texas. Disease was no respecter of loyalties as cholera struck both Union and Confederate refugee camps. This dread malady took fifty Union Seminole lives and swept through several Cherokee communities. Malnutrition was widespread, and hundreds of Indians perished of starvation during the winter of 1865–66. This, added to the thousands who died of wounds and disease on the battlefield, in military camps and on the trail, added to the high mortality rate in the refugee camps, reduced the population of the Five Civilized Tribes by 25 percent or more.

The Choctaws and the Chickasaws fared best, for only the northern perimeters of their nations suffered Union despoilment. Their resources, however, had been severely taxed in the attempt to assuage the hunger and suffering of the Confederate Cherokee, Creek, and Seminole refugees.

The three Indian nations north of the Canadian were a melancholy wasteland. Throughout the war the Cherokee, Creek, and Seminole domains had been plundered by foraging armies. Poor quartermaster systems in both the Union and the Confederate armies were used by the combatants as an excuse to live off the land and the people. Looting by free companies and guerrilla bands accounted for the additional destruction and appropriation of property. Even after the Confederate capitulation the misery of the Five Civilized Tribes knew no end. Though the country north of the Canadian was under Union occupation, more than 300,000 head of cattle worth nearly $5 million were rustled by well-organized stock thieves and driven to Kansas. Subsequently many of these animals were slaughtered and sold to government contractors at Fort Gibson for feeding Indian refugees.

Confederate Indian refugees were hesitant about moving back to their homes north of the Canadian and the Arkansas because they feared reprisal from Union tribesmen. When they finally returned, they found their farms, plantations, towns, schools, and churches in ruins. Houses and barns were charred piles of rubble; stone chimneys marked homesites like stark sentinels; fields were taken over by weeds and scrub growth; fences were destroyed; and moveable property, including plows and tools, were gone. They were confronted with a scene of desolation—a wasteland.

The principal postbellum problem facing the Five Civilized Tribes, aside from grinding poverty and pervasive ruin due to war, was rampant lawlessness. Before 1861, Oklahoma's five Indian republics had maintained well-organized governments that provided such a high degree of law and order that visitors often commented that life and property were safer in Indian Territory than on the streets of Philadelphia or Saint Louis. After the war the Five Civilized Tribes lacked the financial means to carry on effective, organized government. It should be remembered that there were no taxes in Oklahoma in those times. The chief source of support for the tribal governments had been the annuity payment—the annual income from the invested proceeds of eastern land sales paid by the United States to each of the Five Civilized Tribes. The war had cut off this flow of money. The treaties of 1866 provided for resumption of annuity payment, but, as usual, the government was slow in paying.

The Cherokee, Creek, and Seminole governments had the added problem of factionalism. Organized Confederate and Union partisans were struggling to gain control of the government in each of these nations. This factionalism weakened tribal strength almost to the point of anarchy, and disorders and lawlessness flourished. It was a trying period for those interested in recovering from the ravages of war.

Oklahoma's Indian republics were under military occupation like the rest of the former Confederacy, but the troops in Indian Territory were spread thinly over the region. Most United States forces were concentrated on the western border to pacify the tribes, and thus were of little help in maintaining order. Tribal agents were military men from the regular army. Major John Craig was assigned to watch the Cherokees; Captain G. T. Olmstead maintained surveillance over the Choctaws and the Chickasaws; Captain F. A. Field was the Creek agent; and Captain T. A. Baldwin served the Seminoles. The military agents were in charge of the agencies for the Five Civilized Tribes until 1870, when the federal government adjudged these tribesmen reconstructed and assigned civilian agents to Indian Territory. The Indian agents were under the direct supervision of the top official of the Southern Superintendency, with headquarters at Fort Smith. In 1869 the Southern Superintendency was abolished. Thereafter, tribal agents reported directly to the commissioner of Indian affairs. The four agencies of the Five Civilized Tribes were consolidated in 1874 into the Union Agency under a single federal official, the superintendent of the Five Civilized Tribes, with headquarters at Muskogee.

In the absence of effective restraint, every type of desperate character and renegade had an easy time in the Indian Territory. A principal source of disorder immediately following the war was the freedman. The Radical Republicans were in control of the national government, and this group sought to gain for the former slaves of Indian Territory all the political rights enjoyed by Indians, along with an equal share in tribal annuities, lands, and other benefits. This viewpoint was reflected in the Reconstruction treaties of 1866. In addition, the Republicans in Congress seriously considered colonizing former slaves from the Confederacy on lands taken from the Five Civilized Tribes. While that plan never came to pass, the "forty acres and a mule" idea was spread abroad and had the effect of encouraging blacks to immigrate from Texas, Arkansas, and Missouri to Indian Territory. These vagabonds formed colonies, squatting on Cherokee and Choctaw lands or gathering in the settlements of the former slaves of the Five Civilized Tribes.

Indian Territory was poverty-stricken and there was no means of providing gainful employment. To sustain themselves, many of the former slaves raided corn cribs and smokehouses of Indian householders, and stole chickens, cattle, hogs, and horses. The Choctaws and the Chickasaws formed vigilante committees to check the thievery and soon mounted patrols maintained surveillance over the Indian nations. Since blacks were protected by federal law enforced by the troops of the army of occupation, these vigilante committees met secretly. They developed systems of signals and maintained communication through special couriers. At secret meetings the members determined punishment for violators of the vigilante code. At times night riders raided black settlements to intimidate the inhabitants. Once warned, blacks discovered away from their communities were whipped. If caught with a stolen hog, cow, or horse, a freedman was executed on the spot. The success of the Choctaw-Chickasaw vigilante committees in checking errant freedmen caused the Cherokees, Creeks, and Seminoles to adopt this method of private action in the absence of public tribal law enforcement.

The lack of law and order in Indian Territory after 1865 also attracted white renegades. The western border during the Civil War had produced many wild, lawless men. While the war was in progress, they used it as an excuse to rob, burn, rape, and plunder as did the members of the Quantrill gang and other semiofficial guerrilla bands. The close of hostilities ended this quasi license, but these miscreants, unable or unwilling to take up a law-abiding way of life, continued their lawless activities. Many used the Indian Territory as a sanctuary from which to make raids on banks, stagecoaches, trains, and businesses in adjacent states. Herds of cattle and horses gathered from Texas ranches were driven into Oklahoma for resale to dealers with no compunctions about brand registrations and bills-of-sale. These desperadoes also killed and robbed Indian Territory citizens. The Choctaw and the Chickasaw vigilantes did succeed in capturing and hanging a gang of Texas horse thieves, but the spawn of crime was far too widespread and the gangs too powerful and well organized to be dealt with by the limited resources of the Indian nations.

Railroad construction across Indian Territory after 1870 brought additional disorder to the future Sooner State. Each of the railheads and construction camps became a sort of Satan's paradise. These migrant communities had, in addition to the rough and ready, brawling construction crews, a regular assortment of tinhorn gamblers, thieves, prostitutes, whiskey sellers, and assorted hoodlums. Gibson Station, a typical rail camp, was reputed to have at least one killing each night.

The reputation of Indian Territory spread

Creek freedman's cabin and dooryard.

far and wide as "the Robbers' Roost" and "the Land of the Six-Gun" and its shame was epitomized in the widely broadcast slogan: "There is no Sunday west of Saint Louis—no God west of Fort Smith." Tribal leaders, finally convinced of their inability to cope with this crisis in crime, appealed to the federal government for help in ridding their nations of this torment. In their entreaties they pointed out that no traveler was safe; that even the tribal treasuries had been robbed by white intruders; and that, as an example, at Caddo—a railroad town on the Missouri, Kansas, and Texas Railroad in the southern Choctaw Nation—fifteen murders had been committed with impunity in less than a year.

The federal government responded to these pleas in 1871 by moving the Western Arkansas Federal District Court from Van Buren to Fort Smith. A succession of federal judges was charged with responsibility for cleaning up the situation in Indian Territory. It was not until 1875, however, when Isaac Parker was named federal judge at Fort Smith, that the situation improved. In a very short while, Parker was known around the world as a judge who meted out the swift and final punishment

of hanging. He appointed an army of two hundred United States deputy marshals, who traveled over the Indian nations singly and in squads in a massive outlaw roundup.

During Parker's first court term at Fort Smith eighteen outlaws were charged with murder, fifteen were convicted, and eight were sentenced to hang. Of these, one died in an escape attempt and a second had his sentence commuted to life imprisonment. Of the six executed, three were white men, two were Indians, and the sixth was a black. The first public hanging at Fort Smith was greeted as if it were a carnival. More than five thousand persons gathered to witness the work of Parker's hangman, George Maledon. A score of newspapermen attended the event and their descriptions of the execution gave rise to Parker's grisly sobriquet—"the hanging judge of Fort Smith."

Parker's cadaverous executioner, George Maledon, became a celebrity nearly as famous as the judge and took great pride in his work. Parker's heavy docket saw 160 men sentenced to the Fort Smith gallows; on review, however, many sentences were commuted to long prison terms, generally for life. Maledon hanged a

Isaac Parker, the Hanging Judge of Fort Smith.

total of sixty of the seventy-nine convicted criminals executed at Fort Smith. He conscientiously selected hand-woven hemp rope from Saint Louis, with his specification that each rope be impregnated with pitch to prevent slipping. His gallows carried the sign: "The Gates of Hell." Nearly 9,000 persons were convicted of various crimes by Judge Parker's court. His jail, which was in the basement of one of the old military buildings, sometimes had as many as 200 prisoners awaiting trial. Prisoners likened Parker's jail to the fabled "Black Hole of Calcutta."

Most of the big names in western crime felt the stern justice of the federal court at Fort Smith. These included Wyatt Earp, who was involved for a time with a horse-stealing ring in Indian Territory. Probably the most colorful and notorious character who appeared in Judge Parker's court was Belle Starr, famous as a lover, horse thief, and bandit queen. A product of the guerrilla wars on the border during the Civil War, Myra Belle Shirley married Jim Reed, a renegade who operated between the Missouri settlements and north Texas. Reed was suspected of robbing the Creek nation's treasury and of using a hideout on the Cana-

dian at Tom Starr's place. Upon Reed's death, Belle consorted with various criminals, including the Youngers. A bend on the Canadian River in eastern Oklahoma, known as Younger's Bend, identifies a spot where Belle held lovers' trysts with one of the members of this famous gunman family.

Belle's marriage into the Starr family brought her the professional name by which she is known in history. In 1882, Belle was arrested on a horse-stealing charge. Judge Parker must have been indifferent to her charms, for the bandit queen received a federal prison sentence.

The Indian nations produced a number of famous badmen, too. Most notorious was the "Cherokee Bandit," Ned Christie. His career in crime began in 1885 when he shot a federal deputy marshal at Tahlequah. Shortly thereafter he collected a group of followers, and the Christie gang became a terror on the border. Christie's escapades became legendary among the Cherokees. So great was his daring that deputy marshals dreaded receiving an assignment to search for him. On one occasion a federal posse cornered Christie in a log house in the Cherokee Nation, and capture seemed certain; but on the second day of siege the bandit chief shot his way to freedom. The arrogant Christie built a log fort near Tahlequah and stocked it with food and ammunition. This fort served as his base of operations. In November, 1892, however, a posse of deputy marshals from Fort Smith tracked Christie and two of his gang to the outlaw haven. The marshals brought up a three-pound cannon and blasted Christie's fort. Thirty shots didn't even shake out the chinking between the logs. Determined to get their man, the officers obtained some dynamite. Under cover of night, they placed the explosive against the walls of the fort. When detonated, the dynamite blew out one wall and set the sagging fort afire. Christie, attempting to shoot his way out, was mortally wounded.

The federal court at Fort Smith and its army of deputy marshals eventually purged crime from Indian Territory, but Indian citizens came to fear and hate this law enforcement agency. Many tribal leaders charged that the court and the deputy marshals, once such a vital factor for the well-being of the Indian nations, gradually became an instrument of tyranny. Most of the conflict grew out of questions of jurisdiction. The Federal District Court at Fort Smith held jurisdiction in all criminal matters where one or both parties were white, and in all cases where whites and Indians were charged with violation of federal laws. As the Indian nations recovered from the ruin of war and reconstruction, each reorganized its government and appointed Indian officials to enforce tribal laws. Indian offenders were then tried in tribal courts.

The most famous case of conflict between federal and Indian courts was the Going Snake Courthouse affair. On April 15, 1872, the Cherokee court at Going Snake Courthouse was in session to try a tribal citizen, Ezekial Proctor, for the murder of a fellow Cherokee. During the trial a posse of deputy marshals from Fort Smith arrived. The federal officers entered the log courthouse and attempted to take Proctor with them to Fort Smith for trial on another charge. Cherokee officials resisted, and in the lively gun battle that followed, eleven men were killed, seven marshals and four Cherokees. The exchange wounded the trial judge, a juror, and several spectators.

In declaring their resentment of the Fort Smith court and its army of deputy marshals, Indian leaders charged that tribal rights were violated, and that federal officials manufactured charges in order to drag innocent Indians to Fort Smith to enable marshals to collect their mileage and per diem costs. To alleviate the problem of distance, the federal government in 1889 placed the western Choctaw Nation and the Chickasaw Nation under the jurisdiction of the Federal District Court at Paris, Texas.

Partly because of the outlaw problem, rejuvenating the governments of Oklahoma's five Indian republics was a slow process. The Cherokee Nation remained politically divided after the Reconstruction Treaty of 1866. Most of the Confederate Cherokees took up residence in the Canadian District, situated in the southernmost corner of the nation. Upon the death of Principal Chief John Ross in 1866, his nephew, William Potter Ross, became official head of the Cherokees. The younger Ross, lacking the political shrewdness and strength of his uncle, was unable to dominate and con-

Belle Starr, Indian Territory bandit queen.

trol Cherokee affairs as had John Ross. Moreover, the new principal chief displayed the general vindictiveness and bitter partisanship of the Union loyalists toward former Confederates, and his attitude continued the tribal division and slowed reconstruction.

Curiously, the coleader of the full-blood faction, the aged Reverend Evan Jones, longtime Baptist missionary among the Cherokees, and his son, John Jones, tired of the feud and began peace overtures to Stand Watie and the Confederate Cherokees. This action resulted in an alignment of the Jones-led full bloods with the Watie faction to form the Union (Downing) party. In the 1867 election, the leader of this coalition, Lewis Downing, a Baptist minister and colonel in the Union Cherokee Regiment, won the office of principal chief. So ended the Ross dynasty in the Cherokee Nation, although the Ross faction formed the National party to counter the new power of the Union party. The Union party, however, dominated Cherokee politics until Oklahoma statehood in 1907 by electing most of the principal chiefs.

Reconciliation of the Cherokee political factions materially eased the problem of re-

Cherokee national capitol building, Tahlequah.

covery from the ruin of war. A report of conditions in the Cherokee Nation during 1872 revealed that the tribal population numbered fifteen thousand. Order had been restored in most of the Cherokee districts. The Cherokee constitution of 1839 had been amended to conform to the Reconstruction Treaty requirements concerning slavery, and tribal government was functioning in a regular and effective manner. The Cherokee national council met annually to adopt laws to match the new order. District courts protected rights and produced justice as before the war. The *Cherokee Advocate*, the national newspaper, resumed publication, its format including articles in English and Cherokee, based on Sequoyah's syllabary.

Presbyterian, Baptist, and Moravian missionaries returned to the nation soon after the war and reestablished churches and schools. In addition, the Cherokee government organized sixty public schools to accommodate 2,200 Indian students. Three schools were established for the children of former slaves, and special institutions for orphans, the blind, the deaf, and the insane were in operation.

The 1872 report revealed economic re-

covery, too. Cherokee families were housed in 500 frame and brick dwellings and 3,500 log structures. During the year, Cherokee farmers produced 3 million bushels of corn, in addition to abundant harvests of oats, wheat, and potatoes. The Cherokee agricultural production aggregate was greater than that of New Mexico and Utah combined. Their farms and ranches were stocked with 16,000 horses, 75,000 cattle, 160,000 hogs, and 9,000 sheep. The Indians exported much of their surplus to surrounding states and territories on the newly constructed Missouri, Kansas, and Texas (MKT) Railroad.

Cherokee finances received a substantial boost beginning in 1879 when tribal officials began collecting grazing fees from Texas cattlemen who were pasturing their herds in the Cherokee Outlet. By the mid-1800s this source of tribal revenue was producing $200,000 each year. Most of this money was appropriated for schools and other public improvements.

Beginning in 1870, the Cherokees held annual national fairs at Tahlequah. These were well attended. Farmers, ranchers, and householders showed farm products, livestock, crafts, and handiwork. The Cherokee national fair was a precursor of the Territorial Fair, which in turn was an ancestor of today's annual Oklahoma State Fair. Improving conditions attracted two hundred Eastern Cherokees from North Carolina into the Cherokee Nation during 1870–71.

The Creeks faced the same problem of factionalism as did their Cherokee neighbors. During 1867, a Creek National Council dominated by former Confederate mixed bloods met on the Deep Fork near Okmulgee and revised the Creek constitution to meet government demands regarding the abolition of slavery. Elections were held under the new constitution, and Colonel Samuel Checote, a former Confederate officer, became principal chief. His opponent, Oktarsars Harjo Sands, a follower of the late Opothleyaholo and a leader of the Union Creeks during the Civil War, was embittered by the election. Through his opposition to Checote and the mixed-blood dominated government, Sands kept alive the old prewar schism between the Upper Creeks and the Lower Creeks. He voiced the conservative full bloods' discontent with the Creek Reconstruction Treaty that had taken half of the Creek nation. He also opposed the constitution of 1867, claiming that it displaced the old tribal ways. Sands's emphasis of these issues stirred intermittent civil war in the Creek nation that lasted into the 1880s.

Even as late as 1890, Fort Gibson was garrisoned with United States cavalry ready to quell full-blood outbreaks in the Creek Nation. The most serious Creek revolt, called the Sands Rebellion, occurred during 1870–72 when the Creek rebels were in control of the National Council House at Okmulgee. Checote's constitutional government forces crushed the full bloods in 1872. Sands died in 1877, and with the passing of his vigorous leadership, it appeared the outbreaks would cease, but the conservatives found a new leader in Isparhechar, who continued the tradition of trouble for the mixed-blood government. Isparhechar's greatest effort occurred in 1881 and is known as the Green Peach War. Bloody battles were fought at Wewoka and Okemah.

Despite the intermittent turbulence, the Creek Nation, through the enlightened leadership of principal chiefs like Samuel Checote and J. M. Perryman, made progress along the road to recovery from the ruin of the Civil War. The new constitution adopted in 1867 vested law-making powers in a national council consisting of the house of kings and the house of warriors. Each of the forty-seven Creek towns was permitted to send one representative to the upper house (house of kings) and from one to three to the lower house (house of warriors) in proportion to local population. Executive power resided in a principal chief and second chief, both elected every four years. The Creek judiciary consisted of a supreme court, its five members selected by the national council, and of six district courts. The nation was divided into six districts—Cowetah, Okmulgee, Muskogee, Eufaula, Deep Fork, and Wewoka. Each district had a judge, a prosecuting attorney, and a company of lighthorsemen (a captain and four privates), all elected by the district voters every four years. The new Creek constitution and the laws passed by the national council were published in both Creek and English.

To encourage rapid economic recovery and to check the rampant brigandage, the Creek council passed a stern criminal code with punishment prescribed: flogging for the first offense and branding for the second. This deterred crime, at least among the Indians, and promoted order in the nation. Aside from periodic outbreaks incited by the full bloods, the people prospered with abundant harvests and growing livestock herds.

The Creek national council gave close attention to rehabilitating the nation's school system. Tullahassee and Asbury, the academies in the nation before the war, had been used as Confederate barracks and were in bad repair. The Reconstruction Treaty of 1866 provided a federal fund for restoring these institutions, and by 1896 the Creeks supported seventy public schools, six boarding schools, and various separate schools for the children of former slaves.

Long famous on the frontier as leaders in intertribal activities, the Creeks led again in 1875 by forming, along with Cherokee, Choctaw, Chickasaw, and Seminole representatives, the International Publishing Company. This association was incorporated by the Creek national council, and it published the *Indian Journal*, a periodical devoted to informing and educating the citizens of Indian Territory on current issues of common interest, including reports of relations with the federal government and railroads, and reports of aggressions by white intruders.

The Seminoles were more harshly treated during the Reconstruction than any of the other Five Civilized Tribes. Their prewar nation was appropriated by the United States through the Reconstruction treaties of 1866; as a consequence, the tribe was forced to settle and develop a new nation. The extortionate land dealings to which these people were subjected are still puzzling. Through their Reconstruction Treaty, they were forced to sell their prewar domain to the United States for fifteen cents an acre. Then, they were required to purchase a new home of 200,000 acres on the western border of the new Creek Nation for fifty cents an acre. After they had established settlements on what they were assured was their new domain, a survey demonstrated that the Seminoles had settled east of their boundary on Creek land. A third trans-

Seminole Nation election, 1898.

action was necessary to settle this problem. To bring the settled area into their nation, the Seminoles were required to purchase an additional 175,000 acres from the Creeks at one dollar an acre.

Like the Creeks and the Cherokees, the Seminoles were divided into two factions. One, led by John Chupco and numbering about twelve hundred people, had gone to Kansas with Opothleyaholo in 1861. Many of the warriors had returned to Indian Territory as Union troops. The other faction, of about the same numbers and led by John Jumper, had joined the Confederacy. The cleavage in this tribe bore an interesting relation to the members' religious affiliations. Chupco's Union faction was predominantly Presbyterian, while Jumper's Confederate following was almost entirely Baptist. Thus, when the Seminoles arrived on their new lands, they settled in two broad communities based on Chupco's and Jumper's leadership. The nation had no constitution and followed the old town pattern of tribal government, each of the fourteen towns headed by a village chief who, with a warrior delegation from his town, met from time to time with delegations from the other towns.

The town delegations joined with the principal chief as the Seminole National Council. This council transacted the business of the nation and served as the legislative assembly. It also functioned as the criminal court of the nation. Because of the Chupco-Jumper division, the Seminoles really had two governments, although on basic matters Jumper deferred to Chupco. One political advance the Seminoles made in the post–Civil War period was to commit their laws to writing.

Gradually the animosity of war passed, old differences were settled, and the Chupco and Jumper bands finally fused into a single nation during the 1880s. The union is dated from the elevation of the capable John F. Brown to the office of principal chief or governor of the Seminole Nation. The national capital was fixed at Wewoka.

The courage and determination of the Seminoles to recover from the ruin of war is illustrated by their agent's report on their vigorous opening of the new nation:

They at once commenced the erection of cabins and providing themselves with suitable places for winter. The land on which

Nuyaka Mission School, Creek Nation.

they were located was new, uncultivated and for the greater part covered with timber. On this land and without any farming implements, except such as had been transported with them from Kansas and Fort Gibson, and without any seeds furnished them except corn, they were told that they must raise sufficient for their own subsistence after the first day of July, 1867, as the government had determined to furnish no more supplies after that time. Using every exertion possible with the means at my command, I procured them sufficient axes, wedges, and other tools, so that each band could fence a field in common. During the winter they made more than 100,00 rails; some bands of 100 persons fencing 500 acres, by carrying the rails on their backs. ... They raised more than 110,000 bushels of corn and a correspondingly large amount of vegetables and garden produce. By a system of government enforced by the chief and headman, every man and woman was compelled to work; and any neglect on the day appointed was visited with a fine of $5.00 per day and the amount was immediately collected even though it took the last blanket the person slept on, or the last penny in the family. There has been a large surplus of corn raised this year. They have been careful of the moneys paid them, and have invested all in their power in hogs and

stock and the coming year will show a prosperous, contented people.

The Choctaws and the Chickasaws were least ravaged by the war and therefore were quicker to recover from the destruction of the conflict. Both tribes were almost unanimous in their support of the Confederacy and thus avoided the debilitating schisms and factional political conflicts suffered by the Cherokees, the Creeks, and the Seminoles. Both nations revised their constitutions regarding slavery, as required by the Reconstruction Treaty of 1866, but tribal leaders for both nations were reluctant to make the extensive provisions for their former slaves expected by the federal government. This resulted in controversy between government officials and Choctaw-Chickasaw delegations that lasted up to the time of allotment around 1900.

Rapid economic development in both nations eased the economic pinch for these two tribes and accelerated recovery from the Civil War. The Choctaw Nation, especially, was the scene of extensive railroad building, which stimulated the tribal economy and expanded trade. Soon after 1870 a coal-mining boom near McAlester produced a score of mining towns and resulted in the importation of colorful immigrant mining families from Europe. This had the effect not only of diversifying the culture of the Choctaw Nation but also of enrich-

Cherokee Female Seminary at Tahlequah, completed in 1888.

enriching its national treasury since the nation collected a royalty on every ton of coal mined. With such an excellent source of income the Choctaws rehabilitated their public school system and developed it even beyond its remarkable prewar level. Various other public improvements were made possible by the coal royalties.

The Chickasaws found a source of tribal funds in the expanding range-cattle industry and in a tax on white settlers. The great Chisholm Trail crossed the Chickasaw Nation. Indian inspectors collected a trail tax on every animal driven through the nation. Later, Texas cattlemen leased great ranges in the Chickasaw Nation and paid substantial sums of "grass" money into the Chickasaw treasury every year. After the Civil War, there also had been a flood of white farmers into the Washita valley of the Chickasaw Nation. For the privilege of living there and tilling the soil, these people purchased annual permits from the Chickasaw government. It is to the credit of the Chickasaw national council that most of the tribal income each year was appropriated to support Chickasaw schools.

Intertribal cooperation for mutual benefit and improvement was one of the most conspicuous developments among the Five Civilized Tribes in the postbellum period. The International Publishing Company was one example of the cooperative effort; another was the organization of the International Indian

Territory Fair Association. The first International Indian Territory Agricultural Fair was held at Muskogee in 1873, and it swiftly became a heavily attended event. Representatives from the Five Civilized Tribes and the Plains tribes exhibited handiwork, agricultural products, livestock, and crafts. The program included musical and educational performances and entertainment, sporting events, and "exciting horse races with fleet buffalo ponies." Before statehood, the fair was the most eagerly anticipated event in Oklahoma each year.

The most important experience in intertribal cooperation, largely because of the political experience it provided, was the annual International Council, usually sponsored by the Creeks, and customarily held at Okmulgee, although the delegates sometimes gathered at Eufaula. The Reconstruction treaties of 1866 contained a provision committing each signatory tribe to work for an eventual united territory, complete with a single territorial government. The federal government urged tribal leaders in this direction, but local interests, fearing sacrifice of tribal sovereignty and privilege, prevented the development of enthusiastic support for this treaty obligation.

In 1867, Congress even went so far as to appropriate money to pay the expenses of the delegates, thus removing at least one excuse for noncompliance. The council convened at Okmulgee, but was attended only by the Creeks and the Cherokees and delegations

Jones Academy, Choctaw Nation.

from the small tribes located in northeastern Oklahoma. Little was accomplished. There was a very strong practical reason why the tribes did not move rapidly toward creating an inclusive territorial government: establishment of such a government would require that the railroads building through Indian Territory be granted substantial right-of-way land grants from the various tribal domains. It was common knowledge among all tribal leaders that the railroads were strongly supporting the organization of a new territorial government for Indian Territory.

Under strong pressure from the federal government, a second intertribal council met at Okmulgee in 1869. Delegations from all five major tribes were in attendance. Although the delegates did little to achieve the expected organization of the territorial government, they gained valuable experience from working together toward the common goal of preserving the integrity of their respective nations.

An impatient United States Congress went to work on the matter. Senator Benjamin F. Rice of Arkansas introduced a bill providing for organization of "the Territory of Oklahoma." This bill alarmed Indian leaders. They forwarded strong resolutions against the Rice bill to the Congress, but it became abundantly clear that either the Indians must act or the action would be taken for them, perhaps on terms not to their liking. As a result, the Inter-

tribal Council was summoned to meet at Okmulgee in emergency session on September 27, 1870. Forty delegates attended. A committee headed by Cherokee William P. Ross—John Ross's nephew, a gifted writer, an editor of the *Cherokee Advocate*, a former principal chief, and a Princeton graduate—was assigned the task of drafting a constitution for the proposed unified Indian Territory and future Indian state. The council then recessed until December 6. When it reconvened, Ross's committee submitted the famous Okmulgee Constitution, a well-drafted document that included a bill of rights. The delegates adopted the constitution, and it was submitted to the federal government. Congress refused to approve it on the grounds that the Five Civilized Tribes were unduly insisting on the honoring of treaty rights, and as one observer put it, "Congress was unwilling to concede the measure of independence for Indians set in the terms" of the Okmulgee Constitution.

The enlightened efforts of the Okmulgee council delegates were not wasted, however. For one thing, the experience gained through these cooperative channels stood the Indians' leaders in good stead as the Oklahoma statehood movement developed. For another, the Okmulgee Constitution demonstrates conclusively that a tradition of creative constitution writing was well established in the Sooner State long before the Oklahoma Constitutional Convention gathered at Guthrie in 1906.

Notes on Sources, Chapter 11

The reader seeking additional information about the Reconstruction era in Oklahoma should first read Annie H. Abel, *The American Indian Under Reconstruction* (Cleveland, 1925). Other useful sources on this subject are Joseph H. Thoburn, *History of Oklahoma,* vol. 1 (Chicago, 1916); Morris L. Wardell, *A Political History of the Cherokee Nation, 1838–1907* (Norman, 1938); Edward E. Dale and Jesse L. Rader, eds., *Readings in Oklahoma History* (Evanston, Ill., 1930); Thomas F. Andrews, "Freedmen in Indian Territory: A Post-Civil War Dilemma," *Journal of the West* 4 (July, 1965): 367–76; Ohland Morton, "Reconstruction in the Creek Nation," *Chronicles of Oklahoma* 9 (June, 1931): 171–79; Arrell Morgan Gibson, *The Chickasaws* (Norman, 1971); Lewis Kensall, "Reconstruction in the Choctaw Nation," *Chronicles of Oklahoma* 47 (Summer, 1969): 138–53; and Hanna Warren, "Reconstruction in the Cherokee Nation," *Chronicles of Oklahoma* 45 (Spring, 1967): 180–89.

Lawlessness in the Indian Territory and the eventual curbing of it by the federal court at Fort Smith is discussed in Edwin C. Bearss and Arrell M. Gibson, *Fort Smith: Little Gibraltar on the Arkansas* (Norman, 1969; 2d ed., 1979); Glenn Shirley, *Law West of Fort Smith* (New York, 1956); Homer Croy, *He Hanged Them High* (New York, 1952); Fred H. Harrington, *Hanging Judge* (Caldwell, Idaho, 1951); and Burton Rascoe, *Belle Starr: The Bandit Queen* (New York, 1941).

Chapter 12

The Second Trail of Tears

By 1885, Oklahoma was divided into two large Indian communities. The eastern half of the Sooner State was occupied by the Five Civilized Tribes. The western half, taken from the Five Civilized Tribes by the Reconstruction treaties of 1866, was used by the federal government as a colonization zone for tribes from various parts of the United States. Several of the western tribes were peaceful; others were fierce, turbulent, and intractable, and had to be subdued by military force before they settled into peaceful living.

Because of their depredations in Kansas, Colorado, New Mexico, and Texas during the Civil War, the Kiowas, Comanches, Cheyennes, and Arapahoes were regarded as belligerents; in 1865 the federal government was eager to bring them to terms. The wide range covered by these fierce buffalo hunters and their inherent suspicion of the Americans made them difficult to reach. Two famous frontier scouts and traders, Jesse Chisholm, a Cherokee mixed blood, and Black Beaver, a Delaware, both trusted by the Plains tribes, were instrumental in persuading the chiefs to come in for a council, and during the Fort Smith Council in 1865, General William S. Harney, one of the United States delegates, was ordered to attend a second council at the mouth of the Little Arkansas near present Wichita, Kansas.

On October 10, 1865, the Little Arkansas Council began. Government commissioners were General John B. Sanborn; General Harney; Thomas Murphy, head of the Central Superintendency; Indian agent Jesse H. Leavenworth; William Bent, the trader; the famous scout Kit Carson; and James Steele, a representative of the Bureau of Indian Affairs.

The tribal delegations were led by Black Kettle, Little Raven, Seven Bulls, and Little Robe for the Cheyennes and the Arapahoes; Rising Sun, Buffalo Hump, and Ten Bears for the Comanches; Lone Wolf, Black Eagle, Satanta, and Stinking Saddle Blanket for the Kiowas; and Poor Bear, Iron Shirt, and Wolf Sleeve for the Plains Apaches.

The treaties signed at the Council of the Little Arkansas ceded to the United States all lands north of the Arkansas River. The Cheyennes and the Arapahoes, through a special treaty, were assigned the land between the Arkansas and the Cimarron in southwestern Kansas and northwestern Oklahoma. The Kiowas and the Comanches accepted all of present western Oklahoma and the Texas panhandle between the Cimarron and the Red, extending west from the 98th meridian to the 103d meridian. The Plains Apaches were confederated with the Cheyennes and the Arapahoes.

In less than two years it became apparent that the tribal domains assigned by the Little Arkansas treaties would have to be reduced to satisfy the land hunger of homesteaders. Settlements were intruding upon the treaty-assigned ranges, hunters were trespassing and slaughtering the wild game so essential for the survival of these tribes, and there was a heavy flow of traffic along the rivers and the old trails across the tribal ranges. These territory violations were irritants that invited retaliation by the restless Plains Indians. A second peace council was convened in 1867 as a result of demands from the settlers and the governments of the states and territories on the rim of the treaty-assigned ranges that the Indians be constrained to smaller areas.

During October of that year, a United States delegation, which included Commissioner of Indian Affairs Nathaniel G. Taylor, Senator John B. Henderson of Missouri, Samuel F. Tappan, John B. Sanborn, General Alfred Terry, General Harney, and Colonel Christopher C. Augur, met with the chiefs and head men of the Kiowas, Comanches, Cheyennes, Arapahoes, and Plains Apaches at the famous Medicine Lodge Council. Its name was taken from the meeting place on Medicine Lodge Creek in southern Kansas, seventy miles south of Fort Larned and just north of the Indian Territory border. Principal Indian spokesmen at Medicine Lodge included Stumbling Bear, Black Eagle, Satanta, and Satank for the Kiowas; Ten Bears, Little Horn, and Painted Lips for the Comanches; Wolf Sleeve, Poor Bear, and Brave Man for the Plains Apaches; and for the Cheyennes and the Arapahoes, Black Kettle, Bull Bear, Spotted Elk, Whirlwind, Little Raven, and Tall Bear.

It was probably the most colorful assemblage ever gathered on the plains. Buffalo-hide tipis were scattered along the stream for miles. More than seven thousand Indians gathered to watch their chiefs match wits with the federal commissioners and to receive gifts of cloth, paint, and beads sent to them, according to the issue sergeant, by their Great White Father in Washington. The importance of the Medicine Lodge Council is indicated by the presence of several newspaper correspondents who covered the proceedings. The most famous was Henry M. Stanley from the *Missouri Democrat*, later prominent in the Stanley-Livingstone episode in Africa.

The treaties negotiated during the Medicine Lodge Council are of great importance historically, and the Indian oratory, expressing the pathos of these harassed people, provided a rare insight into their characters. The American commissioners warned that the buffalo would soon disappear and that, for their own good, the chiefs must lead their people to settled lives on reservations in Indian Territory and set examples for their followers by taking up farming and peaceful living.

Ten Bears and Satanta made the most forceful rejoinders. First to speak was the Kiowa chief, Satanta, acknowledged as "the orator of the plains. . . . He was a tall man and good-looking, with plenty of long shiny black hair, dark piercing eyes, a consuming vanity, and a quick temper. His presence was commanding and he was able to sway the councils of his people. He was respected, too, as a warrior." He faced the commissioners and declared:

All the land south of the Arkansas belongs to the Kiowas and Comanches, and I don't want to give away any of it. I love the land and the buffalo and I will not part with any. . . . I have heard you intend to settle us on a reservation near the mountains [Wichitas]. I don't want to settle there. I love to roam over the wide prairie, and when I do it, I feel free and happy, but when we settle down we grow pale and die. . . . A long time ago this land belonged to our fathers, but when I go up to the river, I see a camp of soldiers, and they are cutting my wood down, or killing my buffalo. I don't like that, and when I see it, my heart feels like bursting with sorrow. I have spoken.

The Comanche chief Ten Bears spoke next:

My heart is filled with joy, when I see you here, as the brooks fill with water, when the snows melt in the spring, and I feel glad, as the ponies do, when the fresh grass starts in the beginning of the year. I heard of your coming, when I was many sleeps away, and I made but few camps before I met you. . . . My people have never first drawn a bow or fired a gun against the whites. There has been trouble on the line between us, and my young men have danced the War Dance. But it was not begun by us. It was you, who sent out the first soldier, and it was we who sent out the second. Two years ago, I came upon this road, following the buffalo, that my wives and children might have their cheeks plump, and their bodies warm. But the soldiers fired on us, and since that time there has been a noise, like that of a thunderstorm, and we have not known which way to go. So it was upon the Canadian. Nor have we been made to cry once alone. The blue-dressed soldiers and the Utes came out of the night when it was dark and still, and for camp fires, they lit our lodges. Instead of hunting game, they killed my braves, and the warriors of the tribe cut short their hair

Cheyenne-Arapaho Sun Dance encampment near Fort Reno.

for the dead. So it was in Texas. They made sorrow come into our camps, and we went out like the buffalo bulls, when the cows are attacked. When we found them, we killed them, and their scalps hang in our lodges. The Comanches are not weak and blind, like the pups of a dog when seven sleeps old. They are strong and far-sighted, like grown horses. We took their road, and we went on it. The white women cried, and our women laughed. But there are things which you have said to me which I did not like. They were not sweet like sugar, but bitter like gourds. You said that you wanted to put us upon a reservation, to build us houses and to make us medicine lodges. I do not want them. I was born upon the prairies, where the wind blew free, and there was nothing to break the light of the sun. I was born where there were no enclosures, and where everything drew a free breath. I want to die there, and not within walls. I know every stream and every wood between the Río Grande and the Arkansas. I have hunted and lived over that country. I lived like my fathers before me, and like them, I lived happily.

Despite these poignant utterances, the will of the commissioners prevailed, and before the council closed, the chiefs assented to drastically reduced ranges. By the terms of the treaties of Medicine Lodge, the Kiowas and

Comanches were assigned a reservation on lands taken from the Choctaws and Chickasaws by the Reconstruction treaties of 1866, in the Leased District. The Kiowa-Comanche Reservation was bounded on the east by the 98th meridian, the northern limit along the Washita to a point thirty miles (by river) west of Fort Cobb, thence on a line due west to the North Fork of Red River. The North Fork and the Red River formed the western and southern boundaries. The twelve hundred Kiowas and seventeen hundred Comanches thus received a three-million-acre domain. Three hundred Plains Apaches confederated with the Kiowas and the Comanches.

The Cheyennes and the Arapahoes were assigned a reservation home in the Cherokee Outlet, bounded by the Cimarron and Arkansas rivers. These tribesmen, numbering about two thousand Cheyennes and twelve hundred Arapahoes, settled south of this reservation on the North Canadian. An executive order in 1869 established a new Cheyenne-Arapaho reservation, containing nearly five million acres, south of the Outlet line between the 98th and 100th meridians, extending to the Kiowa-Comanche line on the Washita. In 1872 the Cheyenne-Arapaho domain was reduced by about 600,000 acres when the government established a reservation on the Washita for about eleven hundred Wichitas, Caddoes, Absentee Delawares, and the remnants of Texas tribes brought into the Leased District before the Civil War (including Keechies, Anadarkos, Ionis, and Wacos).

One of the larger Indian communities assigned to Indian Territory during the postbellum period was the Osage. These people had in earlier times lived in northeastern Oklahoma and had been relocated in what later became southern Kansas in order to make room for the Cherokees. Osage chiefs signed a treaty with the federal government in 1865 which made preliminary arrangements for removal to Indian Territory, and in July, 1870, the United States Congress passed a law providing for an Osage reservation. A definite assignment consisting of 1 million acres, situated between 96° longitude (western boundary of the Cherokee Nation proper), and the Arkansas in the Cherokee Outlet was made the following year.

The removal agreement included a provision that Osage mixed bloods who wished to do so could accept allotments on the Osage Reservation in Kansas and remain, thereby becoming landowners and citizens of the United States. Their treatment at the hands of the land-hungry Kansans following allotment was reminiscent of the harassment suffered by the Creeks thirty-five years earlier at the hands of the Alabamans. The commissioner of Indian affairs announced that very shortly the mixed-blood allotments were overrun by settlers and that the

> outrages and persecutions perpetrated upon them . . . shames humanity. All except eight have abandoned their homes, or taken what they could get for them. Some of their homes were burnt by mobs of white men; and one half-breed died from injury received. . . . The murderers were arrested, went through the forms of a trial, and were discharged. The eight still remaining will probably lose their land, as they have not the means to engage in a long contest of law.

Between 1871 and 1872, fifteen hundred Osages moved back to Oklahoma. Their domain, although extensive, was rough upland meadow and hill country, most of it apparently fit only for grazing. It is a conspicuous irony of Sooner State history that the Osage Reservation, considered one of the poorer and less desirable assignments, became one of the richest tracts of land in the world. In later years, vast oil deposits were found beneath this rough, hilly, grass-covered domain, and the Osages became the wealthiest community in the United States. For years every man, woman, and child in the tribe received more than $10,000 a year in oil royalties.

The Kaws (Kansas), closely related to the Osages by language and culture, disposed of their reservation in Kansas by successive treaties, and during 1872 agreed to relocate in Oklahoma. A 100,000–acre tract in the northwest corner of the Osage Reservation on the Arkansas River was set aside for them, and during 1873 the five hundred members of this tribe settled on their new reservation home in Indian Territory. The Osage and Kaw tribes were under the supervision of the Osage Agency at Pawhuska.

Another postwar agency developed from the assignment of the Sac and Fox to Oklahoma. Formerly two separate tribes domiciled in the Old Northwest, these people, numbering sixty-four hundred in 1825, ravaged by frontier wars and disease, had been reduced to fewer than a thousand in 1865. During February, 1867, about five hundred members of the Sac and Fox tribe assented to a treaty through which they surrendered their lands in Kansas for a 480,000–acre tract in Indian Territory situated west of the Creek Nation between the Cimarron and North Canadian rivers. By 1869 these Algonkian-speaking tribesmen were settled on their new lands, working their small farms and adjusting to life on the Oklahoma frontier.

The Sac and Fox Agency, established to administer the affairs of this affiliated tribe, soon had attached to it four additional tribes who were settled adjacent to the Sac and Fox lands; these were the Potawatomis, the Absentee Shawnees, the Iowas, and the Kickapoos. Certain segments of the Potawatomi tribe in Kansas signed a treaty with the United States in 1867, agreeing to relocate on a reservation in Indian Territory. A tract of 575,000 acres just west of the Seminole nation was assigned to the Potawatomis. When these people, numbering about 540, reached their new home, they found that the Absentee Shawnees had already occupied the northern portion of their domain. An arrangement was worked out providing for joint occupation, with the Kansas immigrants settling in the central and southern portions of the reservation.

The Iowas, living on the Kansas-Nebraska border, began drifting into Indian Territory in 1876 in protest against government pressure to partition their northern reservation. The Iowas collected in a community in the Sac and Fox country, their status uncertain in the absence of treaties. Finally, in 1883, by executive order a 225,000–acre reservation, situated between the Cimarron and the Deep Fork, was established for the 185 members of this tribe.

The most dangerous and intractable Indians settled within the Sac and Fox jurisdiction were the Mexican Kickapoos. These fierce people, originally from the Old Northwest, had moved west and south of the American settlements until a large portion of the tribe settled in Coahuila in northern Mexico during the Civil War. The Mexican government welcomed these Algonkian-speaking Indians and gave them a reservation home and complete freedom from governmental interference in return for protection of the northern Mexican frontier from raids by the Kiowas and Comanches. Kickapoo warriors met this obligation quite effectively but also involved themselves in an extended war against Texas settlements. Kickapoo raids from south of the Río Grande between 1865 and 1873 caused numerous ranches to be abandoned. Texan demands for respite from the Kickapoo peril led to a special expedition carried out by Colonel Ranald Mackenzie and his famous Fourth Cavalry. During 1873, Mackenzie crossed into Old Mexico, smashed the Kickapoo villages at Nacimiento, and coerced a large part of the tribe, more than 350 people, into returning to the United States and accepting a reservation in Indian Territory. By 1874 these fierce raiders from the Remolino were settled on a 206,000–acre reserve situated between the Deep Fork and the North Canadian.

The Ponca Agency, west of the Osages and Kaws, supervised the Poncas, the Pawnees, the Otoes, the Missouris, the Nez Percés, and the Tonkawas. The Poncas, a Siouan-speaking people from Dakota Territory, had lived briefly in Nebraska but were confronted with removal in 1876 when Congress passed an act

Fox woman weaving.

providing for the relocation of the 680 members of this tribe on a reservation in Indian Territory. The Ponca migration began during 1877. Chief Standing Bear led his people first to the Quapaw Reservation in northeastern Oklahoma, where they remained while tribal leaders looked over the Cherokee Outlet for a permanent home. Standing Bear finally decided upon a 100,000–acre tract between the Chikaskia and Arkansas rivers.

Hardship and suffering marked every tribal relocation, but none can surpass the Ponca removal for pathos. Soon after the Poncas arrived in Indian Territory, Standing Bear's young son died. The grieving Ponca leader could not endure the thought of burying his child in the new land. He felt compelled to return him to the land of his ancestors for last rites. A mounted escort of thirty mourning Ponca warriors accompanied the wagon bearing the chief and the small shrouded body of his son. This slow-moving column alarmed settlers on the frontier, who feared an Indian outbreak, and frantic appeals were made to the military. General George Crook and a cavalry force were sent after the Poncas, and the party was arrested and lodged in the Omaha, Ne-

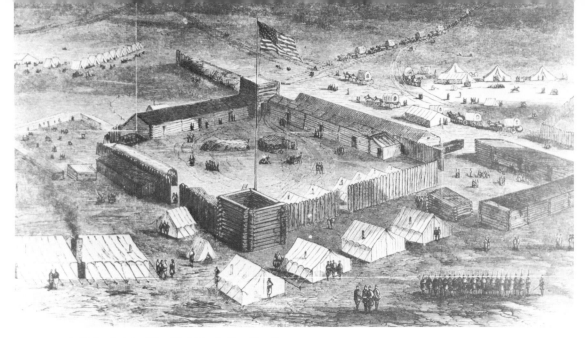

Artist's sketch of Fort Supply, Indian Territory.

braska, jail to await forced return to Indian Territory.

For once, however, the people on the frontier took the side of the Indian. When it became known why Standing Bear's party was off its reservation, the people of Omaha provided legal counsel for the Indians. Their attorney sought a writ of habeas corpus in United States District Court. Local newspapers carried reports of the incident and public interest was stirred to such a level that the courtroom was filled. Government attorneys asked that the petition for the writ be denied on the ground that Indians were not persons within the meaning of the Constitution and therefore could not invoke the right of habeas corpus. Nevertheless, the judge ruled that the Indian was a person, and thus entitled to the same protection as any citizen. Standing Bear's party was released and permitted to proceed to the ancient Ponca ceremonial ground.

The Otoes and the Missouris, Siouan-speaking people closely related to the Iowas, had fused into one tribe by 1854 when they received a reservation on the Nebraska-Kansas border. This northern domain was taken from them by congressional action in 1880 and tribal leaders were forced to find a new location. The Otoe-Missouri removal to Indian Territory, involving about four hundred members of that tribe, occurred between 1880 and 1883. At first they squatted on lands in the Sac and Fox country, but in 1882 tribal leaders purchased a 130,000–acre tract in the Cherokee Outlet south of the Poncas.

The largest Indian community to be settled in the Ponca Agency jurisdiction was the Pawnees, who mustered a population of more than two thousand at the beginning of removal in 1873. The year before, the Pawnee Reservation in Nebraska was appropriated by the United States, and bands from this tribe began drifting into Oklahoma searching for homes. About three hundred Pawnees settled temporarily near the Wichita Agency on the Washita. During 1874, Pawnee chiefs selected a 283,000–acre reservation between the Arkansas and Cimaron rivers. Most of their land was in the Cherokee Outlet, although the southern portion extended into the area ceded by the Creeks in 1866.

The Nez Percés, a Pacific Northwest people of Shahaptian language stock, lived on a reservation astride present Oregon and Idaho. Settlers seized their lands, the Indians resisted, and the conflict set off a long, bloody war that brought prominence to their leader, the famous Chief Joseph, but brought ruin to the Nez Percés. Finally captured under a flag of truce during 1877, 431 resisting Nez Percés were brought under heavy military guard as prisoners of war, first to Fort Leavenworth, then to the Quapaw Agency in northeastern Oklahoma. A seven thousand-acre tract was assigned to them, but Chief Joseph refused to accept it, and selected instead a reservation in the Cherokee Outlet on the Chikaskia River. Protests by the Nez Percés against the questionable methods used to shunt them off to Indian Territory led to an act by Congress in 1885 that provided for returning the Nez Percés to their old homeland.

The Tonkawas, a Texas tribe, had been moved from south of the Red River to the Leased District during the general relocation of Texas tribes that occurred in 1859. The tribe numbered about 350 at that time. The Tonkawas were harassed by the Kiowas, Comanches, Kickapoos, and other powerful tribes under the claim that they were cannibals. The truth of the matter was that the Tonkawas were excellent scouts and trailers, widely used by frontier military units in searching out the camps of hostiles. As a consequence, the Kiowas, the Comanches, and the Kickapoos hated the Tonkawas and used the charge of cannibalism as an excuse to persecute them. In 1862, during a raid on the Wichita Agency by northern Indians, the Tonkawas were nearly exterminated. The survivors, numbering about a hundred, fled to Fort Griffin in Texas and remained there until 1884 when Indian Bureau officials arranged for their relocation in Indian Territory. The Tonkawas settled temporarily in the Sac and Fox country. The following year they were located permanently on the 91,000–acre reservation recently abandoned by the Nez Percés.

Through its Reconstruction Treaty with the Cherokees, the federal government gained the right to settle certain tribes east of the 96th meridian in the old Cherokee nation. A community of Delawares, numbering about one thousand, had been assigned a reservation in northern Kansas while that area was a part of the Indian Territory. An agreement negotiated in 1876 provided that the Delawares settle among the Cherokees in return for payment of $280,000 to the Cherokees. While a 158,000–acre tract was set aside for the Delawares in the northern Verdigris valley, it was not in the nature of a separate reservation because the Delawares were adopted by the Cherokees and soon became full citizens of that nation. Also in 1867 a band of Shawnees, numbering 722, surrendered their lands in Kansas and worked out an agreement with the Cherokees

similar to that negotiated with the Delawares. The Shawnee immigrants settled in present Craig County.

The Quapaw Agency had a number of tribes under its jurisdiction. The reservation area, situated in the far northeastern corner between the Neosho and Grand rivers and the Missouri border, was carved out during 1832 and 1833 by treaties with the Quapaws, the Senecas, and a small band of Shawnees. Following the Civil War, surplus Quapaw, Seneca, and Shawnee land was taken by the federal government to establish reservation homes for small tribes being relocated from Kansas reservations. These tribes included the Wyandots, Peorias, Miamis, and Ottawas. Most of these relocations occurred as a result of treaties negotiated during 1867. The Quapaw Agency received a colorful Indian group from the far West in 1873 when 153 Modocs, punished for making war on the settlers and forced to surrender their lands in northern California and southern Oregon, were brought to Indian Territory as prisoners of war. A reservation for the Modocs was established in northeastern Oklahoma on land taken from the Shawnees.

The assignment of reservations launched by the Medicine Lodge Council set off a series of relocations that soon made western Oklahoma a checkerboard of Indian holdings. Before the Second Trail of Tears was ended, the federal government had colonized over twelve thousand Indians on reservations west of the Five Civilized Tribes. The cumulative tribal population of Indian Territory by the close of this postwar relocation program, including the populous Five Civilized Tribes, numbered slightly under eighty thousand. By 1889 present Oklahoma had twenty-one separate reservations administered by eight agencies. These agencies were the Kiowa-Comanche Agency at Fort Sill; the Wichita-Caddo Agency near Fort Reno; the Ponca Agency near present Ponca City; the Osage Agency by Pawhuska; the Sac and Fox Agency near present Stroud; the Quapaw Agency, also known as the Neosho Agency, at Wyandotte and later at Miami; and the Union Agency for the Five Civilized Tribes at Muskogee. Each agency had at least two tribes under its jurisdiction, and several agencies had five tribes or more.

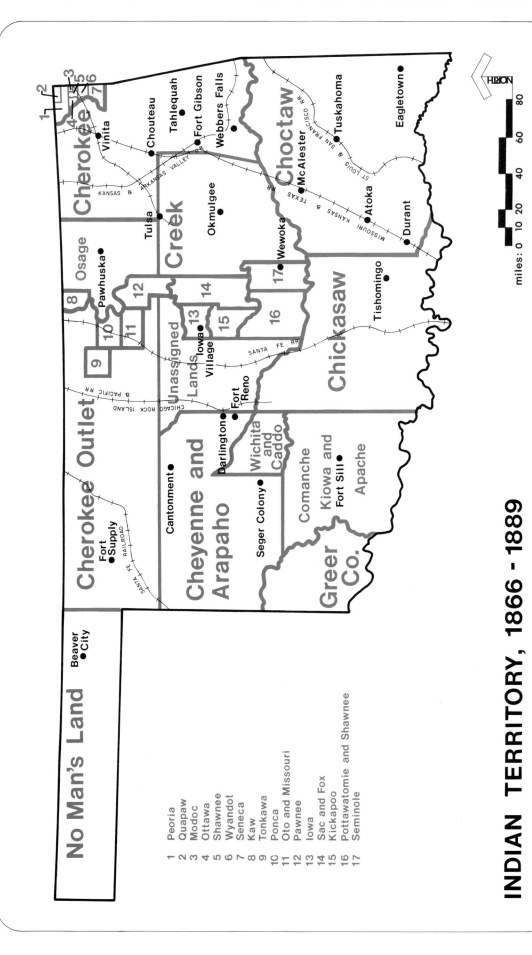

INDIAN TERRITORY, 1866 - 1889

No Man's Land

Beaver City

Cherokee Outlet

Fort Supply

SANTA FE RAILROAD

Cantonment

Cheyenne and Arapaho

Seger Colony

Darlington

Fort Reno

Greer Co.

Comanche

Kiowa and Apache

Fort Sill

Wichita and Caddo

Osage

Pawhuska

8 Cherokee

9
10
11
12
13
14
15
16
17

Creek

Tulsa

Okmulgee

Iowa Village

Unassigned Lands

SANTA FE RR

Wewoka

Chickasaw

Tishomingo

Vinita

Chouteau

Tahlequah

Fort Gibson

Webbers Falls

ARKANSAS VALLEY RR

KANSAS & ARKANSAS VALLEY

Choctaw

McAlester

Tuskahoma

Eagletown

Atoka

Durant

ST LOUIS & SAN FRANCISCO RR

MISSOURI KANSAS & TEXAS RR

CHICAGO ROCK ISLAND & PACIFIC RR

NORTH

miles: 0 10 20   40   60   80

drawn by : S Rogers

1 Peoria
2 Quapaw
3 Modoc
4 Ottawa
5 Shawnee
6 Wyandot
7 Seneca
8 Kaw
9 Tonkawa
10 Ponca
11 Oto and Missouri
12 Pawnee
13 Iowa
14 Sac and Fox
15 Kickapoo
16 Pottawatomie and Shawnee
17 Seminole

Sun Dance, Ponca Reservation, northern Indian Territory.

Aside from Union Agency, the patterns of administration were much alike. Where there were many tribes attached to a major agency, such as the Sac and Fox Agency or the Ponca Agency, the federal government established a subagency for each of the assigned tribes, headed by a deputy responsible to the agent in charge of the total jurisdiction. The arrangement of each, except for Union Agency, was generally as follows: on the agency grounds were the headquarters building, storage sheds for rations and tools, a stable, a school building, and a church. The agency staff included the agent, a clerk, a reservation farmer. a teacher, and a squad of Indian police recruited from among the warriors of the tribe and responsible for maintaining order, confiscating whiskey, and reporting on intruders. Various religious denominations were permitted to locate missionaries among the tribes. The federal government regarded conversion to Christianity as vital for leading the Indians along the "white man's road."

The agent was responsible for watching the Indians assigned to his jurisdiction and for reporting their activities to both the head of the Central Superintendency at Lawrence, Kansas, and to the commissioner of Indian affairs in Washington. The goal of the federal government was to transform the tribesmen into law-abiding citizens, erase tribal lore and native customs, and finally to lead the Indians along the road to Anglo-American civilization,

the Indians to become self-sufficient farmers in the image of the typical American rural family. In order to achieve this, the agent's responsibility was to see that the men were taught farming and animal husbandry, that the women were taught various household crafts, and that schools were established for instructing youth in basic learning and vocational skills. The emphasis on education for the Indians of Oklahoma led to an extension of reservation schools beyond the elementary level. Several Indian schools operating in Oklahoma until recent times date from this period and include Seneca Indian School, Chilocco, and Fort Sill Indian School.

Most of the tribesmen were peaceful and gave their agents no particular trouble other than those caused by their determined efforts to continue the intertribal visits, horse races, gambling, feasts, and dances, and their calculated attempt to avoid farming and other programs thrust upon them by the agents. The Kiowas, the Comanches, the Cheyennes, and the Arapahoes, however, were exceptions. They remained belligerent and continued their attacks on the settlements in surrounding states and territories. To pacify them, the United States government established several military posts—Fort Sill, Fort Reno, and Fort Supply—on Oklahoma's western border. From these bases, hard-riding cavalrymen attempted to maintain surveillance over the fierce Plains raiders.

Federal Indian policy underwent drastic change in the post–Civil War period, and because of the concentration of tribes in Oklahoma, this change had special meaning for the future Sooner State. One of the most revolutionary alterations in Indian policy concerned treaties with the Indian tribes. From earliest colonial times, the tribes had carried on treaty relations with the Europeans and later with the United States. The very act of negotiating such agreements with the tribes ascribed sovereign status to them. In early United States history the tribes were numerous and powerful, and the nation was relatively weak; the result was that the federal government found it desirable to ascribe at least quasi-sovereign status to the Indian communities. The massive military establishment developed by the Union during the Civil War and the national military potential after demobilization made it unnecessary to continue this practice. In March, 1871, the United States Congress passed an act providing: "No Indian nation or tribe within the territory of the United States shall be acknowledged or recognized as an independent nation, tribe, or power with whom the United States may contract by treaty; but no obligation of any treaty made is hereby invalidated or impaired." Thereafter any change in relationship with an Indian tribe was accomplished by executive order or act of Congress. Needless to say, this was a severe blow to the prestige and pride of the Indian tribes.

Another development in federal government relations with the Indian tribes occurred in 1869 with the creation of the Board of Indian Commissioners. Its members were leading citizens, and their functions were to investigate conditions among the tribes, to study Indian administration, and to act in an advisory capacity to the Bureau of Indian Affairs. Board members or their hired investigators spent much time in Oklahoma looking into tribal matters.

The most interesting change in Indian administration during the postbellum period concerned President Grant's encouragement of the "peace policy" as a substitute for the War Department's "force policy" in solving the problems associated with Indians. Shortly after his inauguration, Grant met with a delegation of nationally prominent churchmen, most of whom were Quakers (Society of Friends). These spiritual leaders pointed out that a century of force had failed to solve the Indian problem. Grant heard them out and was impressed by their argument. He offered this challenge: "If you can make Quakers out of the Indians it will take the fight out of them. Let us have peace." He invited the leading religious denominations to recommend their best men to serve as officials in the Bureau of Indian Affairs and as agents on the reservations.

Most of the "peace policy agents" assigned to the Indian tribes of Oklahoma were Quakers. Enoch Hoag, an Iowa Quaker, was appointed to head the Central Superintendency. Brinton Darlington served as agent for the Cheyennes and the Arapahoes until succeeded by another Quaker, John D. Miles. Laurie Tatum worked among the Kiowas and the Comanches; Thomas Miller and later Jonathan Hadley were at the Sac and Fox Agency; Hiram W. Jones was at the Quapaw Agency; Jonathan Richards was at the Wichita Agency; and Isaac T. Gibson worked with the Osages. Laurie Tatum reported his experiences as Kiowa-Comanche agent; they were published in 1899 under the title *Our Red Brothers*. Quakers also served as teachers at the government schools. Thomas C. Battey, who taught at the Kiowa-Comanche school, described his experiences in *A Quaker Among the Indians*, published in 1875.

Before the advent of the Quaker agents, the Kiowas, the Comanches, the Cheyennes, and the Arapahoes left their reservations during the spring of 1868 and resumed their plundering ways. The United States government had failed to deliver the gifts and rations promised by the commissioners at the Medicine Lodge Council, and the warriors claimed that the failure of the United States to keep its promises excused the tribes from observing the treaties. Small predatory bands, well-mounted and heavily armed, raided the frontiers of western Kansas, Nebraska, Colorado, and Texas. Troops found it almost impossible to locate the scattered, fast-moving war parties. General Alfred Sully finally made contact with a village of Kiowas and Comanches in the North Canadian valley, but the truculent attitude of the

Indians caused him to beat a hasty retreat to Fort Dodge.

Steps taken by the War Department during 1868 marked the beginning of the end of the war-making power of the Plains tribes. General Phil Sheridan, commander of United States forces on the frontier, was ordered to establish a military post at a point where hostile bands could be watched and intercepted if a thrust into western Kansas was imminent. The stipulations guiding Sheridan in his choice were that the new post be not more than a hundred miles south of the Arkansas, that it possess natural advantages for a supply depot and operational base, and that its environs have ample wood, water, and winter pasture for a large number of horses. The new military station, which became Fort Supply, was to be used as a base of operations for carrying out a new tactic against the hostiles—a winter campaign.

It was expected that this strategy would be most effective for several reasons. First, the Indians would be concentrated in large villages for winter quarters. Second, it was unlikely that they would be expecting trouble, because the United States military forces usually left them alone during the colder months, largely because the Indians themselves were quiet at this time. And third, the Indians would be unable to defend themselves as effectively as they could during the spring and summer, because their horses would be in a weakened condition owing to sparse forage.

General Alfred Sully selected as a site for the new post the junction of Wolf and Beaver creeks in the far western Cherokee Outlet. During November, 1868, the first contingent, consisting of five companies of the Third Infantry under Major John H. Page, left Fort Dodge for the Cherokee Outlet. Page's orders were to construct fortifications and organize his troops as a garrison force. A train of 450 wagons, loaded at Fort Dodge, carried building materials, provisions, weapons, and ammunition. General George Armstrong Custer and eleven troops of the Seventh Cavalry served as escort for the supply train, which reached Wolf Creek on November 21.

Troops from Fort Lyon, Colorado, Fort Bascom, New Mexico, and the Nineteenth Kansas Cavalry were momentarily expected at Wolf Creek. However, a heavy snowstorm swept into the southern plains. On Oklahoma's western border the snow was reportedly a foot deep, and the Colorado, New Mexico, and Kansas troops were delayed. General Custer, anxious to move on the hostile bands before the warriors learned of his winter campaign, led his Seventh Cavalry, complete with a company band and three scouts—the colorful California Joe and two Osage trailers—south on the cold, snow-covered plains of western Oklahoma.

On the morning of November 27, Custer's scouts located a large Indian village in a bend of the upper Washita. The Seventh Cavalry swept into the settlement and smashed it with a roaring dawn attack. They caught the sleeping Indians by such complete surprise that only the slightest resistance was possible. The massacre that followed was identified in the official reports as the Battle of the Washita. Cheyenne Chief Black Kettle, who had miraculously escaped the Sand Creek Massacre in eastern Colorado in 1864, was leader of the band. As a result of the attack, 102 Cheyenne warriors and numerous women and children were killed. Black Kettle was among those slain. Custer's troopers slaughtered the village herd of 800 ponies and burned every lodge in the encampment. They collected 247 saddles, 573 buffalo robes, arms, ammunition, and the village's winter meat supply. They took more than 50 women and children as prisoners of the government.

General Sheridan followed up the Washita campaign with a thrust south into the Leased District; fifteen hundred troops, including General Custer and his Seventh Cavalry, made up Sheridan's column. From their base at old Fort Cobb, the troopers rounded up scattered bands of Kiowas and Comanches, forcing the Indians to establish their camps near Fort Cobb where the soldiers could watch them. While in the area, Sheridan selected the site for a new post on the edge of the Wichita Mountains. Founded as Camp Wichita on January 8, 1869, this military station shortly thereafter was named Fort Sill in honor of Sheridan's West Point classmate, General Joshua W. Sill. A third link in this defensive chain was constructed near Darlington Agency during 1874

Cheyenne-Arapaho scouts attached to United States cavalry columns at Fort Reno.

in the Cheyenne-Arapaho country and was named Fort Reno for General Jesse L. Reno, who had been killed in the Civil War.

General Sheridan's devastating winter campaign and the relentless watch his troopers maintained over the tribes appeared to pacify the warriors. But an undercurrent of discontent was evident by 1870 and soon threatened to flower into a full-scale uprising. Congress had cut the appropriations for purchasing rations for the reservation tribes, and the agents had to permit small bands of Indians to go to the plains to hunt buffalo. The warriors were sickened and angered at what they saw. A demanding market in the East for buffalo robes had attracted commercial hunters who roamed the plains slaughtering thousands of bison a day, taking only the hides, and leaving the carcasses to rot.

Another disturbing influence that caused great unrest among the wild tribes was the fact that several bands had not yet come to the reservations to surrender to the military. The deadliest group still out was the hostile Quahada Comanche band led by the famous Quanah Parker, son of a Comanche chief and a white girl captive from Texas. Warriors from

the Quahada band slipped into the Kiowa-Comanche reservation and taunted the peaceful Indians, calling them cowards and "squaws," the epitome of Indian derision, and inviting them to join Quanah in his resistance to white domination.

During 1870 small war parties began slipping away from the reservations to attack the settlements. Commonly the warriors made their way on foot to make detection more difficult. Once across the Red River, they prowled about the ranches and stole horses and weapons. Armed and mounted, they began their work of death and destruction. One of the more famous raids was carried out in 1871 by a party of Kiowas led by Satanta, Satank, and Big Tree. Their boldest stroke was near Jacksboro, Texas, where they plundered and destroyed a wagon train.

There were raids more destructive than the Jacksboro incident, but its aftermath was of fundamental significance for the future of the Plains warriors. Satanta, Satank, and Big Tree were arrested soon after their return to the reservation and were held for trial in Texas. This marked a drastic departure from established procedure and set a precedent. Thereafter, hostile band leaders were held responsible for the actions of their warriors. Satanta, Satank, and Big Tree were shackled and hauled by wagon across the Red River to stand trial in the state courts of Texas. Satank slipped his bonds and tried to kill one of his guards. He was shot by the cavalry escort. Satanta and Big Tree were tried and sentenced to death as punishment for the Jacksboro raid, but the Texas governor later commuted the sentences to life imprisonment. The Kiowas on the Fort Sill Reservation petitioned state and federal officials to parole their chiefs. After a while federal agents agreed to use their influence to gain freedom for Satanta and Big Tree if the Kiowas remained on their reservation and kept the peace. The agreement set the release date for late in 1873. The Kiowas scrupulously observed the terms, and Satanta and Big Tree were paroled as promised.

The return of these famous raider chiefs to the Kiowa-Comanche country became a signal for resumption of depredations. The year 1874 was a bloody one on the southwestern frontier, and the many engagements between renegade war parties and wide-ranging cavalry units based at military posts and camps in Indian Territory and Texas during this year are known in military history as the Red River wars. The most famous battle of 1874, oddly enough, involved buffalo hunters instead of United States troops.

On the Canadian River in the Texas panhandle were the ruins of an old trading post known as Adobe Walls. Buffalo had become scarce north of the Arkansas, so hunters moved south to slaughter the herds on the southern plains. Dodge City traders established a station at Adobe Walls, and it became a base for the hide hunters. Their vast harvest of hides soon littered the plains with rotting carcasses. Indian hunters were infuriated by this wanton destruction of their principal food source, and about two hundred Comanche and Cheyenne warriors surrounded the hunters at Adobe Walls on June 27, 1874. The fourteen hunters, with their high caliber, long-range buffalo guns were able to turn back charge after charge by the attacking Indians. Finally, when one of the hunters made an "impossible" hit at a fantastic range, the chiefs called their fighters off and abandoned the assault.

Quanah Parker, Quahada Comanche war chief.

Raider bands were also active in the east during 1874. A Cheyenne war party was known to have attacked Texas cattle herds moving across Indian Territory along the Chisholm Trail. Their most famous coup involved a wagon train hauling supplies from the railroad at Wichita, Kansas, to Wichita Agency in the Leased District. The Cheyenne war party swept down on the train at Buffalo Springs, plundered the wagons, and killed four teamsters, including Pat Hennessey, for whom Hennessey, Oklahoma, is named. Hennessey was tied to a wagon wheel and burned to death.

A major offensive was planned by the federal government during 1874 to end once and for all the military power of the Plains tribes. General Nelson A. Miles was placed in command of a force of eight troops of cavalry, including Colonel Mackenzie's famed Fourth Cavalry; four companies of infantry; a battery of artillery; and a company of guides and scouts, who were principally Delawares. Miles's orders were to comb the region between the Cimarron and the Red for hostiles. Between August and December, 1874, his army maintained relentless pressure on the

Indians, and one by one the renegade bands came in to surrender at Fort Sill. The last to capitulate were the Quahada Comanches led by Quanah Parker.

As each band of Indians surrendered, three things happened: the army appropriated the Indian ponies; the warriors were disarmed; and the chiefs were arrested. Satanta, who had broken parole, was returned to a Texas prison. Seventy-two raider chiefs (thirty-three Cheyennes, two Arapahoes, eleven Comanches, and twenty-six Kiowas) were placed in irons and hauled under heavy guard to military prison at Fort Marion, Saint Augustine, Florida. After three years, twenty-two of the younger chiefs were enrolled in the Indian school at Carlisle, Pennsylvania, where they studied in a rehabilitation program before being returned to Oklahoma.

The followers of the famous Apache warrior Geronimo—407 men, women, and children —were captured in Arizona in 1886 and even-tually transported to the Fort Sill Reservation. At first, however, Geronimo's Apaches were placed in the Fort Marion military prison at Saint Augustine. In 1888 the Apache prisoners were moved to Mount Vernon Barracks in Alabama. Tuberculosis took a heavy toll among the captives, and in 1894 the 296 survivors were resettled on the Kiowa-Comanche Reservation; their status as prisoners of war continued until 1913.

It was not until the warriors on the reservations of western Indian Territory were leaderless, disarmed, and afoot—their horses confiscated and shot or sold to ranchers at auction by military authorities—that they were thoroughly pacified. Disillusioned, they settled into the dull routines of reservation life, most of them demoralized by the drastic changes in life-style confronting them but studiously thwarting the attempt of the agents to lead them along the "white man's road."

Notes on Sources, Chapter 12

Several score of Indian tribes were assigned to reservation homes in Oklahoma after the Civil War. For many tribes this forced move to Indian Territory represented their fourth relocation in fifty years. It was an uprooting that produced considerable suffering and hardship, reminiscent of the melancholy Trail of Tears of the 1830s. Books describing the resettlement of those tribes that came to Oklahoma peacefully are Frederick W. Hodge, ed., *Handbook of American Indians North of Mexico*, 2 vols. (New York, 1959); William E. Unrau, *The Kansas Indians: A History of the Wind People* (Norman, 1971); William T. Hagan, *The Sac and Fox Indians* (Norman, 1958); Muriel H. Wright, *A Guide to the Indian Tribes of Oklahoma* (Norman, 1951); and John Joseph Mathews, *The Osages: Children of the Middle Waters* (Norman, 1961).

Descriptions of the resettlement of the rebelli-ous tribes are found in Douglas C. Jones, *The Treaty of Medicine Lodge* (Norman, 1966); William H. Leckie, *The Military Conquest of the Southern Plains* (Norman, 1963); Mildred P. Mayhall, *The Kiowas* (Norman, 1962; 2d ed., 1971); Ernest Wallace and E. Adamson Boebel, *The Comanches: Lords of the South Plains* (Norman, 1952); Arrell Morgan Gibson, *The Kickapoos: Lords of the Middle Border* (Norman, 1963); Wilbur S. Nye, *Carbine and Lance: The Story of Old Fort Sill* (Norman, 1937; centennial ed., 1969); Robert C. Carriker, *Fort Supply, Indian Territory: Frontier Outpost on the Plains* (Norman, 1970); Keith A. Murray, *The Modocs and Their War* (Norman, 1959); Francis Haines, *The Nez Percés; Tribesmen of the Columbian Plateau* (Norman, 1955); and Marvin E. Kroeker, *Great Plains Command: William B. Hazen in the Frontier West* (Norman, 1976).

Chapter 13

Postwar Economic Development

As noted in Chapter 11, the postbellum period was a time of rapid economic development for the future Sooner State. Of greatest importance was the extensive railroad construction that occurred between 1865 and 1890, an activity that continued well beyond 1900. Oklahoma's railway network nourished many enterprises, including mining, lumbering, ranching, and expanded farming. The coming of the railroads also gave new opportunity to the tenacious, aggressive Boomers. The continued expansion of the railways resulted in the opening of America's last frontier to the homesteaders.

Earlier chapters have reported that Oklahoma's five Indian republics had a fairly well developed system of transportation before the Civil War. Primary reliance for moving goods to Gulf markets was placed on local waterways —the Arkansas River and its tributaries, and the Red River. Steamers, flatboats, and barges carried out cargoes of lead, grain, cotton, animal products (especially furs and buffalo hides), salt, and some lumber. The towns were connected by public and military roads, a postal system, stagecoaches, and ox-drawn freight wagons.

River traffic resumed as the Indian nations recovered from the Civil War. Before 1870 a steamboat line of twenty vessels, each of three hundred tons capacity, plied between Gibson Landing at the mouth of the Grand River and Fort Smith, Little Rock, New Orleans, Memphis, Saint Louis, and Cincinnati. Other steamer lines served the Red River landings in the Choctaw and Chickasaw nations. The *Tablequah, Argos,* and *Fort Smith* were the best-known river steamers on the Arkansas line. Government freight unloaded at Fort Gibson

for military posts and Indian agencies in western Oklahoma amounted to $5 million worth of goods annually.

Before the vast mineral, timber, coal resources, and the almost limitless potential of the soils of Indian Territory could be fully developed, an effective, dependable year-round system of transportation had to be established. The river steamboat service had limitations. Water levels fluctuated, depending on the season, so that the Red and the Arkansas were open for steamer traffic for only part of each year. Railroads, on the other hand, could provide dependable, year-round service on routes that were more flexible.

By 1861 several railroad lines had been extended from the eastern seaboard to the Mississippi River. During the war, Congress chartered a number of transcontinental railways, and with the close of hostilities construction resumed in a rush. The railway companies were powerful enterprises with strong friends in the federal government. Through the railroad lobby's influence, clauses were written into the Reconstruction treaties providing for rights-of-way across the Indian Territory.

The Indian governments feared the entry of railroads into their domains, not only because of the disturbing influences it was assumed that railway construction would bring to Indian Territory but also because of the threat of losing more land from their nations by lavish land grants to the railway companies. It was customary for the states and federal government to make grants of land to railroads as construction subsidies. However, the Indian nations reluctantly granted to railroads planning to build across Indian Territory rights-of-

Freight line serving Indian Territory settlements before the coming of the railroads.

way only two hundred feet wide. The railroads expected more. One line, the Missouri, Kansas, and Texas (MKT or Katy) publicly declared that it was entitled to 3 million acres as a subsidy for building its north–south line across Indian Territory. The fear of having to give up large blocks of tribal land to the railroads caused Indian leaders to do everything in their power to keep the railroads from entering their territories. Failing in this effort, they harassed the railroad companies with claims for damages to land, livestock, orchards, and timber.

During July, 1866, Congress passed an act authorizing the Union Pacific to extend its southern branch, the Missouri-Kansas-Texas, from Kansas through Indian Territory to Fort Smith. Several competing lines were racing for the Indian Territory border. The act provided additionally that if the MKT arrived ahead of its competitors, it would have the privilege of establishing a line all the way to Preston, Texas.

The MKT completed its survey for a roadbed across Oklahoma during 1870, following the old Texas Road. The laying of the track began on the Cherokee border in June, 1870, and by February, 1871, MKT trains were running to Muskogee. Early in 1872, MKT workers laid track across the Red River into Texas at Colbert's Ferry. The feverish construction pace had resulted in the line progressing at the rate of one and a half miles of track a day.

A competing line, the Atlantic and Pacific Railway Company (later the Saint Louis and San Francisco, or "Frisco"), built a line from Saint Louis south through Neosho to Seneca on the southwestern Missouri border. This line entered the Quapaw Agency jurisdiction in May, 1871, and before the end of the year it had crossed the Cherokee nation to meet the MKT line. At this strategic location, a rail station and town grew, and the Indian-railroad controversy that followed illustrates well the conflict between the Indian tradition of common (tribal) ownership of land and the private land ownership system to which the railroad officials were accustomed.

The Cherokee council had passed an act reserving to the Cherokee Nation an area of one square mile around each railroad station in the nation. This law provided that each railroad station reserve was to be surveyed and the town lots sold only to Cherokee citizens. Before the official Cherokee survey of the land surrounding the station at the MKT-Frisco junction could be made, Elias C. Boudinot entered the picture. Boudinot was a prominent Cherokee mixed blood, the son of the famous Elias Boudinot (Buck Watie), and a controversial figure among Indians because of his espousal of the white man's cause, especially of railroad construction. He was one of the Southwest's most successful railroad attorneys and spent most of his time in Washington. Boudinot prevented the official Cherokee survey at the Frisco-MKT junction by exercising his right as a Cherokee citizen to establish a claim to 1,000 acres surrounding the junction.

Boudinot made his own survey, opened city lots, and named his proposed town Vinita for his friend, the noted sculptress Vinnie Ream. Cherokee officials refused to recognize Boudinot's action, named the town Downingville, and harassed the Cherokee railroad attorney in every possible way. They even destroyed his Vinita Hotel. Although Boudinot finally lost in his attempt to control the railroad junction, he did ultimately win on one score—that of having the name of the town changed back to Vinita, as it is known today.

In 1882 the north branch of the Frisco crossed into the Creek Nation to Red Fork and Tulseytown, now Tulsa. Construction to the west was resumed in 1898 when the Frisco, under a subsidiary line called the Saint Louis and Oklahoma City Railway Company, built a line to Oklahoma City. The other fork of the Frisco had been extended to Fort Smith, then southwest across the Choctaw Nation to Paris, Texas. This branch was completed in 1887.

After the MKT and Frisco became well-established in the Indian nations, several additional lines were constructed to tap the rich coal and timber resources of the eastern parts of the Choctaw, Cherokee, and Creek nations. The year 1886 was a busy one for railroad building in the future Sooner State. Congress authorized the Kansas and Arkansas Valley Railway to lay tracks from Fort Smith up the Arkansas valley into Kansas. This company, also known as the Iron Mountain Railway, passed Wagoner and arrived in Coffeyville, Kansas, in 1889.

Another railway chartered during 1886 was the Denison and Washita Company, organized at Denison, Texas, to extend across Red River into the coal fields of the Choctaw Nation. Construction began in 1888 and reached the coal camps of Lehigh and Coalgate during the next year. The Denison and Washita Company eventually came under the control of the MKT. The third line authorized to build into Indian Territory during 1886 was the Kansas City, Fort Scott, and Gulf Railway. The following year the Chicago, Kansas, and Nebraska Rail-

way Company received permission to cross Indian Territory, and in 1888 the Fort Smith and El Paso Railway, the Kansas City and Pacific, and the Parsons, Choctaw, and Little Rock lines were organized. Northeastern Oklahoma, as well as Stilwell, Poteau, and Siloam Springs, Arkansas, were served by the Split Log Railroad. The Split Log holdings were later absorbed by the Kansas City Southern, which completed the Gulf Link as the Kansas City, Pittsburg, and Gulf Railway Company, with its tracks running from Kansas City to Port Arthur.

Construction began on the Midland Valley Railway in 1900. This line ran from the Arkansas coal fields north to Arkansas City, Kansas, with its 277 miles of track serving Muskogee, Tulsa, and Pawhuska in the Indian Territory. Also in 1900, the Fort Smith and Western line built from Fort Smith through the Choctaw Nation coal fields into what is now McCurtain County.

One of the most ambitious and colorful railroad enterprises attempted in Indian Territory was the vast network of track laid by the Choctaw Coal and Railway Company. Incorporated in Philadelphia during 1887, with general offices in Minnesota, this line was developed to tap the coal reserves of Indian Territory. The Choctaw line began construction at Wister Junction on the Frisco, and extended west to the MKT line at McAlester. From El Reno, construction extended eastward through Oklahoma City and eventually linked with the eastern branch at McAlester. Financial difficulties caused a foreclosure sale during 1894, and the company was reorganized as the Choctaw, Oklahoma, and Gulf Railway Company. Under new management, the Choctaw line built west from Weatherford to Amarillo, Texas. Another subsidiary, the Choctaw and Northern, laid track from Geary, Oklahoma Territory, to Anthony, Kansas.

Several short lines were constructed for special services; these included the Mineral Belt Railway in northeastern Oklahoma to serve the rich lead and zinc fields in Ottawa County. By 1905, there were 5,231 miles of railroad in Oklahoma. Consolidation of holdings, so common in American business and industry at the turn of the century, occurred especially often in transportation. Four major

Railroad building in northern Oklahoma Territory.

lines eventually controlled most of the rail facilities in Oklahoma—the Santa Fe, the Rock Island, the MKT, and the Frisco.

The Atchison, Topeka, and Santa Fe line, popularly known as the "Santa Fe" and chartered as a transcontinental line, established several branch lines in Indian Territory. Two of its subsidiary companies, the Southern Kansas Railway, and the Gulf, Colorado, and Santa Fe, began construction in Oklahoma during 1884. The northern branch, the Southern Kansas Railway, built south from Arkansas City, its stations including Oklahoma City and Norman; and the southern link, the Gulf, Colorado and Santa Fe, built north from Red River, arriving at Purcell on the Canadian, joining the Southern Kansas line in 1887. The Santa Fe also ran a line from Kiowa, Kansas, southwest across the Cherokee Outlet to Canadian and Amarillo, Texas, during 1887.

The Rock Island line built south from Caldwell, Kansas, to Fort Reno (soon to be El Reno) in 1889–90, and two years later reached Terrel, Texas. Six years before Oklahoma statehood, the Rock Island constructed a line across the Oklahoma Panhandle to compete with the Santa Fe, and the Rock Island Company became the principal Oklahoma carrier in 1902 when it absorbed the sprawling Choctaw line.

The effects of railroad development in Oklahoma were numerous. One of the more dramatic was the introduction of nearly instantaneous communication through the telegraph, for telegraph poles were set and lines run on the railroad right-of-way. The MKT brought the first telegraph system to eastern Oklahoma in 1871. The first telegraph line in western Oklahoma was established in 1876 and connected Wichita, Kansas, with Fort Reno. The first operating telephone lines in the future Sooner State connected Fort Reno and nearby Darlington Agency in 1884.

Railroad development in Oklahoma strongly influenced place names. Of course, Oklahoma's Indian heritage provided the richest source of place names, but railroads were the next most productive source. Many of the towns that grew up along the new rail lines were named for railroad company officials and their friends, and for hometowns of the railroad builders. For example, on today's Santa Fe railroad between Purcell and Red River, the towns of Ardmore, Berwyn, Marietta, Overbrook, Wayne, and Wynnewood are namesakes of towns west of Philadelphia where railroad stockholders lived.

Another powerful impact of railroad development in Oklahoma was pressure by the railroads for the eventual opening of Indian Territory to the homesteader. The lines building across the Indian nations had hoped to receive large land subsidies as a reward for the risks of their uncertain transportation ventures. As pointed out earlier, one company, the MKT, declared that it alone was entitled to 3 million acres of Oklahoma land. Sustained resistance by the Indian nations defeated the railroads, and one observer wrote, "The only way to recoup their investment and hope for future profitable operations was to populate the country . . . build towns, stimulate agriculture and business enterprises. To this end the railroads maintained a powerful lobby in Washington to promote legislation for the opening up of the Indian Territory to settlement."

Yet another effect of railroad development in Oklahoma was to make possible the delivery to the markets of the world the vast bounty of nature available in the Indian nations. Time, money, and sustained lobbying were required to overcome the opposition of the Indian nations to opening the territory to homesteaders, so the railroads occupied themselves with developing coal, lead, and zinc mines and mills and handling shipments of grain, cotton, and cattle. In many enterprises, notably coal mining and lumbering, the railroads were not only the carriers but the operating companies as well.

In Oklahoma's economic history, four minerals have played a leading role, not only bringing prosperity to the Sooner State but also giving it renown as a world leader. In order of development, these have been coal, lead, zinc, and oil. Before the Civil War vast coal deposits were known to exist in the Cherokee, Creek, and Choctaw nations. Limited demand and lack of adequate transportation facilities resulted in only local use of the coal veins, principally to fuel blacksmith forges.

At about the same time that Oklahoma's first railroad, the MKT was thrusting southward across the Indian nations, in 1871–72, the first commercial coal mines were opened. J. J. McAlester, a Confederate veteran and trader in charge of a store at the Cross Roads, a town on the Texas Road later to be named McAlester, is credited with organizing the first coal mining company. When McAlester married a Chickasaw girl, he gained the benefits of Choctaw-Chickasaw agreements concerning tribal citizenship and mineral rights. The Choctaw and Chickasaw governments had worked out an arrangement by which a citizen

of either nation had equal privileges in both nations. A tribal citizen of either nation who discovered a mineral deposit or other valuable product had the right to establish exclusive claim to that particular locality. He could work the claim himself or lease it to others for development. Any royalty collected was shared, one-half for the claimholder, and one-half for the Choctaw-Chickasaw governments.

In his memoirs McAlester revealed that during the war he obtained a set of field notes from an eminent Arkansas geologist who had traveled over eastern Indian Territory before 1861 and made copious notes on local rocks and minerals. The geological papers included a description of coal seams near the Cross Roads. At about the time that the MKT reached his trading post, McAlester, as an intermarried tribal citizen, established his claim to the deposit described as a "four foot vein of fine bituminous coal." He organized the Oklahoma Mining Company, and when the workings showed certainty of success, a group of financiers joined McAlester to form the Osage Coal and Mining Company.

The first Oklahoma mines were opened by stripping, that is, the earth overburden was removed to expose the shallow coal beds. Later, both strip pit mining and shaft mining were used. In the early days of coal mining in Indian Territory, this fuel customarily sold for ten cents a bushel. The royalty the operators paid was one cent a bushel until, with expanding use, the measure unit became the ton, at which time the royalty was increased to ten cents per ton. Between 1882 and 1897, two companies alone paid out over $2 million in royalties. The Choctaws and the Chickasaws received about $250,000 each year.

The rapid development and expansion of the coal-mining industry in Indian Territory led to the opening of mines in the Cherokee and Creek nations. Near Muskogee during 1887, more than a thousand bushels of coal were mined, but the full development of coal reserves in the Cherokee and Creek nations came after statehood. The only extensive mining activity before 1907 was in the Choctaw nation. In 1894 ten companies controlled all of the Choctaw mines; at the turn of the century thirty-nine companies produced 1.5 million tons of coal. During 1907, fifty companies

Livery stable, El Reno, Oklahoma Territory, showing contemporary conveyances.

mined 3 million tons, rated as the "best steam coal" west of Pennsylvania. The railroads held interests in many mines and controlled vast coal-land leases negotiated with the Choctaw government. Through these arrangements, the railway companies prospered as producers as well as carriers.

The rapid development and expansion of the coal-mining industry in the Choctaw Nation had important social effects. The Choctaws were not interested in going into the pits to mine coal, so the railroads imported skilled miners from Pennsylvania to open the mines. Since new, rich coal deposits were found with startling regularity, a vast labor supply was required. During 1873 railway companies sent agents to Europe to recruit foreign miners. Soon these railroad representatives had a steady stream of immigrants traveling to the Choctaw Nation. They came from Great Britian (Irish, Scots, English, and Welsh miners), from Italy, and from Poland. Labor recruiters even persuaded Lithuanian, Slovene, Magyar, Russian, Dutch, German, Belgian, and French families to seek their fortunes in Indian Territory, with the result that by the mid-1800s the foreign-born miners outnumbered native-born miners in the Choctaw nation two to one. The coal-mining labor force grew to 3,300 in 1894, to 4,000 in 1901, and by 1907 there were 8,000 workers. Most of the miners brought their families and came as permanent settlers, thus sharply increasing the number of foreign immigrants. They brought their languages, customs, foods, and religions, and added a new dimension and color to the kaleidoscopic culture of Indian Territory. Today this color survives throughout the state. One of the few Russian Orthodox churches in the Trans-Mississippi West is situated at Hartshorne, Oklahoma. Ethnic groups maintain their identity through such organizations as Sons of Italy and by holding annual festivals celebrating their heritage.

The immigrants gathered in settlements near the mine workings where company towns were established. The company town is a common feature of coal-mining communities all over America. Some of the better-known Oklahoma company towns were Krebs, Hartshorne, Alderson, Wilburton, Lehigh, Coalgate, Midway, Savannah, Cavanal, Dow, and Haileyville. The pattern that formed for developing and controlling a company town in the Choctaw Nation is illustrated by the following statement:

The coal-mining community . . . was an appendage to the coal mine. It came into existence because the mines were far away from the developed centers of population. All structures were owned by the company and were built on leased land. These semi-feudalistic characteristics of the early mining camp were reflected in the relations between the miners and the operators. Miners were usually paid in scrip, exchangeable only at the company store. Rent for the company house, at the rate of $2.00 a room, was subtracted from the wages. A physician was hired by the company whose salary was paid by monthly deductions of $1.00 from the miner's wages.

The men worked underground ten to twelve hours a day, six days a week, for an average wage of two dollars a day. In addition to paying the tribute levied by the company town, each worker also had to buy an annual residence permit from the Choctaw government that cost $2.50; without the permit a man and his family would be classed as intruders and expelled from the Indian Territory.

Mining was dangerous work. Each day the men faced sudden death in the pits. Mass casualties caused by underground explosions, poisonous gases, cave-ins, and underground flooding were common. Protests against hazardous conditions in the mines caused Oklahoma's first labor strikes and encouraged the organization of the future Sooner State's labor unions. Mine operators retaliated by importing strikebreakers, but the Indian Territory labor movement generally was ineffective until Pete Hanraty came upon the scene. His dedication to the cause of the mine workers put the miners' union on a solid footing.

Hanraty was born in Scotland, worked as a miner in Pennsylvania, and came to Indian Territory in 1882. He labored as a miner at Krebs to support his family, and at night and on Sundays organized the workers into the then popular Knights of Labor. On several occasions he led his followers out on strike against the operators, chiefly in protest against the dreadful working conditions. The Knights of Labor faded as a workingman's society during the 1890s and was replaced in Indian Territory by the United Mine Workers (UMW).

A regional constituency for the UMW, known as District 21, was organized under Hanraty's direction and began enrolling miners in Arkansas, Texas, and Indian Territory. In 1900 he became president of District 21. During the next eight years, he increased the membership of his union from 400 to more than 8,000. He was active in organizing the Twin Territories (Oklahoma Territory and Indian Territory) Federation of Labor in 1903, and served as its president. This organization was the ancestor of the modern-day Oklahoma AFL-CIO. Hanraty was so popular in Indian Territory that he was elected delegate to the Oklahoma Constitutional Convention, and when that body met at Guthrie, Oklahoma Territory, in 1906, he served as its vice-president.

Another pre-statehood mineral industry was lead and zinc mining. From the earliest historical times, trappers, traders, and Indians gathered lead along the valley of Spring River and its tributaries. They smelted the ores over chip fires and molded the metal into shot. In 1884 commercial mining was well under way on the southwestern Missouri border. Pioneer miners floated pig lead out of the area on flatboats down the Grand River to New Orleans.

Northeastern Oklahoma ores were exploited only on a limited and primitive basis until 1891, when prospectors, following the ore beds from southwestern Missouri and southeastern Kansas into Indian Territory, made a rich strike at Peoria. Although Peoria then became Oklahoma's first lead-mining camp, it had been a town since 1882, with a post office, a general store, and a school. A New Jersey corporation, the Peoria Mining, Construction, and Land Company, negotiated the first lease on Indian mineral lands around the town, giving a three to five percent royalty. Within a month after the lead strike, Peoria was a boom town with 1,500 miners. With the discovery at Peoria, the fabulous Tri-State District—southwestern Missouri, southeastern Kansas, and northeastern Oklahoma—was a reality.

Most district mining men agreed that Peoria was the southern-most extension of the Tri-State District, and their estimate appeared to be corroborated when no new strikes were made within a five-mile radius of Peoria. In 1897, however, an accidental discovery occurred that completely shifted the district's mining equilibrium—it moved from Joplin, Missouri, and Galena, Kansas, to Miami, Indian Territory. In that year, a farmer digging a shallow well struck rich lead ore on a tract four miles north of Miami. Additional strikes west of this one resulted in the emergence of sev-

Salt factory in northwestern Oklahoma Territory.

eral new mining camps that eventually became Oklahoma towns. In tapping these rich
lodes, a single rule was applied—follow the
ore. The leading camps were Tar River, Commerce, Hattonville, Douthat, Saint Louis,
Hockerville, Quapaw, Sunnyside, Lincolnville,
and Century. The camps followed the ore
deposits, and new discoveries extended the
limits of each camp. Quapaw, Lincolnville, and
Sunnyside, each following the ore deposits of
its sector, coalesced finally into Quapaw. Tar
River and Hattonville eventually met over an
ore seam and came to be designated Commerce. The Picher Lead Company of Joplin,
while drilling prospect holes in an isolated
farming area northeast of Commerce in 1914,
made a rich strike and almost overnight a new
camp developed. The camp was named
Picher, and several satellite camps also came
into being.

A billion dollars worth of lead and zinc ores
was mined in the Tri-State District between
1900 and 1950, most of this produced in
Oklahoma's sector of the fabulous mineral
zone. In contrast to the coal camps of Indian
Territory, the lead-mining camps escaped the
despotism of the company town and the at-

tendant abuses, including scrip and production quotas.

Oklahoma's greatest fame as a mineral
producer has come from the petroleum industry. A strong beginning for preeminence as
a world leader was made on the eve of statehood with the discovery and development of
such heavy producers as the Glen Pool wells.
Between 1904 and 1907, Indian Territory oil
production jumped from 1 million to nearly
45 million barrels annually.

Oil was known in Oklahoma from earliest
times, appearing as a slick, or green oil, on
water in certain springs and streams. The
Chickasaw Nation was noted for its oil springs.
Oil was believed to have therapeutic qualities,
especially in the treatment of chronic diseases
like rheumatism and dropsy. So well known
were the Chickasaw oil springs that people
from as far away as Arkansas and Texas visited
these petroleum spas for their cures. At Boyd
Springs in the Chickasaw Nation near Ardmore, natural gas spewed from subterranean
crevices. The Indians used the place for a
council ground, and they lighted their camp
with natural gas by placing a tube or gun barrel
into the ground to control the gas flow and
serve as a burner.

The principal uses of petroleum before the
era of the automobile were as an illuminant
(kerosene or coal oil), a lubricant (axle
grease), and medicine. Oklahoma's first oil
well came in during the same year as the
famous Pennsylvania wells at Titusville in
1859. Lewis Ross, a Cherokee and brother of
Chief John Ross, operated a salt works on
Grand River in present Mayes County. While
digging a well to increase the saline flow at one
of his salt springs, he struck oil. His well flowed
at ten barrels a day for a year until the gas
pressure producing the free flow was dissi-
pated.

The pioneer Oklahoma wildcatter was Dr.
H. W. Faucett of New York. Faucett came to
Indian Territory from the Pennsylvania oil
fields during 1882 seeking petroleum concessions from the tribal governments. At his
encouragement the Choctaw council passed
an act creating the Choctaw Oil and Refining
Company and granted Faucett exclusive rights
for oil exploration. During the same year the
Cherokee council passed a similar act and

Steam sawmill in Indian Territory pine forest.

established the National Oil Company as the development firm for the Cherokee Nation. Backed by New York capitalists, Faucett set up drilling rigs at two locations, one in the Choctaw Nation on Boggy River, twelve miles west of Atoka, and the other at Alum Bluff on the Illinois River in the Going Snake District of the Cherokee Nation. Faucett drilled the Boggy River well to 1,400 feet and produced a show of oil and gas. Before he could sink a well in the Cherokee Nation, his financiers deserted him and he became ill and died. This ended both ventures, and commercial oil development was not resumed until just before statehood.

Another of Oklahoma's earliest industries was lumbering. Pine and mixed hardwood forests, concentrated for the most part in eastern Indian Territory, had long been the source of building material, furniture, and fuel. Water-powered sawmills were in operation before the Civil War. In 1868 steam-powered mills were introduced, but within six years the railroads really established Oklahoma's commercial lumbering industry. The first important lumber center was on the MKT line at Stringtown in the Choctaw Nation. Pine logs were cut in the mountain and plateau forests and hauled to the huge steam-powered mill. Rough, heavy saw logs emerged from the mill as planed lumber, ready for construction use.

The major lumber companies, notably the Long-Bell Lumber Company and the Fort Smith Lumber Company, came to the Choctaw forests during the 1890s. The Dierks enterprise began operations in 1898 as the Dierks Lumber and Coal Company, on a contract with the Kansas City Southern Railway Company to manufacture, sell, and ship lumber along that line.

The principal products fashioned from Indian Territory forests were railroad ties, bridge timbers, shingles, telegraph poles, fence posts, staves, cordwood, lath, mining timber, and construction lumber. Lumberjacks slashed away at Oklahoma's primeval forests, annually producing lumber shipments running into the millions of board feet. They took their heaviest toll in the pine forests, although ash, cottonwood, oak, hickory, cypress, walnut, and cedar also were used. The vast walnut stands in the Creek Nation were cut into logs, sawed into blocks, and shipped to Germany to be made into gunstocks.

A short-lived but action-charged economic activity in western Indian Territory was buffalo hunting. Before the Civil War a vast bison herd, possibly numbering 15 million, ranged the grand concourse of the Great Plains from Canada to the Río Grande. So great were the numbers and so overpowering was the influence of the bison that the range of these giant hairy beasts was known as "Buffalo Country." One writer claimed to have "traveled through buffaloes along the Arkansas

Buffalo hunters' camp. Skinners processing hides and tongues.

River for two hundred miles, almost one continuous herd, as close together as it is customary to herd cattle."

For centuries the plains tribes had been sustained by these herds. Their life-styles, migrations, religions, seasons, and cultures generally revolved around the buffalo. The resourceful Indian women used every part of the animal. They dried the meat for winter use, and they saved the tallow for seasoning and cooking grease. They dried the sinews and separated them into threads and bowstrings. They scraped the hair from the hide and wove it into ropes and coarse cloth. The bones were adapted as hoes, mattocks, scrapers, and other tools. Gall was saved for yellow paint, and buffalo chips served as fuel in a treeless country.

Nothing was wasted. The women cleaned the intestines, tied the ends, and used them for carrying water. Buffalo hides were stretched, dried, and tanned, then sewed together and used for tipi covers. The tanned hides were also used for making bullboats, clothing, footwear, bags for packing camp gear, and riding paraphernalia. Strips of hide were braided into lariats. Green hides were stretched and fitted for warriors' shields.

Warm buffalo robes required the most careful, skilled attention. The animals were killed at the season when their hair was longest, and the hair was left on the hide. The hide was stretched on pegs, fleshed, softened by a mixture of buffalo brains and water, and kneaded from time to time until it became a cured, soft, and pliable robe. The Plains Indians especially esteemed the rare albino or white buffalo and considered it sacred. A commercial hunter killed one during 1874 and sold the robe from it to a Dodge City trader for $1,000.

After the Civil War, the transcontinental railroads brought the commercial buffalo hunters to the Plains. The railroads also provided a means for shipping hides and meat, which was usually the hindquarters, tongues, and "jerked" or dried meat, to eastern markets. As the industry developed, the hide hunters became involved in a highly competitive, feverish race, wantonly slaughtering the bison for the harvest of hides but leaving the carcasses to rot. Soon the plains of western Oklahoma were littered with the bones of countless buffalo. Many men whose names were famous in the American West scouted for buffalo on the Sooner State's western margins. They included Buffalo Bill Cody, Pawnee Bill

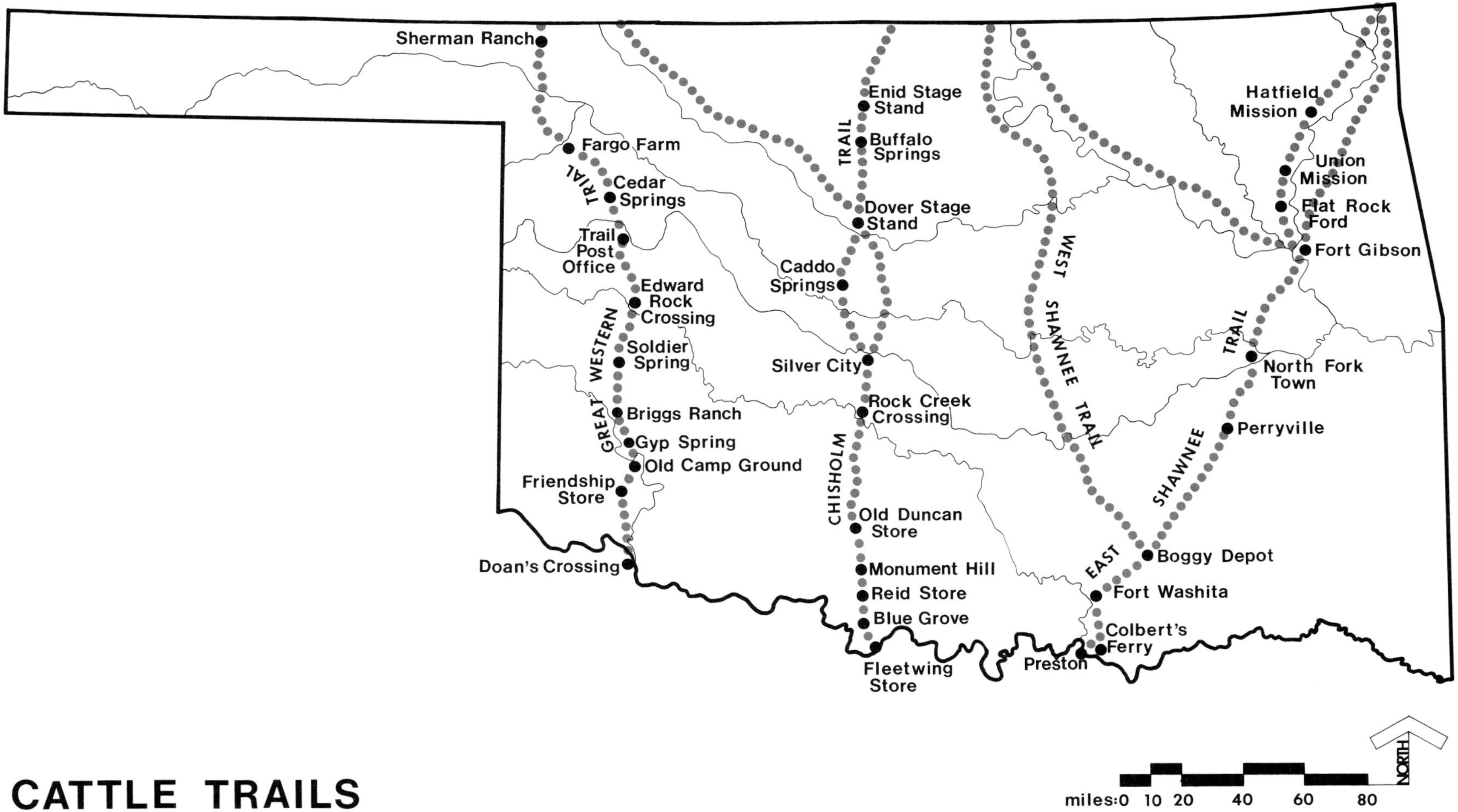

CATTLE TRAILS

Sherman Ranch

Doan's Crossing

Friendship Store

GREAT WESTERN

Gyp Spring

Old Camp Ground

Briggs Ranch

Soldier Spring

Edward Rock Crossing

Trail Post Office

Cedar Springs

TRIAL

Fargo Farm

Silver City

Caddo Springs

CHISHOLM

Fleetwing Store

Blue Grove

Reid Store

Monument Hill

Old Duncan Store

Rock Creek Crossing

Dover Stage Stand

Buffalo Springs

TRAIL

Enid Stage Stand

Preston

Colbert's Ferry

Fort Washita

EAST

Boggy Depot

SHAWNEE

Perryville

WEST SHAWNEE TRAIL

North Fork Town

TRAIL

Fort Gibson

Flat Rock Ford

Union Mission

Hatfield Mission

miles: 0 10 20 40 60 80

NORTH

drawn by : S Rogers

Lillie, Wild Bill Hickok, Pat Garrett, and Billy Dixon. Dixon recalled in his autobiography that

> the hunting was started by a firm of eastern hide-buyers, whose agents came to Hays City and other towns near the buffalo range and offered prices that made hide-hunting a profitable occupation.... The first offers were $1.00 each for cow hides and $2.00 for bull hides, which enabled us to make money rapidly. As the slaughtering increased and buffalo grew scarcer, prices were advanced, until $4.00 was being paid for bull hides by the fall of 1872.... Generally there were three or four men in an outfit, each having contributed his share for necessary expenses. They went where the range was best and buffalo most plentiful. A dug-out worth having was one with a big open fireplace, near the edge of a stream of good water, with plenty of wood along its banks. We often occupied the same dug-out for a month or more. Then, as the buffalo grew less plentiful, we shifted our camp and built a new dug-out, which was easily and quickly done. From where the buffalo were killed on the range, we hauled the hides to market.... I always did my own killing, and generally had two experienced men to do the skinning. A capable man could skin fifty buffaloes in a day, and usually was paid fifty dollars a month. I have paid as high as twenty cents a hide to a good skinner. We often killed the buffalo the day before they were to be skinned.

A herd of 40,000 buffalo was reported on the North Canadian near Fort Supply in 1877. A year later it had been so reduced by commercial hunters that Cheyenne-Arapaho hunters, seeking their winter meat supply, could bag only 218 bison, and in 1879 the Indian hunt was virtually a failure. A small herd was sighted in the Oklahoma Panhandle in 1885, and the last wild buffalo in Oklahoma, "a lonely old bull," was killed at Cold Spring in Cimarron County in October, 1890. The explanation for this phenomenal decline and destruction of the once great bison herds is found in the reports of kills made by commercial hunters. One Kansas newspaper announced that "the best kill on record . . . is that of Tom Nickson,

who killed 120 at one stand in forty minutes, and who, from September 15th to October 20th, killed 2,173 buffaloes." In one season Robert Wright, a trader at Dodge City, shipped by rail 200,000 hides, 200 cars of hindquarters, and two cars of buffalo tongues.

The prodigious slaughter of the buffalo in western Indian Territory opened the area for another important industry—the range cattle industry. One of Oklahoma's leading business enterprises today is stock raising. This industry was established among the Five Civilized Tribes before the Civil War, but it underwent drastic expansion after 1865, becoming a part of America's first billion-dollar industry. The key role played by Indian Territory in this giant postwar enterprise was twofold: first, it was a great cattle highway connecting Texas ranches and rail shipping points at the cow towns of Kansas; and second, during the 1880s, it was the ranchman's last frontier when the vast public domain pastures of the Great Plains were taken over by homesteaders.

After the war, the Texas ranges, largely untouched by foraging armies, were crowded with beef animals and locally each was worth only three to five dollars. Beef was scarce in the East, where cattle brought thirty-five to forty dollars a head. In 1866 some Texas cattlemen drove their herds north to take advantage of these favorable market conditions. The northward passage crossed Indian Territory and this led to the establishment of Oklahoma's first cattle highway—the East Shawnee Trail. Entering Indian Territory at Colbert's Ferry, this trail pushed north to Boggy Depot, then generally up the Texas Road to Baxter Springs, Kansas. From there north, the drovers encountered serious trouble. Settlers on the border, claiming the Texas cattle were carriers of disease that infected local stock, stampeded the immigrant herds and caused trouble generally. Only a few herds were able to reach the railroad at Sedalia, Missouri.

Joseph McCoy, an Illinois stockman, learned of the situation and developed a plan to market Texas cattle. The Kansas Pacific Railroad was building a line across Kansas to connect Kansas City and Denver. On the railroad at Abilene in north-central Kansas, well beyond the line of settlement, McCoy constructed loading pens and accommodations for the cowboys. He advertised the market in Texas, and during 1867, thirty-five thousand head of cattle reached Abilene, the first of the famous Kansas cow towns; seventy-five thousand were delivered the next year.

The Santa Fe, also building west across Kansas, was south of the Kansas Pacific and therefore closer for the Texans. New cow towns soon developed on this line. Of course, the same railroads that carried the Texas cattle to eastern markets brought homesteaders west. Their fenced farms soon closed the open range around the cow towns, forcing the cattle markets to move west. The Kansas towns of Newton, Ellsworth, Wichita, and Caldwell each had its heyday as a ripsnorting cow town. The last of these, Dodge City, the "Queen of the Cow Towns," was the most notorious of all.

The western movement of cow towns influenced the direction of cattle trails across Indian Territory. The Shawnee Trail branched at Boggy Depot to form the West Shawnee Trail, connecting with Newton and Wichita. The most famous cattle highway in western history was the Chisholm Trail, named for Jesse Chisholm, a mixed-blood Cherokee trader who blazed a trail from the mouth of the Little Arkansas (present Wichita) into the Leased District. Crossing at Red River Station, the Chisholm Trail followed a route fairly close to the 98th meridian into Caldwell and Wichita. The fourth Indian Territory cattle highway, the Dodge City or Great Western Cattle Trail, crossed the Red River at Doan's Store and went northwest across Indian Territory to Dodge City. Over 300,000 head of Texas cattle went up the trails in 1870, 600,000 in 1871, and during the first ten years of the northern drive, more than 3 million head crossed Oklahoma to the cow towns of Kansas.

The wealth being realized from stock raising in the American West attracted eastern and foreign capital, and corporate ranching rapidly developed on the Great Plains. Since these vast grasslands were a part of the federal public domain, homesteaders soon appeared on the scene and filed on choice quarter sections here and there, with the result that many cattlemen had to look elsewhere for ranges. The Indian Territory attracted many stock growers displaced by the nesters, as the set-

tlers were called. The possibilities of ranching in the Indian nations and reservations had been under consideration for some time before the 1880s. During the era of the northern drives, Texas cattlemen had allowed their herds to fatten on the grasslands adjacent to the trail, and beef contractors supplying the reservations of western Indian Territory had used Oklahoma ranges to bring their herds to prime condition before issue to the tribes.

Large-scale ranching came to Oklahoma around 1880. Cattlemen negotiated grass leases with the Cherokee, Choctaw, Chickasaw, Creek, and Seminole nations, but the pastures available were limited because many of the tribesmen were already established in stock raising and needed the grass themselves. Cattlemen had their greatest successes in finding new ranges on the reservations in western Indian Territory. By 1890 a portion of each reservation west of the Five Civilized Tribes was under lease to cattlemen. Virtually every acre of grass on the Kiowa, Comanche, Cheyenne, and Arapaho reservations was leased to ranchmen. During 1882, through their agent John D. Miles, the Cheyennes and Arapahoes negotiated an agreement with seven cattlemen, organized as the Cheyenne-Arapaho Stock Growers Association, for the use of 3 million acres of their reservation at two cents per acre per year. This syndicate grazed 200,000 head of cattle on the vast Indian reservation range. Their operation included publishing a newspaper called the *Cheyenne Transporter*, its columns devoted largely to articles of interest to stockmen, on such topics as brand registration and identification and the problem of cattle rustling.

The most extensive ranching enterprise in Oklahoma during this period was in the Cherokee Outlet. While the eastern third of the Outlet had been taken from the Cherokees by the federal government for the purpose of relocating tribes, about 6 million acres of choice grassland remained unassigned. In the late 1870s cattlemen began occupying, more or less permanently, certain ranges in the Outlet. The occupants increased each year with the result that this sixty-mile ribbon of grassland, extending from the Arkansas River to the 100th meridian, became one of the most famous ranges in the West.

Indian Territory ranch scene—branding.

Cherokee Nation officials at Tahlequah soon learned of this appropriation of their land by cattlemen, and they sent representatives west with authority to collect grazing fees. At first the annual levy was twenty-five cents a head. The grazing tax collected from the Outlet stock growers became such an important source of revenue for the Cherokee government that the treasurer of the nation came each year to Caldwell, Kansas, opened an office, and sent his deputies riding through the Outlet to collect grazing fees.

To gain exclusive use of the Outlet and to protect their ranges from rustlers, a group of cattlemen met at Caldwell, Kansas, in 1883 and established the Cherokee Strip Live Stock Association. Its membership consisted of more than a hundred individuals and corporations collectively owning more than 300,000 head of cattle. A five-year lease at $100,000 a year was negotiated with the Cherokee Nation for the exclusive use of the Outlet. This lease was renegotiated in 1888 for $200,000 a year. Association officers hired brand inspectors to police the range for rustlers and to inspect and record livestock shipments, adopted roundup schedules and rules, surveyed and mapped the Outlet, assigned particular ranges to members, and set rules for fencing ranges.

Cowboys watched over the herds of the Cherokee Outlet ranchers. One old rider who worked for various cattle companies around Fort Supply recalled that typical cowboy gear included a fancy saddle, a poncho and bedroll or blanket, a coiled lariat, and a pair of leather chaps to protect the rider's legs when riding through the brush. Nearly all his "compadres" were armed with six-shooters and Winchester rifles and wore large handkerchiefs about their necks. On Sundays the riders entertained themselves with riding and breaking the wild horses that in the early days ranged in herds over western Oklahoma. Later, ranch remudas were maintained with mustangs shipped in from farther west.

An important factor in the rapid postwar economic development of Indian Territory was the steady increase in the non-Indian population. After 1865 great numbers of people migrated to the states and territories of the American West. Except for the Indian Territory, settlement on land in the public domain not only was legal but was strongly promoted. There was a shadow over the rights and legal status of settlers in Indian Territory, so their entry into the future Sooner State was referred to as the "silent migration." The cumulative effect of this extralegal entry was shown in 1907 when the Twin Territories—Oklahoma Territory and Indian Territory—were fused into Oklahoma and admitted to the Union as the forty-sixth state. Oklahoma at statehood had a population of nearly 1 million. The domain of the Five Civilized Tribes, comprising at statehood the eastern half of Oklahoma, had a total population of about 750,000,

Preparing for the trail drive, Indian Territory ranch.

with the ratio of non-Indians to Indians at least seven to one.

The phenomenal tenfold increase in population in eastern Oklahoma can be accounted for in several ways. Federal laws made it a criminal offense to enter the limits of any Indian nation or reservation without proper authority. To meet the requirements of the law, or to evade it, the intruders and the Indians worked out complex arrangements. Marriage was one approach. By marrying an Indian girl, a man gained the privileges and benefits of tribal citizenship, including exemption from taxes and free use of tribal land. By 1877 it was reported that seven hundred outsiders had married Cherokee women, sixty had taken Creek wives, and fifteen hundred were married to Choctaw and Chickasaw women. One intermarried Chickasaw had imported a hundred families as tenants on his vast Washita valley farm. In 1886 it was reported that the Washita valley was almost one continuous farm for fifty miles, most of the holdings farmed by white and black tenants; one operation covered eight thousand acres, another four thousand.

To hasten economic reconstruction, the tribal governments adopted permit laws that allowed mechanics and laborers and their families to settle in their respective nations. The permit system was an important source of revenue for the Five Civilized Tribes. The annual license or permit cost $2.50 for la-

borers, and five dollars for mechanics and farmers. Indian leaders claimed the new source of labor was essential to replace the slaves who had been liberated by the Civil War, and they used both the tenant and share-cropper systems to develop Indian Territory farms. Most of the farm labor force emigrated from Arkansas, Alabama, and Mississippi. In addition, many professional and business people came to Indian Territory during these times. They included lawyers, bankers, coal and timber operators, and railroad promoters. By 1907 the Choctaw Nation alone reported 200,000 Indians, whites, and blacks. The sizeable foreign immigration to the coal camps has already been noted.

One of the most interesting early postwar enterprises in Indian Territory was the tobacco industry. The Cherokee Reconstruction Treaty of 1866 included a clause that permitted tribal citizens to produce, manufacture, ship, and market any product throughout the United States without restraint, exempt from any federal tax. During 1868, Elias C. Boudinot and Stand Watie purchased a tobacco factory at Hannibal, Missouri, and moved it to the Cherokee Nation. At their settlement, called Boudiville, near the Arkansas line, Boudinot and Watie produced chewing tobacco, snuff, treated leaf, and pipe tobacco. Although they sold their products all over the United States, their principal market was the adjoining southwestern states.

Tobacco dealers wailed that their markets in Missouri, Arkansas, and Texas had been wiped out by the untaxed, and thus cheaper, tobacco produced at Boudiville. Powerful business interests were involved, and Congress passed revenue laws annulling this Cherokee privilege. A posse of federal deputy marshals, responding to a complaint from the commissioner of internal revenue in Washington, seized the Boudinot-Watie tobacco works. The Cherokee owners were arrested on a charge of violating the federal revenue laws and their plant confiscated and dismantled.

The Indian defendants were convicted in the lower federal courts, but they gained a hearing in the United States Supreme Court on a writ of error. The Cherokee attorneys claimed an invasion of rights under the historic principle that the United States Constitution and treaties comprised the supreme law of the land, superior to laws made by Congress. The High Court handed down its decision in 1870 in the famous "Cherokee Tobacco Case." The Supreme Court Justices in effect drew a distinction between treaties made with foreign nations and treaties made with Indian tribes, declaring that the 1868 revenue laws did supersede the Cherokee Treaty of 1866, thus upholding the lower courts' ruling.

One writer observed:

> The proposition that an act of Congress could be intended to, and did in fact, supersede and qualify any provision of a treaty made with an Indian tribe, was a startling innovation that alarmed the Indians. It emboldened the whites to predict, and the Indians to fear, that the new principle would be used to break down the protection they had found in the terms of their treaties against white aggression.

This is exactly what happened. A scant three months after the "Cherokee Tobacco Case" decision, Congress passed the famous act that provided that no additional treaties would be made with the Indian tribes. Thereafter, all tribes were subject to the laws of Congress and the executive orders of the president.

Notes on Sources, Chapter 13

Oklahoma was the scene of intensive economic exploitation during the period between 1870 and 1900. Information on the Indian Territory mining, transportation, lumbering, hunting, and ranching enterprises is found in V. V. Masterson, *The Katy Railroad and the Last Frontier* (Norman, 1952); James L. Allhands, "Construction of the Frisco Railroad Line in Oklahoma," *Chronicles of Oklahoma* 3 (September, 1925): 229–39; J. F. Holden, "The Story of an Adventure in Railroad Building," *Chronicles of Oklahoma* 11 (March, 1933): 637–66; Walter A. Johnson, "Brief History of the Missouri, Kansas-Texas Railroad Lines," *Chronicles of Oklahoma* 24 (September, 1946): 340–58; Fred Floyd, "The Struggle for Railroads in the Oklahoma Panhandle," *Chronicles of Oklahoma* 54 (Winter, 1976–77): 489–518; Arrell M. Gibson, *Wilderness Bonanza: The Tri-State District of Missouri, Kansas, and Oklahoma* (Norman, 1972); Paul Nesbitt, "J. J. McAlester," *Chronicles of Oklahoma* 11 (June, 1933): 758–64; Frederick Lynne Ryan, *The Rehabilitation of Oklahoma Coal Mining Communities* (Norman, 1935); S. B. Bayne, *Derricks of Destiny* (New York, 1924); Wilbur F. Cloud, *Petroleum Production* (Norman, 1937); Angie Debo, *Tulsa: From Creek Town to Oil Capital* (Norman, 1943); Wayne Gard, *The Great Buffalo Hunt* (New York, 1959); James H. Cook, *Fifty Years on the Old Frontier* (New Haven, Conn., 1923); Olive K. Dixon, *The Life of Billy Dixon* (Dallas, 1927); Wayne Gard, *The Chisholm Trail* (Norman, 1954); Evan G. Barnard, *A Rider in the Cherokee Strip* (Boston, 1936); Edward E. Dale, *The Range Cattle Industry: Ranching on the Great Plains from 1865 to 1925* (Norman, 1930; new ed., 1960); Charles Francis Colcord, *Autobiography of Charles Francis Colcord* (Tulsa, 1970); and William W. Savage, Jr., *The Cherokee Strip Live Stock Association* (Columbia, Mo., 1973).

Chapter 14

Oklahoma Territory

For a few years after the Civil War, it appeared that Oklahoma, checkered with tribal nations and reservations, would remain a permanent Indian community. However, by the late 1870s most of the arable, well-watered land in the Trans-Mississippi West had been homesteaded, and land-hungry settlers began casting covetous glances at the Indian Territory. The future Sooner State was off limits to non-Indians in the postwar period except for the cattlemen with grazing leases in the western part and permit holders among the Five Civilized Tribes. The chronicle of devious actions that broke the barriers to settlement and opened the Indian nations to the homesteaders makes the western railroad promotions, the mining prospectuses, and the beef bonanza schemes seem tame by comparison.

It was recorded in Chapter 13 that the railroads were prominent in the movement to open Indian Territory to settlement. The MKT, Frisco, Rock Island, and Santa Fe lines crossed the Indian country and linked the Missouri and Kansas trade centers with the greater Southwest. The sparsely settled Indian nations and reservations made only small use of these lines, except in the mining and timber regions of eastern Oklahoma, as noted by a Katy official who complained that his was the first railway company in history to construct a line "two hundred and fifty miles through a tunnel." Of course, the railroad companies were hopeful that Indian Territory would soon be settled with a farmer on every quarter section, that thriving towns would develop along the tracks, and that tons of produce would be freighted to distant markets.

Equally interested in opening Oklahoma to settlement were officials of banking and mercantile firms in Saint Louis, Kansas City, Topeka, and Wichita, who saw the Indian Territory as a new source for investments and markets. Because railroads, banks, and large business combines were generally unpopular with the public, a direct campaign by them to open Indian Territory to settlement probably would have aroused hostility. The homeseeker, more closely connected with the image of American democracy, therefore was selected as a likely stalking horse for the corporate interests. Once the territory was opened, it was argued, all would benefit, including the homeseeker.

The authority for removing the barriers to settlement had to come from Congress. The railroad lobby, one of the real powers behind the scenes in the national government during the post–Civil War era, was responsible for most of the dozens of bills introduced in Congress between 1866 and 1879 proposing Indian Territory for statehood. Interesting names were proposed by these bills for the future Sooner State, including Neosho and Lincoln. On March 17, 1870, Senator Benjamin F. Rice of Arkansas introduced a measure providing for the organization of Indian Territory under the name Territory of Oklahoma.

Each proposal met vigorous opposition. Of course the leaders of the Five Civilized Tribes opposed the move, and the next most powerful group working against the opening of Indian Territory was the cattlemen's lobby. Arrayed against these guardians of the Indian Territory were regional railway companies, banks, farm machinery manufacturers, and wholesale distributors. They hired professional promoters called "Boomers" to mobilize the homeseekers. T. C. Sears, an attorney

Elias C. Boudinot, Cherokee, who introduced the idea of opening the Unassigned Lands to settlement.

for the MKT, early in 1879 announced through the newspapers that he and Elias C. Boudinot, the Cherokee attorney, had examined the treaties laws, and land title question for Indian Territory. He claimed they had found that 14 million acres of land in Indian Territory belonged to the public domain of the United States, subject to entry by qualified homeseekers. "These lands are among the richest in the world," Sears declared. "Public attention is being called to them and my opinion is that, if Congress shall fail to make suitable provision for the opening of the Territory within a very short time, the people will take the matter into their own hands and go down there and occupy and cultivate those lands."

On February 17, 1879, the *Chicago Times* published an article written by Boudinot on the land question in Indian Territory. The Cherokee attorney reiterated his claim that 14 million acres in the Indian country awaited the homeseeker. An accompanying map showed this vast tract to be situated in the Kiowa, Comanche, and Cheyenne-Arapaho reservations, the Unassigned Lands (the so-called Ok-

lahoma District containing nearly two million acres), and Greer County, then in dispute with Texas. Special attention was given to the Oklahoma District. Boudinot's article was widely copied by newspapers over the United States.

Boudinot's article and his many public speeches on the subject, along with a massive distribution of Boomer literature describing the wondrous bonanza opportunities awaiting the homeseeker in Indian Territory, had the desired effect. Three "Oklahoma colonies" were organized during the spring of 1879—one at Topeka, one in north Texas, and a third at Kansas City. The third Oklahoma colony, promoted by Charles C. Carpenter, was the most extensive effort of this period. Branches of Carpenter's Oklahoma colony were established near the Cherokee border at Independence and Coffeyville, Kansas. Carpenter, an adventurer in the mold of Buffalo Bill Cody, had led a caravan of settlers into the forbidden Black Hills country of the deadly Sioux in Dakota Territory. Indeed, his success in the Black Hills invasion led him to hope for an equally fortunate outcome in the Indian Territory.

Carpenter's Oklahoma colony gathered on the Cherokee border in preparation for a thrust into the rich farming lands of Indian Territory. His enthusiastic followers captured the attention of the press, and newspaper stories of Carpenter's scheme reached the governments of the Five Civilized Tribes. The principal chiefs protested, and the secretary of war stationed troops at strategic crossings into the "Promised Land." Carpenter was officially warned and his following faded.

On the heels of Carpenter's fiasco, the "Big Three" in the Boomer movement—David L. Payne, William L. Couch, and Samuel Crocker—launched their campaign to open Indian Territory to the homesteader. Inspired and encouraged by the writings and speeches of Boudinot, a steadily increasing stream of homeseekers from all points of the compass began arriving in the south Kansas towns during 1879. Captain David L. Payne was the Boomer leader who organized them into a well-disciplined group and eventually gained for each the right to a homestead in Indian Territory. Payne, Indiana-born, came to Kansas Territory in 1858, and as a frontier guide and scout became acquainted with much of the Southwest. He served in the Union Army, was elected to several terms in the Kansas legislature, and held minor political posts in Washington. During 1879, Payne appeared in the south Kansas towns to organize the homeseekers. Quickly he established a string of tidy Boomer camps on the environs of Arkansas City, Caldwell, Hunnewell, and other border towns. Collectively, these were called Payne's Oklahoma Colony. He regularly visited the camps and made speeches to keep the hopes of his followers high. He also published a newspaper called the *Oklahoma War Chief*, which aided morale.

The regimen of Boomer camp life had heavy religious overtones. With words alone, the eloquent Payne kept his followers enthusiastic for years. His favorite biblical quote was "and the Lord commanded unto Moses, 'Go forth and possess the Promised Land,' " and the marching song for the homeseekers was "On to Beulah land." Each member paid Payne two dollars for a certificate guaranteeing a quarter section or twenty-five dollars for a town lot in Oklahoma.

Between 1879 and 1884, Payne led several Boomer expeditions into Indian Territory. His most impressive sortie occurred during the spring of 1880 when a column of homeseekers marched to the North Canadian in central Oklahoma. Payne's colonists erected a stockade, platted their town, and began opening fields for planting. When government scouts discovered their location, United States cavalry from nearby Fort Reno arrested Payne and the colonists and escorted them to Kansas. Captain Payne was aware of the publicity value of these Boomer raids and always took newspaper reporters on his excursions.

Later, Payne used the federal courtrooms at Fort Smith, Wichita, and Topeka as a forum to popularize the notion of the homeseeker's rights in the Indian country. On one occasion he was arrested on a charge of conspiracy against the United States and was tried in United States District Court at Topeka. Federal Judge C. G. Foster dismissed the government charge on the grounds that title to the Oklahoma lands was vested in the United States; this placed them in the public domain, the settlement thereon by citizens was not a

David L. Payne, leader of the Boomers.

crime. This naturally gave much encouragement to Payne's followers who looked forward to obtaining homes in the new land.

The Boomer colonies were an enduring protest against the barriers to settlement in Indian Territory, and Boomer raids were in effect demonstrations that evoked widespread interest and sympathy. Payne maintained an incessant pressure on the federal government. Once the Oklahoma colonies on the Kansas border were well-established, he set to work organizing Oklahoma colonies in north Texas, and launched Boomer forays across the Red River into Indian country.

When the Boomer chief died mysteriously in a Wellington, Kansas, hotel room in November, 1884, his lieutenants, Captain William L. Couch and Samuel Crocker, succeeded to the leadership of the Oklahoma colonies and continued the Boomer raids. Although in each case the colonists were ejected as trespassers, their tenacity attracted national publicity and eventually produced the desired result.

Harassment by federal officials continued. Crocker was arrested on July 10, 1885, on a charge of inciting insurrection and seditious conspiracy. The *Oklahoma War Chief* editor was held in jail for a month; suddenly the prosecution dismissed the charges and he was released. Another Boomer leader, W. H. Osburn, at one time Payne's secretary, organized the Osburn Oklahoma Colony soon after the death of the famous Boomer chief and published the *Oklahoma Pilgrim*, a paper similar to the *Oklahoma War Chief*. He, too, endured considerable harassment from government officials.

Nevertheless the Boomer campaign to popularize the Indian country and win support for removing the barriers to settlement was having a telling effect. Boomer charges of inequity and injustice in the use of Indian lands, such as cattlemen being treated as a privileged group, won over the Knights of Labor and other powerful groups. One labor leader delcared, "The cause of Oklahoma colonists was the cause of the poor man, the laborer."

Meanwhile, the Boomer cause was winning powerful friends in Congress. Chief among the sympathetic congressmen were James B. Weaver of Iowa, Charles G. Mansur of Missouri, and William Springer of Illinois. Sidney L. Clarke, former congressman from Kansas, was also active for the cause. Weaver, Mansur, and Springer regularly introduced bills that provided for opening the Indian country. Government attorneys pointed out that the Creeks and the Seminoles had what was called a "residual interest" in the lands of western Oklahoma, especially the Unassigned Lands, which had been taken from them for the purpose of resettling tribes, and that the area had not been used for this treaty-designated purpose. Until this interest was quieted, federal legal counsel claimed the land did not properly belong to the public domain. Negotiations were begun during 1889 to remove this obstacle. Pleasant Porter, a Creek leader, agreed to relinquish to the United States all Creek claims to western lands in return for payment to the Creek nation of $2,280,000. A Seminole delegation headed by John F. Brown signed a similar agreement quieting that nation's claim to any western lands in return for payment of $1,912,000.

Just before Congress adjourned on March 3, 1889, a rider, called the Springer Amendment, was attached to the Indian Appropriation Bill providing for the opening of the Oklahoma District or Unassigned Lands. President Benjamin Harrison issued a proclamation that declared the Unassigned Lands would be opened to settlement on April 22, 1889.

Until this time, in populating the public domain of the American West, there had been such an abundance of desirable land available for homeseekers that the settlement rate had been continuous. By 1889 most of the good land had been taken and the number of homeseekers far exceeded the homesteads available. Because the eventual opening of Indian Territory had been popularized by the Boomers, and because the Unassigned Lands represented such a small settlement area (about 2 million acres), government planners responsible for the opening realized that there would be many more homeseekers than claims available. To give equal opportunity to all interested persons, it was decided to settle the area by a novel procedure—the land run. The rule against trespassing on Indian Territory lands was lifted three days previous to the date of the run to allow homeseekers time to gather on the four borders of the Unassigned Lands. Within a few hours homesteader camps crowded to the southern boundary of the Cherokee Outlet, east in the Sac and Fox country, south along the Canadian in the Chickasaw Nation, and west in the Cheyenne-Arapaho country.

Monday, April 22, 1889, dawned clear and bright. Fifty thousand homeseekers thronged the borders of Captain Payne's "New Canaan," awaiting the starting signal. Then from the detachment of United States cavalry assigned for the day to supervise the race for homesteads there emerged a booted trooper:

Riding to a high point of ground, where he could be seen for miles each way with a flag in one hand and a bugle in the other, the signal officer took his position. At precisely 12 o'clock he raised the bugle to his lips and gave the signal blast, long and loud, waving and dropping the flag at the same moment. Then began the race for homes. . . . It was a race free for all. None was barred. Neither sex, age, nor circumstances were imposed as conditions. The government was the

Arrested "Sooners," homeseekers entering Oklahoma Territory before the designated opening day, being ejected.

starter, and the American people were the racers. Cheers and shouts from fifty thousand souls, a refrain to the bugle notes, sent their echoes o'er hill and plain, arousing into life the solitude of the enchanting surroundings. The race began. The fleet racer and plow horse are given free rein, and plied with whip and spur. The long railway trains, too, with ear-piercing shrieks from their engine whistles, joined in the race. From the windows of every coach came shouts of cheer and the waving of flags and handkerchiefs to those that were racing to the south on either side of the fast-flying trains. The ranks of the racers are diminishing on every side; they are seen to leap from their horses; a happy shout, a waving of their hat, the setting of a flag or stake. They have taken a homestead.

By evening, nearly every homestead claim and town lot (townsites included Guthrie, Kingfisher, Oklahoma City, and Norman) in the settlement zone had been staked. Tents, wagon boxes, dugouts, and crude cabins sheltered the original settlers of Oklahoma Territory, although one enterprising lumberman met the settlers at Norman with a railroad boxcar full of building lumber. A. D. Acres established the first lumber yard in Norman, one that is still in existence.

Congress, in its rush to open the Unassigned Lands, had failed to provide for territorial government. For well over a year the settlers, using grass-roots democracy and vigilante action, provided the essential rudiments of law and order for this raw frontier community. In each town citizens organized a local government usually consisting of an elected mayor and a town marshal. Citizen boards were established to arbitrate disputes over land claims, and schools were organized and supported on a subscription basis.

During the summer of 1889, local conventions at Guthrie and Oklahoma City met to organize a territorial government. Because many of the delegates were of the opinion that only Congress had this authority, the conventions helped publicize the need for a legally constituted government by sending petitions on the subject to Washington. Finally, on May 2, 1890, Congress passed the Oklahoma Organic Act. This became one of the most important laws for the Oklahoma Territory because from it present Oklahoma state government evolved. In addition, the Oklahoma Organic Act marked the beginning of a tutelage period during which the people of Oklahoma Territory received experience in self-government preliminary to statehood.

The Oklahoma Organic Act provided for a territorial governor and a supreme court of three judges (later increased to five, then to seven as the territory grew), who also served as district judges, all appointed by the president of the United States. A bicameral legislative assembly (the house to contain twenty-six members, the council thirteen members) and a delegate to Congress were to be elected by the people. The laws of Nebraska were to apply to Oklahoma Territory until the assembly adopted a code for the territory. County and township governments were to be organized, and until the people elected officials for local government posts, the governor was to fill these positions by appointment. The Oklahoma Organic Act contained an important provision for the growth of Oklahoma Territory in that all reservations in western Indian Territory, when opened to settlement, were automatically annexed to Oklahoma Territory.

The Organic Act attached No Man's Land to Oklahoma Territory. This ribbon of land had been a sort of governmental orphan, its domain evolving from incidents of national history. Its eastern boundary was established at 100°W longitude by the Adams Onís Treaty in 1819. The southern boundary came from the annexation of Texas in 1845 and the Compromise of 1850, which took some land from Texas and set that boundary at 36°30'N latitude. The western boundary at 103°W longitude evolved from the Mexican War conquest, the Treaty of Guadalupe-Hidalgo in 1848, and the organization of New Mexico Territory in 1850. Its northern boundary was established by the organization of Kansas Territory in 1854 with a southern boundary at 37°N latitude.

Called No Man's Land because it was not a part of any state or territory, Oklahoma's Panhandle also had other names—Public Land Strip, Cimarron Territory, and Robber's Roost. The last name was given to the area after the Civil War because, free from the jurisdiction and law enforcement of any state or territory, it became known throughout the West as a rendezvous for outlaws, cattle rustlers, gamblers, and the general run of frontier riffraff. During the 1880s, cattlemen and nesters began settling No Man's Land. They found life and property in constant danger because of the lawless men who flourished at Beaver, Hardesty, and other settlements. During 1886 the law-abiding citizens banded together in vigilante committees and purged No Man's Land of its renegade population.

In order to establish regular and enduring law and order, the vigilante committees began a movement to organize the Panhandle into a formal territory of the United States. In 1887 in a grass-roots democracy fashion, the six thousand people of No Man's Land elected delegates for a convention which met at Beaver City. The convention organized Cimarron Territory, established government for the area, and elected J. R. Linley governor. O. G. Chase was elected as territorial delegate to Congress. Chase's purpose was to gain congressional recognition and approval of the action taken by the Beaver City convention. The Congress had other plans for Cimarron Territory, however, and by the Oklahoma Organic Act of 1890 the Panhandle area was absorbed by Oklahoma Territory.

The Organic Act provided for the future Sooner State's first seven counties. Logan, Oklahoma, Cleveland, Canadian, Kingfisher, and Payne counties were organized in the Unassigned Lands. The seventh was Beaver County in the Panhandle. Beaver County was eventually divided into Cimarron, Beaver, and Texas counties.

The Organic Act designated Guthrie as the territorial capital, and Oklahoma territorial government began during the summer of 1890 with the arrival in the capital of Oklahoma's first official family. President Harrison had appointed George W. Steele of Indiana to the office of governor. Robert Martin of El Reno received appointment as territorial secretary; Horace Speed of Guthrie was appointed United States district attorney; and Warren S. Lurty from West Virginia became United States marshal. The first justices of the Territorial Supreme Court were Edward B. Green from Illinois, Abraham J. Seay of Missouri, and John B. Clark from Wisconsin.

At the first election on August 5, 1890, Oklahoma voters selected members for the legislative assembly. The political composition of the house was fourteen Republicans, eight Democrats, and four legislators from the People's Party Alliance. The council consisted of six Republicans, five Democrats, and two People's Party Alliance members. When the First Assembly convened on August 29, 1890,

Downtown Oklahoma City, April 30, 1889.

the Republicans and Democrats were divided, and the People's Party Alliance members, though a minority in the assembly, were assertive and highly capable, and therefore managed to dominate both houses. People's Party Alliance member George W. Gardenhire became president of the council, and his fellow party member, Arthur N. Daniels, won election as speaker of the house. Oklahoma Territory's second election, November 4, 1890, was held to select a delegate to Congress. Joseph McCoy, the cattleman famous for developing the northern drives from Texas ranches to the Kansas cow towns, ran as the Democratic candidate. His Republican opponent, David A. Harvey, won the election and became Oklahoma's first territorial delegate to Congress.

Much basic work faced the legislative assembly members in activating the government set forth in the Organic Act. Most of their time, however, was spent in quarreling over the future location of the capital, for Oklahoma Territory already had generated a number of vigorous, aggressive towns. Guthrie, with a population of 5,884, was the largest, followed by Oklahoma City with 5,086; Kingfisher, 1,234; Norman, 764; Stillwater, 625; and El Reno, 519. The leading contenders for the capital were Guthrie, Oklahoma City, and Kingfisher. Bills were passed establishing the capital first at Oklahoma City, then at Kingfisher, but Governor Steele vetoed both pro-

posals. Norman, Stillwater, and Edmond benefited from this struggle by shrewd application of their support, through which Norman was assigned the Territorial University, Stillwater was assigned the Territorial Agricultural and Mechanical College, and Edmond was designated as the site of the Territorial Normal School.

Governor Steele alienated various factions by his vetoes of the bills to establish the capital either at Oklahoma City or at Kingfisher. Unable to gain acceptance of his legislative program, Steele finally resigned on October 18, 1891, and left to his successor the unresolved and growing problems of territorial administration. Complexity was assured by the Springer Amendment to the Indian Appropriations Bills of 1889, which had provided for the original land opening, and which also authorized the president to appoint a commission to negotiate with the tribes of western Indian Territory to make their surplus lands available for settlement. The Organic Act itself contained a provision that declared that as the reservations of western Indian Territory were opened to settlement, each automatically became a part of Oklahoma Territory. The new governor was thus assured of an enlarged jurisdiction.

President Harrison appointed the commission authorized by the Springer Amendment in July, 1889. Known in Oklahoma history by two names—the Jerome Commission and the

Downtown Oklahoma City, September 1, 1889.

Cherokee Commission—the membership of this group consisted of Chairman David H. Jerome, former governor of Michigan; Warren G. Sayre of Indiana; and Alfred M. Wilson of Arkansas. In fewer than five years the Jerome Commission completed agreements with most of the tribes holding reservations in western Indian Territory. The common pattern of negotiations was to obtain an agreement with the leaders of each tribe that provided for the assignment of a 160–acre allotment in severalty to each man, woman, and child whose name appeared on the tribal roll. The remaining land was declared surplus and purchased by the federal government for homesteading.

Two years after the first land opening, the Sac and Fox, Potawatomi, Shawnee, and Iowa surplus lands, amounting to about 900,000 acres, were opened to settlement. On September 22, 1891, more than 20,000 persons, three times the number of claims available, made the run for homesteads in the Sac and Fox country. Payne, Cleveland, and Logan counties were expanded from portions of this addition to Oklahoma Territory, and two new counties, Lincoln and Pottawatomie, were created from the remainder.

On April 19, 1892, the 3.5 million surplus acres of the Cheyenne-Arapaho country were made available to homeseekers. Only 25,000 participated in this land run, and nearly 2 million acres in the western portion of the

Cheyenne-Arapaho country were passed over by the settlers, principally because the land was regarded as unfit for farming. These avoided claims were taken up by farmers and ranchers on a more leisurely basis. From this accretion, Oklahoma Territory received six new counties: C County became Blaine; D County became Dewey; E County became Day; F County became Roger Mills; G County became Custer; and H County became Washita. Additions were made to the already established counties of Kingfisher and Canadian. Later, Day County was abolished by the Oklahoma Constitutional Convention, and part of it was attached to Ellis County and part to Roger Mills County.

One of the attractive portions of Indian Territory was the Cherokee Outlet. The Jerome Commission spent many difficult sessions at Tahlequah with the officials of the Cherokee nation before it won an agreement to transfer title of the Outlet's six million acres to the United States for $8,595,736. Two tribes settled in the Outlet, the Tonkawas and Pawnees, also negotiated allotment agreements with the Jerome Commision, so that their surplus lands were included in the great area opened to homeseekers on September 16, 1893. More than 100,000 settlers raced for the 40,000 claims in the Outlet. In the earlier land runs, it had been customary to reserve sections 16 to 36 of each township for schools. In the Outlet, in addition to the school reserves,

Downtown Oklahoma City, September 1, 1906.

section 13 was reserved for territorial educational institutions and section 33 was set aside for public buildings. Pawnee, Kay, Noble, Grant, Garfield, Woods, and Woodward counties were established initially, and additional counties were to be created by the Oklahoma Constitutional Convention.

The format for modern northern and western Oklahoma was nearly completed after the Outlet run. The Kickapoos were finally brought to terms and their tiny reservation, situated just east of the old Unassigned Lands, was opened by run in 1895. This small reservation had so little surplus land that, to sate the land-hungry settlers, the Kickapoos received allotments of only eighty acres each.

With each land run there had been an increase in Sooner activity. A Sooner was a homeseeker who illegally entered the settlement zone before the scheduled run. He would select a choice homestead, hide in the brush, and at the propitious moment appear to stake his claim. Unlawful entry was so widespread by the time of the Kickapoo run that many officials charged that possibly half of all claims were filed by Sooners. To thwart these cheats, the United States government searched for a foolproof method for opening additional Indian reservations.

Before another opening occurred, Oklahoma Territory received a land increment by court action. From surveys of southwest Oklahoma dating as far back as 1852 when Ran-dolph B. Marcy and George B. McClellan led expeditions across the region, the North Fork of Red River had been regarded as the major branch of the stream separating Indian Territory from Texas. In 1880 cattlemen entered the area and a Texas county named for Texas Lieutenant Governor John A. Greer was organized with Mangum as the county seat. The federal government discovered the error in original surveys and mapping, and claimed that because the North Fork was only a tributary of the Red, Greer County belonged to Indian Territory. In July, 1884, President Cleveland issued a proclamation warning people not to settle Greer County until the dispute was settled, but his order was ignored by the Texas cattlemen. Suit was filed in federal court to determine title to Greer County in 1890. The United States Supreme Court rendered its decision against Texas on March 16, 1896, and directed that Greer County be attached to Oklahoma Territory. The awarded territory contained about 1.4 million acres.

Congress then passed a law in 1896 that permitted long-time settlers to file on 160 acres already occupied. The law also gave these settlers the privilege of purchasing an additional quarter section at one dollar an acre. In Greer County there remained about four thousand homesteads available for entry under the land laws of the United States. This new addition to Oklahoma Territory remained as Greer County until the Oklahoma Constitutional Convention in 1906 divided it into Jackson, Greer, Harmon, and a portion of Beckham counties.

Governmentally, western Oklahoma was nearly in its present form in 1896; in August, 1901, the last remaining Indian land in that section was opened to settlement. By that year the Kiowa, Comanche, Wichita, Caddo, and Apache lands had been allotted, and the surplus, amounting to more than 2 million acres, was opened. Instead of the customary run for opening a settlement zone, a lottery was used. Hopeful settlers numbering 165,000 registered at Fort Sill and Fort Reno for a drawing to distribute the 15,000 claims. There was no "soonerism" because the number of claim tickets drawn equalled the number of homesteads available. Several areas were reserved before the opening, including sections 16, 36, 13, and 33; the Fort Sill Military Reservation of 56,000 acres; the Wichita Mountain Forest Reserve of 58,000 acres; and the Big Pasture Reserve of 480,000 acres. In addition, half a section in each of the three counties (Kiowa, Comanche, and Caddo) was set aside to provide income for public purposes. The Big Pasture Reserve, which included land in both Comanche and Tillman counties, was later sold at public auction in 1906. Interested parties could bid on several 160-acre tracts but could buy only one tract each. Big Pasture land sold at this auction for about ten dollars per acre.

Small enclaves of Indian land west of the Five Civilized Tribes still remained under tribal control after 1900. The Ponca, Otoe, Missouri, and Kaw reservations, by act of Congress in 1904, were opened and attached to Oklahoma Territory. After allotment, the Ponca Reservation contained only 320 acres of surplus land; the Kaw Reservation was divided entirely among the tribal members; and on the Otoe and Missouri Reservations there were 51,000 surplus acres for sale to settlers. The Osage nation was attached to Oklahoma Territory for court purposes by an act of Congress in 1893, but this tribe had been exempted from allotment under the Dawes Act of 1887. Therefore, in 1906, Congress passed an act providing for liquidating this last reservation west of the Five Civilized Tribes. There was no surplus for the settlers in the Osage nation because all of this land went to the Indians, with each tribal citizen receiving more than 500 acres.

The energy, tenacity, and ambition of the homesteaders soon converted central and western Oklahoma from a wilderness to a thriving agricultural region. Most of the early settlers were poor. Cash crops eventually were adapted to this erratic prairie-plains environment, but in those early, harsh days, survival was a clear and constant question. Lacking money, the nesters bartered butter and eggs for salt, sugar, and coffee, and it was common to trade a horse or cow for a year's supply of flour. The men gathered buffalo bones on the prairie and sold them to fertilizer companies for seven to nine dollars a ton. Some settlers cut cedar posts and sold them to ranchers at two cents a post. After the crops were in, many fathers and sons followed the wheat harvest northward to Kansas to earn money to equip their frontier farms.

Many settlers were from the East, and drastic adjustment, not only in personal habits but also in farming techniques, was required of them. The soil was carpeted with deep-rooted, thick buffalo grass. Special tools were used to cut this cover and to open fields for planting. The sod plow, already in use on the northern plains, accomplished this efficiently. Two kinds of sod plows were widely used—the Jack Rabbit and the Nebraska. Each was pulled by a two-horse team and worked on the same principle, but the Nebraska plow was shorter and lighter than the Jack Rabbit. Instead of a moldboard, commonly found on regular turning plows, the sod plow had steel rods set four inches apart and curved after the fashion of a moldboard. The tough sod was cut vertically and horizontally in shallow furrows by a knife edge set near the point of the plow. The rods turned the sod bottom side up in long ribbons or slablike layers.

Pioneer dwellings were built from the resources of this new land. Immediately after each run, homesteaders used tents or canvas-covered wagon boxes for temporary shelter. If there was a timbered canyon on his claim, the homesteader cut logs and constructed a crude cabin to house his family. Most of the country in central and western Oklahoma was grassland; lacking timber for cabins, settlers set up housekeeping in soddies, dugouts, half-dugouts, and sod fronts in banks of low-lying hills. The soddy or sod house was the most widely used kind of dwelling.

During the early hard-scrabble days, home-steaders often were pressed even to find sufficient fuel for heating their crude dwellings and for cooking fires. Wood on most claims was scarce and chief reliance was placed on "cow chips." The women found that a bucket of dried cow dung, kindled by dried grass tapers, made a good bed of cooking coals. Because so much was used, this fuel became scarce across western Oklahoma, and many homesteading families placed sideboards on their wagons and went across the 100th meridian to the great cattle ranges of Texas on cow chip-gathering expeditions. Each family member would take a washtub, tie a short rope to one handle, and drag it across the range while filling it. When full the tub was emptied into the wagon. One settler recalled that his family built a winter fuel pile fifty feet long, twelve feet wide, and eight feet high.

Homesteader's fare was simple and reflected the resourcefulness of the people. Game was abundant; in 1894 one settler killed a wagonload of wild turkeys in a day at Boiling Springs. Another reported that after a severe snowstorm he went along the creeks near his claim, gathering up prairie chickens and quail in a grain sack, for coveys of these birds had frozen during the cold. He thawed and cleaned them and fed his family through a difficult period.

A popular wild fruit was the sand plum. It made excellent pies and jellies and was of great value to the settlers. When a household exhausted its supply of canning jars, the remaining plums were cooked into a batter; spread on cloths made from flour sacks; dried in sheets, then removed from the cloths; rolled up; and put away for winter. During hard times, pioneer families even subsisted on boiled kaffir corn, and it "became a polite art that first winter to . . . gracefully and quietly spit the hulls out while at the table."

One of the early concerns was establishing schools and churches. In the absence of territorial support for early-day education, the settlers built their schools through public subscription. The men donated their labor for hauling material and erecting the buildings. Some of these pioneer schoolhouses were of the sod-house kind. Others were constructed of split cedar posts placed in picket walls (vertical rather than horizontal, as was customary in constructing log buildings). The only textbooks at first were those books the parents had brought from their original homes. One early-day student remembered that "spelling, ciphering, and geography matches with an occasional 'speaking' relieved the monotony of the regular school life."

The students at one school carried water from a spring situated a quarter mile from the schoolhouse. Toilet facilities would be "two privies . . . located on the back of the school yard, and you held up two fingers in a V shape to get permission to leave the room." During pioneer days on the Oklahoma frontier, schools seldom operated for more than three months of twenty days each. Teachers received about twenty-five dollars each month. One teacher "was given a cow . . . as a consideration for teaching a fourth month."

At first there were no church buildings, but the settlers still worshiped, meeting in the schoolhouses or in homes whenever a circuit rider came through the country. One pioneer remembered that "everyone went to these meetings [revivals] as they were outstanding events, regardless of the denomination of the preacher. We had what was called free or shouting Methodists, regular Methodists, Baptists, and Christian preachers, who received little pay and stayed with the neighbors."

Just as the settlers energetically opened farms on the prairies and in the rich river valleys, they also established towns. One of the most exciting towns in Oklahoma Territory was Woodward, a northwestern community that developed after the run of 1893. Woodward's first town ordinance, according to one of its founders, admonished its five hundred citizens: "If you must shoot, shoot straight up." An early visitor to Woodward recalled:

The crooked old main street was lined on both sides with mostly old frame buildings, and we got our first sight of a real western frontier cow town. Woodward in those days, while on a little "milder scale" was

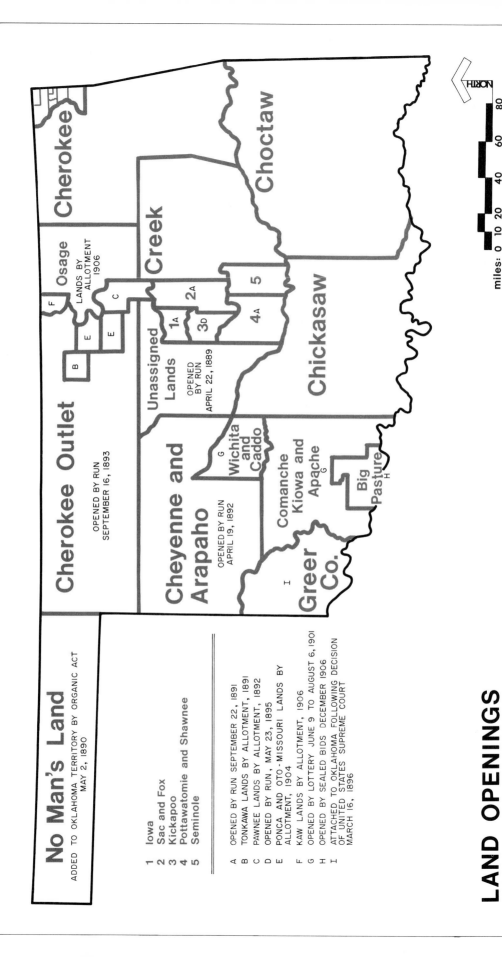

No Man's Land

ADDED TO OKLAHOMA TERRITORY BY ORGANIC ACT
MAY 2, 1890

Cherokee Outlet

OPENED BY RUN
SEPTEMBER 16, 1893

Cherokee

Osage

LANDS BY
ALLOTMENT
1906

F

B

E

E

C

F

Creek

1A

2A

3D

4A

5

Unassigned
Lands

OPENED
BY RUN
APRIL 22, 1889

Choctaw

**Cheyenne and
Arapaho**

OPENED BY RUN
APRIL 19, 1892

Wichita
and
Caddo

G

Comanche
Kiowa and
Apache

G

Big
Pasture

H

Chickasaw

**Greer
Co.**

I

1   Iowa
2   Sac and Fox
3   Kickapoo
4   Pottawatomie and Shawnee
5   Seminole

A   OPENED BY RUN SEPTEMBER 22, 1891
B   TONKAWA LANDS BY ALLOTMENT, 1891
C   PAWNEE LANDS BY ALLOTMENT, 1892
D   OPENED BY RUN, MAY 23, 1895
E   PONCA AND OTO-MISSOURI LANDS BY
    ALLOTMENT, 1904
F   KAW LANDS BY ALLOTMENT, 1906
G   OPENED BY LOTTERY JUNE 9 TO AUGUST 6, 1901
H   OPENED BY SEALED BIDS DECEMBER 1906
I   ATTACHED TO OKLAHOMA FOLLOWING DECISION
    OF UNITED STATES SUPREME COURT
    MARCH 16, 1896

NORTH

miles: 0 10 20   40   60   80

drawn by : S Rogers

LAND OPENINGS

about like Dodge City. It was quite a shipping point for range cattle of those days, and it was naturally full of cowboys. The hitchracks were lined with saddle horses. A few buggies and wagons could be seen, and occasionally a covered homeseeker's wagon.

The focus of the winding main street, with its false-front buildings and board sidewalks, was the Cattle King Hotel. As late as 1901, there was only one brick building in the town. Water was scarce and businessmen and householders used the barrel system. For twenty-five cents a townsman could have a barrel on his porch filled each day from a horse-drawn tank wagon. Restaurants, dry goods and general stores, the Sing Lee Laundry (the proprietor conspicuous with his queue), two banks, and twenty-three saloons completed the town's leading business establishments. Hard liquor was legal in Oklahoma Territory until statehood in 1907, and Woodward claimed some of the leading resorts in the West, complete with mahogany and walnut bars, nude paintings, and female faro dealers.

Such a promising farming center and cattle town could be expected to receive the attention of the outlaws who roamed the frontier like predatory wolf packs. On March 14, 1894, the notorious Bill Doolin gang held up the Woodward railroad station. The loot included a safe full of currency for the Fort Supply payroll.

Other prominent robber bands that roamed the Oklahoma Territory frontier included Red Buck Waightman's riders and the notorious Dalton gang. During the 1880s and 1890s, the "Wanted Dead or Alive" posters scattered over the territory carried such names as Dynamite Dick Clifton, Zip Wyatt, Tulsa Jack Blake, Bitter Creek Newcomb, Little Dick West, Black-Faced Charley Bryant, and Arkansas Tom Jones. At times, no train, stagecoach, or bank was safe from the daring raids of these plunderers. Sheriffs, their deputies, and citizen posses did their best to hold the outlaw gangs in check, but the most effective work was done by United States deputy marshals. Evett D. Nix, a respected citizen and fearless officer, was assigned as United States marshal with headquarters at Guthrie, the territorial capital. His best-known deputy marshals were Frank Canton, Heck Thomas, Chris Madsen, and Bill Tilghman. These federal officers matched their outlaw adversaries in bravery, and by the turn of the century had fairly well purged the territory of brigandage.

The theme of anomaly, conspicuous throughout Oklahoma history, is especially apparent in the Sooner State's political development. From statehood in 1907, Oklahoma has been characterized largely as a one-party state, the Democrats winning most of the elections and wielding a sustained, powerful influence over state affairs. This one-party domination by the Democrats becomes all the more curious in view of the political situations in territorial times when the Republicans dominated the political scene. As a matter of fact, Oklahoma Territory appeared so safe for Republicans that leaders in the United States Congress and Republican Presidents William McKinley and Theodore Roosevelt seriously considered admitting Oklahoma Territory as a state, separate and distinct from Indian Territory. The following table illustrates the one-party domination of the office of governor for the period of 1890 to 1907:

George W. Steele	May 22, 1890 to Oct. 18, 1891	Republican
Robert Martin	Oct. 18, 1891 to Feb. 2, 1892	Republican
Abraham J. Seay	Feb. 2, 1892 to May 7, 1893	Republican
William C. Renfrow	May 7, 1893 to May 24, 1897	Democrat
Cassius M. Barnes	May 24, 1897 to May 12, 1901	Republican
William M. Jenkins	May 12, 1901 to Nov. 30, 1901	Republican
William C. Grimes	Nov. 30, 1901 to Dec. 9, 1901	Republican
Thompson B. Ferguson	Dec. 9, 1901 to Jan. 13, 1906	Republican
Frank Frantz	Jan. 13, 1906 to Nov. 16, 1907	Republican

Land Rush opening the Cherokee Outlet, 1893.

This pattern of Republican domination was borne out in other respects. Between 1890 and 1907, the following men served as territorial delegates to the United States Congress: David A. Harvey, 1890 to 1893; Dennis Flynn, 1893 to 1897; James T. Callahan, 1897 to 1899; Dennis Flynn, 1899 to 1903; and Bird S. McGuire, 1903 to 1907. All were Republicans except Callahan, a Populist. He won election in November, 1896, through a fusion of Populist and Democratic voting.

Republicans also fared well in the territorial assembly. It will be remembered that the First Legislative Assembly, elected in 1890, had a Republican majority, though that majority did not effectively control the assembly. The Republicans held a substantial majority in both houses of the Second and Third Legislative Assemblies. The Fourth Assembly, 1897 to 1899, was dominated by a fused Populist-Democratic majority. At the same time, this combination elected the territorial delegate to Congress. The Republicans controlled both houses of the Fifth Assembly, 1899 to 1901. During the Sixth Assembly, 1901 to 1903, the Democrats dominated the council; the Republicans dominated the house. The Seventh Assembly saw the majorities reversed, with the Democrats controlling the house, the Republicans the council. The Eighth Assembly, 1905 to 1907, was Oklahoma's last as a territory and was dominated by Republican majorities in both houses.

Unfortunately for the Republicans, their advantage at the polls was reduced by intra-party strife over patronage and party leadership, where the territorial capital would be, and the statehood question. Among the people of all parties in the territory there was resentment at the tendency of the presidents to appoint outsiders to important posts in the territorial government. This practice came to be called "carpetbag government," and added to the troubles of the Republicans. The people of Oklahoma Territory had intense pride, and they firmly believed that there were well-qualified persons in the territory who should receive these appointments. Governor Steele's stormy administration was, in large measure, because of local resentment against an outsider. Territorial political leaders and citizens alike regarded his appointment as merely political and not in the best interests of the territory.

A pioneer's sod house on a prairie claim.

Following Steele's precipitate resignation, Robert Martin, the territorial secretary, served as governor until February, 1892, when President Benjamin Harrison appointed Abraham J. Seay, a Territorial Supreme Court justice and a former resident of Missouri. Seay's administration, though brief, witnessed a large accretion to Oklahoma Territory brought about by the Cheyenne-Arapaho opening during April, 1892. As governor he faced the duty of dividing this addition to Oklahoma Territory into counties and organizing local government for the area. Caring for territorial prisoners was another problem that faced Seay, for Oklahoma Territory had no prison for its criminals. In November, 1890, Oklahoma Territory made a contract with the state of Kansas that allowed the courts of Oklahoma to place convicted criminals in the Kansas state prison at Lansing. During Seay's term, a system of employment was worked out so that the Oklahoma prisoners were leased to the Kansas coal mines for their board and keep. This was continued for several years.

In 1892 the election of Democratic presidential candidate Grover Cleveland initiated a brief period when Democrats held appointive offices in Oklahoma Territory. During the spring of 1893, Democratic appointees replaced Republican officeholders and President Cleveland attempted to refute the charge of "carpetbag rule" by selecting local men. Thus William C. Renfrow, a banker from Nor-

man, was appointed governor. During Renfrow's administration, Oklahoma Territory nearly achieved its present geographical limits through the opening of the Cherokee Outlet (1893), the Kickapoo opening (1895), and the transfer of Greer County from Texas to Oklahoma Territory (1896). Oklahoma's only Democratic territorial governor approved a series of bills that advanced the program of education: one created the Colored Agricultural and Normal University at Langston; another established Northwestern Normal at Alva; and a third provided for the first uniform textbook system for Oklahoma. Although the problem of territorial prisoners had been settled, that of the mentally ill continued. Until Renfrow's term, Oklahoma's mentally ill had been committed to an asylum at Jacksonville, Illinois. He gained legislation from the Territorial Assembly that provided for their care in a private sanitarium at Norman.

The presidential election of 1896 swept Republican William McKinley into office and produced extensive changes in the personnel of Oklahoma territorial government. Democratic officeholders were replaced by Republicans. Cassius M. Barnes, from New York and a Union Army veteran (a common preferment for public office in those times), was appointed governor. Barnes had come to Oklahoma Territory in 1889. He had held various public offices including a federal appointment in the United States Land Office at Guthrie. In 1894 he won election to the Territorial Assembly. During Governor Barnes's administration, Oklahoma educational facilities continued to expand with the establishment of University Preparatory School at Tonkawa and Southwestern Normal. Granite and Weatherford each sought to gain Southwestern Normal, and the contest finally was won by Weatherford.

Two other major developments occurring during the Barnes administration were the participation of Oklahoma in the Spanish-American War and passage by Congress of the Free Homes Bill. Two troops of cavalry were recruited in Oklahoma at the outset—one from Oklahoma Territory and one from Indian Territory. Oklahoma troopers comprised units in the famous Rough Riders commanded by Colonel Theodore Roosevelt. This military association of Oklahomans with the dynamic Roosevelt had great influence on Oklahoma politics because it established a basis for political preference after Roosevelt became president, and its ramifications extended into later state and national elections. On the second call for recruits for the Spanish-American War, Oklahoma raised a battalion of four companies, composed of men from both Indian Territory and Oklahoma Territory, as a component of the First Regiment, Territorial Volunteers. Other troops were recruited in Arizona and New Mexico territories. Captain Allyn K. Capron, commander of the Indian Territory cavalry, was killed in the charge at San Juan Hill.

Aside from the Oklahoma Statehood Bill, the Free Homes Bill was probably the most sought-after federal law promoted by Oklahomans during the territorial period. Chief advocate of the Free Homes Bill was congressional delegate Dennis Flynn, who won election to this office more times than any other Oklahoman largely because of his sustained promotion of this proposal. Flynn, probably the most powerful Republican in Oklahoma throughout the territorial period, came to Oklahoma Territory from Kiowa, Kansas, where he had edited a newspaper and had served as postmaster. He arrived in Guthrie on the day of the 1889 land run, and opened the first post office there. More than anything else, his service in Congress amounted to a crusade

for free homes. While the provisions of the Homestead Act applied chiefly to Oklahoma Territory, much of the land was not free, as was the case for most of the public land in the West. To open Indian Territory land to home-seekers, the federal government first had to extinguish Indian title by purchasing each tribe's surplus land. This cost was passed on to settlers, generally running about $1.25 an acre, and Flynn's Free Homes Bill proposed to repeal these charges. When Congress finally passed the Free Homes Bill in 1900, it saved Oklahoma settlers an estimated $15 million.

A Democratic-dominated assembly, elected in 1898, attempted to embarrass the governor and other Republican appointive officials in the territorial government through extensive investigations. This heightened the turmoil of territorial politics, already turbulent enough with such issues as location of the territorial capital and the statehood question. Governor Barnes assured a split in his party as well as Democratic denunciation by his veto of a vast public works bill, though the veto was well intentioned because of the huge expenditure involved. The bill provided for a territorial penitentiary, an asylum for the insane, a school for the deaf and blind, reformatories for youthful offenders, and government buildings at Guthrie, including a supreme court building.

Barnes's four-year term came to a close in 1901. William McKinley had won reelection the preceding November, thus Republicans could expect continued preference in Oklahoma Territory affairs. Despite his good record, Barnes had irritated powerful territorial Republicans, notably Dennis Flynn, and with Flynn's encouragement, President McKinley passed over Barnes and appointed William Jenkins, secretary of the territory, to the office of governor. The most conspicuous occurrence of Jenkins's tenure as governor was the opening of the Kiowa, Comanche, Wichita, Caddo, and Apache reservations to settlement in 1901. The vast addition nearly completed Oklahoma's geographic format.

President McKinley fell to an assassin's bullet in September, 1901; Vice-President Theodore Roosevelt succeeded to the presidency, and in a few weeks he removed Jenkins. The stated reason was official misconduct growing

The governors of Oklahoma Territory.

out of Jenkins's ownership of stock in the sanitarium at Norman, which held the contract to care for the mentally ill of Oklahoma Territory. While Roosevelt looked over the list of Oklahoma Republicans for a possible gubernatorial appointee, Secretary of the Territory William C. Grimes served as acting governor.

Roosevelt's eventual choice was Thompson B. Ferguson, a newspaper editor and prominent territorial Republican from Watonga. Ferguson came to Oklahoma from Kansas during the opening of the Cheyenne-Arapaho country. He founded the *Watonga Republican* and served as postmaster of the town under an appointment from President McKinley. Governor Ferguson's administration continued into 1906, the eve of statehood. A shrewd political leader, he reduced the bitter factionalism among territorial Republicans. More important, he was a most capable public official, and through his wise administration of territorial affairs, he was able to assure congressional leaders that Oklahoma was ready for statehood. Among other achievements, he corrected the situation at the Norman sani-

tarium by securing legislation from the Territorial Assembly that allowed transfer from the federal government of the facilities of Fort Supply to be used as a territorial public insane asylum. The transfer of this old post occurred in 1903. By the close of Ferguson's administration in January, 1906, Oklahoma Territory's population had increased to 700,000, a more than tenfold increase from Oklahoma's first census in 1890 of 60,000.

Oklahoma's last territorial governor was Frank Frantz, who came to Oklahoma Territory at the time of the Cherokee Outlet opening in 1893. During the Spanish-American War, he served with Colonel Roosevelt and the Rough Riders, advancing to the rank of captain. His rise in politics after the war demonstrated the advantage of having been a Rough Rider. Frantz received appointments as postmaster at Enid and as Osage agent at Pawhuska before the president elevated him to the governor's chair in Oklahoma Territory in January, 1906. About the only distinction Frantz could claim as territorial governor was that of being the youngest—he was thirty-four years old. His administration was brief and was concerned primarily with the transition from territorial status to statehood. The Territorial Assembly did not meet during the Frantz administration, and the governor spent most of his time at-tempting to unify his party in order to provide an effective challenge to the Democrats in the upcoming elections for delegates to the Oklahoma Constitutional Convention.

Notes on Sources, Chapter 14

The period of the Boomers in Oklahoma history is the subject of Carl Coke Rister, *Land Hunger: David L. Payne and the Boomers* (Norman, 1942); George Rainey, *The Cherokee Strip* (Guthrie, Okla., 1933); Dan W. Peery, "Captain David L. Payne," *Chronicles of Oklahoma* 13 (December, 1935): 438–56; and Hamilton S. Wicks, "The Opening of Oklahoma," *Chronicles of Oklahoma* 4 (June, 1926): 129–42.

Land openings and the growth of Oklahoma Territory are discussed in Robert E. Cunningham, *Stillwater: Where Oklahoma Began* (Stillwater, Okla., 1969); Orrin B. Burright, *The Sun Rides High: Pioneering Days in Oklahoma, Kansas, and Missouri* (Wichita Falls, Texas, 1975); George Rainey, *No-Man's Land* (Norman, 1948); Emma A. Estill, "The Great Lottery," *Chronicles of Oklahoma* 9 (December, 1931): 365–81; Roscoe E. Harper, "Homesteading in Northwestern Oklahoma Territory," *Chronicles of Oklahoma* 16 (September, 1938): 326–36; G. E. Lemmon,

"Reminiscences of Pioneering in the Cherokee Strip," *Chronicles of Oklahoma* 22 (December, 1944): 435–57; and Sidney Thiel, *The Oklahoma Land Rush* (New York, 1973).

The evolution of Oklahoma political parties is explained in Mrs. Thompson B. Ferguson, *They Carried the Torch* (Kansas City, Mo., 1937); John Alley, *City Beginnings in Oklahoma Territory* (Norman, 1939); Gerald Forbes, *Guthrie: Oklahoma's First Capital* (Norman, 1938); Roy Gittinger, *The Formation of the State of Oklahoma* (Norman, 1939); LeRoy Fischer, ed., *Territorial Governors of Oklahoma* (Oklahoma City, 1975); Dora Ann Stewart, *Government and Development of Oklahoma Territory* (Oklahoma City, 1933); Dan W. Perry, "George W. Steele, First Governor of the Territory of Oklahoma," *Chronicles of Oklahoma* 12 (December, 1934): 383–92; and John B. Meserve, "The Governors of Oklahoma Territory," *Chronicles of Oklahoma* 20 (September, 1942): 218–27.

Chapter 15

The Forty-sixth Star

From the first land run in 1889, the people of Oklahoma Territory worked for statehood, but it was eighteen years before this goal was achieved. The Oklahoma statehood question was another of the anomalies in which the history of the Sooner State abounds. Most of the American states created from the classic pattern of the old Northwest Ordinance began life as territories with the future land area for statehood already established. The germ of Oklahoma statehood, however, began with the Unassigned Lands. This nucleus of land was expanded through the years by land runs, congressional action, and a United States Supreme Court decision until, in 1906, Oklahoma Territory encompassed all of present western Oklahoma. The drive for statehood came from Oklahoma Territory, and every year from 1889 until 1907 statehood conventions were held in various towns over the territory. Regularly this sentiment was crystallized in the statehood proposals introduced in the Congress by the delegates from Oklahoma Territory.

Congress showed good judgment in thwarting these early but enthusiastic proposals. Although Oklahoma Territory quite early had sufficient population for statehood (400,000 citizens in 1900), there were fundamental problems that had to be resolved before the territory could properly take its place in the Union. One was public finance—statehood would require a source of revenue. The principal basis for supporting state and local government in those times was a tax on land, and much of the land of Oklahoma Territory was nontaxable. For a substantial portion of Oklahoma land this was only a temporary situation because when settlers met certain Homestead Act requirements, including five years of residence on their claims, titles would be issued and the property would be taxable. A more vexing problem was that a substantial part of the land of Oklahoma Territory consisted of Indian allotments. These were restricted in that title for each allotment was held in trust by the federal government for twenty-one years, and throughout the restricted period Indian homesteads were exempt from taxation.

Geography was another deterrent to early statehood. Oklahoma Territory occupied an area of about 40,000 square miles. Most of the states of the Trans-Mississippi West were at least twice this size. Certain congressional leaders pointed out that in fairness to future generations, Oklahoma Territory should not seek statehood with such a limited domain.

Politics entered the picture, too. Early Republican successes in local elections raised hopes among national Republican leaders that a safe Republican state could be established in a traditionally Democratic Southwest. Uncertainty caused the Republican leadership to wait to see how strong and permanent its party's showing in Oklahoma Territory would be. Democratic congressional leaders, notably Joe Wheeler of Alabama, wanted Oklahoma Territory admitted at an early date because of his confidence that Democratic majorities would eventually triumph in the new land. Speaker Joe Cannon of the United States House of Representatives, a power in the Republican party, was alleged to have deliberately held Oklahoma statehood in abeyance because of the substantial number of political appointments available to his party in the territory. These appointments would be lost with statehood.

Isparhecher, Creek traditionalist and opponent of absorption by Oklahoma Territory.

Any consideration of Oklahoma statehood inevitably brought up the matter of Indian Territory. During the 1890s and early 1900s, the leaders of the Five Civilized Tribes were satisfied with their situations, and for years they resisted every attempt by the federal government to interfere with what they regarded as the best arrangement possible for their people.

Out of the extended campaign for Oklahoma statehood there eventually emerged four definite plans. The first was known as the "single or joint statehood" plan. Many prominent persons in Oklahoma Territory, both Republicans and Democrats, wished to join with Indian Territory. There were sound historical grounds for this proposal, for with the exception of the Panhandle and Greer County, all of Oklahoma Territory had once belonged to the Five Civilized Tribes as a part of the Indian Territory. Fusion with Indian Territory would nearly double the size of the future state, and thus answer one objection to statehood advanced by Congress. Single statehood advocates pointed out the economy of having one state government rather than two. Okla-

homa Territory business leaders emphasized the economic advantages of fusing the two territories into a single state. They claimed a combination of Indian Territory minerals and timber with Oklahoma Territory farm and range land would assure a balanced economy for the future state.

A second plan for handling the statehood question was known as "double or separate statehood," that is, creating two states from the Twin Territories. The leaders of the Five Civilized Tribes favored this plan if statehood was to be inevitable. Their anxiety about joining Oklahoma Territory in order to create a single state grew out of the fear that Oklahoma Territory politicians, with experience in territorial government, would dominate affairs in the new government. (As events proved, however, Indian Territory politicians underestimated their talents.) Understandably, the probable loss of personal status by certain aristocrats among the Five Civilized Tribes figured in this resistance to joining with Oklahoma Territory.

In addition, there was the very practical matter of public institutions, such as the Territorial University, the Agricultural and Mechanical College, the normal schools, and the capital, all already established in Oklahoma Territory. Tribal leaders feared that Indian Territory would be neglected in the location of major institutions.

Certain Republicans and Democrats were in favor of two states rather than one. The Democrats hoped to balance new Republican states in the Northwest, their reasoning being that double statehood meant two certain Democratic senators from Indian Territory, and with the predicted decline of Republican strength in Oklahoma Territory, two Democrats from there, also. The two-state Republicans in Oklahoma Territory feared that fusion with Indian Territory would reduce their power. They were confident that they could keep Oklahoma a Republican province, and they foresaw a party disaster if they were joined with the Democratic Indian Territory. This Republican faction in Oklahoma Territory pleaded with Congress not to "obliterate her [the Oklahoma Republican party] identity by casting her into the arms of a Democratic majority in the Indian Territory."

When it appeared that fusion with Indian Territory would not occur in the near future, Dennis Flynn, the Oklahoma Territory congressional delegate, introduced a third plan, known as "piecemeal absorption." This formula proposed to grant immediate statehood to Oklahoma Territory and permit the absorption by Oklahoma of various Indian nations as they were prepared for statehood. The fourth plan, one of last resort, was to admit Oklahoma Territory to the Union and leave Indian Territory and the Five Civilized Tribes to their own devices.

Soon after 1900, it became apparent that the single or joint statehood plan would prevail. Because Indian Territory was regarded by Congress as unprepared for union with Oklahoma Territory, Oklahoma statehood faced an additional delay. Indian leaders continued to oppose joining their nations to Oklahoma Territory. Their opposition, however, was not an insurmountable obstacle for Congress clearly had had the power since 1871 to do nearly anything it chose to do with the Five Civilized Tribes. The two really serious complications with which Congress had to deal in preparing Indian Territory for union with Oklahoma Territory were liquidating the Indian governments and changing the Indian land ownership from communal to private.

Long before the statehood question arose, Congress had been reducing the prerogatives of the Indian governments. The series of federal laws applicable to Indian Territory, enacted in the 1880s and 1890s, were primarily to protect the rights of the ever-increasing number of non-Indians living in the Indian nations. By 1906 they outnumbered the Indians at least seven to one. Yet, Indians retained all political authority and their tribal governments owned all the land. In addition, tribal schools were open only to Indian children. Even in the towns, non-Indian business and professional men could not own the land occupied by their stores, banks, and office buildings. To provide a more convenient and effective means for protecting the rights of non-Indians, Congress in 1889 authorized the establishment of a federal court at Muskogee. Its criminal jurisdiction was limited to such offenses as were not punishable by death or imprisonment. Felony cases involving non-

Indians were tried at Fort Smith, Arkansas; Paris, Texas; and Fort Scott, Kansas. The laws of Arkansas were to be applied to Indian Territory insofar as non-Indians were concerned.

Between 1890 and 1895, Indian tribal courts and Indian law suffered severe reductions in authority through the expansion of federal courts in Indian Territory. Reflecting the increase in non-Indian population and the concomitant increase in judicial business for this period, federal law divided Indian Territory into three judicial districts. Courts were established at South McAlester with jurisdiction over the Choctaw nation; at Ardmore, with jurisdiction over the Chickasaw and Seminole nations; and at Muskogee, with jurisdiction over the Cherokee and Creek nations and the Quapaw Agency. The three Indian Territory judges sat twice each year at South McAlester as a court of appeals to review decisions of the trial courts. Under this arrangement, the three federal courts for Indian Territory tried all cases that formerly had gone to federal court at Fort Smith, Paris, or Fort Scott.

The Curtis Act delivered further devastating blows to the courts, laws, and general government of Oklahoma's five Indian republics. Written by Congressman Charles Curtis of Kansas, a mixed-blood Kaw Indian (later United States senator and vice-president of the United States), this measure became law on June 28, 1898. The Curtis Act in many respects was a sort of organic act for Indian Territory in that it provided for the survey and incorporation of towns; gave townsmen the right to vote; authorized the establishment of free public schools; and abolished tribal courts. All persons in Indian Territory, Indian and non-Indian, thereafter were subject to federal law and the laws of Arkansas as applicable in the particular cases coming before the federal courts of Indian Territory.

In preparing Indian Territory for statehood, the federal government found that persuading the Indians to accept the Anglo-American concept of private ownership of land was going to be as difficult as abolishing the Indian governments. The ancient belief of all North American tribes had been that land was to be used—lived upon, cultivated, hunted and fished upon—by anyone, but the concept of

Chitto Harjo (Crazy Snake), Creek traditionalist and opponent of allotment in severalty.

individuals owning land was alien to them. When the Five Civilized Tribes formed their nations, the land was held in common, or "owned," by the tribe. Even after the formation of their nations into Indian Territory, and even though acculturation had produced a modernization of attitudes among the tribes, notably in the mixed-blood community, the practice of communal landholding was followed and defended by all Indian citizens.

Congress, however, insisted that the communal land ownership must be altered to conform with the land-holding practice in the United States, that of private ownership of land in fee simple, allowing the ownership of the land to be passed to heirs. Thus statehood for the Indian Territory would not be possible until private ownership of the Indian land was accomplished.

The change of title from tribal to individual ownership of land was carried out by the Dawes Commission, whose name is taken from that of its senior member, Senator Henry L. Dawes of Massachusetts. The Jerome or Cherokee Commission had been given authority to deal only with Indian land west of the

Five Civilized Tribes. Senator George Vest of Missouri proposed a rider to the 1893 Indian Appropriation Bill authorizing the president to appoint a commission to negotiate with the Five Civilized Tribes for the allotment of tribal lands, which was approved on March 3, 1893. Senator Dawes, Archibald S. McKennon of Arkansas, and Meredith H. Kidd of Indiana were the original members of the Dawes Commission.

The Dawes Commission met with leaders of the Five Civilized Tribes for the first time at a council at Checotah during February, 1894. The federal commissioners received a cool reception, with the Indian representatives refusing to discuss allotment. The Dawes Commision then visited each Indian capital—that of the Cherokees at Tahlequah, the Creeks at Okmulgee, the Seminoles at Wewoka, the Choctaws at Tuskahoma, and Chickasaws at Tishomingo—and received a similar rebuff. Repeated attempts by the commission to gain allotment agreements ended in utter failure; thereupon, in 1896, Congress gave the commission authority to survey tribal lands and enroll allottees without waiting for tribal assent. Earlier legislation had increased the Dawes Commission to five members, and Thomas B. Cabaniss and Alexander B. Montgomery were appointed as the new commissioners. Frank C. Armstrong replaced Meredith H. Kidd on the Commission.

Apparently the leaders of the Five Civilized Tribes saw in the new authority the futility of further resistance, for on April 23, 1897, the federal commissioners negotiated the Atoka Agreement with Choctaw and Chickasaw leaders and this became the basic allotment formula for these two tribes. The Choctaw-Chickasaw capitulation paved the way for agreements with the Seminoles in 1898, and the Cherokees and the Creeks came to terms in 1901.

Through Dawes Commission negotiations with the Five Civilized Tribes, it was agreed that all tribal governments were to cease operation during 1906. Since the Curtis Act preempted their judicial functions, the Indian governments then operated until statehood only on a caretaker basis, with most of their activities devoted to liquidating public property. The Cherokee government functioned on a limited basis until 1914 because of its extensive public properties.

Dawes Commission surveys of the domain of the Five Civilized Tribes showed that the Cherokee Nation held 4,420,068 acres; the Creek nation, 3,079,095 acres; the Seminole Nation, 365,852 acres; the Choctaw nation, 6,953,048 acres; and the Chickasaw Nation, 4,707,903 acres.

In addition to supervising the surveys, the Dawes Commission enrolled the allottees and determined eligibility. Determining eligibility was a vexing problem because more than 300,000 persons claimed citizenship rights in the Five Civilized Tribes. Their qualifications were judged by the commission, and 101,526 persons were entered on the rolls for allotment. Preparation for the enrollment began on June 28, 1898, and extended to March 4, 1907, when the rolls were closed. The Dawes Commission enrolled 26,794 full bloods, 3,534 Indians of three-fourths Indian blood or more, 6,859 of one-half to three-fourths Indian blood, and 40,936 persons of less than one-half Indian blood. The last category included adopted and intermarried whites. In addition, the Commission enrolled 23,405 former slaves and their descendants.

Of the 19,526,966 acres composing the land of the Five Civilized Tribes, 15,794,400 acres were allotted to persons whose names appeared on the tribal rolls. The remainder was accounted for by land taken for townsites, schools and other public purposes, and segregated coal and timber lands. Most of the latter was sold at public auction, and the proceeds were placed to the credit of the tribes holding such lands. Thus there was no surplus land for homesteading in Indian Territory, as there had been in Oklahoma Territory.

Allotments varied in size. Each Choctaw and Chickasaw received about 320 acres; each Cherokee about 110 acres; Creek allottees, 160 acres each; and Seminoles, 120 acres each. Cherokee, Creek, and Seminole former slaves and descendants shared equally with the Indians in size of allotment, while Choctaw-Chickasaw freedmen and descendants each received an allotment of 40 acres. Most allotments were held in trust by the federal government.

Congress terminated the Dawes Commission on June 30, 1905. Its work was continued by a federal agency (headed by Tams Bixby) known as the Commission to the Five Civilized Tribes. The tribes of the Quapaw Agency jurisdiction, except the Quapaws, were allotted by special assignment between 1889 and 1892. The Quapaws delayed in protest over the federal government proposal that they be satisfied with eighty-acre individual allotments. Knowing there was substantially more land than this available on their reservation, the members of this tribe resisted until 1893 when each Quapaw received an allotment of two hundred acres.

The various laws passed by Congress to phase out tribal governments and prepare the Indian Territory for statehood contained provisions granting United States citizenship to the Indians. A United States law of 1890 provided that members of the Five Civilized Tribes could apply to the federal court at Muskogee for United States citizenship. Few Indians took advantage of this because of pride in tribal citizenship. Later, in each of the allotment agreements negotiated by the Dawes Commission there was a provision for transfer from tribal to United States citizenship, and the Dawes Allotment Act of 1887 provided that citizenship was automatically granted to each Indian upon assignment of an allotment. A congressional act passed in 1901 finally made all Indians of Indian Territory citizens of the United States.

Allotment did not go smoothly even after tribal leaders committed their respective nations to submit to the government program of allotting tribal estates. Resistance developed in each nation, primarily among the full bloods who believed that the Great Spirit had ordained certain things for the Indians including their land ownership system; to them, taking an allotment was a violation of a sacred religious ordinance. The full-blood Keetoowah society among the Cherokees demonstrated, and five thousand refused to be enrolled for allotments. The Dawes Commission had to assign federal marshals to carry out the full-blood allotments. The best-known resistance to allotment occurred among the Creeks, where Chitto Harjo led a protest movement known as the Crazy Snake Rebellion. Harjo presumed to establish a new Creek govern-

Green McCurtain, Choctaw chief, a Sequoyah Convention leader.

Pleasant Porter, Creek chief, president of the Sequoyah Convention.

ment based on old tribal law and custom, and his followers arrested people who accepted allotments and whipped them in public. Chief Pleasant Porter called on the United States government for help, and cavalry from Fort Reno rounded up ninety-four Creek rebels. They were tried at Muskogee in federal court and finally accepted allotments as a condition of being set free.

The inevitability of statehood and the dreadful prospects of being attached to Oklahoma Territory to form the new state of Oklahoma fired the leaders of the Five Civilized Tribes to action. Beginning in 1902, Indian delegates met regularly to develop plans to obstruct fusion with Oklahoma Territory. Principal chiefs W. C. Rogers of the Cherokees, Pleasant Porter of the Creeks, and Green McCurtain of the Choctaws issued a call during 1905 for a statehood convention, scheduled to meet at Muskogee on August 21, 1905. Its purpose was to prepare a constitution for an Indian state to be called Sequoyah. The 182 delegates elected Porter president of the convention and a vice-president was selected from each of the Five Civilized Tribes. The vice-presidents were W.

C. Rogers for the Cherokees; Green McCurtain, Choctaws; John F. Brown, Seminoles; Charles N. Haskell, Creeks; and William H. ("Alfalfa Bill") Murray for the Chickasaws. Haskell, a non-Indian, was a railroad promoter from Muskogee, and Murray was an intermarried Chickasaw and tribal attorney for the Chickasaw Nation. Through years of diligent study, Murray had become steeped in basic law and was regarded as a leading authority on constitutional government. Alexander Posey, popular Creek poet and political essayist, was elected secretary of the convention.

The work of the Sequoyah Convention resulted in a well-written document that followed closely the traditional pattern of American constitutional government. A referendum for adoption of the Sequoyah Constitution by the voters of Indian Territory provided an overwhelming vote of approval. When the Sequoyah constitution was presented to Congress, however, that body was ready to act definitively on the Oklahoma statehood question, and the Hamilton Statehood Bill, named for Congressman Edward L. Hamilton of Michigan, was signed into law on

June 16, 1906. This bill became the Oklahoma Enabling Act.

The Oklahoma Enabling Act must rate with the Oklahoma Organic Act and the Curtis Act as one of the three most important pieces of federal legislation in the evolution of the Sooner State. It set the formula for achieving Oklahoma statehood. The Twin Territories were to be joined. A constitutional convention was authorized, consisting of fifty-five delegates from Indian Territory, fifty-five from Oklahoma Territory, and two from the Osage Nation. These 122 delegates were to assemble in convention at Guthrie. The Enabling Act established guidelines for the delegates to follow in preparing the constitution: the instrument of government for the new state was required to provide for a republican form of government; to establish religious liberty; to prohibit polygamous marriages; and to guarantee suffrage regardless of race, color, or previous condition of servitude. Two curious mandates were placed on the delegates by the Enabling Act: the new constitution had to provide for prohibition in Indian Territory and the Osage Nation for twenty-one years, and the new state capital had to be located at Guthrie, with no change permitted until 1913. Congress appropriated $5 million for the support of public schools to offset the loss of sections 16 and 36 in each Indian Territory township that had been allotted.

By August, 1906, the 112 constitutional convention districts had been established in the Twin Territories. Territorial Governor Frank Frantz supervised the determination of districts for Oklahoma Territory, and W. H. Clayton, senior federal judge for Indian Territory, was in charge of eastern Oklahoma. The election of delegates was held on November 4, 1906. While the candidates campaigned principally as Democrats and Republicans, various groups interjected their ideas of how the constitution should be written, and these became issues providing a kind of political platform on which the delegate candidates could campaign. In addition to the railroads, corporations, and the saloon interests, the most active groups were the Farmers Union and organized labor, both strong in the Twin Territories.

The Republicans, long in power in Okla-

Allen Wright, Choctaw chief who was first to suggest the name "Oklahoma."

homa Territory, hoped to elect enough delegates to control the convention and write a constitution friendly to their partisans. It was devastating when they were defeated badly in this most basic election. Of the 112 seats in the constitutional convention, the Democrats captured 100, and thus won the privilege of organizing the convention.

The delegates assembled in Guthrie on November 20, 1906. The Democrats, with their strong majority, elected William H. Murray of Tishomingo as convention president, Pete Hanraty, the labor leader from McAlester, as vice-president, and Charles N. Haskell of Muskogee, majority floor leader. Except for Henry Johnston of Perry, the Democratic caucus chairman, the convention officers were from Indian Territory. In fact, thirty-four delegates had served in the Sequoyah convention.

While the spectrum of economic, social, and political interests of the Twin Territories was represented, a farm-labor bloc dominated the convention. Background studies of the delegates show that forty-seven farmers, twenty-seven lawyers, twelve merchants, three teachers, six clergymen, two doctors, and one student (Carlton Weaver from the University of Oklahoma) were included in the membership. The Oklahoma Constitutional Convention was composed generally of young men; President Murray was only thirty-seven. The average age was forty-three, and the delegates demonstrated the spirit and enthusiasm of youth in going about their work.

The leader of the Republican minority was Henry Asp of Guthrie. He had been in Washington at the time of passage of the Oklahoma Enabling Act, and it was commonly known that through his influence the clause designating Guthrie as capital of the new state had been included. This raised old controversies over the capital location and in itself would have provided the Democrats a lively campaign issue, because Guthrie was regarded by many persons as a "Republican nest." In addition, Asp was a highly successful attorney and head of the legal division for the Santa Fe Railroad in Oklahoma. It will be recalled that at this time railroads and trusts generally were regarded as public enemies because of high rates, abusive practices, and general disregard of the public interest. Throughout the Twin Territories, Democrats pointed to Asp's election to the constitutional convention as evidence of a long-suspected tie between the Oklahoma Republican party and the railroads. Thus it was charged that the railroads and trusts, through Asp, would attempt to control the convention and write the constitution. While both Murray and Haskell hammered on these themes to discredit Asp and the Republicans, both later admitted they esteemed Asp for his talent and high character.

This was the age of muckrakers and emerging progressivism. Ida Tarbell, Lincoln Steffens, and other writers were using their literary talents to expose contemporary political, social, and economic evils. It was also a time of political ferment and change. Daring reformers were developing plans to purge corruption from government, control abusive trusts, and restore the government to the people. Thus the Oklahoma Constitutional Convention came at a critical juncture in national history. Its delegates, especially the convention president, Bill Murray, were steeped in the new thought, and their dedication to the ideals of reform made the Oklahoma Constitutional Convention a sort of political laboratory.

So exciting were the prospects of producing a new social and political order at Guthrie, that leading national newspapers and magazines sent writers to cover the convention. The *Saturday Evening Post* correspondent wrote of the goal of the delegates: "It was not merely the birth of a new state, it was the birth of a new kind of state." The same writer provided future generations with a graphic word picture of the colorful Alfalfa Bill Murray and the high-handed manner in which he ran the convention:

> Chairman Bill Murray mounts the platform and sweeps the hall with his piercing glance. Down comes his gavel with repeated crashes of the table. The tumult ceases. "The convention will come to order!" Murray shouts, with a final blow of the gavel. "Delegates will take their seats, loafers and lobbyists will get out! We will begin by singing that grand old hymn, 'Nearer, My God, to Thee.' "

Oklahoma's founding fathers produced a constitution that followed the general American pattern of three coordinate departments (executive, legislative, and judicial), a system of checks and balances, veto and impeachment powers, a bill of rights, and they added certain popular reforms, which included the long ballot. Twelve constitutional officers were defined and made elective on a statewide basis, which reduced the appointive power of the governor and according to the delegates would deter executive tyranny. By constitutional definition, the judicial power of the state was vested in a supreme court, district courts, county and municipal courts, and justices of the peace. The judiciary was made elective and thus responsive to the people. The constitution was inordinately long in text due to the determination of the delegates to spell out their intent and reduce opportunity for loose judicial interpretation.

Election for governor was to be in off years, making it impossible for a candidate to ride to office on the popularity of a presidential candidate. The term of office for the chief executive was set at four years, with the restriction that no governor could succeed himself. This

Allotment assignments for the Five Civilized Tribes, Muskogee, Indian Territory.

was to reduce the chances of a governor building personal power through long tenure.

The most powerful branch of the state government, deliberately so placed because the delegates regarded its members closer to the people, was the legislature. Established as a bicameral body, the house members were to serve two-year terms, members of the senate, four-year terms. Provision was made for a continuing membership in the state senate by setting the first terms of half of that body at two years.

The legislative function was shared with the people through the then-revolutionary initiative and referendum. The new constitution provided that 8 percent of the voters could initiate a constitutional amendment by petition, and 5 percent of the voters by petition could obtain a referendum on an act of the legislature.

Additional political reforms embedded in the constitution included an eight-hour work day on public projects and in the mines, and prohibition of child and convict labor. The primary was adopted as the method for nominating candidates for public office, thus reducing the power of party conventions and machines, and providing the people a voice in the selection of candidates. Machinery for controlling trusts was established in the Corporation Commission.

Even the revolutionary idea of women's suffrage was favorably considered and almost written into the constitution. It failed at the last moment due to claims by opponents that giving the ballot to Oklahoma women would "unsex them." Prohibition also was a popular social reform of the times, and the Enabling Act required the convention to apply prohibition to the Indian Territory and Osage Nation for twenty-one years. In response to lobbying by the Anti-Saloon League and other dry groups, the delegates decided to extend prohibition to the entire state. Strategy considerations, however, led the Democratic managers to handle this issue separately. Murray, Haskell, and others feared that if prohibition were included in the original draft of the constitution, a combination of Republican and liquor interests might defeat the constitution at the polls. Thus a prohibition amendment, separate from the constitution, was offered to the voters at the election held to approve the constitution.

The constitutional convention displayed bigotry as well as enlightenment. Of the 112 delegates, seventy-five were natives of the South. This group attempted to inject into the constitution "Jim Crow" provisions that would have discriminated against blacks. Haskell objected, pointing out that "statehood was the all-important question" at that time, but implying that those interested in such a program could take care of the matter after Oklahoma was admitted to the Union.

The convention worked hard to wind up its work by the spring of 1907. Its effort had been

Oklahoma Constitutional Convention, Guthrie, Oklahoma Territory.

monumental in view of the challenge—that of fusing two diverse cultural communities, the Twin Territories, into a political unity, and satisfying 1.5 million people. It had to lay out counties in Indian Territory and select county seats, both thorny problems. In all, the convention established seventy-five counties across the Twin Territories. Two additional counties were later added by law. In addition to providing for state government, the delegates had to make provision for county and local government.

The Democratic majority, proud of its work, was irritated by the negative attitude of the Republican minority. Under Asp's leadership, this group produced its own version of what the constitution for the new state should be. When the Republican draft was voted down, the minority party members attempted to obstruct the work of the convention, and failing there, sought to keep the constitution from going into effect by injunctions and other methods. Unfortunately for the future of the Republican party, this negative approach only sealed its doom and assured one-party domination until the 1960s for Oklahoma. Most Oklahomans, tired of territorial status and

longing for statehood, listened to Democratic exploitation of what was called Republican obstructionism, and voted for the Democratic candidates and the constitution.

President Theodore Roosevelt showed his displeasure with the constitution when a draft was submitted to him by declaring that his thoughts on it "were not fit to print," and he pressured the convention to change those sections providing for progressive reforms that he found objectionable. He also sent William Howard Taft to Oklahoma to speak against the constitution and recommend that the people vote against it, so that what he called "a better constitution" might be produced. This infuriated the Democrats. The current favorite of farm, labor, and other western interests was William Jennings Bryan, and the Democrats invited him to Oklahoma to counter Taft's effort. Bryan followed Roosevelt's representative across the Twin Territories praising the constitutional convention and the constitution, declaring it was one of the "great documents of modern times," and assuring Oklahomans "you have the best constitution today of any state in the Union."

The constitution was submitted to the

Statehood Day, November 16, 1907, Guthrie, Oklahoma.

people of the Twin Territories on September 17, 1907. It was ratified by a vote of 180,333 to 73,059. The separate prohibition amendment carried, 130,361 to 112,258. Elections for governor and other state offices, were held on the same day. Earlier, on June 8, 1907, in a preferential primary sponsored by the Democratic party of the Twin Territories, Haskell sought his party's nomination for governor. He was contested by Lee Cruce and Thomas Doyle. In a closely fought contest, Haskell won the Democratic nomination for governor. The Republicans chose Frank Frantz, governor of Oklahoma Territory. The Socialist party, soon to be a power in Oklahoma politics, nominated C. C. Ross. At the general election on September 17, Haskell won, receiving 137,559 votes, Frantz netted 110,292 votes; and Ross received nearly 10,000 votes.

In the Democratic senatorial preferential election, held on the same day, the Democrats also selected their United States Senate candidates. Earlier this party had worked out a so-called gentleman's agreement whereby, to demonstrate the unity of the Twin Territories, one senatorial candidate should come from Indian Territory and one from Oklahoma Ter-

ritory. The three top candidates were Robert L. Owen, with 48,885 votes; Henry M. Furman, with 39,113 votes; and Thomas P. Gore (blind, but a brilliant lawyer and scintillating orator), with 38,288 votes. Owen was from Muskogee, Furman was from Ada, and Gore lived in Lawton. Although Furman ran second, because both he and Owen were from Indian Territory, he withdrew in favor of Gore, to fulfill the gentleman's agreement. At this time the state legislature elected the United States senators, so this preferential vote merely had the effect of nominating the candidates. The legislature could not meet to transact business of this sort until the president proclaimed statehood.

The Enabling Act allocated Oklahoma five congressmen. By the September 17 elections, four Democrats, Scott Ferris (Lawton), James Davenport (Vinita), Charles D. Carter (Ardmore), and Elmer Fulton (Oklahoma City) won seats in the United States Congress. Bird S. McGuire (Pawnee), former territorial delegate, was the sole Republican congressman elected. Also in the September 17 elections, the Democrats swept all state offices, established heavy majorities in both houses of the legislature, and won most of the county and local offices as well. Still, everything was contingent upon the president approving the constitution and proclaiming statehood—and the president was frankly critical of the document.

The convention under Murray's leadership had scrupulously followed the Enabling Act, and the president had no grounds for withholding approval except personal antagonism. Reluctantly, at 10:16 in the morning of November 16, 1907, he signed the statehood proclamation and the tidings were telegraphed to Guthrie. A vast crowd had gathered for the occasion. Just before noon Charles N. Haskell took the oath of office and was installed as Oklahoma's first governor. In demonstration of the fusion of the Twin Territories, symbols of these two diverse communities, a woman representing the Indian Territory and a man from Oklahoma Territory, were bound in a mock wedding.

A writer for the *Muskogee Phoenix* reported the mood of the day:

But yesterday, we were a million and a half of political orphans, misunderstood, misgoverned in administration. Today we stand erect, clothed with the full panoply of American citizenship, in all things the equal in fact as well as in name, of the proudest people of the nation. But yesterday, to all the other states we were strangers. Today we have entered into our inheritance . . . to take our place in Columbia's household as the most favored of all the nation's children. But yesterday, the long range government by appointment, by political favorites, by telegraph and by misinformation, was the rule. Today we begin a new era with the ideal government of the immortal Lincoln, "a government of the people, by the people, and for the people." . . . we turn with confidence to the future, proud in the record of yesterday, masterful in the strength of today, and meet the future, secure in the belief that tomorrow will bring to us but additional triumphs.

Notes on Sources, Chapter 15

Several plans were proposed to achieve statehood for Oklahoma Territory and Indian Territory. Thomas H. Doyle, "Single versus Double Statehood," *Chronicles of Oklahoma* 5 (March, 1927): 18–41; and Grant Foreman, "Oklahoma and Indian Territory," *The Outlook* 82 (October 5, 1907): 550–52, explain these proposals.

The altering of the land ownership and institutions of Indian Territory as a preliminary to statehood is discussed in Loren B. Brown, "The Dawes Commission," *Chronicles of Oklahoma* 9 (March, 1931): 71–105; Loren B. Brown, "Establishment of the Dawes Commission for Indian Territory," *Chronicles of Oklahoma* 18 (June, 1940): 171–81; Imre Sutton, *Indian Land Tenure* (New York, 1975); Wilcomb E. Washburn, *Red Man's Land, White Man's Law* (New York, 1971); Harold M. Hyman, ed., *The Assault on Tribalism: The General Allotment Act (Dawes Act) of 1887* (Philadelphia, 1975); and D. S. Otis, *The Dawes Act and the Allotment of Indian Land* ed. Francis Paul Prucha (Norman, 1973).

Indian leaders attempted to form the separate all-Indian state of Sequoyah to avoid absorption by Oklahoma Territory. Their efforts are detailed in Amos D. Maxwell, *The Sequoyah Constitutional Convention* (Boston, 1953); and C. M. Allen, *The Sequoyah Movement* (Oklahoma City, 1925).

The Oklahoma Constitutional Convention's work, and finally statehood for Oklahoma on November 16, 1907, are explained in Irvin Hurst, *The Forty-Sixth Star: A History of the Oklahoma Constitutional Convention and Early Statehood* (Oklahoma City, 1957); Gerald Forbes, *Guthrie: Oklahoma's First Capital* (Norman, 1938); Albert H. Ellis, *A History of the Constitutional Convention of the State of Oklahoma* (Muskogee, 1923); William H. Murray, "The Constitutional Convention," *Chronicles of Oklahoma* 9 (June, 1931): 126–38; and Blue Clark, "Delegates to the Constitutional Convention," *Chronicles of Oklahoma* 48 (Winter, 1970–71): 400–15.

Chapter 16

Oklahoma Politics: The Early Years, Part 1

Oklahoma political history from statehood to the present can be divided into three periods: Early—1907 to 1943, Middle—1943 to 1955, and Modern—1955 to the present. Certain qualities distinguish each period. The early period, from the administration of Governor Charles N. Haskell to that of Governor Leon Phillips, is conspicuous for bold contrasts: there was daring gubernatorial leadership and intimidated chief executives; there was liberalism and reaction, enlightenment and bigotry; there was a recurring conflict between local interests and broad state interests; and there was raw frontier "rambunctiousness" and general diversity.

One of the most capable men ever to hold public office in Oklahoma was Charles N. Haskell. From a poverty-ridden youth in Ohio, this handsome, dynamic adventurer won and lost several fortunes before arriving in Muskogee to promote Indian Territory railroads. His talents are brilliantly exemplified by the fact that after serving as the Sooner State's first governor, he went on to recoup his private fortune. In his message to Oklahoma's First Legislature, Haskell recommended the adoption of laws providing for a guaranty system to stabilize state banking, a compulsory primary election system, the establishment of initiative and referendum, the regulation of trusts and monopolies, and the enforcement of prohibition.

Oklahoma's First Legislature was the busiest in state history. Its primary task was to promulgate the recently approved constitution, and the influence of the constitutional convention was strong in its membership. Henry S. Johnston was elected president pro tempore of the senate and William H. Murray served as

Governor Charles N. Haskell.

speaker of the house. One of the first legislative actions was the election of the two United States senators. At a Tulsa meeting, the Republicans, using the convention method of selecting candidates, had chosen Charles G. Jones of Oklahoma City and Clarence B. Douglass of Muskogee as their Senate candidates. Through their preferential primary the Democrats had nominated Robert L. Owen and Thomas P. Gore. Because the Democrats were in the majority in the legislature (house—92 Democrats, 16 Republicans; senate—39 Democrats, 5 Republicans), their candidates won. Gore drew the short term and was required to run for reelection in 1908.

The Oklahoma judiciary was organized on November 16, 1907, when the State Supreme Court convened for the first time. Robert L. Williams, a delegate to the constitutional convention from Durant, was selected chief justice. Soon thereafter, the Oklahoma judicial hierarchy was completed through legislative enactments, and extended downward from the Criminal Court of Appeals to district, circuit, superior, county and municipal courts, and justice of the peace courts.

The spirit of reform, so strong in the constitutional convention, continued as a pervasive force in the First Legislature. An extensive labor code was adopted and became a forerunner of federal labor reforms promoted by Presidents Woodrow Wilson and Franklin D. Roosevelt. This included a safety code for the mines; a child labor law; a factory inspection law; a health and sanitation code; and employer's liability for workers' job-related injuries. In addition, laws were passed that established a conciliation service in labor disputes; created public employment agencies; prohibited unlabeled convict-made goods; outlawed the yellow dog contract; defined workers' rights; and declared Labor Day a state holiday.

Control of trusts, monopolies, corporations, and railroads was a matter of public concern in the early twentieth century. The Oklahoma Corporation Commission, headed by Jack Love of Woodward, thoroughly checked exploitation and what was then called "corporate greed." Rates for railroads and public service corporations were set by this agency, which allowed railroads to charge only two cents per mile for passenger fare. Lobbyists were required to register with the state. Commissioner Love's devotion to protecting the public interest and his fight to control monopolies made him a popular hero.

Banks were notoriously unstable in the early twentieth century. Because of the lack of trust in management and the fear of loss of savings, bank "runs" by depositors were frequent occurrences. Haskell pointed out that a strong, well-managed banking system was basic to business confidence, credit, and economic development in the new state. To stabilize Oklahoma banks and establish confidence among depositors and investors, he recommended adoption of a bank guaranty law. As passed by the legislature, this measure assessed a one percent tax on the daily balances of participating banks. The proceeds went into a fund to underwrite deposits. Member banks drew on this fund as needed. The bank guaranty system had the desired effect and served as an ancestor of the present Federal Deposit Insurance Corporation.

Public education received considerable attention by the First Legislature. Its enactments established a textbook commission, a system of teacher certification, and a compulsory attendance law requiring enrollment of all children between the ages of eight and sixteen. E. D. Cameron, first state superintendent of public instruction, energetically promoted improvement of instruction by organizing a four-week teachers' institute in each county. Teachers attended these institutes during the summers to improve their knowledge of subjects taught. The school terms ranged from three months in some districts to nine months in others.

Prohibition, another of the reforms adopted in 1907, posed a problem for Haskell and for all public officials until the repeal amendment was adopted in 1959. The First Legislature established an enforcement system. Because the author of the bill was State Senator Richard A. Billups, it was popularly known as the "Billups Booze Bill." The law forbade the manufacture, transportation, and possession of intoxicating liquors. Much lobbying preceded its passage. Two of the most powerful pressure groups in Oklahoma politics, the "dry" interests, including the Oklahoma Anti-Saloon League, the WCTU, and various religious denominations, opposed the "wet" interests, consisting principally of displaced saloonkeepers (Oklahoma Territory had been wet) and liquor manufacturers. A deference to the wets was a provision in the Billups bill authorizing a state dispensary system. Each county was permitted to establish what amounted to a state-owned package liquor store where a citizen with a doctor's prescription could purchase whiskey. This source dried up in 1908, when the voters repealed the state dispensary system.

Robert L. Owen, one of Oklahoma's first United States senators.

Thomas P. Gore, one of Oklahoma's first United States senators.

To raise expense money for the new state government, the First Legislature levied a 2 percent gross revenue tax on pipelines, coal mines, and telegraph lines. An 0.5 percent gross production tax on oil, railroads, telephone companies, and electric utilities proved a definite producer of revenue. In response to reform advocates, a graduated income tax was established of from 0.5 percent on incomes ranging from $3,500 to $10,000, to 3.5 percent on incomes over $100,000.

One of the first matters of legislative business, Senate Bill 1, combined all the racial bias of the constitutional convention in what was known as the "Jim Crow Code." Operating on precedent taken from federal court decisions holding that the white and the black races could be separated if equal facilities were provided the segregated blacks, the legislature adopted laws requiring separate facilities for blacks in public transportation and in all other public facilities. Oklahoma's Jim Crow Code also included segregated public education. That this was not altogether a partisan issue was indicated by passage of the code in the senate by a vote of 37 to 2 and passage in the

house by a vote of 95 to 10. Shortly after adoption of the Jim Crow code, riots broke out in black communities throughout Oklahoma. The most destructive outbreak was at Taft, where a mob burned the Midland Valley Railroad station.

The election of 1908, which selected the members of the Second Legislature, was historic in that Oklahomans participated in their first presidential election. In Oklahoma the Democratic candidate, William Jennings Bryan, triumphed over the Republican candidate and the national winner, William H. Taft, by a vote of 122,363 to 110,474 and thus captured Oklahoma's seven electoral votes.

This election was epochal on two counts. First, a black, A. C. Hamlin of Guthrie, won a seat in the Oklahoma House of Representatives. Second, in the United States congressional races, Republican candidates won three of the five seats allocated to Oklahoma. Both situations influenced future Oklahoma election procedures. Also in the 1908 election, United States Senator Thomas P. Gore sought reelection. He was contested by the famous territorial Republican, Dennis T. Flynn. A

Democrat-dominated legislature selected Gore.

Democratic party leaders were alarmed over Republican victories in the congressional elections. They blamed defeats in the northern districts on bloc voting by the blacks. A common device in the South to control black voting, the so-called "grandfather clause," was instituted in Oklahoma. The bill was submitted to voters in August, 1910. It provided that no person could be registered to vote unless he passed an examination demonstrating his ability to read and write various portions of the state constitution. Exempted from the requirement were lineal descendants of persons eligible to vote on January 1, 1866. This exemption generated the term "grandfather clause." It had the effect of excluding blacks from voting, since election officials could make the literacy test on the state constitution as difficult as they chose. Oklahoma Socialists, Republicans, and certainly the blacks fought the adoption of this proposal, but it carried by a majority of 35,000 votes.

Aside from restricting suffrage, the Second Legislature was primarily concerned with balancing the distribution of major institutions. It will be remembered that one objection Indian Territory raised to joining Oklahoma Territory had been the concentration of public institutions in the western half of Oklahoma. A few of the new institutions were placed in old Oklahoma Territory by the Second Legislature, but most of them were situated in former Indian Territory. The state prison, for example, was established at McAlester. Oklahoma prisoners, earlier placed by contract in the Kansas state prison at Lansing, were brought by railroad under heavy guard to a compound near McAlester, where they helped build the prison walls and buildings.

Other institutions established during the Haskell administration included a Confederate veterans home at Ardmore, the Industrial Institute and College for Girls at Chickasha, Northeastern Normal at Tahlequah, East Central Normal at Ada, Southeastern Normal at Durant, Eastern Oklahoma Preparatory School (Claremore Junior College) at Claremore, the Oklahoma School of Mines at Wilburton, mental hospitals at Enid and Vinita, the Training School for Delinquent Boys at Pauls Valley,

the School for Delinquent Girls at Wynnewood, the State Reformatory at Granite, Whitaker Home for Orphans at Pryor Creek, the School for the Blind at Fort Gibson, the School for the Deaf at Sulphur, a mental hospital for blacks at Taft, Murray School of Agriculture at Tishomingo, Cameron School of Agriculture at Lawton, and Panhandle A and M College at Goodwell.

Governor Haskell's most daring move was to transfer the state capital from Guthrie to Oklahoma City. The Oklahoma Enabling Act had required that the capital remain at Guthrie at least until 1913. Haskell contemptuously referred to the place as a "Republican nest," and he and other Democratic state officials were under constant attack through intemperate editorials by Frank Hilton Greer in the *Oklahoma State Capital*. Obviously, the governor rankled under the regular snubbing he received from Guthrie's Republican aristocracy.

A proposition concerning the capital location was submitted to the voters on June 11, 1910, with no mention made as to when the move would occur. The candidate-cities were Guthrie, Oklahoma City, and Shawnee. The count showed Oklahoma City received 96,261 votes; Guthrie, 31,301; and Shawnee, 8,382.

On the night of June 11, when the results of the election were clear, Haskell sent his secretary to Guthrie for the state seal. The next morning, Haskell, with the state seal in his possession, declared the Lee Huckins Hotel in Oklahoma City to be the new capitol. The shocked citizenry of Guthrie protested, but thereafter the governor conducted the state's business in Oklahoma City. Gradually various state offices moved to the new capital. Until a suitable building was constructed, state government was carried on in rented buildings in Oklahoma City.

Guthrie civic leaders brought suit for recovery of the capital. The state supreme court in *Coyle* vs. *Oklahoma* (1911), by a three-to-two decision, upheld Haskell's action. On appeal to the United States Supreme Court, in *Coyle* vs. *Smith* (1911), it was held that a state could determine the location of its capital city, despite an enabling act mandate.

In the 1910 primaries to select candidates

for the governor's race, William H. Murray competed with Leslie P. Ross of Lawton and Lee Cruce of Ardmore for the Democratic nomination. Joseph W. McNeal, a Guthrie banker; Thompson Ferguson, a former territorial governor; and John Fields, an editor, sought the Republican nomination. Since no runoff primary was held to produce a majority-vote winner, Cruce defeated Murray and Ross—Cruce, 52,262; Murray 40,166; and Ross 26,792. McNeal won the Republican nomination with 30,491 votes over Ferguson's 23,276 votes. Fields polled 17,985 votes. In the general election in November, Cruce won over McNeal, 120,218 to 99,527. The Socialist party also showed strength when its candidate, J. T. Crumbie, drew 24,767 votes for governor. The results showed that the "grandfather clause" clearly reduced the vote; before its adoption, the black vote numbered about 30,000, and after 1910 it dropped to less than 1,000.

Democrats made gains in both houses of the legislature and won back a congressional seat. Thus, Democratic congressmen from Oklahoma outnumbered Republicans three to two. In 1910 the voters also made a decision on modifying prohibition through local option, turning it back with a 25,000–vote margin.

Oklahoma's second governor, Lee Cruce, was a Kentuckian who had arrived in Ardmore before statehood, and had become an intermarried citizen of the Chickasaw nation. Trained as an attorney, he practiced law and engaged in banking. His previous political experience included an unsuccessful quest for the Democratic nomination for governor in 1907 and serving as a member of the University of Oklahoma Board of Regents. Cruce's cautious nature was demonstrated by his actions during the inaugural. After taking the oath of office at Oklahoma's new capital in Oklahoma City, he went to Guthrie and had the ceremony repeated.

Cruce campaigned on a platform of economy and made every attempt to keep the cost of government below that of the first administration. In this he was unsuccessful. Haskell's first legislature had appropriated nearly $4 million. Cruce's first legislature authorized expenditures totalling nearly $9 million. His attempts at economy eventually caused him

Governor Lee Cruce.

considerable trouble with the legislature because the governor's plan for paring state expenditures included abolishing certain state colleges and tightening control over surviving institutions of higher learning, including the University, through the new State Board of Education. This administrative change necessarily excluded the agricultural and mechanical colleges at Stillwater, Goodwell, Warner, Broken Bow, Helena, Tishomingo, and Lawton, since they were under the direction of the State Board of Agriculture.

Rumblings, auguring trouble, sounded in the legislature. Leaders in the law-making branch of government were irritated by the governor's tampering with local interests through his efforts to reduce the number of colleges, but they also were annoyed by his thwarting their congressional reapportionment proposal. The 1910 census showed Oklahoma, with a population of 1,657,155, was entitled to three additional seats in Congress. The Democrat-dominated legislature attempted to gerrymander Republican pockets of strength out of existence. Cruce threatened to veto the reapportionment bill whereupon the matter was deferred until 1913, with

Governor Robert L. Williams.

the three new congressmen to be elected at-large in 1912.

One area in which the governor and legislature worked in notable harmony concerned roads. The number of automobiles was increasing in Oklahoma, and the driving public demanded improved roads. On Cruce's recommendation, the legislature established the State Highway Department in 1911. Sidney Suggs, an editor from Ardmore, was named director. Income for the new state agency came from a one-dollar license fee charged for each vehicle.

Additional counties were created during Cruce's administration. Harmon County, in the southwestern corner of the state, became a separate political entity in 1909. Cotton County was carved from lower Comanche County, and Swanson County had a short life, for it was in existence less than a year.

The 1912 election was an interesting one for Oklahomans for three reasons. First, former Governor Haskell attempted to win the Democratic nomination for senator from incumbent Senator Robert L. Owen, but Owen triumphed, 80,204 to 44,483. Haskell's defeat set a trend, for thereafter no governor until

Robert S. Kerr was able to leave the governor's office popular enough to win a United States Senate seat. Owen went on to defeat J. T. Dickerson, the Republican candidate, and John G. Wills, the Socialist contender. Second, there was a national split in the Republican party. William H. Taft was the choice for president of the conservative wing of the party, while Theodore Roosevelt was the nominee of the so-called Bull Moose insurgents. Woodrow Wilson, the Democratic candidate, carried Oklahoma and the nation. Eugene Debs, Socialist candidate for president, received 46,262 votes in Oklahoma, his strength in the Sooner State due largely to an alliance of Farmers Union members and the United Mine Workers. And third, in the at-large—elected on a statewide basis—congressional elections to select the new members allocated to Oklahoma, the Democratic candidates, who included William H. Murray, won all three seats.

The Democratic legislature elected in 1912 therefore came to Oklahoma City angry at the governor and the administration generally for proposing to liquidate such vital local interest projects as colleges, and for the thwarting of the Democratic attempt to gerrymander congressional districts. Much of the legislatures' time was spent in investigating executive departments and conducting impeachment proceedings. The entire session of the Fourth Legislature was the forerunner for actions of this sort in subsequent legislatures. The governor himself escaped impeachment by a single vote in the investigating committee. The state auditor, state insurance commissioner, and state printer were impeached— that is, charges were brought by the house for trial by the senate. The state auditor and the insurance commissioner resigned. The senate convicted the state printer on a charge of approving illegal claims against state funds, and he was removed from office.

Governor Cruce held strong convictions on certain matters, notably capital punishment, with the result that no convicted criminal was executed during his administration. He commuted twenty-two death sentences to life imprisonment. This was the time of attempted moral reform through the adoption of "blue laws" by cities to enforce Sunday closing of businesses, and to prevent prize fighting, gambling, bootlegging, and horse racing. On several occasions, Governor Cruce, in an attempt to support local reformers, called out the militia to stop horse races and prize fights. On April 14, 1914, he declared martial law in Tulsa to stop a scheduled horse race.

While Cruce lacked the swashbuckling energy and daring of Governor Haskell, he was a man of high integrity, patience, and vision. He is credited with being the first state leader to see the need for long-range planning to promote industrial development in Oklahoma, in order to diversify the economy of the young state. Through his efforts, state and federal government surveys were made of Oklahoma coal, oil, other mineral resources, and water-power sites, and a long-range plan for highway development was formulated.

In the last year of Cruce's administration, World War I erupted in Europe. The nation, however, was more preoccupied at the time with local matters. In Oklahoma the consuming interest was the forthcoming election. In the gubernatorial primary, the Democratic party's candidates included Chief Justice Robert L. Williams; James B. Robertson of Chandler; and Al Jennings, best known as a train robber who had served a prison term for his brigandage. Jenning's notoriety produced 21,732 votes, enough to gain third place. Robertson, with 33,504 votes, barely lost to Williams with 35,605. The Republicans chose John Fields as their candidate. Division in the Oklahoma Republican party continued, with an insurgent Bull Moose candidate, John Hickam, polling 4,189 votes in the general election. Williams defeated Fields for the governor's office, 100,597 to 95,905. Fred Holt, a United Mine Workers official and the Socialist gubernatorial candidate, drew 52,703 votes. The election of 1914 marked the high tide of socialism in Oklahoma. In the same election Socialist leader Oscar Ameringer was almost elected mayor of Oklahoma City.

Thomas P. Gore, Democrat and United States Senate incumbent, defeated Republican John Burford and Socialist candidate Pat Nagle in the first popular United States Senate election held in Oklahoma. In the congressional races, the Democrats won seven of the eight seats, and the state legislature continued with a Democratic majority in both houses.

Oklahomans also voted on an initiative petition to reduce the legislature to a single (unicameral) body of eighty members. It almost passed, receiving a vote of 94,686 to 71,742 in favor of the proposition. This was 30,000 votes short of the prescribed majority. Thus, in effect, the silent vote killed the proposition.

Oklahoma's third governor was from Alabama. Robert L. Williams studied for the Methodist ministry, was licensed to preach, and served as a circuit rider in Texas. He then taught school and studied law. Williams came to Oklahoma in 1893 during the Cherokee Outlet opening, and he practiced law briefly at Orlando. After a return to Alabama, he came back to Indian Territory and settled at Durant in 1896. He played a key role in developing the Democratic party in eastern Oklahoma and served as a national committeeman from Indian Territory. He won election as a delegate to the constitutional convention in 1906, and a year later was elected to the State Supreme Court and became its chief justice. He resigned from the court in 1914 to make the race for governor.

Governor Williams, an assertive, determined administrator, was distressed by the sprawling maze of boards, commissions, and agencies making up the structure of state government, each more or less autonomous, going its own independent way. He consolidated several governing boards for state institutions through the State Board of Affairs, and played a directive role in their administration by making appointments and setting salaries. Through his concentration of power, Williams probably was Oklahoma's strongest chief executive.

Governor Cruce had broken ground for a new state capitol situated in northeast Oklahoma City on July 20, 1914; eager to complete it, Governor Williams made himself chairman of the commission supervising construction. Williams moved into the new building on January 1, 1917, although it was not completed until July 1 of that year. The plans called for a capitol dome and footings were poured to carry it, but because of lack of funds and the wartime steel shortage this characteristic feature of state capitols was omitted. The total cost of the building which housed all three

The Oklahoma state capitol building constructed during Governor Williams's term.

branches of state government, was $1.5 million.

Williams stressed economy and had greater success than his predecessor in achieving it. Taxes were raised and appropriations for all institutions were trimmed in an effort to reduce state indebtedness. Connell A and M College at Helena and Haskell A and M College at Broken Bow were abolished. The physical plant at Helena was converted into a reformatory, and the girls' reformatory at Wynnewood was moved to Tecumseh. Oklahoma's institutional development continued as the state purchased the private mental hospital at Norman for $100,000 and renamed it Central State Hospital.

Legislative action during Williams's administration included appropriation of funds to expand Oklahoma's highway system in cooperation with the federal government's program of matching funds. Social and economic legislation provided a minimum hour law for women in industry; welfare laws to support widows and orphans, including a stipend of ten dollars per month to be administered by the county commissioners; and laws regulating warehouses. Cotton gins were made public utilities and thereby became subject to state regulations.

Legislative action included continuation of investigations and impeachments. A corporation commissioner was impeached, con-

victed, and removed from office on a charge of accepting loans from companies which appeared before him. An insurance commissioner, impeached on a charge of improper relations with insurance companies, was acquitted.

One of the two major developments occurring during the Williams administration was the *Guinn* vs. *United States* decision, handed down by the United States Supreme Court in 1915. State election officials in certain counties had been indicted by federal grand juries on charges of violating federal election laws by enforcing Oklahoma's "grandfather clause." Several officials were convicted and sentenced to prison. Later they were pardoned, but the decisions were appealed. The High Court declared that the "grandfather clause" amendment to the state constitution was invalid because it violated the Fifteenth Amendment of the United States Constitution. Williams called the legislature into special session in 1916, and two methods were adopted to check Negro suffrage. One was a proposition submitted to the voters providing for the customary literacy test for voter registration but making military service the basis for exemption. This proposition was voted down by the people, 133,140 to 90,605. The other suffrage restriction device consisted of setting an extremely brief registration period for voters not already eligible, which included most blacks. This law was in force until 1939 when the *Lane* vs. *Wilson* decision declared it unconstitutional.

The 1916 election was a tame one for Oklahoma. There was no United States Senate contest and, since it was a presidential election year, there was no governor's race to spice the proceedings. President Woodrow Wilson was challenged by Republican Charles E. Hughes and Socialist Eugene Debs. Oklahoma's presidential vote was Wilson, 148,113; Hughes, 97,233; and Debs, 46,527. The Democrats won six of the eight congressional seats and heavy majorities in both houses of the state legislature.

The second big development of Williams's administration was the involvement of the United States and Oklahoma in World War I. Oklahoma was somewhat prepared for the American declaration of war in the spring of 1917 because the state militia was already on active duty as a part of the force mustered under General John Pershing to crush the Pancho Villa outbreaks on the Mexican border. Governor Williams energetically mobilized the resources of the state for the war effort. He assisted in mustering troops through local draft boards; encouraged maximum farm production; promoted the saving of food and fuel for the troops in Europe; and led Liberty Bond drives to help finance the war. More than 91,000 Oklahomans, including 5,000 blacks, saw active military duty. Of these, 1,064 were killed in action; 502 were reported missing in action; 4,154 were wounded; and 710 died from disease, primarily from Spanish influenza, which spread over Europe and the United States in epidemic proportions. The epidemic struck in Oklahoma, too, taking a heavy toll.

Turmoil erupted on the home front in political actions by extreme left-wing and extreme right-wing groups. On the left were the Socialists and the IWW (Wobblies), agitators who preached that the struggle in Europe was a "rich man's war and a poor man's fight." These extremists encouraged resistance to the military draft. A ragtag band of antidraft demonstrators roamed the countryside in Pottawatomie, Hughes, and Seminole counties during the summer of 1917, burning bridges and committing general mischief. This

Governor James B. Robertson.

"Green Corn Rebellion" ultimately was crushed by posses and the leaders were arrested. On the right were members of the American Protective League and the Knights of Liberty; in their white robes they watched for subversion and disloyalty. Innocent citizens who failed to buy their quota of Liberty Bonds were publicly scorned as "slackers." Failure to heed the warnings of the "silent watchers of disloyalty" often led to the tar and feathers treatment or orders to leave the state.

The 1918 elections were held during the last months of the war. In the Democratic primary, James B. Robertson defeated William H. Murray, 48,568 to 24,283, and met the Republican candidate, Horace McKeever, in November. The disenchantment of Oklahomans with socialism, partly as a result of the "Green Corn Rebellion," was reflected in the small vote received by the Socialist candidate for governor, Pat Nagle, who received only 7,438 votes. In the United States Senate race, Robert L. Owen won over Republican W. B. Johnson, 105,000 to 77,000. The Democrats obtained seven of the eight congressional seats and elected a heavy majority in both houses of the legislature. The outgoing governor, Robert L. Williams, was appointed judge for the United States District Court for eastern Oklahoma by President Wilson. He was elevated to the Federal Circuit Court of Appeals in 1937 by President Franklin Roosevelt.

Oklahoma's fourth governor, James Brooks Robertson, was born in Iowa and reared in Kansas. He trained as an attorney and settled at Chandler during territorial days. He taught school, practiced law, and entered politics, progressing from county attorney to membership on the State Supreme Court Commission. Robertson sought the Democratic nomination for governor in 1914, losing to Williams, but made a strong comeback and was successful in 1918. Significantly, he was the Sooner State's first governor from old Oklahoma Territory.

One of Robertson's principal goals was to improve Oklahoma roads. He attempted to gain voter approval on a $50 million bond issue for highway construction, and although he lost, he did manage to squeeze out sufficient state revenue to construct 1,300 miles of highways, more than the total mileage produced by his three predecessors combined. Through his promotion of farm marketing cooperatives, these organizations flourished in the Sooner State, especially in the west.

As governor, Robertson backed away from the centralized power structure built by Governor Williams. At his instigation the control of colleges by the State Board of Education was abolished and institutions of higher learning were again governed by separate boards of regents. In the institutional changes occurring during the Robertson administration, Tonkawa Preparatory College became a junior college; Eastern Preparatory College at Claremore became Oklahoma Military Academy; a school of mines was established at Miami in the heart of the famous Tri-State District lead and zinc field; and the six normal schools became teachers' colleges.

Governor Robertson was distressed by the generally low academic levels of Oklahoma schools, especially by the great number of districts unable to maintain school for more than three months per year. His interest led to the appointment of a special commission consisting of leading national and state educators, headed by William T. Bawden of the United States Bureau of Education, which was assigned the task of making a searching study of Oklahoma schools. From the Bawden study came such reforms as improvement in the preparation and certification of teachers, upgrading of curricula, beginnings of consolidation of rural schools; a subsidized textbook program, and state aid to poorly financed districts. During the second biennium of the Robertson administration, an appropriation of $100,000 was made as a response to the state aid recommendation. This began the system of school finance which in recent years has become an important source of support for public schools.

With Robertson's encouragement, the legislature approved the Eighteenth Amendment (national prohibition) and the Nineteenth Amendment (national women's suffrage) to the United States Constitution. An interesting and important development of the Robertson administration was the settlement of the Red River boundary. Controversy over jurisdiction grew out of the discovery of oil in the broad riverbed. Both Texas and Oklahoma executed leases and prepared to collect taxes on production. Texas declared jurisdiction over the southern half of the river channel, while Oklahoma claimed that its boundary extended to the foot of the bluffs on the south side. Injunctions were issued and Oklahoma national guardsmen faced Texas rangers where Tillman County, Oklahoma, abuts the famous stream. In three decisions handed down between 1921 and 1923, the United States Supreme Court defined the boundary. The south shore was declared to be the cut-bank, and not the foot of the bluffs as Oklahoma claimed. Oklahoma had jurisdiction, said the High Court, to the middle of the stream.

The second half of the Robertson administration was a time of turmoil and disorder. Only the determined efforts of the governor prevented disaster. Pervasive trouble had its roots in a postwar recession that developed into a full-blown depression in Oklahoma, principally because of the state's primary dependence on agriculture and oil production. Inflated wartime prices had encouraged farm expansion and increase in debt, and the postwar decline in grain and beef prices caused extensive foreclosures and bank failures. The bank guaranty system could not stand the strain and it too collapsed, causing additional economic anguish. Beginning in 1919, strikes became widespread, and 9,000 miners were out in eastern Oklahoma alone. Business leaders blamed IWW agitation, and Robertson sent two regiments of national guard troops to Henryetta, Coalgate, and McAlester. Martial law was declared in the troubled zone. Labor protests spread to the railroads, building trades, and manufacturing plants.

The election of 1920 produced a revolution in Oklahoma politics. General disillusionment with President Wilson's crusade to make the world safe for democracy, the League of Nations issue, and the paralyzing depression caused Oklahomans to show their disenchantment with the Democratic party by overthrowing its long-standing domination of state politics. In this, the first general election in which Oklahoma women voted, the Sooner State's electoral vote went to the Republicans for the first time in state history. Republican Warren G. Harding carried Oklahoma with 243,831 votes to 217,753 for the Democratic candidate, James M. Cox. Socialist Eugene Debs polled 25,716. In the United States Senate race, Democrat Scott Ferris, who had beaten incumbent Thomas P. Gore in the primary, lost to Republican John W. Harreld. This was another first for the Oklahoma Republican party.

Republican candidates won five of the eight congressional seats. One of the Republican victors in the congressional contests was Alice M. Robertson of Muskogee, a grandaughter of Samuel Austin Worcester, the great Cherokee missionary and educator. The first woman elected to Congress from Oklahoma, she was at the time of her election, only the second in the United States. The Republicans won several state offices, including seats on the supreme court. For the first time in state history, Oklahoma's minority party won a majority of seats in the Oklahoma House of Representatives, with a final division of fifty-five Republicans and thirty-seven Democrats. The senate, with its one-half holdover membership, remained Democratic, twenty-seven to seventeen.

The Republican dominated house of repre-

Patrick J. Hurley, Oklahoman who was President Herbert Hoover's secretary of war.

sentatives investigated the governor and several other Democratic officials. Governor Robertson missed impeachment by one vote; an ailing Democratic house member was carried from his sickbed by an ambulance to cast the crucial vote turning back the governor's impeachment. Lieutenant Governor Martin E. Trapp was charged with "fraudulent conspiracy" and impeached by the house, but he was acquitted in the senate on a strict party-line vote.

The most dreadful occurrence of the Robertson administration was the Tulsa race riot, although it was not the first instance of racial turbulence in Oklahoma. A Negro-white outbreak had occurred in Guthrie during territorial days, but the Tulsa riot on May 31, 1921, was much more serious. Dick Rowland, a black, was arrested on a charge of molesting a white girl, and a mob of whites gathered at the jail apparently intent on lynching him. Violence flared when a countering mob of blacks sought to protect Rowland. The struggle spread to the black section of Tulsa where fire gutted two miles of homes and businesses. Seventy blacks and nine whites died in the rioting and order was restored only by the entry of the national guard and application of martial law.

There was considerable postwar concern in Oklahoma over the threat of the radical left. The legislature passed laws to control criminal syndicalism; forbade desecration of the American flag; and banned the teaching of foreign languages in the first eight grades of public schools.

The Knights of Liberty, the American Protective League, and other superpatriot groups active in Oklahoma during World War I fused into a national movement known as the Ku Klux Klan. The leader of this organization in Oklahoma was Clay Jewett, who headed a state membership probably exceeding 100,000. The Klan was the champion of white supremacy and claimed to be the "defender of traditional white Anglo-Saxon native-born Protestant values." It was anti-Catholic, anti-Semitic, anti-Negro, opposed to immigration, international involvement by the United States in such activities as the League of Na-

tions, and was antilabor and probusiness. The Klan with its regalia, initiations, and secret operations appealed to citizens much like a lodge or social club. Klan members were, as one observer put it, "bigots in bed sheets." The Klan enforced its own code of private moral law by warnings, whippings, mutilation, and burning crosses. If a victim reported Klan action, he was brutalized again, so that few reports were made to authorities. Political activity was a logical step beyond the Klan's vigilante activities, and it became a power in Oklahoma politics. As one observer pointed out, "it used violence to further its politics and politics to protect its violence."

Many claim that the Klan took an active part in Oklahoma politics in 1922 to check the extreme program proposed by the Farm Labor Reconstruction League. The League and the Klan and their interactions with Oklahoma's established political parties set off personal rivalries and political struggles which remain among the stormiest experienced by the Sooner State.

Notes on Sources, Chapter 16

Oklahoma's post-statehood political evolution is in part an extension of its ethnic composition. *Newcomers to a New Land*, a recent series of works interpreting Oklahoma's diverse racial makeup, edited by a committee chaired by H. Wayne Morgan, confirms this point: Kenny L. Brown, *The Italians in Oklahoma* (Norman, 1980); Patrick J. Blessing, *The British and Irish in Oklahoma* (Norman, 1980); Richard C. Rohrs, *The Germans in Oklahoma* (Norman, 1980); Douglas Hale, *The Germans from Russia in Oklahoma* (Norman, 1980); Rennard Strickland, *The Indians in Oklahoma* (Norman, 1980); Richard M. Bernard, *The Poles in Oklahoma* (Norman, 1980); Jimmie L. Franklin, *The Blacks in Oklahoma* (Norman, 1980); Michael M. Smith, *The Mexicans in Oklahoma* (Norman, 1980); Karel D. Bicha, *The Czechs in Oklahoma* (Norman, 1980); and Henry J. Tobias, *The Jews in Oklahoma* (Norman, 1980).

Early Oklahoma politics are presented in Oscar P. Fowler, *The Haskell Regime: The Intimate Life of Charles Nathaniel Haskell* (Oklahoma City, 1933); Gordon Hines, *Alfalfa Bill* (Oklahoma City,

1932); William H. Murray, *Memoirs of Governor Murray*, 3 vols. (Boston, 1945); Oscar Ameringer, *If you Don't Weaken* (New York, 1940); Edward E. Dale and James D. Morrison, *Pioneer Judge: The Life of Robert L. Williams* (Cedar Rapids, Iowa, 1954); and Keith L. Bryant, *Alfalfa Bill Murray* (Norman, 1968).

Prohibition, a recurring issue in Oklahoma politics, is discussed by Jimmie L. Franklin in *Born Sober: Prohibition in Oklahoma, 1907–1959* (Norman, 1971); and in "Prohibition in Oklahoma," *Chronicles of Oklahoma* 43 (June, 1965): 19–34.

Radicalism in Oklahoma politics before 1922 is discussed in Orben Casey, "Governor Lee Cruce and Law Enforcement, 1911–1915," *Chronicles of Oklahoma* 52 (Winter, 1974–75): 456–75; Sherry Warrick, "Radical Labor in Oklahoma: The Working Class Union," *Chronicles of Oklahoma* 52 (Summer, 1974): 180–95; and Howard L. Meredith, "Agrarian Socialism and the Negro in Oklahoma, 1900–1918," *Labor History* 11 (Summer, 1970): 227–84.

Chapter 17

Oklahoma Politics: The Early Years, Part 2

Oklahoma's Farm Labor Reconstruction League was an outgrowth of the Non-Partisan League of North Dakota. In 1917, L. N. Sheldon came to Oklahoma from North Dakota and began spreading Non-Partisan League doctrine. At the time the League was advocating a graduated land tax; a rural credit bank operating at cost; public ownership of utilities, warehouses, flour mills, stockyards, packing plants, cotton gins, and coal mines; and the exemption of farm improvements and tools from taxation. The Oklahoma Farm Labor Reconstruction League, consisting of the Farmer's Union, a remnant of the Socialist party, and labor groups including the railroad brotherhoods, was organized at Shawnee on September 17, 1921. The Oklahoma group adopted many of Sheldon's ideas. John Simpson, Farmer's Union president, proposed that the new league use the apparatus of the Democratic party to achieve its goals rather than organize a third party. League officials adopted Simpson's proposal. This action set the stage for a split in the Democratic party.

Jack Walton, mayor of Oklahoma City, announced early in 1922 his intention to run for the Democratic nomination on a platform espousing the league proposals. Conservative Democrats sponsored Judge Thomas H. Owen of Muskogee. Robert H. Wilson, who was state education superintendent and allegedly endorsed by the Klan, also sought the Democratic nomination. When Walton won the primary, conservative Democrats formed the Constitutional Democratic Club to support the Republican candidate, John H. Fields. In the general election, Walton defeated Fields, 280,206 to 230,469. Walton's campaign was a "rip-snorter," the liveliest campaign in state history. His crowd-attracting activities included string bands and spellbinding oratory. Democrats won seven of the eight congressional seats and a solid majority in both houses of the legislature, although many of the new Democratic members were Klansmen hostile to Walton.

John C. (Jack) Walton, Oklahoma's fifth governor, was born in Indiana in 1881, traveled west as a youth, and lived in Nebraska before coming to Oklahoma Territory to work as an engineer. His political career began in 1917 when he was selected commissioner of public works in Oklahoma City. He was mayor of Oklahoma City at the time of his nomination as Democratic candidate for governor. Walton served the shortest term of all elected Oklahoma governors, from January 9 to November 19, 1923. His inauguration was the happiest time of his brief tenure as chief executive, for soon thereafter grief and disappointment were his constant companions, brought on largely through his own ineptitude and political inexperience. He eschewed the traditional elegant inaugural ball, preferring in the Jacksonian tradition a party where all the people of Oklahoma could participate—a giant barbecue and square dance, the noisiest, most colorful inaugural in Sooner State history.

The Ninth Legislature was cool to much of Walton's Reconstruction League program, drafted by a group known as the Committee of Twenty-One and promoted by Pat Nagle. Mild reforms adopted by the legislature included an expanded farm cooperative program; revision of the Workman's Compensation Law to provide improved benefits; stronger warehouse inspection laws to satisfy wheat and cotton farmers; the state's first free textbook law; and

Governor Jack Walton.

aid for poorly funded schools to the amount of nearly $1 million.

Walton's trouble began when he vacillated between league advisers and the conservatives in the legislature. Both groups pressured him; as the governor sought to placate first one group and then the other, he succeeded only in alienating both. His greatest problems grew out of patronage. One observer wrote that Walton "looked on his office as a patronage distribution center," and that to appease the conflicting factions he thought it necessary only to find more jobs for them, or as he put it, his duty was "finding a place for the boys." After he had loaded every department in state government with appointees, Walton turned to the institutions of higher learning for fresh rewards for his friends and for persons whose support he sought. Tampering with the University of Oklahoma and the A. and M. College at Stillwater caused his downfall. At the University he applied pressure from the board of regents to the president and the faculty in his search for places for gubernatorial favors. His pressure on University President Stratton D. Brooks ended in Brooks's resignation. At Oklahoma A and M College he managed to

force the resignation of President J. B. Eskridge to make room for George Wilson, president of the Farm Labor Reconstruction League. Faculty members also were forced to resign.

Walton's summary actions caused demonstrations at Stillwater among students and townspeople, and a military guard was necessary to place Wilson in the president's office. Meanwhile, Stratton D. Brooks became president of the University of Missouri, and his loss to Oklahoma caused additional denunciation of the governor.

Klan activity over the state increased during 1923 as beatings, mutilation, and intimidation occurred daily. Okmulgee County was especially notorious for nocturnal orgies by hooded Klansmen. In June, 1923, Governor Walton placed the county under martial law. Reports of Klan beatings in Tulsa likewise caused the governor to place that county under martial law, with the additional penalty of suspension of habeas corpus, the latter step clearly prohibited by the state constitution.

When an Oklahoma City grand jury prepared to investigate the governor's office, Walton placed the entire state under martial law on September 15, 1923, with "absolute martial law" applicable to the capital. Walton claimed he took this drastic step to thwart "the enemies of the Sovereign State of Oklahoma, the deadly Invisible Empire."

The governor's actions caused several leading state newspapers to demand his impeachment. When legislative leaders responded to these demands and attempted to convene the law-making body in special session without the constitutionally required call by the governor, the legislature was dispersed by national guard troops. Thereupon, Campbell Russell, a Democratic leader, circulated an initiative petion that called for allowing the legislature to assemble on its own motion. The success of the petition placed the proposition on the ballot for a special election already scheduled for October 2, one calling for a vote on a soldier's bonus. The bonus measure failed, but the legislative meeting proposal carried 209,452 to 70,638.

Walton called the legislature into special session on October 11 to consider a proposal to "unmask the Klan and destroy its power." The legislature refused to consider the governor's request. It recessed but met again on October 17 at the call of Speaker of the House W. D. McBee. The house formulated twenty-two charges against the governor and voted for impeachment. On October 23, Jack Walton was suspended from office and Lieutenant Governor Martin E. Trapp became acting governor. Tulsa house member Wesley E. Disney headed the prosecution against Walton in the senate, which was presided over by the chief justice of the State Supreme Court. Eleven charges were sustained, including illegal collection of campaign funds, padding the public payroll, suspension of habeas corpus, excessive use of the pardon power, and general incompetency. On November 19, 1923, Jack Walton was convicted and removed from office.

Martin E. Trapp came to Oklahoma from Kansas during the Run of 1889, and settled at Guthrie. After an early career in newspaper work, he turned to politics and became the epitome of the professional politician, working up through the ranks of elective office until 1914, when he became the perennial lieutenant governor, winning that office again in 1918 and 1922.

After the Walton episode, Oklahomans were ready for quiet, conservative leadership, and Trapp provided just that. He restored the credit of the state by gaining repeal of $10 million worth of Walton's planned expenditures, primarily related to institutional building. His economies included a one-third reduction by the legislature in the school aid appropriation, and the repeal of Walton's free textbook program. With a three-cents per gallon increase in the gasoline tax, Trapp carried out a vast highway construction program. He managed public finances so carefully that when he left office there was a $2 million surplus in the state treasury. Because of his interest in the outdoors, he provided leadership and initiative in establishing a forestry commission, a conservation commission, and a fish and game commission. Trapp showed great courage in promoting the passage of an antimask law which eventually reduced the power of the Klan, although at the time the "invisible empire" in Oklahoma was still powerful. Trapp also promoted legislation that improved enforcement of prohibition.

Governor Martin E. Trapp.

The 1924 election saw a curious turn of events when Robert L. Owen, senatorial incumbent since statehood, decided to retire and Jack Walton won the Democratic nomination for United States senator. The anomaly of Walton's nomination, following so closely on the heels of his impeachment, is explained in part by the fact that he was the only candidate who publicly condemned the Ku Klux Klan. The Klan was at its peak in political power in 1924, both in Oklahoma and in the nation. So effectively had the Klan infiltrated the Democratic party across the nation that the "invisible empire" was able to thwart the nomination of Catholic Al Smith of New York for the presidency. Public repugnance toward the Klan in Oklahoma increased as its membership became more arrogant and intemperate in its attacks on the persons and property of innocent citizens. The fact that Walton's opponents in the Democratic primary failed to condemn the Klan, and that Walton's closest primary competitor had direct Klan endorsement probably account for the former governor's nomination.

William B. Pine, Okmulgee millionaire, was Walton's Republican opponent in the general

Governor Henry S. Johnston.

election. The former governor went down to crushing defeat, 339,646 to 196,417, as Oklahoma elected its second Republican United States senator. The presidential contest pitted Democrat John W. Davis against Republican Calvin Coolidge. While Coolidge won nationally, Oklahoma returned to the Democratic fold for its electoral vote, providing Davis with a 30,000–vote margin. Democrats won six of the eight congressional seats and majorities in both houses of the state legislature.

Trapp had studiously refused to acknowledge that his tenure in the state's highest office was any more than that of acting governor, and as the election of 1926 approached, the reason became apparent. He had ambitions to run for governor and there was a constitutional rule that a governor could not succeed himself. Trapp had been a conservative, capable administrator; he enjoyed widespread popularity, and his chances of winning the nomination appeared good. To clarify his status, the State Supreme Court took the matter under study and in *Fitzpatrick* vs. *McAlister*, it ruled that Trapp had been governor in fact and that the constitutional limitation applied.

With Trapp removed, the field of Democratic nominees narrowed to Henry S. Johnston of Perry, a leader in the constitutional convention and favorite of prohibition forces and Protestant churchmen of Oklahoma; O. A. Cargill, the mayor of Oklahoma City; and William Darnell, a farm leader. Johnston reportedly was favored by the Klan, while his principal opponent, Cargill, was bitterly against the Klan. When the votes were in, the results indicated the hazards of opposing the Klan, even as late as 1926, for Cargill placed third with 45,993 votes. Darnell took second place with 73,922 votes, and Johnston won with 87,840 votes. Johnston's Republican opponent in November was Omer K. Benedict, Tulsa postmaster and the former editor of the *Oklahoma City Times*. Johnston won in the general election, 213,167 to 170,714. At the same time, incumbent Republican Senator John W. Harreld was up for reelection, and Elmer Thomas, congressman from Lawton, was his Democratic opponent. Thomas won, 195,312 to 159,287, and launched a career in the United States Senate that extended to 1950. Democrats also won seven of the eight congressional seats and returned majorities to both houses of the state legislature. In view of the legislature's growing obsession with its impeachment power, the lieutenant governor's race was becoming important in state politics. The winner of this office in the 1926 election was William J. Holloway, former president pro tempore of the senate.

The Eleventh Legislature, led by Speaker D. A. Stovall in the house and President pro tempore Mac Q. Williamson in the senate, received Governor Johnston's inaugural legislative program. No augury of trouble was evident in legislative approval of such enlightened proposals as establishing a crippled children's hospital and increasing the school aid appropriation to $1.5 million, the highest public school subsidy in the state history to that time.

However, revolt against the governor began when he proposed to enlarge the State Highway Commission from three to five members. Patronage in the State Highway Department became a lively issue. This in turn developed into a bitter controversy over the relative advantages of asphalt and concrete as basic highway materials, and it seemed the legislature was spoiling for a fight. Legislative leaders missed no opportunity to criticize the governor. Their customary prerogatives and free access to the governor apparently were of no consequence to Johnston's private secretary, Mrs. O. O. Hammonds, who controlled the governor's appointments; in exercising her duties she turned powerful legislators away from the governor's door. Mrs. Hammonds then became a center of violent legislative criticism. It was charged that she made executive decisions, and it was but a natural step to accuse the governor of neglect of duty.

After the close of the regular session of the Eleventh Legislature, house and senate leaders kept alive a determined campaign to discredit Governor Johnston. In late November, 1927, the legislature planned to meet in special session under authority of the adopted initiative proposition which had spelled Walton's doom. The declared purpose was to investigate the governor. Shortly before the scheduled meeting date, the State Supreme Court ruled the initiative proposition unconstitutional, which meant that the legislature could meet only in regular session or at the call of the governor. When it appeared that the legislature would convene in defiance of the court ruling, a district court in Oklahoma City issued an injunction forbidding the legislature to assemble unless called by the governor. House and senate leaders ignored the ruling and the injunction and called the legislature together. The members were turned away from the capitol by national guard troops placed there on Johnston's orders, whereupon the legislature convened in the Huckins Hotel in downtown Oklahoma City. E. P. Hill replaced Stovall as speaker of the house, and Representative Tom Kight was appointed chairman of the committee to investigate the governor. Impeachment charges were voted, and the senate convened in the hotel as a court of impeachment. Impeachment charges also were brought against Chief Justice Fred Branson and Harry P. Cordell, chairman of the State Board of Agriculture. Taking a more deliberate view of the matter, since the courts were on the governor's side, and concerned over the legality of their convening, the senate

Prohibition agents destroying a moonshine still seized in Oklahoma City.

turned down the charges and the legislature adjourned.

Johnston was vindicated, his poise under fire had won support, and his restraint in using the courts rather than martial law proved him a tactician superior to Walton. All things being equal, he could have served out his term without additional legislative harassment, but his political doom was sealed by the election of 1928. The Democrats, meeting at Houston, Texas, in national convention, selected Al Smith of New York for their presidential candidate. In addition to being a Catholic, Smith was an acknowledged advocate of repeal of prohibition. During the campaign he appeared in Oklahoma City for a speech in which he denounced the Ku Klux Klan, prohibitionists, and religious bigots. This aroused the Klan, the WCTU, and the Anti-Saloon League, and the Protestant clergy of Oklahoma.

The governor's fatal slip was campaigning for Smith across the state, making four or more speeches a day on behalf of the Democratic candidate. Herbert Hoover, the Republican candidate, carried the state with an overwhelming majority of 170,000 votes and for

Ku Klux Klan rally at Bartlesville.

the second time since statehood the Republicans captured Oklahoma's electoral vote. Hoover also won the Deep South generally and achieved a decisive national victory over Smith. Republican candidates exploited the situation to win several state offices, including three seats on the State Supreme Court, a near-majority in the lower house of the legislature, substantial gains in the senate, and three of the eight congressional seats.

All Democratic wrath was heaped on Henry Johnston, for he was held responsible for the disaster. Principally, it was charged that he had worked for the nomination of Smith and thus made a Hoover victory inevitable. Ironically, Johnston's heaviest condemnation came from his erstwhile supporters, the dry forces, the Ku Klux Klan, and the Protestant clergy.

The day after the Twelfth Legislature convened in regular session during January, 1929, a combination of Republicans and insurgent Democrats set in motion a second impeachment effort. Thirteen charges were presented to the senate, eleven of which were accepted. Johnston was suspended from office on January 21, and Lieutenant Governor Holloway became acting governor. Johnston's impeachment trial began on February 6 and extended over six weeks. The governor took the stand in his own defense and the prosecution was unable to ruffle him. His answers to the charges, many of them trivial, were strong and challenging. Even so, it was clear that he was convicted before the trial ever began. On March 20 the governor's ordeal ended when the senate voted to remove him from office on the charge of general incompetency.

Governor Holloway's political reputation had been established through years of service in the senate as a friend of the teaching profession and an advocate of educational reform. In his dignified, measured way, he restored executive rapport with the legislature and managed to gain adoption of a new mining code requiring operators to provide improved health and sanitary conditions for their workers. He also obtained passage of a law that extended protection to the state's youth by expanding the child labor laws. Because of the large number of automobiles now on the state's highways, a forty-five mile per hour speed limit was set. Holloway won from the legislature a revision of the State Highway Commission, and its membership was reduced to three commissioners. To carry out his pledge of bipartisan management of road construction, he appointed Lew Wentz, a prominent Republican and oil millionaire, as chairman of the Highway Commision.

Probably the most important reform of Holloway's announced goals was to keep biennial expenditures under $30 million. In this he succeeded, but the Great Depression developed in 1929, and the governor had to extend every effort to keep the state solvent in time of crisis. During the Holloway administration, the "invisible empire," the Ku Klux Klan, faded as a power on the Oklahoma political and social scene.

The closing months of the Holloway administration were enlivened by the 1930 election to choose a new governor. The Great Depression of 1929 had worsened to disastrous proportions in Oklahoma. Factories and mines closed, the oil market was depressed, and unemployment was the highest in history, as hungry, poverty-stricken citizens formed long lines at public soup kitchens. From the number of candidates filing for nomination, it appeared that many of the displaced workers were seeking employment by election to public office. One hundred three candidates filed for election to the fifteen state positions in 1930 and this total did not include a proportionate number seeking the legislative, judicial, and congressional offices. The trend increased throughout the depressed 1930s in Oklahoma until 1938 when more than one thousand candidates filed for political office with the State Election Board. At the primary election the voters were confronted with what was called the "bed sheet ballot."

Oklahoma Republicans, the party of President Herbert Hoover, carried the stigma of depression, so Democrats appeared to have things their own way. Leading candidates for governor were former Governor Trapp and Frank Buttram, Oklahoma City oil millionaire. The latter was endorsed by the *Daily Oklahoman* (Oklahoma City). Absent from the Oklahoma political scene for years had been Alfalfa Bill Murray, who had led a colony of Oklahomans to Bolivia. Now he had returned in time to file for governor, an office he had sought several times. In keeping with the Depression theme, Murray began his campaign on what he called "$40 of borrowed money." Murray supporters purchased a paper at Roff, Oklahoma, the *Blue Valley Farmer*, and it became famous as a mouthpiece for Alfalfa Bill. Murray condemned the "metropolitan press" (Oklahoma City and Tulsa newspapers) and claimed to be the champion of "little people" —the poor, struggling farmer, and the unemployed city worker.

A reincarnation of the frontier politician, complete with the homey touch, Murray ran well ahead of the other Democratic candidates in the primary. In the first vote he led Buttram, his closest rival, 134,243 to 69,501, and he easily won the runoff. Oklahoma Republicans selected Ira A. Hill, state senator and attorney from Cherokee, as their gubernatorial candidate. Alfalfa Bill won in November by a vote of 301,921 to 208,575. Incumbent Republican United States Senator William B. Pine lost reelection to a resurgent Thomas P. Gore, 255,838 to 232,589. Democrats won seven of the eight congressional seats and healthy majorities in the state legislature.

No governor before or since faced the prob-

Governor William "Alfalfa Bill" Murray.

lems that Murray had to deal with. He attacked the $5 million deficit in the state treasury, mass unemployment, mortgage foreclosures, and bank failures with an aplomb, which, if not always effective, was at least entertaining. Emergency relief to mitigate the pervasive economic suffering was Murray's first concern. From the Thirteenth Legislature he obtained a $600,000 appropriation to provide free seed for planting gardens and emergency commodities. Murray collected money from state employees, businessmen, and even gave much of his own salary (over the years his gifts amounted to nearly $6,000) to feed the destitute. No federal relief program of consequence had as yet been formulated and Murray became a leader in developing a broad concern for the victims of the Great Depression by calling a national council for relief which met at Memphis in June, 1931.

State government faced bankruptcy not only because of the $5 million deficit but because most taxpayers lacked the means to pay their county and state obligations. In this emergency, Murray led the legislature to create the State Tax Commission. The new agency soon demonstrated its worth by estab-

Western Oklahoma Dust Bowl scene.

lishing safeguards against tax evasion and showing the alarming drainage of taxable wealth from the state. Murray also encouraged the Board of Equalization to equalize tax assessments. The board eventually claimed to have so righted injustices of assessment that small homeowners' tax burdens were reduced by a total of $141 million, while corporate property taxes were increased by $65 million.

There was no doubt about who was running the state when Murray was governor, and there was rarely a dull moment during his administration. He talked economy, and he meant what he said. The one possible extravagance he allowed was free textbooks. This program had been adopted earlier, repealed, and then reenacted on Murray's recommendation. Perhaps this action was because of the governor's big-hearted if rough concern that children of all economic and social groups have equal opportunity.

Murray directed the Thirteenth Legislature to pare its appropriations, which the members refused to do. Alfalfa Bill countered with this warning: "You fellows go ahead and pass these appropriations . . . and I'll veto every damned one of them. And if you've got any impeach-

ment ideas in your heads, hop to it. It'll be like a bunch of jack rabbits tryin' to get a wildcat out of a hole."

These were hard times, and Murray exploited the emergency situations to justify extensive use of the national guard and martial law. He used state troops to enforce his bank moratorium order, which was aimed at stopping bank runs and checking bank failures. He used national guard troops and martial law to enforce segregation in Oklahoma City, and to collect tickets at University of Oklahoma football games while the school's athletic department was under investigation. One of his most widely publicized uses of state troops concerned the Red River bridge episode. The Durant-Denison Bridge Company operated toll bridges across Red River. The Oklahoma Highway Department constructed a free bridge on Highway 69. A federal court injunction forbade use of the free bridge and ordered it closed. Murray charged that the courts were protecting toll bridge investors to the detriment of public welfare and ordered the national guard to close the toll bridges and keep the free bridge open. State troops successfully opened the free bridge.

Governor Murray's soup line in Oklahoma City.

Alfalfa Bill's most effective use of military power was applied to restraining oil production. Heavy production from new fields in east Texas and in the Seminole and Oklahoma City fields glutted the market. Producers ignored the attempts of the Oklahoma Corporation Commission to regulate production, and prices plunged to fifteen cents a barrel. Murray became concerned because a principal source of state revenue was the gross production tax on oil. The industry faced disaster, along with state finances in general. The governor acted on August 4, 1931, and placed 3,106 wells under martial law. Production stopped until a quota—the forerunner of the present daily allowable—was assigned each well. Oklahoma troops guarded the oil fields and supervised production until April 11, 1933.

Murray accused the Sinclair and Wilcox oil companies of violating production quotas. He claimed that Wilcox had exceeded its quotas by 600,000 barrels, and at the governor's instigation this company was assessed a pro-rata production tax that paid for the cost of keeping state troops in the field as oil well guards.

Murray saw that oil production was not local but a regional problem, extending throughout the vast Mid-Continent Field. He met with the governors of Texas and Kansas, and both agreed to join him in controlling production. This cooperative action saved the petroleum industry from collapse and marks the beginning of interstate control of oil pro-

duction. The price of oil improved, moving to eighty-five cents a barrel, and by the close of Murray's administration, the price had climbed to a dollar a barrel.

In his economy efforts, Murray hounded departments and institutions about expenditures. He ordered a cut in state government personnel, harassed institutions of higher learning, and threatened to cut college faculties 30 percent. Murray was critical of higher education generally, claiming it made "high-toned bums" of college students.

Governor Murray was ambitious for higher office and at the Democratic National Convention in Chicago in 1932, he announced his candidacy for the presidency. His old constitutional convention friend, former Governor Henry S. Johnston, made the nominating speech. Murray received the support of two state delegations—Oklahoma and North Dakota, where brother George Murray was active in politics. Franklin D. Roosevelt of New York won the Democratic nomination, however, and the Republicans nominated President Hoover.

In the Oklahoma primaries, incumbent United States Senator Elmer Thomas had a battle with Gomer Smith, an Oklahoma City attorney who was an old-age pension advocate and a perennial candidate for public office. Smith forced Thomas into a runoff, but the incumbent won, going into the general election to meet the Republican candidate, Wirt

Migrants fleeing the Dust Bowl for California.

Franklin, an Ardmore oil man. Thomas received 426,130 votes to his opponent's 218,854. The 1932 election was historic because of the overwhelming majorities built up by Democratic candidates. In Oklahoma, Roosevelt defeated Hoover 516,464 to 188,165. Democrats swept the statehouse, including heavy majorities in both branches of the legislature and won all seats allocated to Oklahoma in Congress. It was significant that Ernest W. Marland, founder of the Marland Oil Company (later Conoco) of Ponca City, won election to Congress as a Democrat over the Republican incumbent Martin Garber of Enid.

The 1930 census showed Oklahoma's population had increased to 2,396,000, which entitled the state to a ninth congressman. The congressional districts were not reapportioned, and this seat was filled by at-large voting each election until it was abolished in 1943. Will Rogers, a Moore schoolteacher and Democrat, capitalizing on the name of the famous entertainer, won this at-large congressional seat in each of five consecutive elections.

During the closing years of the Murray administration, the federal government under President Roosevelt's leadership launched a series of revolutionary programs that had far-reaching effects on Oklahoma and other states of the American Union. One was the adoption of the Twenty-first Amendment to the Federal Constitution, which had repealed the Eighteenth (Prohibition) Amendment. Oklahoma was one of few states that remained dry. Sooner State voters compromised this status somewhat in 1933 by adopting a proposition that legalized the sale and consumption of 3.2 beer (defined as nonintoxicating), by a vote of 244,598 to 129,582.

Another Roosevelt program was the establishment of a system of emergency relief for the nation's destitute. The Depression persisted; unemployment increased, and an extended drought blistered crops, withered pastures, and reduced farmers to ruin. Nearly 93,000 Oklahomans were on relief, drawing commodities and clothing from the new federal-state distribution system.

Most of the emphasis of the Roosevelt administration was directed toward rehabilitating the American economy through the New Deal programs of revitalizing factories, mines, farms, and transportation systems, and provid-

CCC workers restoring an eroded field in Oklahoma County.

ing purposeful work for the unemployed until private industry could provide jobs. A vast program of public works—the PWA, the WPA, and the CCC—was inaugurated in the states by the federal government. Oklahoma's participation in the New Deal was barely underway when the Murray administration ended.

Oklahomans went to the polls in 1934 to choose a successor to the irrepressible Alfalfa Bill Murray. Fifteen candidates filed for governor. In the July primary, the three Democratic frontrunners were Congressman Ernest W. Marland, Tom Anglin, veteran legislative leader, and Jack Walton. Marland received 165,885 votes, Anglin, 101,689, and Walton, 85,616. No runoff primary was held because Anglin withdrew to support Marland. Oklahoma Republicans nominated William B. Pine, former United States Senator.

Marland campaigned on the pledge to bring the New Deal to Oklahoma. The tendency of certain factions of the Oklahoma Democratic party to defect was shown in the gubernatorial campaign. Alfalfa Bill had come to despise President Roosevelt and the New Deal, while Marland had been a New Deal congressman. The latter campaigned for governor on the pledge to bring all the rehabilitating machinery of the New Deal to Oklahoma. Murray threw his support to Pine, and promoted his election through the columns of the *Blue Valley Farmer*. Despite Murray's apostasy, Marland won in November, defeating Pine

363,992 to 243,841. Democrats again swept the state offices, the legislature, and elected all nine congressmen. One of the new members of Congress was a University of Oklahoma professor, Josh Lee, soon to be heard from in another political quarter. The Socialists made a mild comeback in these hard times when S. P. Green, that party's candidate, polled 16,688 votes.

The Sooner State's new governor, Ernest W. Marland, had come west from Pennsylvania about the time of Oklahoma statehood to develop a vast oil empire. His first big strike was on the Miller Brothers' 101 Ranch, and by 1920, his personal fortune was estimated at $85 million. Marland's monument is the beauty of Ponca City; his faith in the frontier spirit of Oklahoma is epitomized in his greatest gift to the state—the *Pioneer Woman* statue.

An unfortunate association with the J. P. Morgan interests of New York destroyed Marland's oil empire, and by 1930 he had lost his wealth. Vengeful toward the eastern "economic royalists," he became an ardent New Dealer and won election to Congress in 1932, the first Democrat to win in the traditionally Republican Eighth District.

Governor Marland's program as presented to the Fifteenth Legislature stressed rehabilitating Oklahoma's lagging economy and restoring the army of unemployed citizens to productive work. Nearly 150,000 Oklahomans were unemployed, and 700,000 were

Governor Ernest W. Marland.

on relief. To achieve this aim he recommended establishing 115,000 subsistence homesteads; developing a system of conservation, including terraces, check dams, cover crops, and reforestation to halt destructive erosion and restore soil production; constructing multiple purpose dams on Oklahoma's rivers to provide hydroelectric power, flood control, and manufacturing and recreation sites; setting up old-age pensions; upgrading education; reducing state indebtedness, which was $20 million in 1935; and creating a planning board to develop the state's bounty and to attract industry. There was an inconsistency in Marland's program to get the state back on its feet—reducing indebtedness on the one hand and increasing state expenditures on the other, at a time when revenue was hard to come by—and this inconsistency was exploited by the legislature to thwart his program.

The Fifteenth Legislature, led by Speaker of the House Leon Phillips, was bent on economy, and most of Marland's "Little New Deal" foundered. Revenue bills were adopted, but more for the purpose of producing state solvency than in expanding its operations. The

sales tax, a new and monumentally effective revenue producer, was widely used by the states during the Depression to raise revenue for welfare purposes. In Murray's time, a one percent sales tax was adopted. During Marland's administration, in 1936, this was increased to two percent. Sales tax revenues were used to match federal funds to provide old-age assistance and support for dependent children and the handicapped. A special election in 1935 provided for partial exemption of homesteads from taxation. This reduction of the ad valorem levy saved many homes from tax sale, but at the same time it created additional pressure for state funds because property taxes had been a principal source of support for schools. To replace it, the legislature increased school aid to $8.2 million.

Phillips bitterly opposed Marland's program. He led a successful movement in the legislature not only to scrap most features of the Little New Deal but also to slash appropriations for institutions and departments to a level that allowed only minimum operation. About the only state operation not to suffer from legislative stringency was the Highway Department, and an expanded road construction program provided thousands of new jobs for Oklahoma's army of unemployed.

Marland won on his state planning board proposal. Renamed the Oklahoma Planning and Resources Board in 1937, this agency became an important vehicle for shifting the emphasis of the Oklahoma economy from nearly total dependency on oil and agriculture to a more diversified economy.

The 1936 election attracted considerable attention, notably because United States Senator Gore was up for reelection. Several prominent politicians filed for the nomination. The principal ones were Governor Marland; Congressman Josh Lee, a favorite of President Roosevelt; and Gomer Smith, by this time a champion of old-age pensioners and leader of the Oklahoma Townsend Club movement. The Townsend movement was a scheme to provide each old-age pensioner with an income of $200 a month for the purpose of restoring prosperity to the entire economy. Lee was frontrunner in the primary with 168,030 votes, followed by Marland, 121,433; Smith, 119,585; and Gore 91,581. Lee defeated Marland in the runoff primary, 301,259 to 186,899. Oklahoma City attorney Herbert Hyde was Lee's Republican opponent in November. Lee won this one, too, 493,407 to 229,004. President Roosevelt won another victory in Oklahoma, defeating Republican Alf Landon, 501,069 to 245,122. In the state legislature, the Republicans won only three house seats, and for the first time in state history the senate was unanimously Democratic. A proposal for repeal of prohibition went down to defeat, 391,083 to 267,285.

When the Sixteenth Legislature met, the bitterly anti-Marland legislator Leon Phillips was turned back in his bid for reelection to the speakership, and the more compatible J. T. Daniel won the post. The new legislature generally was more favorable to Marland's Little New Deal. It adopted a series of laws providing for state-federal action in social security, welfare, and public works. Before the close of Marland's administration, nearly 90,000 workers were employed on 1,300 WPA projects which ranged from sidewalks to courthouses.

Marland's most enduring contributions as governor were providing leadership in the eventual development of the Oklahoma Highway Patrol, the establishment of the Oklahoma Planning and Resources Board, and the Interstate Oil Compact. Murray had led the way on the compact by his agreement with the governors of Texas and Kansas, which brought some improvement in crude oil prices in the Mid-Continent Field. Marland followed Murray's progress with initiation of the Interstate Oil Compact, an agreement among oil-producing states to practice petroleum conservation and control production to assure a stable oil price. His plan included a commission to direct the compact program and Marland was elected its first president.

Oklahomans went to the polls in 1938 to select Marland's successor. Nine candidates sought the Democratic nomination, including two former governors—Walton and Murray. Leon Phillips and General William S. Key, state WPA administrator, were the favored candidates. The returns showed Phillips barely ahead of Key, 179,139 to 176,034. Murray drew 148,398 votes and Walton, 45,760. The runoff primary had been abolished in 1937;

Governor Leon Phillips.

thus Phillips won the nomination with only 30 percent of the vote. In the general election, Phillips was contested by Ross Rizley, a prominent Republican leader from Guymon. Phillips, bitterly anti–New Deal and pledged to economy, won endorsement by most of the state's larger newspapers and conservative leaders, and defeated Rizley, 355,740 to 148,861. Elmer Thomas, candidate for reelection to the United States Senate, won the Democratic nomination over Governor Marland and Gomer Smith, and went on to defeat Republican Harry O. Glasser in November, 307,936 to 159,734. The Democrats again swept all nine congressional seats, and among the victors was A. S. "Mike" Monroney of the Fifth District.

State institutions, public services, and education faced a grim future with Phillips's declared plan to cut appropriations and to reduce the state indebtedness, which in 1939 amounted to nearly $26 million. The new governor received authorization from the legislature to issue bonds in the sum of $35 million. The bonds funded the state debt and provided a small surplus to assure a balanced budget. The legislature slashed institutional

United States Senator Josh Lee.

and educational appropriations 20 percent, and increased taxes on automobiles, cigarettes, and gasoline (from four to five and a half cents per gallon). To ensure against a recurrence of state deficits, Phillips proposed a budget-balancing amendment to the constitution. It passed 163,886 to 85,752.

The Phillips administration was enlivened by the fiery governor's battle against the construction of multiple purpose dams on Oklahoma's waterways. He called out the national guard to prevent completion of the Grand River Dam project but was thwarted by a federal court injunction. He also attempted to check construction of Denison Dam, which impounded the waters of Red River to form Lake Texoma.

In the 1940 election, President Roosevelt sought an unprecedented third term. He was opposed by Republican Wendell Wilkie. Oklahomans gave Roosevelt a state victory, 474,313 to 348,872, but the Republicans won their first seat in Congress since 1930 when Ross Rizley defeated Democrat Phil Ferguson in the Eighth District. An initiated proposition to repeal prohibition lost, 374,911 to 290,752.

The second half of the Phillips administra-

tion was absorbed in mobilizing the state for World War II. Construction of military training stations in Oklahoma and development of war industries helped ease the economic pinch and produced full employment for the first time since the 1920s.

It seems that the essence of politics in a free society is opposition. The Oklahoma Republican party, with its Hoover Depression image and the devastating Roosevelt landslide of the 1930s, was so weakened that it could not provide effective opposition for Oklahoma Democrats. The result was that the necessary opposition developed within the Democratic party itself. This phenomenon appeared in the election of 1942. Although the election was held principally to select Phillips's successor, attention centered on the United States Senate race.

As Josh Lee approached the end of his first term, he was esteemed by President Roosevelt and popular with his United States Senate colleagues. Phillips's resentment of Lee, Roosevelt, and the New Deal was shared by a growing and powerful element in Oklahoma. Lee had promoted the building of dams to which the governor was strongly opposed. Phillips suspected that Lee had worked for General Key during the 1938 election, and Senator Lee had thwarted Phillips in his efforts to block WPA projects.

William B. Pine won the Republican nomination as Lee's opponent. Pine died suddenly on August 25, 1942, and Ed H. Moore, Tulsa oil millionaire and conservative Democrat, was selected by the Oklahoma Republican Central Committee as a substitute candidate. Phillips broke with the Democratic party and joined the Republicans in their effort to unseat Lee. Senator Lee, deeply involved in war work in Washington, had little time to campaign before the November election. Anti–New Deal and anti-Roosevelt sentiment aroused by Phillips crystallized in a major upset. The Republicans elected their third United States senator since statehood: the vote was 204,163 for Moore and 166,653 for Lee.

The 1940 census showed Oklahoma's population as 2,336,434, and the decline from the 1930 figure resulted in the Oklahoma congressional delegation being reduced to eight. The Democrats won seven of the seats; Ross

Rizley was the lone Republican victor. Robert S. Kerr, the Democratic nominee for governor, was opposed by Republican William J. Otjen. Kerr won, 196,656 to 180,454, to launch a long political career. His election marked the end of the turbulent, often violent politics of the early years.

Notes on Sources, Chapter 17

Materials used in preparing this chapter, which covers the period betwen 1922 and 1942, include biographies of Oklahoma leaders, exposés of the Ku Klux Klan, and special studies of Oklahoma government: John Joseph Mathews, *Life and Death of an Oil Man: The Career of E. W. Marland* (Norman, 1951); Russell D. Buhite, *Patrick J. Hurley and American Foreign Policy* (Ithaca, N.Y., 1973); Parker LaMore, *Pat Hurley: The Story of an American* (New York, 1932); Ernest T. Bynum, *Personal Recollections of Ex-Governor Walton* (Oklahoma City, 1924); Marion Monteval, *The Klan Inside Out* (Claremore, Okla., 1924); Howard A. Tucker, *History of Governor Walton's War on the Ku Klux Klan, the Invisible Empire* (Oklahoma City, 1923); Brookings Institution, *Report on a Survey of the Organization and Administration of Oklahoma* (Oklahoma City, 1935); Robert C. Carr, *State Control of Local Finance in Oklahoma* (Norman, 1937); Horace C. Peterson and Gilbert C. Fite, *Opponents of War, 1917–1918* (Madison, Wis., 1957); Gilbert C. Fite, "The Nonpartisan League in Oklahoma," *Chronicles of Oklahoma* 24 (July, 1946): 146–57; Rudia Halliburton, Jr., "Statewide Legislation Banning Teaching of Evolution," *Proceedings of the Oklahoma Academy of Science* 43 (1962): 190–98; and "The Nation's First Anti-Darwin Law: Passage and Repeal," *Southwestern Social Science Quarterly* 41 (1960): 125–29; Garin Burbank, *When Farmers Voted Red: The Gospel of Socialism in the Oklahoma Countryside, 1910–1924* (New York, 1976); and Ed Gill, *Oklahoma in the 1920s* (Muskogee, 1974).

Chapter 18

Oklahoma Politics:
The Middle Years, 1943 to 1955

The Phillips administration marked the end of an era—an age of self-interest and locally dominated, frontier-type politics. The inauguration of Robert S. Kerr in January, 1943, ushered in a new political epoch and a new approach to state problems. It marked the beginning of a broad awareness of the need for pervasive changes and a willingness for state government to serve as a vehicle to produce these changes. During this "middle years" period, there was a wider participation by Oklahoma in the affairs of the nation and the world, a resurgence of state pride and spirit, and a broad determination to improve the Sooner State image to overcome the scorn unintentionally generated by John Steinbeck's *Grapes of Wrath*.

Robert S. Kerr was Oklahoma's first native-born governor. His birthplace was a log cabin in the Chickasaw nation. Spurred by an ambitious family, he attended East Central State College (later University) at Ada, Oklahoma Baptist University at Shawnee, and finally the University of Oklahoma, where he studied law. During World War I, Kerr served with the American Expeditionary Force in France as an artillery officer. Through his military service he later was elected commander of the American Legion, Oklahoma Department. He became well known in Oklahoma as an attorney and lay leader in the Southern Baptist Convention. Besides serving as a church officer, Kerr eventually became president of the Oklahoma Baptist Convention. As his wealth grew, he contributed large sums to religious institutions, colleges, hospitals, missions, and orphanages.

Kerr soon became prominent as an oil producer. He organized a drilling company in 1926 and helped develop the Oklahoma City field. Ten years later he formed a partnership with Dean McGee, a successful geologist, and from their association emerged Kerr-McGee Industries. Success in the oil industry led to Kerr's election in 1936 to the presidency of Mid-Continent Oil and Gas Association, Kansas-Oklahoma Division. His personal wealth by 1942 was estimated at $10 million.

Kerr was an energetic worker in the Oklahoma Democratic party. Although not a candidate for elective office until 1942, he served for several years as a Democratic national committeeman; held an appointment as a special justice on the State Supreme Court in 1931; and was a member of Governor Marland's unofficial pardon and parole board. Active in election campaigns, he played key roles in the Marland and Phillips victories.

Kerr sprinkled his speeches with an earthy, subtle humor that succeeded with the voters. In an obvious criticism of outgoing Governor Phillips, he promised in his inaugural address to avoid "smearing the reputations of persons who did not agree with the administration." The new governor declared that he would support the national administration and asserted that a friendly attitude toward Washington was essential in order to bring dams, roads, and other projects to Oklahoma.

Governor Kerr maintained good relations with the legislature and provided effective leadership in managing state affairs. He was firm but not arrogant, and instead of denouncing his opponents, he attempted to win them over with reason and patronage. His first legislature, the nineteenth, consisted of ninety-four Democrats and twenty-four Republicans in the house, and forty Democrats and four

Republicans in the senate. Harold Freeman of Pauls Valley served as house speaker and Tom Anglin of Holdenville was president pro tempore of the senate. Kerr's program for the legislature included mobilizing Oklahoma's resources for World War II; extending the free textbook program; assuring a full nine-month term for public schools; and an aggressive industrial recruitment program to diversify the Oklahoma economy.

Before the lawmakers gave serious attention to Kerr's proposals, they adopted the Ballot Separation Law. This was a strategic move by the Democrat-dominated legislature to reduce the effects of an anticipated Republican sweep in the 1944 election. It was not the first time the legislature had changed the ballot make-up to serve Democratic party interests. Following the Harding and Hoover victories in 1920 and 1928, both of which swept Republicans into state offices, the legislature adopted a law providing for a ballot for presidential electors separate from the ballot containing the names of candidates for state offices, the legislature, and the United States Senate and House. This had seemed protection enough; but 1942 had not been a presidential-election year, and all nominees were on a single ballot. Disdain for Roosevelt and the New Deal had cost Josh Lee his United States Senate seat, and Kerr had won the governorship by only 15,000 votes. In 1943, President Franklin Roosevelt was known to be seeking an unprecedented fourth term. Conservative Oklahoma Democrats, linked with Republicans, had elected a conservative United States senator in 1942, and it appeared that defection from Roosevelt was increasing.

The Ballot Separation Law was hailed as a "new Oklahoma brand of G.O.P. storm insurance." As one legislator frankly admitted, "If there is a national Republican victory next year and it includes Oklahoma, there is no need for it to catch us Democratic legislators if we can avoid it. This separation of the ballots gives us the best protection we can provide." Thereafter at each election Oklahoma voters were confronted with separate ballots: one for legislators, one for congressional and United States Senate nominees, one for state office nominees, others for constitutional questions,

Governor Robert S. Kerr.

and still another for electors during presidential elections years.

When Kerr took office, a major problem was the $37 million state debt. The war boom and general prosperity, along with increased taxes on income and gasoline, soon swelled state revenues. The governor emphasized that failure to achieve solvent state finances would be a deterrent to attracting new industries to the state. Accordingly, he suggested that the way to get the state out of debt was to commit the surplus revenue to a sinking fund that would be used to retire bonded indebtedness. Submitted as State Question 313, this proposal was adopted on July 11, 1944, by a vote of 145,039 to 63,816. The plan worked and when Kerr left office in 1947, Oklahoma was free of debt.

Another state question promoted by Kerr and approved by the voters at the July 11 election in 1944 authorized the establishment of the Pardon and Parole Board. Loose administration of the state prison system, notably Walton's so-called "open door policy," had brought strong criticism to every governor since statehood. This reform authorized the appointment of a board to consider applications for commutations of sentences, pardons, and paroles. Under the new system, reprieves and leaves of absence from prison were restricted to sixty days, and the governor was required to report all acts of clemency to the legislature.

Anxious to reform the management of Oklahoma's system of higher education, Kerr recommended that the boards of regents for the University of Oklahoma and the agricultural and mechanical colleges be removed from politics by extending regents' terms to seven years and allowing dismissal of members only for cause. Voters approved these changes, together with State Question 312, which provided for resumption of the runoff primary system.

Much of the energy and time of the governor, the legislature, and business, labor, and professional leaders, as well as the general public were absorbed by the war effort. Because of a mild climate that permitted ground and air training most of the year, Oklahoma was the center of intensive military construction. Twenty-eight army camps, the best-known being the artillery center at Fort Sill, provided training for hundreds of thousands of troops for action in Europe and in the Pacific. Thirteen naval bases were constructed, notably the Technical Training Center at Norman where 15,000 naval aviation personnel were trained. In addition, several Army Air Corps stations were established, including Will Rogers Field near Oklahoma City, Cimarron Field near Yukon, and Vance Field at Enid. The huge Tinker Field at Midwest City became the largest air material depot in the world. Named for Major General Clarence Tinker, an Osage Indian from Pawhuska who was killed in a bombing raid on Japanese installations in the Pacific, the facilities at Tinker kept the B-17s, B-24s, and B-29s of the Army Air Corps in flying order. Heavy bombers were adapted at Tinker Field for the atomic bomb strikes on Hiroshima and Nagasaki. In addition, pilot training facilities at Miami and Ponca City were used for instructing British and Canadian pilots.

Another interesting kind of military installation in Oklahoma was the prisoner-of-war compound. As United States military forces swept across Europe, recapturing territory taken by the Axis, vast numbers of the enemy troops were taken prisoner. Many were transported to the eight POW compounds in Oklahoma. The two largest were at Fort Sill and Fort Reno, and others were located at Tonkawa, Chickasaw, Alva, Tipton, Okmulgee, and Camp Gruber near Muskogee.

As in World War I, the Sooner State rallied enthusiastically to the cause. Of the 193,000 Oklahomans who enlisted in the armed forces, 125,000 joined the army; 7,500 became marines; and 60,000 chose the navy. An additional 300,000 men were included into the armed forces through Selective Service. Oklahoma's battle casualties ultimately included 6,500 slain and 11,000 wounded.

On the home front Oklahomans in the cities produced weapons of war or performed vital services, while miners, oil field workers, farmers, and ranchers supplied vast quantities of metals, fuel, grains, and meat for the national arsenal. The University of Oklahoma, the Oklahoma A and M College, and the various state colleges adapted their curricula to the wartime situation and provided military training under the V-12 and other service programs. Like other United States citizens, Oklahomans submitted to a comprehensive system of rationing, which allocated scarce gasoline, tires, meat, sugar, butter, and other critical items, and controlled prices and rents.

With the capitulation of Germany and Japan in 1945 and the demobilization of American fighting might, hundreds of thousands of veterans flooded the nation's college campuses and trade schools to study under the so-called GI Bill. Thousands of war veterans learned trades and received agricultural training, and college enrollments in Oklahoma doubled and then tripled.

A presidential election occurred in the year before the close of World War II. The Republicans in 1944 nominated Thomas E. Dewey, governor of New York, while President Roosevelt sought a fourth term as the Democratic nominee. Governor Kerr, one of the few southern Democratic leaders who had remained loyal to the New Deal, presented the convention's keynote address at Chicago. This was the first time an Oklahoman had received this honor, and observers rated his speech "the ablest keynote speech in a Democratic convention in our generation." Kerr's oratory "stirred lagging Democrats."

Sparked by Kerr's leadership, the Democrats in Oklahoma turned an apparent disaster into a victory. Improving war fortunes helped. D-Day in Europe occurred a month before the Oklahoma primary, and Pacific naval victories during the summer of 1944 sustained President Roosevelt's claim to the need for crisis leadership and assured for him a fourth term. He carried Oklahoma by 401,549 votes to 319,424 for Dewey. Elmer Thomas won re-election to the United States Senate over Republican William J. Otjen, 390,851 to 309,222. Democrats also won six of the eight congressional seats and majorities in the legislature.

Oklahoma's Twentieth Legislature was led by Johnson Davis Hill as speaker of the house and Homer Paul as senate president pro tempore. Early in the session the legislature turned to investigating an alleged textbook scandal that had festered through the years. Dixie Gilmer, Tulsa prosecuting attorney and soon to be heard from in state politics, kept the issue alive. Superintendent of Public Instruction A. L. Crable received the brunt of legislative attention and escaped impeachment by only four votes in the house. During the session, Speaker Hill resigned and was replaced by H. I. Hinds, representative from Tahlequah.

Through a series of legislative acts and voter-approved referenda, Kerr achieved his goal of improved school financing. Aid based on average daily attendance was set at a $42 minimum per student, and the maximum ad valorem levy was raised from ten to fifteen mills in all districts voting for the higher tax. Oklahoma public schools were segregated at this time, and a special levy was passed to upgrade schools for blacks. Furthermore, a free textbook amendment was added to the state constitution in 1946.

The Twentieth Legislature expanded the functions of the Planning and Resources Board. Its fifteen members, all appointed by the governor, set to work collecting information on the industrial potential of Oklahoma and disseminating their findings to interested agencies across the country. Anticipating the cessation of hostilities, Kerr recommended and received authority from the legislature to appoint a Division of Postwar Planning.

Governor Kerr's interest in Oklahoma's future and his efforts to promote the state brought a gradual change in its image. He traveled 400,000 miles promoting the agricultural and industrial potential of Oklahoma. He sought an improvement of freight rates for the postwar era by pointing out that rates approved by the Interstate Commerce Commission for the Southwest hampered industrial development. In his many speeches to eastern business executives, he challenged them to bring "the 'colonial regions' to the average level of national income which would produce an increase of ten billion dollars in purchasing power," and thus help all the nation. One result of Kerr's ceaseless promotion of the state was the National Governors Conference held in Oklahoma City in 1946.

Oklahoma's first postwar election in 1946 saw public interest focused on the gubernatorial race. The Republicans nominated Olney Flynn, former Tulsa mayor and son of the famous Republican territorial delegate to Congress, Dennis Flynn. Roy J. Turner, oil producer and rancher, was the Democratic nominee. National issues influenced local candidates and platforms. Some wartime restrictions, notably Office of Price Administration (OPA) price controls, were still in force, and the Democratic administration favored continuing them during the transition to a peacetime economy in order to check inflation. Republicans advocated abolishing price controls.

Robert R. Wason, president of the National Association of Manufacturers, actively campaigned for an end to OPA. In a speech before the Tulsa Chamber of Commerce he linked OPA to what he called "the oppressive Oklahoma tax system which prevents industry entering Oklahoma and invites industries you have to leave Oklahoma." Wason sounded the general postwar reaction against the long Democratic domination in Oklahoma and across the nation.

In the election, Republicans won control of both houses of Congress. Although Democrats won most of the races in Oklahoma, their margins of victory were close, and Turner defeated Flynn by only 32,000 votes. Democrats won majorities in both houses of the legislature and six of the eight congressional seats, but the contests were close in the latter races. A. S. ("Mike") Monroney had just won the Colliers Award as the nation's most valuable congressman, but he was nearly defeated in Oklahoma by Carmon C. Harris, 47,173 to 43,508. A new name—Carl Albert, war veteran, McAlester attorney, and Rhodes Scholar—appeared in the Oklahoma congressional delegation.

Oklahoma's thirteenth governor, Roy J. Turner, was a native of Lincoln County and a World War I veteran. He entered the oil business in 1926; developed a world-famous ranch near Sulphur; and served as president of the American Hereford Breeders Association. Turner had campaigned on a platform espousing economy, a reformed highway commission, expanded use of state resources, soil conservation, and development of Oklahoma's recreational facilities. He also advocated a tax reduction to attract industry to Oklahoma; encouragement of agriculture through a reform of the State Board of Agriculture; educational improvement by increasing district property assessments to percent of real value and reducing the number of schools; and long-range highway development.

The Twenty-first Legislature was led by C. R. Board as speaker of the house and James Nance as president pro tempore of the senate. Among other things it conducted two controversial investigations. One concerned Oklahoma's public welfare program, the other highways. Ora Fox, president of the Oklahoma Welfare Federation, pressed for a raise in the monthly allowance for recipients of old-age assistance. The legislative investigation that followed showed that 97,728 persons already were on the old-age assistance rolls. In addition, 23,706 families with dependent children and 2,581 blind persons were receiving monthly welfare payments. The report further disclosed that Oklahoma ranked first in the nation in the ratio of welfare expenditures to population. Economy advocates pointed to the cost, $2 million each month, and recommended that 20,000 welfare recipients be cut off the rolls. Even so, welfare proponents had sufficient

strength in the legislature to pass two bills providing for raises in monthly payments. Governor Turner vetoed both measures but later approved another boosting old-age assistance to $58 per month.

The second legislative investigation resulted from a report released by the house on April 14, 1947, which disclosed that, "Oklahoma spent more for construction and maintenance of highways than did Kansas, Arkansas, Missouri, and Texas." Legislators blamed

> undue exercise of political pressure and influence for the fact that costs in Oklahoma were thirty-three per cent greater than in the surrounding states. Political pressure resulted in inefficiency by securing the discharge of capable employees and by securing the appointment of some employees having doubtful ability.... Oklahoma was far behind the other states in the hiring and training, and use of inspectors to check the work of the contractors.

This report provoked two reform movements. One sought to establish a state merit system to remove public employees from political pressure, and the other to change the Highway Commission membership. When Governor Turner declared his support for the concept of removing the state employees from patronage and placing them under a civil service merit system, the legislature drafted a bill similar to the Louisiana Merit System Act. For some unknown reason the governor withdrew his support of the proposal and the matter was dropped. The legislature did pass a bill to reform the Highway Department. It provided for a new eight-member board, one from each congressional district, and a full time director. H. E. Bailey became the first engineer to hold this office.

Turner was well-informed on education, having served as a member of the Oklahoma City School Board for several years. His plan for reforming public education included increased local levies, with supplementary aid only for weak districts, and the elimination of 500 rural schools through consolidation. His efforts to reform public education generally were thwarted, however, because many members of the legislature were teachers and the Oklahoma Education Association, like the Oklahoma Welfare Federation, had by this time become a power bloc in state politics.

Turner sought to continue Kerr's program of recruiting industry to diversify Oklahoma's economy by tax reduction, reorganization of the Planning and Resources Board, and personal visitations. At his encouragement, the legislature reduced personal and corporate income taxes by one-third in partial answer to the charge that Oklahoma's tax system suppressed industry and drove it from the state. The legislature revamped the Planning and Resources Board to consist of five appointive and four ex officio members, the ex officio members to be the president of the State Board of Agriculture; the director of the State Highway Commission; the director of the State Game and Fish Commission; and the governor. Each member was assigned new responsibilities in developing and advertising the state's industrial and recreational potential.

Business experts rated personal visitation as the most effective recruitment practice. Oklahoma businessmen raised $150,000 to finance a special train of fifteen railroad cars loaded with "made in Oklahoma" exhibits. Governor Turner personally called on eastern industrialists and played a leading role in organizing the industrial tour. The excursion extended over seventeen days and stopped at the principal northern and eastern cities where 162 volunteers explained to businessmen the Sooner State's potential for industrial development. The emphasis was on abundant mineral resources; low-cost power, water, and natural gas; the state's central location and its transportation facilities; its freedom from labor disputes; and its liberal tax laws. The Oklahomans told the executives that more than twenty communities had raised between $100,000 and $500,000 each to construct plants for out-of-state firms. This vigorous recruitment drive soon bore fruit and Oklahoma industrial development advanced 36 percent during 1948 compared to 10 percent for the nation overall.

The 1948 presidential election was one of the most dramatic in history. The Democrats nominated President Truman, while the Republicans renominated Thomas E. Dewey. Republican chances for capturing the presidency appeared excellent because the Demo-

Governor Roy J. Turner.

cratic party was badly divided. One faction formed the Progressive party and nominated Henry Wallace, former secretary of agriculture and vice-president. A second insurgent group called itself the Dixiecrats. Formed to oppose the Democratic party's civil rights program, this party nominated Governor Strom Thurmond of South Carolina.

Oklahoma played a key role in this election in that Governor Turner, ignoring pressure to join the Dixiecrats, remained loyal to his party. He served as national president of the Truman-Barkley Clubs (Alben W. Barkley was the Democratic vice-presidential candidate), and worked diligently for Truman's election.

The president campaigned intensively, including in his schedule two days in Oklahoma. He hammered away at what he called "that do-nothing 80th Republican Congress," and to the great surprise of many observers, he defeated Dewey in the state and in the nation. His Oklahoma vote was 452,782 to 268,817. An Oklahoma Dixiecrat group led by Ross Lillard and William H. Murray had met in Oklahoma City in August to organize a local branch of this party and to select presidential electors. They were not permitted a place on the ballot because of the mandatory primary law. The Oklahoma Progressive party, campaigning for Henry Wallace, was denied a place on the ballot for the same reason.

The Truman momentum swept Democratic candidates into state and federal offices. The Democrats won all eight congressional seats, including the traditionally Republican Eighth District. George Howard Wilson of Enid accomplished a virtually impossible feat in winning in this congressional constituency, while Tom Steed of Shawnee won the first of what would become a long series of congressional victories. One of Oklahoma's United States Senate seats was up for election in 1948. Ed Moore, the aging and ill incumbent, was not a candidate for reelection. Ross Rizley, state Republican leader and former congressman, won the Republican nomination. Former Governor Robert S. Kerr was the Democratic nominee, and he won election by a vote of 441,690 to 265,169. Also in the 1948 election, Oklahoma voters approved a constitutional amendment providing for a board of regents for state colleges similar to the system already in effect for the University of Oklahoma and the Oklahoma A and M colleges through which the regents were freed from undue political influence.

Governor Turner was rewarded for his role in President Truman's election by the offer of appointment as secretary of agriculture. The governor declared his appreciation of this consideration but refused on the claim that so far he had accomplished only half of his state program. In 1950 he was offered the position of national director of civil defense, which he also rejected.

The Twenty-second Legislature, which convened in January, 1949, was led by Walter Billingsley as speaker of the house and Bill Logan as president pro tempore of the senate. Since it did not adjourn until May 28, the Twenty-second Legislature was exceeded only by the First Legislature in time spent in transacting the state's legislative business. Only in recent times has this record length of a legislative session been exceeded. The extended session of the Twenty-second Legislature is explained by the important legislative business it transacted, including development of a toll road program, a vote on repeal, a $36

million bond issue, constitutional reform, and desegregation of higher education.

In 1947 a group of Oklahoma City and Tulsa civic leaders called on Governor Turner to discuss a plan for a new superhighway to carry the heavy motor traffic between the two cities. The businessmen declared that Highway 66, a major transcontinental artery, would not be modernized for some time because of the competition for public road money throughout the state. They proposed a turnpike built by self-liquidating bonds, the bonds to be retired by tolls charged for the use of the superhighway. Oklahoma City, Tulsa, and Sapulpa businessmen advanced $48,000 for initial expenses, and the legislature created the Oklahoma Turnpike Authority.

The plan was bitterly opposed by the smaller towns—Chandler, Stroud, and Bristow—along the route. Their spokesmen in the legislature attempted to repeal the act creating the Oklahoma Turnpike Authority. Failing there, they carried the fight to the State Supreme Court, and finally on appeal to the United States Supreme Court, but without success. In deference to the opposition the new road was surveyed to run within half a mile of each town with toll gates at these points.

The cost of the turnpike was estimated at $41 million. The governor first attempted to obtain financing from the Reconstruction Finance Corporation, but he finally sold the turnpike bonds to private investment companies. Construction began on the eighty-eight miles of four-lane road in December, 1949, and rising construction costs required a new $7 million loan in 1952. Oklahoma's first modern toll road, named the Turner Turnpike, was completed and opened to traffic on May 17, 1953.

The question of repeal of prohibition, a recurring issue in Oklahoma history since statehood, arose during Turner's administration. When the governor refused to include it in his program, an initiative petition brought it before the voters. Wet forces in Oklahoma were encouraged by the action of Kansas, a dry state that had repealed prohibition in 1948. After a stirring campaign by both wet and dry forces, the vote on September 27, 1949, showed the drys still in the majority, 323,270 to 267,870.

Turner's legislatures set new records for spending, the Twenty-first Legislature appropriating $104 million, which was $29 million over the previous biennium, and included a doubling of funds for mental hospitals. Yet the state faced a crisis in institutional buildings. Rising college and university enrollments taxed every classroom and laboratory on the campuses. Prisons and mental hospitals were in dire straits with old, dilapidated buildings that lacked even minimal facilities for the comfort, care, and rehabilitation of inmates and patients. No additional state money was available for these critical institutional building needs, so Governor Turner proposed to solve the problem by submitting to the people a $36 million bond issue. The proposition allowed the legislature to issue twenty-five-year bonds financed by a tax of two cents on each pack of cigarettes sold. The building bond issue was submitted to the voters in a special election along with the prohibition-repeal proposal. The building bond issue carried 343,900 to 239,190.

One of the most important matters considered by the Twenty-second Legislature was whether to revise the state constitution or draft a new one. The governor invited a committee of 150 citizens to meet with a legislative council of fifteen house members and ten senators, and to make recommendations for change. A strong movement soon developed against any change in the constitution. Former Governor William H. Murray refused to attend the citizens' conferences and spoke out bitterly against revision. Former governors Johnston and Phillips attended the meetings but declared opposition to change. After nineteen months of preliminary work, the proposal for calling a constitutional convention was submitted to the voters on November 7, 1950, and was defeated 347,143 to 159,903.

Probably the most significant development occurring in the Turner administration was the desegregation of higher education. All Oklahoma schools, from elementary through graduate college level, had been segregated since statehood. Under license of the "separate but equal" doctrine of the 1896 *Plessy* vs. *Ferguson* decision, Oklahoma's First Legislature had established separate schools for blacks. The segregation statute prescribed

Ada Lois Sipuel Fisher, whose application for admission to the University of Oklahoma Law School began the drive for desegregation of Oklahoma higher education.

heavy fines for any administrator or teacher who taught classes where the white and black races were mixed.

The college at Langston, which had been founded in territorial days, provided black students with instruction leading to the bachelor's degree. For those black students seeking professional training in medicine, law, pharmacy, engineering, nursing, and graduate professional education, Oklahoma followed the traditional southern practice of out-of-state tuition grants, whereby the state paid the expenses of black students and sent them to various universities in northern states where black applicants were accepted. Between 1907 and 1946, almost 2,000 Oklahoma blacks had studied under this out-of-state grant system.

In January, 1946, Ada Lois Sipuel, a black student from Chickasha and a Langston University honor graduate, applied for admission to the University of Oklahoma Law School. University officials rejected her application, as they were required to do under the terms of the Oklahoma segregation statutes. Roscoe Dunjee, editor of the *Black Dispatch* and a director of the National Association for the Advancement of Colored People (NAACP), engaged Amos T. Hall, prominent black attorney from Tulsa, to represent Miss Sipuel. Hall applied in Cleveland County Court for a writ of mandamus to direct University of Oklahoma officials to admit Miss Sipuel. Judge Ben T. Williams ruled that neither an administrative board nor officials could be forced to disobey a state law, and the writ was ended.

The *Sipuel* case was appealed to the State Supreme Court in January, 1947. Thurgood Marshall, legal counsel for the NAACP, came to Oklahoma to represent the appellant. Marshall claimed that segregation was an abridgment of the Fourteenth Amendment. He added that, "segregation itself amounts to unlawful discrimination. . . . Equality under a segregated system is a legal fiction and a judicial myth. . . a device for keeping the Negro in his place, *i.e.* in a constantly inferior position." The state's highest court sustained the lower court ruling, however, and on September 20, 1947, the Sipuel attorneys appealed to the United States Supreme Court on a writ of certiorari.

The nation's High Court reversed the Oklahoma decision on January 12, 1948, and declared that the student was "entitled to secure a legal education offered by a state institution," and that "the state must provide it as soon as it does for any other group." State Attorney General Mac Q. Williamson held that the decision did not strike down Oklahoma's system of segregated education. It merely required the state to provide Miss Sipuel with a legal education. Thereupon the State Supreme Court directed the state education officials to establish a law school for blacks.

The State Regents for Higher Education established the Langston University Law School, with classes in the state capitol building; hired three attorneys for a faculty; and declared the state library's legal collection as the law library for the new school. The new Langston University Law School was then officially declared to be equal to the University of Oklahoma Law School. Marshall immediately charged that the new law college was a Jim Crow law school and pledged that his client would not enroll there. Miss Sipuel again applied to the University of Oklahoma Law School and was denied admission.

In January, 1948, six Oklahoma City blacks applied for admission to the University of Oklahoma Graduate College, but University officials were directed by the attorney general to reject their applications. Governor Turner and legislative leaders called on the regents for higher education to establish graduate facilities at Langston University by June, 1948. A committee of deans from the University of Oklahoma and Oklahoma A and M College was appointed to study the matter and make recommendations. The committee report disclosed that to meet graduate study needs for blacks, fifty to sixty departments offering graduate study would have to be established at Langston to provide equal facilities. The cost of constructing a new graduate physical plant at Langston was estimated at $12 million, and recruiting competent graduate faculty posed an additional problem. The committee recommended that in view of the expense and faculty recruitment problem, qualified black applicants should be admitted to the University of Oklahoma and Oklahoma A and M College for advanced work.

Matters came to a head in June, 1948, when George W. McLaurin, one of the blacks who had been rejected in January, petitioned the Cleveland County Court for a writ of mandamus to direct the University of Oklahoma to admit him to its graduate college. Later, he dropped his suit in Cleveland County Court and filed for similar remedy in federal court. When McLaurin applied for admission again on September 16, 1948, he was turned away. Two weeks later the Federal District Court for Western Oklahoma directed officials at the University of Oklahoma to admit McLaurin. Governor Turner, the university regents, and school officials met in an emergency meeting to work out a method to permit McLaurin to attend classes and still abide by the state segregation laws. On October 13, 1948, McLaurin was admitted for graduate study in the College of Education. A classroom in the Carnegie Building was adapted by constructing an alcove (called by NAACP officials a broom closet) adjoining room 104, separated from the classroom by a wooden railing with an entrance off the hall. The alcove was equipped with lights, desk, and chair. Though various classes using room 104 were large, no one left in protest. Lecture sessions were livened by reporters and photographers from *Time* magazine and other national periodicals covering this revolution in Oklahoma education.

Anticipating additional black requests for admission, Attorney General Williamson recommended that the legislature amend the segregation statutes to allow qualified blacks to enroll for graduate study. The legislature complied during May, 1949. A month later, twenty-six blacks applied for admission to the University of Oklahoma Graduate College for the summer term. A lack of faculty prevented use of separate classrooms for the new enrollees because forty different courses were involved, but railings were erected in various classrooms to separate white from black students. During this summer session Ada Lois Sipuel was admitted to the College of Law.

McLaurin protested the railing, the separate table in the library with his name on it, and segregation in the campus cafeteria. His attorneys appealed to the United States Supreme Court, claiming, "such restrictions impair and inhibit his ability to study, to engage in discussion, and exchange views with other students, and in general to learn his profession."

The Court replied that "state imposed restrictions which produce such inequalities cannot be sustained," and annulled segregation at the graduate level in higher education on June 5, 1950. Following the 1954 United States Supreme Court ruling in *Brown* vs. *Board of Education* which forbade segregation in public schools, the Oklahoma State Regents for Higher Education announced in July, 1955, that qualified black applicants would be accepted in all colleges, schools and departments of higher education in Oklahoma. This decision was a turning point in civil rights development in the United States and in the school systems of Oklahoma.

In 1950, Oklahomans went to the polls to select Governor Turner's successor. Phil Ferguson, Frank P. Douglas, William O. Coe, and Johnston Murray filed for the Democratic nomination. Murray and Coe led in the first primary, and in a painfully close runoff Murray won, 235,830 to 234,980. The Republican

Governor Johnston Murray.

primary nominees were Bruno H. Miller, 4,415; Rexford B. Cragg, 3,886; Earl F. Winsel, 2,890; Jo O. Ferguson, 36,292; and Ernest Albright, 7,928. The light primary vote for Republican nominees compared to the general election tally for this party's candidate (313,205) is instructive of a trend Oklahoma Democrats call "primary raiding."

Probably some of the strong Republican showing in the general election as compared to the light Republican primary vote can be accounted for by Democratic defection and opposition to Murray as their party's candidate. According to veteran observers, however, this also was indicative of a trend by Republicans in their attempt to overcome one-party Democratic domination. State election laws require citizens to vote in a primary election as they are registered, but they can vote as they please in the general election. Many Republicans register as Democrats, some so as to have a voice in selecting the best candidate possible offered by the Democrats, who have won most of the state elections; others register as Democrats in an attempt to elect the Democratic nominee that their Republican candidate can more easily defeat in

November. Murray won in the general election, 329,308, to 313,205 for Jo O. Ferguson, the Republican candidate.

The 1950 United States Senate race attracted wide interest. Congressman Mike Monroney sought the Democratic nomination from veteran incumbent Elmer Thomas. Monroney was successful, and in November he was challenged by the Republican nominee, the Reverend Bill Alexander, a world-famous evangelist and pastor of the Oklahoma City First Christian Church. Monroney defeated Alexander, 345,953 to 285,224.

In the congressional elections Republican Page Belcher of Enid won the Eighth District seat, and John Jarmon, Oklahoma City Democrat, won the congressional seat vacated by Monroney. In this election the Democratic margin in the Oklahoma delegation was six to two. Democrats also won substantial majorities in the state legislature.

Oklahoma's fourteenth governor, Johnston Murray, the son of Alfalfa Bill, was born in the Chickasaw Nation at Emet. He accompanied his father to Bolivia in the 1920s and later became an attorney. Murray's political experience included service in various county positions, chairman of the State Election Board in 1941, and secretary of the School Land Commission in 1948. His "just plain folks" campaign slogan, and the nostalgia of old-timers for "Bill's boy" are said to have increased his support. The irrepressible Alfalfa Bill administered the oath of office to his son at the inauguration on January 9, 1951.

The Twenty-third Legislature was led by James M. Bullard, speaker of the house, and Boyd Cowden, president pro tempore of the senate. The new governor's program for the legislature stressed economy, no new taxes, and a continuation of the program to recruit industry for Oklahoma.

Economy moves by the legislature included defeating a proposal to increase the sales tax to 3 percent, thus holding the line on expenditures, and reducing welfare assistance by closer scrutiny of qualifications of recipients. Before Murray's administration, approximately 9 percent of the state's population received some form of welfare payment. The cutback reduced it to slightly over 7 percent. The 1950 census revealed Oklahoma's

population to be 2,223,351, a drop of 103,000 over the 1940 count. This was the second consecutive decade showing a decline. One effect of this was the loss of two seats in Congress, which required a reapportionment of congressional districts by the legislature.

The legislature referred to the people a constitutional amendment permitting women to serve on juries. This won approval on July 1, 1952, by a vote of 236,546 to 131,743. In November, the legislature submitted for popular approval a veteran's bonus proposal, which was rejected 639,226 to 233,094, and a proposition to extend suffrage to citizens eighteen years of age, also defeated, 593,076 to 268,223. The proposal to increase the sales tax to 3 percent, promoted by the Oklahoma Welfare Federation and defeated in the legislature, came before the voters in the same election on an initiated petition but failed 727,540 to 115,592.

In 1952, Oklahomans went to the polls to elect a new president. The Republicans nominated General Dwight Eisenhower, a hero of World War II, who promised to end the unpopular war in Korea. Senator Robert S. Kerr was a candidate for the Democratic nomination, but the National Democratic Convention selected Adlai Stevenson, governor of Illinois and a strong advocate of civil rights. Eisenhower defeated Stevenson in Oklahoma and the nation. The Sooner State vote was 518,045 to 430,939, the heaviest presidential vote in state history. Democratic candidates won majorities in the legislature and five of the six congressional seats. Republican Page Belcher proved unbeatable in the newly apportioned First District. Democrat Ed Edmondson from Muskogee won the Second District congressional seat to begin an extended tenure in Congress.

The Twenty-fourth Legislature was led by James Nance, speaker of the house, and Raymond Gary, president pro tempore of the senate. Governor Murray's legislative program included continued consolidation of schools to improve instruction; revised ad valorem assessments to return a major part of school financing to local districts; and expansion of highway and toll road systems. The legislature improved the Oklahoma mental health program by increasing appropriations, enabling the hospitals to expand staffs and upgrade rehabilitation of patients. Expansion of Oklahoma Turnpike Authority functions made possible the construction of the Will Rogers Turnpike, a toll highway nearly ninety miles long connecting Tulsa and Joplin, Missouri. Cost of the superhighway was $68 million. Governor Murray was credited with the most extensive use of the executive veto in forty years of Oklahoma politics—forty vetoes in four years.

Murray established the Governor's Joint Committee on Reorganization of State Government and commissioned "privates" in a "Broom Brigade to sweep the statehouse clean" of unnecessary personnel. While operating only as an advisory group, the committee consisted of house and senate members and private citizens whose recommendations pointed the way for future changes.

Another scheme was advanced by Murray, which, though it did not gain acceptance, became a subject of continuing discussion. This was a plan for building 400 miles of canals to connect lakes in the well-watered Ozark foothills with cities on the dry western plains. An Oklahoma water authority, organized like a toll road company, would finance the canals by issuing $125 million in bonds and pay out the bonds from water sold.

The governor and the state's first lady, Willie Murray, created widespread interest with their regular "Open House in Oklahoma." They opened the twenty-room executive mansion each weekend. Citizens from all over the state came to visit the official family, tour the mansion and state capitol, and partake of gubernatorial hospitality.

As Governor Murray's term came to a close, so did an era—the middle years in the Sooner State's political evolution. This epoch was a transition, a bridge between rough-and-tumble frontier politics and a new and emerging sophistication and state-centered polity. Johnston Murray's parting remarks on what Oklahoma needed to achieve greatness presaged the future: reapportionment of the legislature; elimination of homestead exemption; a state merit system to minimize patronage and provide continuity of service; improvement of state buying through a central purchasing agency; consolidation of Oklahoma counties; and a reduction of the power of county commissioners. A review of these needs would be heard again in the campaign platforms of his successors, the modern period governors.

Notes on Sources, Chapter 18

The material for this chapter on Oklahoma politics during the years 1942 to 1954 is drawn from several books, but the most productive sources are articles in periodicals. Walter M. Harrison, *Me and My Big Mouth* (Oklahoma City, 1954), is the best single source for this period. Also useful are H. O. Waldby, *The Patronage System in Oklahoma* (Norman, 1950); H. V. Thornton, *Oklahoma Constitutional Studies* (Oklahoma City, 1950); Arrell Morgan Gibson, *The West in the Life of the Nation* (Lexington, Mass., 1976); and W. Eugene Hollon, *The Southwest: Old and New* (New York, 1961). For articles, see Johnston Murray, "Oklahoma Is in a Mess," *Saturday Evening Post* 228 (April 30, 1955): 20–21; Irving Dillard, "Oklahoma Makes Ready for 1944," *New Republic* 109 (August 9, 1943); Robert T. Elson, "If Not Truman, Who?" *Life* 32 (March 24, 1952): 118–33; and Marquis W. Childs, "The Big Boom from Oklahoma," *Saturday Evening Post* 221 (April 9, 1949): 118–20.

Robert S. Kerr was the dominant political personality in Oklahoma during this period. Anne Hodges Morgan, *Robert S. Kerr: The Senate Years* (Norman, 1977), is the principal study on Kerr.

Chapter 19

Oklahoma Politics: The Modern Period

Since 1955 the Sooner State has undergone great economic, social, and political changes. A shift from heavy reliance on agriculture and oil to a more diversified economy, including vigorous industrial expansion, has been achieved in the modern period. Oklahoma not only arrested a loss in population extending over the previous two decades but enjoyed substantial increases. True, the Oklahoma birth rate has been high in the modern period—at least until about 1970—but much of the population increase is attributable to migration into the state. This is illustrated by the fact that one-eighth of the Sooner State's 1960 population had lived outside Oklahoma in 1955.

Politics during the modern period has been conservative, with Oklahoma political leaders deserting the old liberal heritage of the Populists and Farm Labor Reconstruction League. The emphasis has been on economy in government and "holding the line" on taxes, primarily as an inducement for industries to locate in the state. The modern period has been one of political reform but a slow and deliberate reform aimed at increasing efficiency in government and improving public services. Political leaders have been reluctant to expand social welfare programs. From time to time, however, the old frontier rambunctiousness has asserted itself. The election of 1954, characterized by the press as "such a sizzling one that Governor Murray was taking no chances," saw the chief executive use the national guard and martial law in five counties to maintain surveillance over the polling places. This provoked one national news magazine to declare, "There's always an aroma in Oklahoma at election time." The modern period has witnessed the introduction of controls that have checked "finagling" at the polls. In addition, there has been some reduction of the power of the so-called Old Guard politicians, notably through the epochal legislative reapportionment decision.

In the gubernatorial election of 1954 sixteen candidates sought the Democratic nomination. These included the two frontrunners, William O. Coe with 159,122, and Raymond Gary with 156,376. Mrs. Willie Murray, the former governor's wife, polled 20,336 votes. In the runoff, Gary defeated Coe, 251,902 to 233,079. Rueben K. Sparks, a Woodward attorney and a prominent Republican leader in northwest Oklahoma, was his party's gubernatorial nominee. Gary won in November, 376,386 to 251,808. Democrats also won five of Oklahoma's six congressional seats and majorities in both houses of the legislature.

United States Senator Kerr won the Democratic primary in a field of nine candidates, including former Governor Turner. Turner received 205,241 votes to Kerr's 238,543. Turner withdrew before the runoff to give Kerr a clear-cut nomination. Kerr then defeated the Republican nominee, Fred M. Mock, an Oklahoma City attorney, 335,127 to 262,013.

Oklahoma's fifteenth governor, Raymond Gary, had experience as a schoolteacher, a county superintendent of schools in southern Oklahoma, a businessman, and an independent oil operator. He won election to the Oklahoma senate in 1940 and served continuously for fourteen years. Gary held the office of senate president pro tempore during the Twenty-fourth Legislature.

Governor Gary's first legislature, the Twenty-fifth, was led by Bill Harkey, speaker of the house, and Ray Fine, president pro tempore of the senate. Gary's first legislative message proposed a conservative program of government. He opposed a tax increase, pointing to the need for the state to live within its current means as an inducement to industry. He advocated the organization of a statewide authority to plan and develop water resources to meet the expanding needs of cities and new industries. Gary asked for appropriations to finance studies of upstream flood control projects that would lead to the construction of additional check dams. The lakes thus created would supply water for irrigation, municipalities, and industrial uses. His plan provided for financing the water projects by bolstering local support through county-wide school levies. He announced his goal for highway construction as 2,500 miles of new, first-class roads. In addition, Gary urged the creation of a new department of commerce and industry and a system of personnel management for 20,000 state employees.

The Twenty-fifth Legislature passed legislation increasing appropriations for higher education, public schools, the welfare program, notably old-age assistance, and mental hospitals. Sustained legislative support of the state's mental health program made possible drastic reforms in the care and rehabilitation of the mentally ill. Through this support, Oklahoma, ranking toward the bottom among the states in its provision for care of the mentally ill during the early 1950s, became a leader in mental health program improvement.

Most of the time and energy of Governor Gary and the Twenty-fifth Legislature were consumed in planning for the desegregation of public schools. Oklahoma's institutions of higher learning had been desegregated by the *Sipuel* and *McLaurin* decisions, but the state's public schools continued to operate on a system that separated white and black students. On May 17, 1954, the United States Supreme Court handed down the historic *Brown* vs. *Board of Education (of Topeka, Kansas)*, decision. In effect the nation's highest court declared that segregated schools were not equal and could not be made equal. Thus black students in segregated school systems were held to be denied basic rights guaranteed by

Governor Raymond Gary.

the equal protection clause of the Fourteenth Amendment of the United States Constitution. The Court threw out the long-standing "separate but equal" doctrine of *Plessy* vs. *Ferguson* and ordered all states with segregated school systems to integrate forthwith. The United States Supreme Court allowed the seventeen states, including Oklahoma, that maintained segregated public school systems, a reasonable time to conform.

State officials, led by Attorney General Mac Q. Williamson, pledged to the United States Supreme Court the good intentions of Oklahoma to comply with the decision. Black leaders agreed to go slowly. Dr. F. D. Moon, prominent black educator, declared that "if we attempted to put it into effect immediately, we would have chaos." Tax collections for schools were already underway for the 1954–55 term to meet accepted district budgets, and the state constitution forbade diverting funds from the original purpose of the levy. In September, 1954, Oklahoma parochial schools integrated, but the State Department of Education announced that public schools would operate during the next year under the old system.

Governor Gary took immediate action following his inauguration. First, he met with the state superintendent of education, the chancellor of higher education, and representatives of the Oklahoma Education Association. Second, when the Twenty-fifth Legislature convened on January 4, 1955, he told a joint session that "we may just as well be realistic and face the issues squarely." At the close of his administration he rated his success in handling the public school integration question as his top achievement and recalled that "it was obvious that when the Supreme Court issued its edict, the federal courts would not allow us to collect taxes for a school system that violated that edict. We stood to lose about $8,000,000 a year." He pointed out to the legislature that the first problem was changing the system of separate school financing, and expressed the fear that railroads, power companies, and other business enterprises paying substantial annual sums for the support of schools might object in the courts and thus cripple the school finance system. To counter this possibiity, the governor recommended submitting to the voters a constitutional amendment that would consolidate school finances and end the separate levies in each county. He suggested that the proposed amendment provide for an additional four-mill levy to make up for the loss of separate black school financing. It was his hope that the amendment could be considered before county excise boards undertook their work on the 1955–56 budgets.

The amendment abolishing segregated school finances passed the legislature with overwhelming majorities. Only two negative votes were cast in the house. Gary signed the proposition on March 9, 1955, and set April 5, 1955, to permit members to travel over the state to explain the amendment and promote its adoption. Governor Gary and other state officials also worked for the cause. Called the Better Schools Amendment, and carrying the slogan, "SOS—Support Our Schools," the amendment won by a three-to-one majority— 231,097 to 73,021. While it did not abolish segregation in Oklahoma public education, the amendment did place the state in a position to handle the financial situation when the

final decree came from the United States Supreme Court.

The second *Brown* decision was handed down on May 31, 1955. It required states with segregated schools to make a prompt and reasonable beginning toward full compliance with desegregation. Oklahomans were conditioned to accept integration of their public schools because of the transition through desegregation of higher education. Years of litigation and the publicity of the *Sipuel* and *McLaurin* decisions explain in part Oklahoma's orderly response to the demands of the *Brown* decision. Thus the Sooner State was spared the disorder and shame of riotous episodes such as those that occurred at Little Rock, Arkansas. The prompt compliance and firm leadership of Governor Gary and legislative leaders were of great importance, too. Their conduct is especially noteworthy because the governor and numerous legislators were from Oklahoma's "Little Dixie."

Governor Gary's response to the second *Brown* decision was to advise each school district in the state that it would receive no state aid (more than half of the annual budgets for public schools came from state aid) if it defied federal law. Officials in state government studiously avoided publicity on the question in order not to inflame any segment of the population. Leadership and restraint by public officials in this regard is an example of the spirit of the Modern Period in state politics. No organized opposition to desegregation developed in Oklahoma. Reportedly the governor received fewer than two dozen letters critical of his action; many of these were unsigned, and most of the critical comments came from outside the state.

A national magazine quoted Governor Gary:

No organized opposition ever developed anywhere in Oklahoma, because we didn't allow any to develop. When a segregationist sounded off too loudly, he would be visited by a couple of Crime Bureau agents. They would explain the law to him, courteously but firmly. Then, they would list the penalties for violating the law. This usually quieted him down. The Negro agent worked to keep the Negro community from taking any action that might have inflamed the public. The press gave us invaluable help by pledging to avoid sensationalism; the reporting was most fair, even though some of the reporters were themselves opposed to integration.

At the peak of turmoil and disorder at Little Rock, Arkansas, when President Eisenhower moved federal troops into the stricken town, NAACP officials declared they were "very proud of Oklahoma's attitude" toward integrating public schools, and praised Governor Gary: "We are very happy over the straightforward stand that you took concerning integration in the public schools [of Oklahoma]." Gary led in desegregating other areas, too. At the State Capitol, separate washrooms, drinking fountains, and other reminders of Jim Crow days were removed. The Oklahoma National Guard was integrated, and the governor refused to attend any conference or meeting in the state that was held in a hotel or resort that practiced discrimination.

In the presidential election of 1956, President Eisenhower was again contested by Adlai Stevenson. Eisenhower's popularity remained high, Stevenson's intellectual image persisted, and the Republican president carried Oklahoma and the nation again. His state vote was 473,769 to 385,581 for Stevenson. United States Senator Mike Monroney, up for reelection, defeated the Republican candidate, Douglas McKeever of Enid, 459,996 to 371,146. Democrats carried five of the six congressional seats and won sizeable majorities in the legislature.

An absentee vote and relief-check scandal developed in Wagoner County during the election of 1956. The episode centered on the state senate race between John Russell and Tom Payne. To Governor Gary's credit, he urged the legislature to adopt reforms on absentee ballots and to tighten control of emergency relief.

Gary's second legislature, the Twenty-Sixth, was led by Bill Harkey, speaker of the house, and Don Baldwin, president pro tempore of the senate. The governor and legislature were primarily concerned with Oklahoma's semicentennial celebration and highway construction. Oklahoma's fiftieth anniversary of statehood occurred in 1957. A state agency, the Oklahoma Semi-Centennial Commission, directed the spectacle. All the communities in the state were represented, and cities and states across the nation participated, as did nineteen nations. The event was well advertised and promoted in local, state, and national newspapers. James C. Burge was director of the semicentennial observance. Held at the Oklahoma City Fairgrounds, the celebration drew massive crowds; attendance figures for a three-week period showed 1.5 million visitors. The Futurama showing of automobiles and the Russian exhibit reportedly drew the largest crowds. The focal point of the exposition grounds was the "Arrows to Atoms" tower, epitomizing the semicentennial theme. This tower still stands. Linking the semicentennial celebration to posterity was the burial of a time capsule to be opened in 2007.

Governor Gary's announced goal on highway building was twenty-five hundred miles of new roads in four years. At the close of his term in 1959 approximately thirty-five hundred such miles had been constructed. This increase in road building was made possible by the Federal-Aid Highway Act, passed by Congress in 1956. It provided for forty-one thousand miles of multilane highways, called the National System of Interstate and Defense Highways, with eight hundred miles of this vast grid to be in Oklahoma. The three branches of the Oklahoma portion of the system centered on Oklahoma City. The north-south route was designated as Interstate Highway 35, the east-west route as Interstate Highway 40, and a northeast-southwest route as Interstate Highway 44, to include the Will Rogers Turnpike, the Turner Turnpike, and a projected southwestern toll road. The Federal-Aid Highway Act required that one-half of the national system be completed by 1965, and the remainder by 1972.

Governor Gary succeeded in getting his proposed Department of Commerce and Industry established. This agency advertised Oklahoma's industrial potential around the nation and accelerated the relocation of job-supplying enterprises in the state. The governor himself worked hard at what he called

Governor J. Howard Edmondson.

"balancing our agricultural economy with a variety of industries." In his speeches and writings on the Sooner State's future in industry, he pointed to low tax rates, local inducements to business, and growing water resources.

Throughout his administration, Governor Gary emphasized expansion of water resources. His legislatures passed a water code aimed at expanding urban water resources. One law allowed cities and towns to combine their resources through the organization of water conservancy districts, and to enter into long-range contracts to build and operate water facilities. Another law created the Water Study Commission, with a membership of citizens and legislators, and assigned responsibility for surveying state water supplies and needs. Then on July 1, 1958, voters approved State Question No. 380. This legislative referendum proposal authorized cities and towns to develop water facilities by issuing thirty-year bonds, to be retired from water sales.

In 1958, Oklahomans went to the polls to elect Raymond Gary's successor. Eleven candidates filed for the Democratic nomination. To the surprise of veteran observers, J.

Howard Edmondson, a young Tulsa attorney who campaigned on a pledge to bring a quick vote on repeal of prohibition, placed first in the primary election with 108,358 votes. In second place with 107,616 votes was William P. "Bill" Atkinson, a Midwest City builder. It had been predicted that Edmondson would rate no higher than third place in the primary, for he had virtually no support from the professional politicians. One of the few experienced politicians working for his election was his brother, Congressman Ed Edmondson.

Edmondson had inexperienced but vigorous colleagues who spearheaded his campaign with an accent on youth and slogans such as "Big Red E," "Fresh Breeze," and "Prairie Fire." Edmondson's ability as a public speaker and a highly favorable television image were of considerable influence in his victory. One television rating authority declared, "Edmondson held his audience one night against the Lone Ranger." Edmondson gained momentum in the runoff and defeated Atkinson, 363,742 to 107,616. In the November general election Edmondson received the greatest majority ever accorded a gubernatorial candidate in defeating the Republican aspirant, Phil Ferguson, 399,504 to 107,497. D. A. Bryce, the Independent candidate, polled 31,840 votes. Democrats won five of the six congressional seats and once again rolled up substantial majorities in the legislature.

Oklahoma's sixteenth governor was inaugurated in January, 1959. At the age of thirty-three, he was the youngest chief executive in state history, and the youngest governor in the nation at that time. The accent on youth extended into the office of lieutenant governor, won by George Nigh, a thirty-one-year-old McAlester schoolteacher and former member of the legislature. Edmondson's close advisers were young men, soon to be known as the "crew cuts." Joe Cannon, Edmondson's choice as commissioner of public safety, was leader of the youthful clique.

Though young men controlled the executive branch, the Old Guard dominated the legislature. The inevitable conflict in viewpoint on what was best for the state produced an impasse. In the ensuing power struggle, the legislature, as usual, emerged supreme. Edmondson's first legislature, the Twenty-

Seventh, was led by Clint Livingston, speaker of the house, and Harold Garvin, president pro tempore of the senate.

The new governor pursued his campaign pledge to obtain an early vote on repeal of prohibition, the seventh such vote since statehood. Heretofore the dry forces had successfully turned back the wet interests, but their numbers had declined with each referendum. Soon after the close of World War II, the Anti-Saloon League, the WCTU, and certain church groups comprising the prohibition constituency joined to form the Oklahoma Dry Association. This group hired a full-time director and staff to stiffen the spine of opposition to repeal of prohibition.

The wet forces organized soon after Edmondson's election to launch a full-scale assault against prohibition. Widely publicized reports told of Oklahoma bootleggers doing a gross annual business of $100 million, and disparagingly referred to this "aged blend of piety and politics." Cynics declared, "the Wets have their liquor and the Drys have their law."

The Edmondson strategy was to enforce the prohibition law as it had never been done before. Joe Cannon, commissioner of public safety, and his "crew cuts" became familiar public figures with their midnight raids on Oklahoma bars and clubs. Their announced goal was to dry up Oklahoma. It is said that in those times a favorite cocktail with Oklahoma's drinking constituency was named for the redoubtable commissioner of public safety—"The Cannon Ball," consisting of the legal 3.2 percent beer served in a champagne glass.

A social revolution occurred in Oklahoma on April 7, 1959, when voters went to the polls to consider State Question 386. This legislative referendum proposed to repeal the prohibition amendment to the state constitution. If adopted, it would establish an Alcoholic Beverage Control Board and authorize licensed, privately owned package stores as liquor outlets. The question carried by a vote of 386,845 to 314,380. The Twenty-seventh Legislature implemented the amendment through the Liquor Control Act, and legal liquor sales began on September 1, 1959.

With rising costs of government, pressure for additional revenue, and a reluctance to increase the state sales and income taxes, the wet force had emphasized the revenue-producing benefits of repeal of prohibition. Estimates on new money for the state from the sale of legalized liquor were as high as $27 million annually. Actually, the $2.40 per gallon state tax on liquor produced only $8,252,336 in 1959–60, and $5,942,611 in 1961–62. The liquor revenue is divided between the state and cities, with the state receiving two-thirds and the cities one-third. When the costs of administering the law through the ABC Board, the costs of law enforcement problems inherent in consumption, and the costs of rehabilitating alcoholics are deducted from this total, however, the state scarcely breaks even. Thus revenue production was a fallacious argument for repeal. A more honest argument would have been that repeal legalized a de facto situation. Before repeal, there had been open flaunting of the law with an undemocratic, selective enforcement.

Governor Edmondson also favored a withholding system to assure a more efficient collection of state income tax, a continuation of interstate highway development, a southwestern toll road estimated to cost $54 million, reduction of the spending powers of county commissioners, a state merit system, central purchasing, and reapportionment. The Twenty-Seventh Legislature was in no mood to accept all of Edmondson's reform proposals. The governor did obtain passage of a law providing for the withholding system and the state merit program. The latter was aimed at placing competency above partisanship as a qualification for appointment to state jobs, thus freeing state employees from political interference and insuring security in their positions. The legislature also submitted State Question 393 for referendum consideration. Approved by the voters on July 5, 1960, it established the Oklahoma Industrial Finance Authority. This new agency was authorized to issue bonds to the amount of $10 million for loans to local agencies for industrial development.

Thwarted in his attempts to obtain legislative support for his reform program, Governor Edmondson went to the people through initiative petitions, and three propositions were considered in a special election on September 20, 1960. State Question 396 proposed to

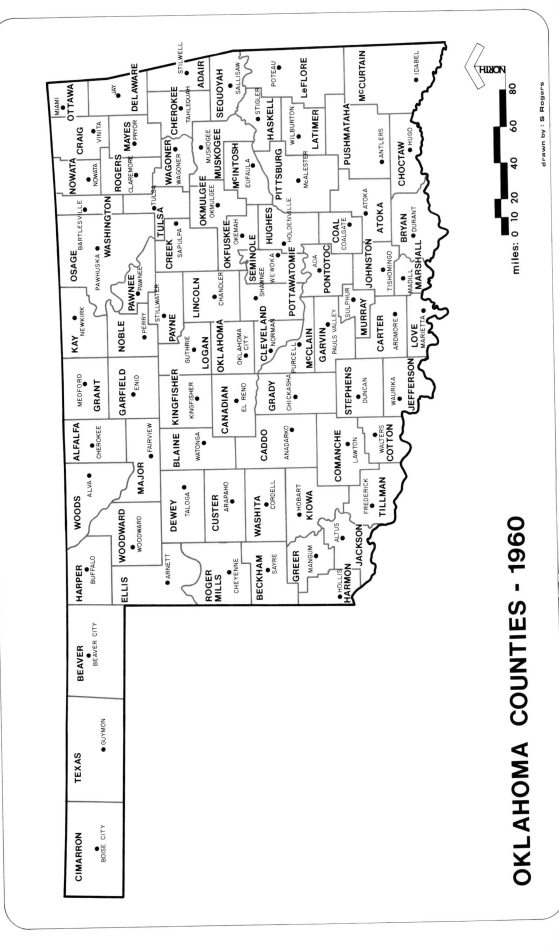

OKLAHOMA COUNTIES - 1960

miles: 0 10 20 40 60 80

drawn by : S Rogers

NORTH

President John F. Kennedy at Big Cedar, Oklahoma.

establish a constitutional highway commission, and in some respects remove this patronage paradise from politics. State Question 397 proposed to reapportion the legislature to adjust Oklahoma's law-making body to the state's population changes and therefore to shift the balance of political power from the rural districts to the cities. State Question 398 proposed to permit the citizens of each county to decide whether their county road money should be administered by the State Highway Commission. This change would mean the transfer of as much as $30 million annually from control of the county commissioners to control of the State Highway Department. Small towns, rural interests, most legislators, and county commissioners—the backbone of support for the Old Guard power structure—rallied in an intensive campaign against the Edmondson proposals. Each proposition went down to smashing defeat.

When Governor Edmondson left office in January, 1963, he was rated by political analysts as the most controversial governor since Alfalfa Bill Murray. These same sources claimed he had less control of the Democratic party than any governor since the strife-ridden

1920s. The genesis of his trouble, and of future trouble for the Oklahoma Democratic party, may have come from Edmondson's obsession for reform and his eagerness to achieve much-needed changes. He stirred up the Old Guard with his three initiative proposals, and many observers claim that this tore the Democratic party asunder because it split the rural and urban factions of the party. Repeal of prohibition had been a touchy issue, too, and its success had antagonized certain church groups and dry leaders. Undoubtedly, all of these factors contributed to Democratic losses in the 1960 and 1962 elections. At any rate, the governor received part of the blame for stirring up the waters of partisan politics.

Edmondson also alienated the Old Guard through his promotion of the presidential nomination of Senator John F. Kennedy. The governor was an early Kennedy supporter, and when he seconded the Kennedy nomination at the 1960 Democratic National Convention he was booed by certain members of the Oklahoma delegation. Kennedy, a Roman Catholic, had a difficult time mustering support in Oklahoma, and in the November general election, Richard M. Nixon, the Republican presidential nominee, carried the state 533,039 to 370,111. This was the third consecutive time Oklahoma's electoral vote had gone to the Republican candidate. Yet, despite his failure to carry Oklahoma, Kennedy won nationally, and Governor Edmondson was vindicated. At the same time United States Senator Robert S. Kerr defeated the Republican candidate, B. Hayden Crawford, a Tulsa attorney, 474,116 to 385,646. Democratic candidates won five of the six congressional seats and control of the legislature.

The Twenty-eighth Legislature, led by J. D. McCarty, speaker of the house, and Everett D. Collins, president pro tempore of the senate, met in January, 1961. The merit system was amended to exempt personnel in departments of elective officials, thus restoring to patronage a substantial number of state employees. An attraction for new industries was a reduction in the rate paid by employers for workman's compensation insurance; business leaders had claimed the previous rate was "a deterrent to industrial development." In a thoroughgoing tax equalization program, the burden of revenue raising was shifted more to the local level. By reducing the need for state aid, this program produced an estimated saving of $5 million in the general fund.

Central purchasing, a controversial practice at first, succeeded in the second half of the Edmondson administration. The governor claimed an annual savings of $8 million was realized through having one agency make purchases for all departments of state government.

An intensive public construction program during the Edmondson administration, together with rapid industrial development, produced an all-time high in nonagricultural employment. More than two thousand miles of highways were built, including an expansion of the interstate system. This construction was carried out under a program of joint funding, with the federal government paying 90 percent of the costs and the state paying 10 percent. Public building projects included two new state office buildings and the new Center for Continuing Education at the University of Oklahoma, the latter made possible by a grant from the Kellogg Foundation with state funds matching the foundation grant.

Limited state revenues and expanding public needs placed inexorable pressures on the legislature. The constitution's budget balancing amendment, adopted in 1941, forbade the state to spend more money than it collected. Public schools, higher education, the Highway Department, welfare, and other state operations demanded more money to meet increasing costs, but few politicians seemed willing to announce for an increase in taxes. Most claimed that holding the tax line and depending on the growth of revenues through concomitant growth in business would solve the state's financial problem. They argued that a tax increase would upset "the favorable business climate" and discourage industries from locating in the state.

Meanwhile, an increase in state bond issues was frequently used to evade or defer the ultimate confrontation on a tax increase. Another method was sought through legal loopholes. For example, Edmondson attempted unsuccessfully to draw into the State Highway Department coffers the $30 million spent annually by the county commissioners. "Raiding" the welfare fund, which was created by earmarking the sales tax, to support certain other state operations—for example, mental health—was another proposal to stretch public funds.

Some of these methods were used by the Twenty-Eighth Legislature to relieve temporarily the pressure for more revenue. After appropriating all funds available under the terms of the budget balancing amendment, the lawmakers then turned to the anticipated surplus. The budget balancing amendment limits appropriations from the general fund to the three-year average of tax collections as set by the State Board of Equalization. Oklahoma's expanding economy consistently has yielded revenues in excess of the three-year average with result that a surplus has accrued for each appropriation period. To make appropriation of the surplus legal, the legislature in 1947 adopted a law creating the emergency appropriation fund. This measure directs that any surplus in the general revenue fund over regular appropriations be transferred to the emergency fund. The law instructs the State Board of Equalization to make an official estimate of the revenue accumulating in the emergency fund, which is subsequently appropriated by the legislature.

The Twenty-eighth and succeeding legislatures, after appropriating the anticipated surplus, have gone one step further. The estimate of the anticipated surplus has been lower than actual collections. Therefore, beginning in 1961 the legislature appropriated according to the formula as allowed by the budget balancing amendment, then appropriated the anticipated surplus. In addition, the legislature made what was called open-end appropriations on a contingency basis, that is, the agencies designated would receive additional funds if and when such money accumulated in the treasury.

The question of state finance and how to solve the crisis of limited funds and expanded services was the leading issue in the gubernatorial campaign in 1962, and the voter response to proposed solutions produced a revolution in Oklahoma politics. The Democrats endured one of the bitterest primary battles in state history. Former Governor Raymond Gary, a leading Democratic candidate, admitted in his campaign that the state needed more money and proposed a multimillion-dollar bond issue to relieve pressure on the general fund. The other Democratic front-runner, William Atkinson, Midwest City builder, declared the only solution to Oklahoma's fiscal crisis was a one-cent increase in the sales tax. Atkinson won the Democratic nomination, but the crippling schism in the party that began in the early Edmondson years persisted, and observers claimed that many Gary supporters either refused to work for Atkinson's election in November, or actually voted for the Republican nominee.

Henry Bellmon, prominent Republican leader and his party's choice for governor, maintained that by rigid economy and dependence on growth revenue the state could operate with its current revenue. He made it clear that if elected he would veto all tax increase bills. Oklahoma voters in November had a choice between an assured tax increase with Atkinson and no new taxes with Bellmon. Bellmon won and became Oklahoma's first Republican governor. Democrats dominated in other elective positions, including substantial majorities in the legislature. United States

Senator Robert S. Kerr, "Uncrowned King of the United States Senate."

Senator Mike Monroney won reelection over B. Hayden Crawford, the Republican nominee. All six incumbent congressmen won reelection: Ed Edmondson, John Jarman, Tom Steed, Carl Albert, and Victor Wickersham, and the lone Republican, Page Belcher.

Senator Robert S. Kerr died suddenly on New Year's Day, 1963. His untimely passing produced a drastic change in Oklahoma political history. According to the state's succession law, the governor had the power to fill the vacancy, with the appointee to hold the office until the next general election in 1964. Kerr had been reelected in 1960, and his term would not have expired until 1966, but the appointee would have to stand for election to a two-year term on November 3, 1964. Nine days before his term as governor ended, Edmondson resigned and Lieutenant Governor George Nigh became Oklahoma's chief executive. To no one's surprise, Governor Nigh appointed Edmondson to the United States Senate.

Oklahoma's eighteenth governor, Republican Henry Bellmon, was inaugurated on January 14, 1963. His position was anomalous in that he was surrounded by elected Democratic officials including Lieutenant Governor Leo Winters, and a predominantly Democratic legislature, the Twenty-ninth. J. D. McCarty became speaker of the house, while Roy Belcher was president pro tempore of the senate.

The new governor maintained cordial relations with the legislature and stressed prudent management of public affairs and the status quo rather than reform. The first half of his administration saw the sale of bonds for a new eastern turnpike to cost an estimated $31 million. The state oil depletion allowance was increased to 27.5 percent, and the merit system was strengthened by establishing an employees retirement system. On the other hand, certain legislative proposals were turned back for lack of support from the governor. One of these would have granted teachers a thousand-dollar pay raise, spread over a six-year period, which Bellmon vetoed.

The legislature considered but did not approve lowering the legal voting age. Several lawmakers favored a proposal granting suffrage to eighteen-year-old citizens. A legislative study showed that Georgia and Kentucky allowed eighteen-year-old citizens to vote; that nineteen was the legal voting age in Alaska; age twenty in Hawaii; but voting age was twenty-one in the other forty-six states, including Oklahoma.

Public finance was the biggest problem facing the Twenty-Ninth Legislature. Among other things it had to honor a commitment on open-end finances made by the Twenty-eighth Legislature, and to appropriate $10.5 million from the treasury surplus. In the hearings on this and other appropriation bills, the entire structure of Oklahoma public finance received careful examination. Studies of the sources of state income disclosed that thirty cents of every dollar spent in Oklahoma state government came from federal grants, most of it for welfare, highways, and education. Principal state sources of revenue were cigarette tax, 3.4 percent; gross production tax, 6.61 percent; income tax, 6.9 percent; sales tax, 11 percent; and gas tax, 11.4 percent. In the division of revenue, the big recipients were welfare, 33 percent; highways, 25 percent;

public education, 16 percent; and higher education, 14 percent.

Of approximately one billion dollars spent by state government during the previous two years, the legislature had controlled only about one-fourth. Most of the remainder had been earmarked for various state agencies and did not require legislative appropriation. The major portion of nonappropriated funds were derived from sales tax revenue, which went directly to the Welfare Department, and gasoline taxes, which went directly to the Highway Department and to county commissioners for road-building purposes. Though some legislators voiced strong opposition to the earmarking practice on the grounds that it prevented a complete examination of all public expenditures, nothing was done to change the system.

The Twenty-ninth Legislature eventually appropriated $255 million to meet the largest budget in state history. This included $22.5 million in anticipated surplus, plus $11.5 million from the welfare fund to improve mental health care and support three schools for the mentally retarded. Public schools received $98 million with the promise of $6 million more early in 1965. Higher education received $62 million and a promised supplementary appropriation of $4.2 million. The Highway Department was allocated $17 million, along with a pledge of an additional grant of $1.5 million from the anticipated surplus. These figures, plus the earmarked monies from the gasoline tax, assured the Highway Department of a record budget of $92 million.

A much more controversial subject faced by the Twenty-ninth Legislature was legislative reapportionment. Over the years the majority of the state's population had shifted from rural areas to the cities, but the state legislature had consistently refused to abide by the constitutional requirement to reapportion the state's districts every ten years. This situation had assured rural control of the state's law-making machinery and serious underrepresentation for city dwellers.

The failure of previous legislatures to reapportion had led Tulsa newspaper editor Jenkin Lloyd Jones to seek remedy in the State Supreme Court as early as the 1940s, but the court refused Jones's petition. Later, Governor J. Howard Edmondson tried to achieve equal representation in the legislature but succeeded only in stiffening the Old Guard's resistance. Then in 1962, in *Baker* vs. *Carr*, a Tennessee case, the federal courts took judicial notice of widespread inequality of legislative representation. Also in 1962, the Federal District Court in Oklahoma City ruled that Oklahoma's legislative malapportionment discriminated against city residents. In declaring the present system null and void, it gave the legislature one last chance to remedy the system.

Just before the March 8, 1963, deadline, the legislature passed a reapportionment act, and the three-member federal court tribunal in Oklahoma City took the plan under study. On July 17, 1963, Federal Judges Fred A. Daugherty, Ross Rizley, and A. P. Murrah disapproved the plan, charging it "provides no relief for a malapportionment." The judges described it as "a patchwork of political maneuvering and manipulation to perpetuate the same invidious apportionment which prevailed," whereupon the judges "reluctantly decided to reapportion the Oklahoma legislature by judicial decree, because we are convinced . . . that the legislature, as now constituted, is either unable or unwilling to reapportion itself in accordance with . . . the requirements of the equal protection clause of the 14th amendment."

Rural and legislative interests appealed the ruling to the United States Supreme Court. On February 7, 1964, Justice Byron White issued an order staying the order of July 17, 1963. Meanwhile, the State Supreme Court finally issued its own reapportionment formula, which increased somewhat the urban quota in both houses of the legislature. Under the state court's plan, candidates would file in February, 1964, for election to the Thirtieth Legislature. After the May, 1964, primary, Democratic candidates in many legislative districts faced no opposition in November, and in the characteristic pattern of states with a one-party system, Democratic legislative leaders met shortly after the primary and organized the Thirtieth Legislature by selecting the speaker, president pro tempore of the senate, and

Governor Henry Bellmon.

committees. Had this election stood, the Thirtieth Legislature would have been the only one elected under the State Supreme Court formula, for at the May 26 primary election, the voters approved State Question 416, a legislative referendum establishing a new reapportionment formula. It allocated twelve house members to Oklahoma County and ten to Tulsa County. Each county was assured at least one house member, and none more than one senator.

Sid White and Norman Reynolds, reapportionment attorneys from Oklahoma City, pushed for a decision by the United States Supreme Court. On June 15, 1964, the federal three-judge tribunal in Oklahoma City ruled the May primary results null and void, and ordered the governor to arrange for a special election to select the Thirtieth Legislature on the basis of a forty-eight-member senate (eight for Oklahoma County, seven for Tulsa County), and a ninety-seven-member house (Oklahoma County receiving nineteen members, Tulsa County fifteen).

A short time later, Governor Bellmon ordered new legislative elections for September

29. Democratic candidates won substantial majorities again and the day after the election they met to organize the new house and senate. J. D. McCarty won the office of speaker of the house for the Thirtieth Legislature and Clem McSpadden won the post of president pro tempore of the senate.

"Right to work" was another lively issue throughout the early part of 1964. The federal Taft-Hartley Labor Act permitted states to enact statutes, commonly known as right-to-work laws, to forbid compulsory unionism. Twenty states, including Kansas, Texas, and Arkansas, already had right-to-work laws, and advocates claimed such a law was necessary for Oklahoma to create a favorable business climate. Oklahoma business and professional leaders organized Oklahomans to support right-to-work legislation, and brought in as executive director the Reverend Ray Armstrong from Kansas, who had led the successful movement there. Organized labor in Oklahoma countered with the Oklahoma Free Marketing and Bargaining Committee. Both groups carried on intensive campaigns. The Oklahoma right-to-work proposition, a proposed constitutional amendment brought up as an initiative petition, appeared on the ballot as State Question 409. If adopted it would have restricted union activity by forbidding compulsory union membership as a condition for employment. In the May 5, 1964, election it was defeated by a vote of 316,670 to 320,871.

The general election in November, 1964, brought to an end one of the most exciting campaigns in Sooner State history. In this presidential election year, Democratic nominee President Lyndon B. Johnson opposed Senator Barry Goldwater, the Republican candidate. Political interest in Oklahoma had been heightened earlier by the right-to-work issue and the primary election for the United States Senate. Democratic Senator J. Howard Edmondson was contested by state Senator Fred R. Harris, former Governor Raymond Gary, and Willard R. Owens. In the primary Edmondson received 177,091; Harris, 162,960; Gary, 152,805; and Owens, 32,050. Fred R. Harris then won in the runoff, 276,000 to 177,000. Jed Johnson, youthful congressional candidate and son of a former congressman, defeated incumbent Victor Wickersham

for the Sixth District Democratic nomination.

The Republican candidates for United States senator were Bud Wilkinson, famous football coach from the University of Oklahoma; Tom J. Harris, Oklahoma City businessman; and Forest Beall, prominent Republican party leader. Wilkinson won the nomination with a vote of 85,211. Harris received 16,100, and Beall placed third with 6,826.

One of the surprises of the 1964 November general election was the remarkable unity of the Democrats. President John F. Kennedy's tragic death in November, 1963, had removed a cause of friction among Oklahoma Democrats. All factions closed ranks behind President Johnson with the result that Oklahoma's electoral vote returned to the Democratic column for the first time in twelve years. President Johnson defeated Senator Goldwater in Oklahoma and across the nation in a landslide vote. The Oklahoma presidential vote was 520,315 for Johnson to 411,272 for Goldwater. Harris defeated Wilkinson, 463,292 to 440,472, thus winning the final two years of the late Senator Kerr's term. The tradition of Democrats winning five of the six seats in Congress continued. Republican Page Belcher appeared invincible in the First District, but Jed Johnson, Democratic winner over incumbent Victor Wickersham in the primary, went on to defeat Republican Bayard Auchincloss. Johnson gained the Sixth District seat at the age of twenty-four, making him the youngest in the United States Congress and second youngest in 167 years. He reached the United States Constitution's required age of twenty-five just before Congress convened in January, 1965.

In the November, 1964, general election Oklahoma voters also passed judgment on four initiated propositions aimed at upgrading Oklahoma public schools. One proposal recommended beginning salaries for teachers at 75 percent of the national average, providing for a base salary of $4,440 with 3 percent increases for each year of teaching experience. Another proposal provided for consolidating weak districts and reducing the number of school districts from 1,160 to 547. A third proposition sought to repeal the five mill emergency levy and allowed a permissive county levy of fifteen mills. The fourth proposition retained the position of county superintendent by expanding the duties of this official. The Oklahoma Education Association (OEA) staff and classroom teachers obtained the required number of petition signers. Strong opposition led by the metropolitan press and the governor developed against the four propositions, especially the minimum salary and county superintendent proposals, and all four propositions were defeated.

Reaction by Oklahoma's twenty-five thousand teachers was immediate, and a rebellion in the teaching profession threatened. Tulsa and Midwest City teachers led the imminent revolt. Agents for the United Federation of Teachers, AFL-CIO, came to the state and attempted to unionize Oklahoma teachers. In the face of the crisis in education, Governor Bellmon called two emergency meetings at Tulsa and Oklahoma City on December 5, 1964. At these sessions the governor reiterated his stand against a tax increase and emphasized reliance on growth increase. He also revealed his "Giant Stride plan to substantially improve Oklahoma's educational system." The focus of his plan was a proposed $500 million bond issue to refinance the state's bond-financed turnpikes, to build five new toll roads and provide $100 million for state highways. By taking care of highways through the bond issue, Bellmon said his plan would provide more than $306 million for appropriation by the legislature. This, according to the governor, would assure teachers an $800 pay increase over a two year span.

The Oklahoma Education Association, demanding a $1,000 increase, requested the National Education Association (NEA) to investigate the Sooner State school situation. A special committee from the NEA's Commission on Professional Rights and Responsibilities came to Oklahoma in December to survey local conditions. From publicity surrounding the NEA hearings on the Oklahoma educational situation, it was disclosed that the national salary average for classroom teachers was $6,250. Oklahoma's average was $5,160, but the starting salary was $3,800. Oklahoma ranked thirty-seventh among the states in teachers' salaries. The report showed that federal aid for Oklahoma public schools during 1964 amounted to $13 million. Most of this

was impacted area subsidy, that is, federal aid to Indian children and children of persons associated with military installations.

The NEA study further showed that with the adoption of the "Better Schools Amendment" in 1955, the school finance load had shifted to the local level, so that while ten years before 50 percent of school finance came from state aid, in 1964 the ratio was 31 percent state aid and 69 percent local support. NEA surveys of school finance revealed that the national average expenditure per student was $455. Oklahoma ranked fortieth among the fifty states in expenditures per child. The NEA report closed with the indictment that "subminimal conditions exist in almost every area of the Oklahoma school program."

Oklahoma's first legislature apportioned by a federal court, the Thirtieth, convened on January 5, 1965. J. D. McCarty and Clem McSpadden, the house and senate leaders, supported by substantial Democratic majorities, paid only token attention to Republican Governor Henry Bellmon's program, built around his proposed "Giant Stride," and developed their own program. The overriding problem continued to be that of finding new revenue to finance expanding state services and to meet OEA demands for increased school support, including a $1,000 salary increase for teachers. Faced with threats from Governor Bellmon to veto a tax increase bill, the legislature went to the people with a sales tax proposition. At a special election on April 27, voters considered State Question 425 providing for a one-cent increase in the sales tax, an institutional building bond issue (State Question 426), and a highway bond issue (State Question 427). All three were voted down, the sales tax proposition losing 292,429 to 170,990.

The sales tax defeat had repercussions in Oklahoma's public schools, for revenue derived from it was expected to eliminate the so-called "subminimal conditions" in the state's educational system. Turned back in November on their initiated proposals, then advised by NEA investigators that their schools ranked fortieth in the nation in public support, Oklahoma teachers, through the OEA, threatened strikes and walkouts. On May 11, the NEA imposed sanctions on Oklahoma and placed the Oklahoma educational system on its national blacklist. In 1963, NEA sanctions had been imposed on Utah, so Oklahoma was the second state to receive professional condemnation by this national teachers' organization. Sanctions meant that out-of-state teachers taking jobs in Oklahoma would be censured. The NEA also established relocation centers in Oklahoma to help local teachers find better positions in other states. Governor Bellmon demanded retraction of this action by NEA officials, and most state newspapers condemned the OEA and the NEA, declaring that several states were in worse shape, and asked, "Why pick on Oklahoma?" Leaders of the NEA answered that while a few states were below Oklahoma, this fact provided no defense when quality education was at issue. Sanctions came to Oklahoma because Sooner State teachers were better organized than those in states with lower ratings than Oklahoma, and the "relatively swift decline" in public support of education in Oklahoma was the principal reason. "In 1950," said the NEA, "the state was spending only one dollar less per student than the national average. In 1964 it was $104 less, and this year [1965] it will be $117 less."

With the defeat of the sales tax proposition, the legislature sought other sources of additional revenue, primarily to reduce the crisis in public education. The lawmakers passed a one-cent increase in the cigarette tax, and despite the governor's pledge to veto any new tax bill, he signed the measure. This action, along with a higher estimate of general revenue, permitted the legislature to appropriate a record $328.7 million for the biennium. Legislative leaders claimed that the Thirtieth Legislature was the first in ten years to finance state government without resorting to open-end appropriations, but critics pointed out that this claim was made possible by use of late estimates on anticipated revenue.

The legislature adopted a new common school code that guaranteed a minimum $380 teacher pay raise, and statisticians estimated that most teachers would receive an average $500 raise, while some increases would amount to as much as $900. In addition, the legislature appropriated $5.2 million for textbooks, which marked the first time the program had been amply financed since the adoption of the free textbook amendment in 1947. In overall appropriations, the Thirtieth Legislature granted a 25 percent increase to common schools, a 26 percent increase for higher education, and mental health received 12 percent more than it had during the preceding biennium.

The legislature also submitted a proposition to the voters whereby school districts could levy an additional ten mills ad valorem tax for local support of schools, to be approved or disapproved in a special election scheduled on September 14. This action, plus the increased common schools appropriation, led the governor and the legislative leaders to expect the NEA sanctions to be lifted. The OEA Board of Directors met at Stillwater on August 11, and much pressure was placed on this group by state leaders and newspapers to request NEA to remove Oklahoma schools from its blacklist. The OEA Board refused to comply, whereupon Governor Bellmon on August 16 requested the state's attorney general to investigate the possibility of bringing suit to force the NEA to drop its sanctions against Oklahoma schools.

The Thirtieth Legislature, in session from January 5 to July 22, 1965, ranked as the second longest in state history. Its length was exceeded only by the Twenty-eighth's session in 1961, which ran from January 3 to July 29. The Thirtieth Legislature had much to do. Besides attempting to abate the public school crisis, this legislature also had to exercise its impeachment power. The impeachments were based on charges of corruption in the State Supreme Court, and grew out of a recent conviction in federal court of former Vice-Chief Justice Nelson Corn on charges of income tax evasion. Justice Earl Welch was convicted in federal court on a similar charge. While in federal prison, Corn provided federal and state investigators with a statement accusing colleagues on the state's highest bench of accepting bribes. Justice Welch resigned from the State Supreme Court a few days before impeachment proceedings began. Corn's statement, however, also implicated Justice N. B. Johnson. The house investigated and voted charges of accepting bribes. A week-long trial in the state senate resulted in Johnson's conviction and removal from the Oklahoma Supreme Court.

The supreme court scandal brought demands for judicial reform, notably a proposal for adoption of the Missouri Plan for selecting justices. While no pervasive cleanup of the Oklahoma judicial system was produced by the legislature, it did adopt a related reform—the District Attorney Law, which replaced the county attorney system. Under this law, the state was divided into twenty-seven districts, each with a district attorney. These officials were elected for the first time in 1966.

One of the most notable acts of the Thirtieth Legislature was the adoption of the Oklahoma Higher Education Code. Oklahoma was the first of the fifty states to take such action. Studies that led to this reform came principally from the chancellor of higher education, Dr. E. T. Dunlap, and his research staff. The code reestablished the fact that the Sooner State higher education system derived its authority from a constitutional amendment adopted in 1941, State Question 300, which created the nine-member Oklahoma State Regents for Higher Education and provided for coordination of public and private colleges and universities through this agency. The administrative staff for the higher education system headed by the chancellor coordinates the Oklahoma public and private institutions of higher learning.

The public institutions, which are locally administered as indicated, include the University of Oklahoma at Norman, by the University of Oklahoma Board of Regents; Oklahoma State University at Stillwater and the A. and M. colleges, Panhandle A and M University (Goodwell), Langston University (Langston), Cameron University (Lawton), Eastern A. and M. College (Wilburton), Connors State Agricultural College (Warner), Murray State Agricultural College (Tishomingo), and Northeastern A. and M. College (Miami), administered by the Board of Regents for Oklahoma State University and the Oklahoma A and M Colleges; Central State University (Edmond), East Central State University (Ada), Northeastern State University (Tahlequah), Northwestern State University (Alva), Southwestern State University (Weatherford), and Southeastern State University (Durant), administered by the Board of Regents of Oklahoma Colleges. The University

Governor Dewey Bartlett.

of Science and Arts of Oklahoma at Chickasha is governed by the Regents for Oklahoma University of Liberal Arts. In addition, there are state-funded junior colleges at Claremore, Tulsa, Tonkawa, Sayre, Poteau, Midwest City, El Reno, Seminole, Altus, and Oklahoma City.

The private colleges and universities coordinating their programs through the Oklahoma System of Higher Education include Phillips University at Enid; Bethany Nazarene at Bethany; Oklahoma Christian College, Oklahoma City University, Southwestern College, and Midwestern College, all situated in Oklahoma City; Wesleyan College at Bartlesville; Tulsa University and Oral Roberts University, both at Tulsa; Bacone College at Muskogee; Hillsdale Free Will Baptist College in Moore; and Oklahoma Baptist University and St. Gregory's College at Shawnee.

The Thirtieth Legislature created the Industrial Development and Park Commission, consisting of seven commissioners, a director, and a full-time lobbyist resident in Washington to work with Congress and the various agencies to attract government contracts to Oklahoma. This action consolidated the Department of Commerce and Industry and the Planning and

Governor David Hall.

Resources Board. In other action, the legislature adopted a law providing for an end to the open ranges and requiring ranchers to fence pastures. Another approved measure requires a special election to fill a United States Senate vacancy, replacing the law allowing the governor to fill the vacancy by appointment. In response to a special interest demand, the legislature passed a new turnpike bill authorizing five new toll roads.

One of the most controversial measures confronting the Thirtieth Legislature was congressional reapportionment. This problem arose because of the tacit threat that legislative failure to balance population in congressional districts would lead to federal court reapportionment, as occurred in reapportioning the state legislature. Governor Bellmon vetoed the first reapportionment bill; a compromise bill was vetoed, but the second veto was overridden by the legislature. The congressional reapportionment bills were controversial chiefly because of the manner in which each bill divided Tulsa County.

Before the Thirtieth Legislature adjourned, it provided for submitting a proposition to the people to allow the governor, secretary of

state, auditor, and treasurer to succeed themselves.

Governor Bellmon's successor was elected in 1966. The Republican party chose as its candidate state Senator Dewey Bartlett of Tulsa. The Democratic party candidate was Preston Moore, former national commander of the American Legion and an attorney from Oklahoma City. Bartlett defeated Moore to become not only the second Republican chief executive of the state but the first Republican to be elected consecutively to that office.

United States Senator Fred Harris, elected in 1964 to serve the last two years of Senator Robert S. Kerr's term, sought a full six-year term in 1966. He was contested by Republican Pat J. Patterson of Oklahoma City. Harris defeated Patterson in the November election.

The Republicans, besides electing their second consecutive governor, for the first time in state history won the office of attorney general with the election of G. T. Blankenship. Democrats maintained control of both houses of the state legislature and won four of the congressional seats. Republicans won two.

Governor Dewey Bartlett had campaigned and won on a platform similar to that of former Governor Henry Bellmon—a no-tax increase promise, with the pledge to manage the state government with existing revenue.

A change in legislative meetings from biennial sessions to annual sessions took place in 1967. The legislature passed a redistricting bill that was based on the population shift from rural to urban areas and provided each congressional district with a better balance of population. The legislature also passed the Unclaimed Property Act that permits the Oklahoma Tax Commission to take under state ownership the accounts in banks, utilities, and oil companies that have lain dormant for fourteen years and convert them to public use.

The State Supreme Court bribery scandal prompted a demand for judicial reform. The legislature passed a court reform proposal and submitted it to a special election on July 11, 1967. The measure provided for the nonpartisan election of members of the Oklahoma judiciary. The measure also abolished the justice of the peace system in Oklahoma. Voters approved the judicial reform proposals.

Governor Bartlett vetoed a number of legislative bills, including a salary increase for several state officials and a statewide kindergarten system. During 1967 the state senate investigated charges of conflict of interest among state officials. The investigation was prompted by revelations that public utility lobbyists had provided cash and other considerations for public officials, including the state corporation commissioners.

Oklahomans went to the polls to vote for a new president in 1968. The Republican party nominated Richard M. Nixon, a former vice-president. The Democratic party nominated incumbent Vice-President Hubert Humphrey. A new political group, the American party, campaigned in Oklahoma. This party's presidential candidate was George Wallace, governor of Alabama. Nixon carried Oklahoma and the nation to win the presidency.

Mike Monroney sought reelection at this time as the Democratic candidate for the United States Senate. His Republican opponent was former Governor Henry Bellmon. Bellmon defeated Monroney; his victory marked the fourth time an Oklahoma Republican had won a United States Senate seat, and the second time a former governor of Oklahoma had won this high office. Oklahoma voters also approved by referendum vote a proposition to repeal the state tax on intangible property.

Inflation, a national economic problem, was affecting state government. Public employees, including schoolteachers, faced reduced real income as modest salary increases failed to keep pace with rapidly rising living costs. The rising costs of supplies and equipment required by state agencies, and contract charges for public construction, particularly highways, placed added stress on the state's financial resources. Governor Bartlett's commitment to no new taxes imposed limitations on increasing public funds to meet rising costs. This dilemma surfaced in the legislature several times during the second half of the Bartlett administration.

The 1968 legislative session was particularly turbulent. Public schoolteachers demanded higher salaries and improved conditions for Oklahoma schools. Their statewide organization, the OEA, presented teacher demands to Governor Bartlett and the

Governor David Boren.

legislature. These included a state-supported kindergarten system, increased funds for educating handicapped children, improved library facilities, and smaller classes.

Early in the session, the legislature adopted several plans tailored to meet the teacher demands. Bartlett vetoed them because each required a tax increase to fund it. In May, 1968, the teachers, through the OEA voted professional sanctions against Oklahoma schools. Legislative leaders, in cooperation with Governor Bartlett, finally adopted a school improvement program that included a salary increase of $1,300 for each teacher, spread over a three year period.

During the 1968 session, the legislature adopted a series of laws putting into effect the judicial reform propositions. Also adopted was a bill that prohibited controversial speakers from appearing in Oklahoma, particularly on college campuses.

Campus disorders were common across the nation during the 1960s. The possibility that these eruptions of student unrest might spread to Oklahoma caused the governor and the legislature great concern. The speaker-ban statute was expected to keep agitators off the

Congressman Carl Albert, Speaker of the United States House of Representatives.

Oklahoma campuses. In 1969 the statute came under attack in the state and federal courts, and a year later Attorney General Blankenship declared the statute unenforceable because it amounted to an abridgment of free speech.

To thwart civil disorders in the state, especially on college campuses, Governor Bartlett in 1968 created the Office of Inter-Agency Coordination. Its function was to gather information on persons suspected of radical tendencies, and to make this information available to state and local law enforcement groups. The Office of Inter-Agency Coordination was attacked from several sources as an invasion of privacy. The agency and its operation became a campaign issue in the 1970 governor's race.

In 1969 and 1970 the legislature attempted to accomplish some reform in the state tax structure. The proposals for equalizing the tax burden ranged all the way from ending the tax-exempt status of Oklahoma insurance companies to requiring more equitable and realistic assessments on real estate.

Another reform proposal was to rewrite the state constitution and bring it up to date. State leaders varied in their views on how to accomplish this. One group favored calling a constitutional convention to draft a new constitution. Another group favored reforming the constitution by amendment, with the legislature directing the process. The matter of writing a new constitution was submitted to Oklahomans for a referendum vote. Also to be voted on was a proposal to authorize state officials to carry out a $70 million industrial bond issue. These issues were defeated.

As the Oklahoma political parties prepared for the 1970 gubernatorial contest, Governor Bartlett came in for considerable criticism by Democratic party leaders for what they called a lack of progressive leadership for the state. The constitutional change allowing the governor to succeed himself made it certain that Bartlett would seek reelection.

The election of 1970 was a very close contest in the governor's race. Governor Bartlett was the Republican candidate, as expected. From an intense Democratic primary, David Hall, Tulsa attorney, emerged as the party's candidate. Initial returns in the November election showed that Hall was the victor but only by a margin of 2,190 votes. Governor Bartlett requested a recount of the ballots, and the recount sustained Hall's margin of victory.

In this election, Republicans won two of Oklahoma's six congressional seats. One of the Democrats returned to Congress was Carl Albert, destined by this victory to achieve high national office. Democrats also won all the state's elective offices and a majority of seats in both houses of the state legislature.

When the United States Congress convened in January, 1971, Congressman Carl Albert was sworn in as Speaker of the House. This is the highest national office ever held by an Oklahoman. For several years Albert had served as majority floor leader of the United States House of Representatives while John McCormack of Massachusetts was speaker.

Governor Hall's first official act was to fulfill a campaign promise to abolish the controversial Office of Inter-Agency Coordination. He saw as the most pressing problem in state government the need for more revenue. A continuation of rising costs caused by the national inflation and increasing revenue needs of state operations were complicated by state income not matching agency needs. The most pressing crisis was in public education. By 1971, Oklahoma ranked forty-fifth among the fifty states in per-pupil expenditure, with only Idaho, Tennessee, Arkansas, Mississippi, and Alabama ranked lower than Oklahoma.

Governor Hall proposed a series of tax increases to raise $82.7 million in additional revenue. The legislature responded by approving increases in the oil and gas tax, the state income tax, and the liquor tax, which together would increase state income by $43 million. Public schools, higher education, and highways received most of the increased revenue.

The legislature approved the Public Kindergarten Law which had been sought by Oklahoma teachers for many years. The legislature also passed a reapportionment law to provide more effective representation in state government for the growing towns and cities of the state.

Besides providing leadership in reducing the crisis in state government finance, Governor Hall carried out an extensive industry recruitment program. State transportation resources were expanded and diversified in 1971 with the dedication of the vast Arkansas River navigation project, which provided Oklahomans a waterway barge connection between Catoosa, near Tulsa, and ports on the Gulf of Mexico.

The remainder of the decade of the 1970s was a time of modest, reluctant reform in Oklahoma politics, occasional public corruption, and a continuing pattern of split-ticket voting. Oklahomans favored Republican presidential candidates throughout the decade and, with one exception, also preferred Republican over Democratic candidates for the United States Senate. Nonetheless, Democrats maintained a five-to-one majority in congressional positions allocated to the state; they were victorious in virtually all executive and judicial elective offices; and they continued to win substantial majorities in the legislature.

In the presidential election of 1972, Richard M. Nixon carried the state and nation over the Democratic candidate, Senator George McGovern. Former Republican Governor Dewey Bartlett defeated Congressman Ed Edmondson, the Democratic candidate, for the United

Governor George Nigh.

States Senate seat held by Fred Harris, who chose not to seek reelection. Two years later David Boren, a Democratic state representative from Seminole, defeated Republican Jim Inhofe, a state senator from Tulsa, for the governorship. Republican Henry Bellmon won reelection to the United States Senate over, once again, Ed Edmondson in 1974. The State Election Board Chairman certified Bellmon the victor, but Edmondson contested the result, claiming that in Tulsa County votes were cast in violation of state law. He contended that if the challenged ballots were excluded, he would be the victor. When the State Supreme Court upheld the Election Board decision, Edmondson appealed to the United States Senate, charging that voting irregularities had deprived him of the office. During the summer of 1975, Senate officials came to the state and investigated the charges. They reported back to the United State Senate, and that body sustained Bellmon's election.

In the 1976 presidential election, former Georgia Governor Jimmy Carter, a Democrat, contested incumbent President Gerald Ford, a Republican. President Ford carried Oklahoma by 13,000 votes, the closest margin in a presidential election since Oklahoma's first presidential election in 1908, but Carter won nationally. However, Democratic congressmen continued their five-to-one majority. Carl Albert, who had served as Speaker of the United States House of Representatives for six years, retired, whereupon Congressman Tom Steed became the most important voice in Washington for Oklahoma.

In the 1978 election, George Nigh, perennial lieutenant governor, won the Democratic nomination for governor and defeated Republican Ron Shotts, an attorney and member of the Oklahoma House of Representatives. Senator Bartlett, ill with cancer, chose not to seek reelection. The Democratic candidate for this United States Senate position, Governor Boren, defeated Republican candidate Robert Kamm, former president of Oklahoma State University. Thus for the first time in six years, a Democrat represented Oklahoma in the United States Senate.

Legislative highlights during the decade of the 1970s included submitting a referendum proposal to reduce the minimum age for voters to eighteen. Oklahomans approved this proposition on December 7, 1971. During the 1972 legislative session, lawmakers adopted a statute extending collective bargaining rights to municipal employees, improved the state employee retirement system, and granted certain majority rights to eighteen-year-olds. The increased levies on oil, gas, liquor, and personal incomes enabled the legislature to appropriate a record-setting $325 million for state agencies and functions.

In 1973 the Oklahoma legislature increased the terms of county officials to four years and adopted a new death penalty law, one of the first states in the nation to do so after the United States Supreme Court voided state death penalty statutes. As state income continued to increase, the legislature set another record in appropriations to support state agencies and functions—$400 million.

The 1974 legislature began a long-needed penal reform program by appropriating funds for construction of two new prisons to relieve overcrowding. It adopted more stringent measures for reporting campaign contributions and political expenditures. This legislature investigated several state officials on charges of public corruption. The house considered a motion to impeach Governor Hall, but legislative leaders decided that the evidence did not warrant further investigation of the charges against him. This body also appropriated well over half a billion dollars to support state agencies and functions.

In 1975 the Oklahoma legislature adopted legislation which eliminated the inheritance tax between spouses, appointed a study committee to survey reorganization of the executive branch, and submitted for referendum vote a proposal to shorten the ballot. The proposition, which authorized the governor to appoint the secretary of state, labor commissioner, and chief mine inspector, was approved. The legislature placed $30 million in a reserve account, and used another $33 million to retire state bonds. It appropriated nearly $700 million to fund state agencies and functions.

Continuing investigation of alleged malfeasance in the executive branch of state government led the house to impeach Secretary of State John Rogers on charges of corruption and incompetency. The house also prepared to impeach Labor Commissioner Wilbur Wright, but legislative leaders chose to defer because Wright faced criminal charges in district court. The senate was to try Rogers on the impeachment charges voted by the house during late summer, but Rogers resigned before the senate trial convened. In 1975 a federal grand jury indicted former Governor David Hall on charges of extortion and conspiracy to commit bribery. He was charged with seeking a $50,000 bribe to influence investment of $10 million of state retirement funds in a private company. He was subsequently convicted in federal court and sentenced to a three-year term in federal prison.

The 1976 legislature improved the Teacher Retirement System; strengthened the state securities law to prevent illegitimate sales of oil and gas leases; and approved a victim restitution bill permitting judges to order criminal defendants to make monetary restitution to victims. A landmark measure approved by this legislature directed transfer of 3.5 percent of sales tax revenues, earmarked for the Welfare Department, to the state's general fund. This legislature restructured the Highway De-

Women in Oklahoma Politics. Above, left, Representative Hannah Atkins; right, Representative Cleta Detherage. Below, left, Patience Latting, mayor of Oklahoma City; right, Norma Eagleton, corporation commissioner.

partment as the Transportation Department, retaining the Highway Commission as its management board, and continued support for penal reform by authorizing additional prision expansion. Governor Boren called the legislature into special session during the summer of 1976 to write a death penalty law to replace the law adopted in 1973 recently declared unconstitutional by the United States Supreme Court.

The 1977 legislature approved measures reforming the state workman's compensation system by increasing payments to discharged workers and tightening eligibility for benefits. It adopted an open meeting law requiring public boards and agencies to publish their agendas and give twenty-four-hour advance notice of meetings. So-called "sunset" legislation required that some ten to twenty agencies be reviewed each year to determine whether or not the continued existence of each is justified. A new law changed the ad valorem assessment on new business property from an unlimited exemption to a ten-year exemption. The automobile tag licensing procedure was changed to provide for five-year tags with annual renewal stickers, issued on a staggered basis. The execution method in death penalty cases was changed from electrocution to injection with a lethal drug. The governor called a special session to permit the legislature to complete its work on seven appropriation bills.

During 1978, as a reflection of the continuing increase in state revenue, inflation, and rising costs of state government, the Oklahoma legislature appropriated over one billion dollars to fund state agencies and functions. The Equal Rights Amendment to the United States Constitution was regularly considered by the Oklahoma legislature during the decade of the 1970s, and each time that body decisively defeated the proposal.

In 1980, at the end of his second term, Senator Bellmon chose not to seek reelection. His U.S. Senate seat was sought by Democrat Andrew Coats, Oklahoma County district attorney, and Republican businessman Don Nickles. The latter triumphed. Also in the 1980 election, President Carter was defeated for reelection by Republican Ronald Reagan in Oklahoma and in the nation.

Throughout the decade of the 1970s the Democratic-dominated Oklahoma legislature sought to keep pace with the rising costs of state government, caused largely by inflation; in 1980 the legislature appropriated $1 billion, the highest in state history. Also in 1980, the national census revealed that Oklahomans had increased from 2,559,253 (according to the 1970 census) to 3,025,266, the first time for the Sooner population to exceed three million persons.

Notes on Sources, Chapter 19

Oklahoma's modern period, 1952 to the present, embraces an often tumultuous era of change in politics. The times and the changes are depicted in Samuel Kirkpatrick, David R. Morgan, and Thomas G. Kielborn, *The Oklahoma Voter: Politics, Elections, and Political Parties in the Sooner State* (Norman, 1977); Samuel Kirkpatrick and David R. Morgan, eds., *Constitutional Revision; Cases and Commentary* (Norman, 1970); Stephen Jones, *Oklahoma Politics in State and Nation* (Enid, Okla., 1974); George L. Cross, *Blacks in White Colleges: Oklahoma's Landmark Cases* (Norman, 1975); Bureau of Government Research, University of Oklahoma, *Oklahoma Votes, 1907–1962* (Norman, 1964); *Directory of the State of Oklahoma, 1961–1980* (Oklahoma City, n.d.); Milton MacKaye, "The Oklahoma Kid," *Saturday Evening Post* 231 (May 6, 1959): 36–37; Raymond Gary, "I Say Oklahoma's O.K.!" *Saturday Evening Post* 228 (July 9, 1955): 27; "Oklahoma: How Wet Is Wet?" *Newsweek* 52 (September 8, 1958): 31–32; "Oklahoma's Nugget Head," *Time* 72 (August 4, 1958): 16; and "Oklahoma: Life Begins at Thirty-seven," *Time* 81 (January 18, 1963): 20.

Chapter 20

The Evolution of Oklahoma's Economy

The ways Oklahomans earn their daily bread have undergone a revolution. Fifty years ago, most Sooner families lived on farms that were nearly self-sufficient units. Produce from gardens and orchards sustained them in season, and they canned the surplus for winter use. They butchered hogs and cattle to supply meat. Cotton, wheat, and corn were the cash crops that provided income for the simple needs of farm families. Now, improved farm technology makes it possible for one farmer to produce enough food to sustain sixty persons, and most Oklahomans live in towns and cities. Workers employed in factories, on construction jobs, and at military installations purchase their food and other consumer needs in stores.

Oklahoma, like so many other southern and western states, was for many years an economic satellite of the industrial North and East, its role that of a supplier of foodstuffs, basic raw materials, minerals, and fuels. This undue reliance on products especially sensitive to national and world markets—oil, cattle, grain, and cotton—caused instability in the state's economy, Thus nowhere in the nation was the economic collapse of 1920 after the boom of World War I more severely felt than in the Southwest. Rock-bottom prices for oil, wheat, and beef caused widespread financial ruin, unemployment, and suffering. Because the state had never fully recovered from the 1920 depression, the economic crash of 1929 did not affect Oklahomans as severely as it did other regions. Oklahoma had little respite from the economic blight and unemployment during the 1930s because of an extended drought that produced the famous "dustbowl" area, which covered portions of Kan-

Wheat threshing, Garfield County, 1910.

sas, Texas, Colorado, and New Mexico as well as Oklahoma.

The lack of job-producing industries in an economic environment where the greatest reliance was placed on agriculture, ranching, and oil finally made an impression on state leaders. Their response to this problem, along with the World War II boom, helped to revitalize the Oklahoma economy. Since 1945 the business community and state government have sought vigorously to diversify the economy by encouraging job-producing industries to locate in the Sooner State. The results have been impressive, as indicated by the fact that

Wheat threshing, Garfield County, 1980.

in 1980 nearly 300,000 Oklahomans were employed in manufacturing, compared with only 30,000 in 1929. At the same time, the annual value of manufactured goods in Oklahoma increased from $150 million in 1929 to more than $3 billion in 1980.

Despite diversification of the Sooner State economy through the establishment of factories and plants that employ the latest developments in technology, electronics, and telecommunications, many of the traditional economic enterprises still persist. These include the fur trade, lead mining, salt processing, agriculture, pecan growing, and lumbering. Another enterprise more recently renewed is that of boat building, which once was an important activity at Chouteau's shipyard on the Verdigris, where barges, pirogues, and bateaus were constructed. Heavy recreational use of the many large lakes scattered across Oklahoma has caused a pleasure and fishing boat industry to develop. With the completion of the Arkansas barge canal connecting Oklahoma City and Tulsa with the principal Gulf ports, barge and other commercial craft construction has resumed.

Since a very early time certain basic manufacturing enterprises have been in operation in the state. These included flour and feed mills, which processed the abundant grain crops harvested annually; zinc smelting, using locally produced and inexpensive natural gas to fire the furnaces; the refining of petroleum

products; meat packing; fruit and vegetable canneries; furniture plants; breweries; oil field equipment manufacturing; and glass and brick plants. These industries have continued, generally have expanded, and have been joined by new ones. Instead of playing the role of drawers of water and hewers of wood, or suppliers of basic materials to more advanced industrial centers of the East, Oklahomans now perform locally more of the steps between production of raw materials and the finished product.

Many of Oklahoma's new industries produce consumer goods in a variety ranging from clothing, gloves, footwear, carpets, and appliances, to automobiles and aircraft. Other industries reflect the national trend toward sophisticated products and research. For example, plants at Tulsa and Oklahoma City produce components for space systems and their ground support equipment. Industrial laboratories at Ponca City, Bartlesville, Tulsa, and Oklahoma City conduct research in missile fuels, metallurgy, and plastics.

In Ottawa County, Miami offers an example of another industrial project. This community has a long history of prosperous business activity with a solid farming and ranching base, and for years it was a banking and trade center for the southern portion of the rich Tri-State Mining District. As mine production faded, city leaders formed an industrial foundation to promote new industry. Their energy and

Pioneer irrigation in western Oklahoma Territory.

efforts were rewarded by the establishment of plants that today produce twenty different manufactured products, ranging from tires, tubes, clothing, and fabricated steel parts, to boats, canvas products, and appliances.

A growing outlet for Oklahoma industrial and agricultural products is foreign export. At least 350 Sooner State firms sell abroad, and this expanding activity provides a total of fifteen thousand jobs and an annual export trade valued in 1978 at $1.5 billion. Items and products exported to foreign markets include oil field equipment, fishing reels, western wear, chemical sprays, wheat, and cotton. Indeed, 40 percent of Oklahoma's wheat enters foreign commerce. Both the Oklahoma Department of Commerce and Industry and the United States Department of Commerce are active in locating new foreign markets, spurred on by such organizations as the Oklahoma City International Trade Club.

Tourism is an expanding industry worth about $1.2 billion a year to the state. Out-of-state visitors each year number approximately 30 million. The intrinsic beauty of the Sooner State and its bold contrasts in landforms and vegetation are especially appealing to those who enjoy outdoor recreation. Moreover, this natural beauty has been enhanced by the construction of several huge dams and lakes on Oklahoma's waterways. In fact, Oklahoma has more than 1,000 square miles of inland water impounded in 230 lakes. These include Lake Texoma (1,730,000 acre-feet), Lake Eufaula (2,378,000 acre-feet), and Grand Lake (1,653,000 acre-feet), each of which is larger than any body of water between the Great Lakes and the Gulf of Mexico. Oklahoma state parks rank seventh in the nation for use by campers and sportsmen, with visitors numbering 19.5 million a year. The United States Game Refuge in the Wichita Mountains attracts two million visitors, and the Chickasaw Recreation Area near Sulphur, four million.

In the Oklahoma economy, the employer providing the greatest number of jobs is government. Of the 206,000 persons in government work of some kind, 50,000 are federal employees, and about 156,000 are state and local government employees. The principal federal installations are Tinker Air Force Base and the Federal Aviation Agency at Oklahoma City. Fort Sill at Lawton, and Altus Air Force Base at Altus.

An inventory of Oklahoma's modern-day economy shows that agriculture, while not involving nearly as many people as in early times, continues as one of the state's leading enterprises. Forty percent of Oklahoma's employed are engaged in work related to agriculture, either as farmers and ranchers, or as handlers and processors of agricultural products. Some 85,000 farms and ranches are operated by 175,000 persons and produce an annual income in excess of $2 billion from a variety of crops, including wheat, cotton,

Modern irrigation in western Oklahoma.

corn, peanuts, vegetables, pecans, poultry, dairy products, and livestock. More capital is invested in Oklahoma agriculture than in any other state industry: nearly $5 billion in land and buildings.

From territorial days to the 1930s, cotton was the most important cash crop. Despite a decline in production by nearly 1 million acres between 1940 and 1954, cotton income increased from $40 million to $54 million. Since 1960 cotton production has averaged about 365,000 bales or $58 million in annual income. As recently as the 1940s more than 40,000 persons were required each fall to hand-pick the crops, compared with fewer than 7,000 pickers needed in 1964. The increased use of mechanical pickers has brought about this revolution. In recent years wheat has replaced cotton as the leading crop. Wheat production reached a record of 217 million bushels in 1979. The five-year average since 1975 has been slightly over 150 million bushels, which brings an income of about $500 million each year.

Wheat is Oklahoma's most important foreign export, with about 40 percent of the annual harvest exported.

Dairy products derived from Oklahoma herds produce income of more than $100 million, or almost twice the value of the cotton crop. Next in importance are poultry and eggs, $51 million; peanuts, $36.1 million; and pecans, approximately $3.5 million annually. For years the Sooner State was the nation's leading broomcorn producer. Corn, historically an important crop, has dropped in production to about 6 million bushels annually.

Stock raising is even more important to Oklahoma's economy than farm produce. The annual income from sheep, lambs, and wool is approximately $3.5 million; from swine, $45 million; and from cattle, 1.25 billion. The ranching tradition, dating from frontier times, is strongly entrenched in the Oklahoma economy. Because of the mechanization of agriculture, less intensive cultivation, and the application of conservation practices, more of Oklahoma's farmland has been returned to grass and livestock support crops in recent years. Currently, annual alfalfa acreage averages about 400,000 acres; forage sorghums, 500,000 acres; and bermuda grass pastures reportedly occupy more space than any single crop except wheat. In 1978 Oklahoma farms

Harvesting cotton in Oklahoma in 1925.

and ranches supported 6.5 million cattle. The Sooner State ranks second in the nation in the number of cows and calves, and the 1978 calf crop at 2.5 million was the largest on record in Oklahoma. The principal outlet is the Oklahoma City Stockyards, rated as one of the leading cattle markets in the nation.

Oklahoma State University (formerly Oklahoma A. and M. College), with its Agricultural Experiment Station headquarters at Stillwater and nineteen regional stations distributed over the state, is preeminent in the field of agricultural research. Its scientists maintain research liaison with the United States Department of Agriculture. In addition, the staff at the University of Oklahoma Biological Station on Lake Texoma near Willis conducts research on plants and animals, an activity related to agriculture and conservation.

Another important development in Oklahoma is irrigated agriculture, virtually unknown in the state until the 1930s. The erratic rainfall in western Oklahoma made irrigation desirable, but as late as 1940 fewer than five thousand acres were artifically watered. Large-scale irrigation came to Oklahoma in 1947 with the opening of the W. C. Austin project near Altus. Within three years nearly fifty thousand acres were under irrigation. In 1964 the total had increased to 340,000 acres, and in 1978 more than a million acres were irrigated, mostly from deep wells. Texas County led with 250,000 acres

irrigated, followed by Cimarron County with 145,000 acres.

Conservation has been another important development in Oklahoma agriculture. Two generations of unwise farming methods, usually the one-crop emphasis common on most early-day farms, caused an estimated one-third loss of topsoil by wind and water erosion. Because of the extended drought and resulting dustbowl tragedy of the 1930s, Oklahoma farmers and ranchers quickly adopted conservation methods promoted by private industries, agricultural college researchers, and state and federal agencies. Contour plowing; gulch control; regrassing and reforestation; and the use of cover crops; shelter belts, and strip farming have advanced the cause of conservation, reduced erosion, and restored the soil.

In 1930 there were 203,866 farms and ranches in Oklahoma, but this figure has gradually fallen to about 85,000 today. The average homestead after 1889 was 160 acres. Today, the typical Oklahoma farm covers about 400 acres, an indication of how farming has become less a way of life and more a commercial activity. Meanwhile, Oklahoma land values have increased fourfold since 1950. In 1945, Oklahoma farmland sold for an average of $31 an acre. This climbed to $52 in 1950, and to near $400 in 1978.

Historically, Oklahoma has had many tenant farmers, as late as 1945 almost half the farmers

Harvesting cotton in Oklahoma in 1980.

in the state were tenants. This is not as significant as it may seem; it can be readily explained by the nature of landholding in the part of Oklahoma where considerable property is Indian land allotted by the Dawes Act of 1887. Under the terms of this act, the allotments were restricted, and most Indians could not sell their homesteads because the titles were held in trust for them by the federal government. Indians could and did lease their allotments, a situation which accounts in large measure for the many tenant farmers. Since World War II, the number of tenant farmers has been falling steadily. Today there are only about ten thousand tenant farmers in the state. This figure represents 20 percent of the total number of farm families.

Certainly one of Oklahoma's principal sources of wealth, employment, and revenue for state government is the petroleum industry. Beginning in 1882 with crude equipment, local production was hardly worth recording, amounting to about thirty barrels of crude oil annually. The chief uses of petroleum products in those days were as medicine, as kerosene or coal oil for illuminating homes and businesses, and as grease for lubricants. Pro-

duction gradually increased to a few hundred barrels each year. The Red Fork Field, near Tulsa, was opened in 1901, and its wells produced the first commercially significant volume of oil. Wildcatters (prospector-drillers) scoured Indian Territory and Oklahoma Territory for favorable oil signs as the demand for petroleum increased. Drillers opened new fields at Coody's Bluff and Cleveland in 1904, and in 1905 the famous Glenn Pool, near Tulsa, spawned a rip-roaring boom town. On the eve of statehood, Oklahoma oil wells produced more than 40 million barrels annually.

Improved equipment and increased demand brought additional exploration or wildcatting and, by 1920, Oklahoma had become the nation's leading oil producer with a production of more than a billion barrels annually. It seems that oil is found nearly everywhere in Oklahoma, even on the state capitol grounds. There, pumps draw on a vast petroleum reservoir beneath the capitol building. Indeed, oil and gas have been found in sixty-five of Oklahoma's seventy-seven counties.

Low oil prices during the 1930s, caused by the opening of new fields and overproduction, forced the application of regional and state controls to production. The Interstate Oil Compact Commission has some regulatory power in checking excessive production, and the Oklahoma Corporation Commission directly controls local oil well output by setting a monthly quota or allowable for each well. These controls, along with depletion of some fields, has caused state production to level off at 550,000 barrels a day, or approximately 200 million barrels of crude oil a year.

One of the richest petroleum fields in the world was discovered in the heart of Oklahoma City in December, 1928. Of the 1,658 wells sunk in the Oklahoma City structure, all but 113 produced oil and gas. Since its opening, the Oklahoma City district alone has yielded more than 700 million barrels of crude oil.

Osage County, famed not only as a rich production area but also for the fabulous Osage Indian oil headrights, entered the petroleum picture in 1904 with the bringing in of wells at Avant. Osage County's wells pumped nearly one billion barrels. By 1957, the Cushing Field, discovered in 1912, had yielded 500

Herefords finishing out in a western Oklahoma feed lot.

Drilling rig opening an oil well in Major County.

million barrels from 1,830 wells. Glenn Pool, with 1,804 wells, produced more than 250 million barrels during its turbulent production history. Both the Wheeler Pool in Carter County and a field near Okmulgee were brought in during 1907. These were followed in a few years by the Hewitt, Garber, and Healdton fields. The vast Healdton Field helped Oklahoma achieve national oil leadership in 1920 by boosting the total production for the state that year to a record of one billion barrels of crude oil. It is said that the wells at Healdton furnished 50 percent of all oil for the Allied Powers in World War I. At the end of

Refining facility, Tulsa.

1957, its 2,046 wells had yielded 250 million barrels.

The Tonkawa and Three Sands fields, opened in 1921, were at the time of discovery the westernmost of Oklahoma's oil-producing districts. Nearly every year throughout the rest of the decade a new field opened. Among the major discoveries were the Sholem Alechem of southern Oklahoma in 1923 and the Saint Louis Field in Pottawatmie County in 1925. The 289 heavily flowing wells in the former yielded 200 million barrels of crude oil by 1957. The Seminole Field opened in 1926 made a record output during the 1930s. The Little River Field was discovered in 1927, followed by the Earlsboro Field in 1930. The Earlsboro Field matched the nearby Saint Louis Field in production. Fitts Field, in Pontotoc County, opened in 1933. In more recent times, the Golden Trend Field, a vast district spreading through Garvin, Grady, and McClain counties, was tapped first in 1946. Along with more recent discoveries at Ringwood and Hennessey, the Golden Trend accounts for many of the new completions recorded since the close of World War II.

Oil provides three-fourths of the nation's energy needs, and the Sooner State is a prime contributor, in 1980 ranking fifth among the states in production of crude. Oklahoma's output from Indian Territory days to the present shows a production record of 11.5 billion barrels valued at $25 billion. Income from gas liquids, crude, and natural gas amounts to more than $2 billion each year. Scattered throughout the state are 85,000 oil wells and more than 6,000 gas wells. The oil industry provides jobs for 60,000 Oklahomans. The state's fourteen refineries, with a daily capacity for handling 425,000 barrels of crude oil, employ 7,500 persons.

An important phase of the oil industry is transportation. Tank trucks, railroad tank cars, and 12,000 miles of pipeline move the daily crude production to market. That the oil business is an expanding industry is attested by sustained exploration. Drillers sank 5,200 new wells in Oklahoma in 1978, the second largest number among all the states. During 1978 drillers brought in nearly 2,000 oil wells and 786 gas wells.

Natural gas is an important element in Oklahoma's petroleum industry. Gas usually occurs in association with oil, but drillers frequently open wells yielding only natural gas. In early oil field history, operators wasted most of the natural gas to get at the more valuable crude oil. Uses of natural gas gradually developed. At first it was used principally as an illuminant; many homes and cities at the turn of the century were lighted by gas. Today natural gas is used for home heating and cooking and to fire the boilers of industry, even those producing electric power. Most of the large gas wells are in western Oklahoma and the Panhandle, but recently in eastern Oklahoma, drillers discovered a new natural gas district called the Arkoma Basin in LeFlore, Latimer, Haskell, and Pittsburg counties. Like crude oil production, natural gas production is regulated by a daily allowable of about two billion cubic feet a day.

As in the case of Oklahoma's agricultural enterprises, research and conservation are basic for the Sooner State's petroleum industry. Oil companies, agencies of state government such as the Oklahoma Geological Survey, and the federal government through the Bureau of Mines, maintain scientific staffs and laboratories in the state. Their findings provide guidance and new direction for the oil industry. For example, researchers have found that only about 35 percent of the oil in a subterranean reservoir is extracted, and further research reveals methods to increase recovery. One method is to pump water into a geological formation to force out more oil. This process, called water flooding, has rehabilitated several abandoned fields.

Another method reinjects natural gas into a formation to restore and maintain sufficient pressure to sustain oil flow. Some operators have injected carbon dioxide, which is the same gas used to carbonate soft drinks, to increase recovery. Deep drilling is another development. In Grady County some wells are deeper than 14,000 feet; and South Alex well records a depth of 17,120 feet.

In the early days much of the gas found in association with oil escaped into the air and was wasted. The Sayre gas field of Beckham County, discovered in 1922, had a life of about ten years. When the gas was near depletion in 1933, a gas company acquired subsurface rights in the area with plans to use the emptied gas reservoirs for storage. The company then purchased gas from the scattered oil wells in western Oklahoma, pumped it back into the Sayre storage reservoirs, and held the fuel for later marketing.

Mining was one of Oklahoma's earliest industries. In northeastern Oklahoma small chunks of lead ore (galena) could be found in the grass. Frontiersmen and Indians followed these mineral signs into the ground with shallow pits to mine the ore veins. The purity of this ore made it possible to smelt it over buffalo chip fires. The lead was molded into bullets, which served as an important item in frontier trade. Commercial mining got under way in the 1890s, and Ottawa County became the southern flank of the fabulous Tri-State District (southwestern Missouri, southeastern Kansas, and northeastern Oklahoma). Lead found at upper levels in the mines gradually gave way to zinc at deeper levels. Some of the Oklahoma mines had central shafts as deep as three hundred feet. From there workers followed the ore deposits laterally, and carved out huge underground galleries that today are tourist attractions. Between 1900 and 1950 more than a billion dollars worth of minerals had been extracted from Tri-State District mines, to establish this region as the world's leading producer of lead and zinc.

Heavy mining, however, has depleted the rich mineral lodes of the Tri-State District. Only marginal deposits remain, and to operate at a profit, mine owners must have some sort of subsidy assistance.

Another important extractive industry of Oklahoma has been coal mining, beginning with the Choctaw Nation pits during the 1870s and extending north of the Arkansas and Canadian into the old Creek and Cherokee nations. Here, strip mining methods were applied to uncover the coal deposits. Until recently, coal mining had gradually declined, because of the development of other power sources, notably fuel oil, gasoline, and natural gas.

The peak year for coal production before 1978 was 1948 when 3,430,152 tons were mined in 111 slope, strip, and drift mines by 2,500 miners. By 1970, Oklahoma coal mines had yielded an average of 1.5 million tons a year, produced by thirty-two companies at thirty-seven mines in ten counties. Since 1970

Coal mining, southeastern Oklahoma.

increased demand for fossil fuels has led to increased coal production from Oklahoma's mines. In 1978, state coal production had increased to 4 million tons each year. Much of the Oklahoma coal is exported to other states, particularly to Saint Louis, Missouri, where the coal's high quality helps to reduce that city's smoke problem, and to East Texas, where it is used in the production of steel. The coal-producing counties are Haskell, Craig, Rogers, Pittsburg, LeFlore, and Sequoyah. Some production is reported in Latimer, McIntosh, Muskogee, and Okmulgee counties. Coal remains one of the Sooner State's most abundant energy resources.

Additional Oklahoma mineral industries include quarrying of limestone and granite for building purposes and crushed rock for building roads and dams. Gypsum deposits are found in several locations across Oklahoma. This material is used for plaster, building board (sheetrock), and soil conditioning. In addition, cement, sand, clay for ceramics and brick manufacture, and tripoli (a soft porous rock used as a fine abrasive and in filters) are elements basic to an increasingly industrialized Oklahoma.

Another industry important to Oklahoma's modern economy is lumbering. Significantly, 13 percent of the state's industries are dependent to some degree on wood products. From eleven commercial sawmills operating in Indian Territory forests by 1889, lumbering has grown to a modern $100 million industry with 103 commercial sawmills, employing 4,500 workers. Oklahoma's largest sawmill is at Wright City, and it has the capacity to process 150,000 board feet of lumber daily. Forests in seventeen eastern counties yield timber averaging 140 million board feet a year.

The principal timber sought is softwood—shortleaf and loblolly pine—although hardwoods are also commercially important. The latter are white and red oak, bois d'arc, ash, elm, hickory, black and sweet gum, sycamore, cypress, maple, black cherry, and walnut. Red cedar is also a widely used commercial wood. Eastern Oklahoma mills turn out construction lumber, bridge timbers, fence posts, telephone poles, cooperage materials, pulpwood, fiberboard, charcoal, and furniture woods. At one time Oklahoma had 13 million acres of forest. More than 10 million acres still are classed as forest, and the timber balance is

Lead and zinc mining, northeastern Oklahoma.

highly favorable because the reforestation rate exceeds the annual harvest.

The most conspicuous feature of Oklahoma's modern economy is the substantial increase in manufacturing, which in total state business income places it ahead of agriculture and oil, long the standby of the Oklahoma economy. This diversification provides the better economic balance sought by state leaders since the close of World War II. In 1900, Oklahoma had 500 manufacturing establishments, involving 2,600 workers, with an annual value of $2.7 million. The number of workers involved in industry rose to 30,000 in 1929, with a value of $150 million. Later figures reflect the results of the industrial recruitment program after World War II: in 1952 manufacturing employed 78,000 workers, with an annual value of $493 million, and in 1978 nearly 300,000 Oklahomans held industrial jobs, and the value of manufacturing exceeded $3 billion.

State and local agencies have worked together to bring new industries into the state. Private groups, including the State Chamber of Commerce, local chambers, and civic committees, have formed industrial trusts that purchase land, provide utilities, construct buildings, and provide financing for new industries. Various state agencies carry on intensive campaigns to advertise Oklahoma's industrial potential. Every governor has been an active advocate of diversification, each

traveling extensively and making speeches, calling on industrialists, and using the prestige of his office to encourage industries to locate in Oklahoma. As mentioned in an earlier chapter, traveling industrial exhibits and businessmen's tours since 1947 regularly have called attention to the opportunities in the Sooner State. The cumulative success of these efforts is demonsrated by the fact that 1964 was the best year in state history for industrial expansion, with six thousand new jobs and nearly $300 million invested in new plants.

Another factor in diversifying Oklahoma's economy and accelerating industrialization has been available capital. During the early years, local capital was generally lacking, and any large development needed the backing of eastern financiers. Their conservative approaches toward assisting emerging enterprises in this frontier state had the effect of arresting the Sooner State's economic development. Since World War II, a number of Oklahoma groups have generated capital reserves sufficient to underwrite many local enterprises, a development that has had the effect of liberating the state from dependence on outside sources. In addition, the prosperous and solvent local environment has had the effect of attracting a heavier flow of eastern capital.

Until the 1940s, Oklahoma Gas and Electric Company and the Public Service Company supplied most of the state's industrial power

An Oklahoma tourism industry attraction, Sequoyah State Park.

needs. Both companies added steam capacity to keep up with the demands of a growing industrialism. When power from the Grand River Dam Authority became available, it was offered to industries. During World War II when the federal government operated GRDA, it furnished power to the nearby Oklahoma Ordnance Works and other war industries. After the war the GRDA acquired the steam plant at the ordnance works and offered industries a "package deal" of low-cost power, water, and process steam. During the 1950s, with the aid of the MKT Railroad, four major industries located in the ordnance works area—a chemical fertilizer plant, a carbide plant, and two paper plants, the largest single industrial increase in the state until the 1970s.

Just as vital as capital to a healthy, expanding economy is a labor force. Oklahoma has been attractive to industries seeking new homes because of its high-quality labor supply. The Sooner State labor force runs the gamut from unskilled migratory workers harvesting vegetables, fruit, cotton, and broomcorn, to highly trained electronic techniques, construction workers, industrial chemists, and space engineers.

In Oklahoma unions have played an important role in improving working conditions for the laborers. Momentum for labor reform was strong at statehood. Unions were respected, and the public generally was sympathetic with the cause of organized labor. It should be remembered that the vice-president of the Oklahoma Constitutional Convention was a prominent labor union official. Labor reforms were written into the new state constitution by the convention meeting at Guthrie in 1906. Early legislatures continued to show interest in the cause of the working man, and Oklahoma pioneered in constructive labor legislation.

Unionism in Oklahoma began in 1882 when the Knights of Labor established assemblies in the coal camps of the Choctaw Nation. Gradually the United Mine Workers took over the organization of workers in the coal fields of Indian Territory. At the same time, building trade unions were active in Oklahoma Territory, and in 1903 these organizations fused into the Twin Territories Federation of Labor. At statehood this organization became the Oklahoma Federation of Labor, an affiliate of the American Federation of Labor. The railroad brotherhoods had the largest membership both before and after statehood when railroads were the principal carriers of men and goods and were major employers.

Agitators attracted unskilled workers and tenant farmers into the Industrial Workers of the World (Wobblies) and the Working Class Union during World War I, but the radicalism of these groups caused their demise. The Committee on Industrial Organization (CIO), an adjunct of the American Federation of Labor, entered the state in the 1930s as a part of the national movement to organize the unskilled and industrial workers. Various units of the CIO seceded and maintained an independent existence until recent years when the national AFL and CIO fused. Today the official designation for organized labor in the Sooner State is the Oklahoma Federation of Labor, AFL-CIO.

Transportation is a vital component of the modern Oklahoma economy. Before statehood an extensive railroad grid of more than six thousand miles of track laced the Sooner State. For many years the Santa Fe, Rock Island, Frisco, and MKT were the principal carriers of both passengers and freight traffic. With the advent of modern highways and universal use of automobiles, most railroad business is freight hauling. Many railway companies have abandoned hundreds of miles of railroad track in the state, but the Sante Fe, Frisco, and MKT lines have actually expanded their southwestern lines recently to connect with new centers of commerce and industry.

A principal rail competitor is the automotive truck, which, as a result of the extensive highway system, can offer flexible service. Air transportation links the principal Oklahoma cities with the world. The most extensive facilities are at Tulsa and Oklahoma City, though several smaller cities maintain commercial fields. Another form of transportation is pipelines for moving oil and natural gas.

Economic development in Oklahoma has been handicapped by discriminatory freight rates set by the federal Interstate Commerce Commission. One Oklahoma editor has pointed out the inequity of transportation costs as illustrated by a new scale of motor freight rates from the eastern United States to Oklahoma. According to him,

a fifty pound key of nails, shipped from New York to Altus would carry a freight cost of $8.12. But at the same time a 100 pound keg of nails can be shipped from New York to Gallup, New Mexito, for $6.31. That fifty pound keg of nails from New York to Vinita would cost $8.12, but would move to Gallup for $7.55. Thus, it is cheaper to have the shipment routed to Gallup, then unload it on the way through Vinita, and 974 miles separate Vinita and Gallup.

Modern lumbering in southeastern Oklahoma's pine forests.

These discriminatory rates have inspired countermeasures. Private interests have turned to the federal government for help. Paradoxically, the Interstate Commerce Commission is the source of the rate handicap. In this connection, it might be well to observe that the federal government has become an increasingly common source of assistance for meeting local problems. The tendency to fall back on the government for help is a controversial question. It evokes such issues as "big centralized government" and "federal handouts," and no defense is made here for this or the opposite point of view. Nevertheless, the practice exists, and more and more it seems that a state's economic growth is in part dependent upon the power and influence that its congressmen and senators can wield in the Congress in obtaining federal projects, grants-in-aid, and contracts for public and private interests in the state.

Oklahoma has been exceedingly well represented in this regard. Former Senator Mike Monroney, with national and international interests, vigorously supported bills in Congress that would help his home state. His special

A new Oklahoma industry, aircraft manufacture.

interest was aviation. At one time he was chairman of the Senate Aviation Subcommittee, and his influence in this key post is shown by the fact that aerospace expenditures in Oklahoma during 1964 amounted to $600 million. This sum included air base expansion, operation, and payrolls; and civilian air field development, communications, services, and equipment. Monroney's long career in Washington demonstrated the influence a congressman or senator can play in bringing job-producing federal projects to the state. As a young congressman he worked with Senator Elmer Thomas to retain Tinker Air Force Base in the state, and after Monroney became a senator, he was instrumental in the choice of Oklahoma City for the Federal Aviation Authority's Aeronautical Center, which is the "civil aviation headquarters for the free world."

Oklahoma's most active and powerful advocate in Washington was Senator Robert S. Kerr. Shortly before his death on January 1, 1963, he had earned the title of "the uncrowned king of the Senate." This title came to him because of the political power he wielded in Congress from the time of his election to the United States Senate in 1948 until his death. He used this power to advance the interests of Oklahoma. One national news publication said of Kerr: "What he sought for Oklahoma— and got—is a saga of the new West. . . . A seaway through Oklahoma and space-age factories on the plains—they were part of Senator

Robert S. Kerr's plans for his state. He reached for many goals before his death."

Even while he served as governor from 1943 to 1947, Kerr carried on a one-man crusade to improve the Sooner State's position in transportation costs. It was, and still is, a simple fact that the punishing rates for goods coming into the state mean higher consumer prices, and products and goods exported from the state face unfavorable competition with areas that have low rates. Kerr's solution was to develop cheap competitive transportation on Oklahoma's waterways. As chairman of the Senate Rivers and Harbors Subcommittee, he was responsible for gaining congressional approval of a vast inland navigation project on the Arkansas River. The Arkansas Basin Project was completed in 1970, and it serves eight states and eight million people. The 500–mile–long waterway extends from the mouth of the Arkansas on the Mississippi River to Catoosa near Tulsa. Four main-stem reservoirs and seven upstream reservoirs control the river, reduce the flood threat, and store water to maintain a year-round navigation channel nine feet deep. There are eighteen locks, each 600 feet long.

The cost in federal funds for the Arkansas Basin Project was an estimated 1.2 billion. Kerr, as chairman of the Senate Rivers and Harbors Subcommittee, managed to get appropriations for his huge canal tripled in 1956, tripled again in 1960, and by 1962 the project was receiving $100 million a year. An extension of the barge canal to a point near Oklahoma City by way of the Deep Fork River will cost an additional $500 million.

Barges plying the Arkansas give Oklahoma producers direct water access to Gulf markets. The United States Geological Survey estimates that the Arkansas barge canal taps one of the nation's greatest sources of energy fuels—Oklahoma's oil, gas, and coal. Besides providing the Sooner State with a water route to the sea, it connects Oklahoma with northern and eastern cities by way of a vast 30,000–mile inland waterway lying along the Mississippi, Missouri, and Ohio rivers. At present transportation rates, the savings for Oklahoma are expected to be similar to this: steel moves from Pittsburg at a saving of ten dollars a ton; fertilizer at a saving of two dollars a ton; and newsprint at a reduction of four dollars a ton. Shippers save more than thirteen cents a bushel on wheat from Oklahoma to New Orleans, well over one dollar a ton on coal, and oil transport prices are substantially lower, too.

That a bright future is in store for the Oklahoma economy is augured in the words of Walter Prescott Webb:

> The North had a trinity of industrial resources in coke and coal, limestone, and iron ore. These ushered in the Age of Steel and gave the North its industrial supremacy. ... [The Southwest] today has a similar industrial trinity—the trinity of hydrocarbons, which are oil and gas, plus coal, sulphur, and water. This is the trinity of the Age of Chemistry. Only in the Southwest do these three elements exist in juxtaposition.

Webb predicted that with these advantages the Southwest bids fair to advance to a position of national economic supremacy.

Notes on Sources, Chapter 20

This chapter on the Oklahoma economy is drawn from various materials. The principal sources have been the business and financial sections of the *Oklahoma Journal* (Oklahoma City), the *Daily Oklahoman* (Oklahoma City), the *Oklahoma City Times*, the *Tulsa World*, and the *Tulsa Tribune*.

Two publications produced by the Bureau of Business Research of the University of Oklahoma, *Statistical Abstract of Oklahoma* and the *Oklahoma Business Bulletin* are useful for current economic trends in the Sooner State.

Annual reports of the State Department of Agriculture, the Department of Industrial Development, and the Department of Tourism and Recreation yield vital data on the Oklahoma business picture.

Also instructive on problems in the Oklahoma economy are Paul B. Sears, *Deserts on the March* (Norman, 1935; 4th ed., 1980); Don Green, *Rural Oklahoma* (Oklahoma City, 1977); Don Green, *Panhandle Pioneer: Henry C. Hitch, His Ranch, and His Family* (Norman, 1979); Max W. Ball, *This Fascinating Oil Business* (Indianapolis, 1940); W. L. Connelley, *The Oil Business as I Saw It: Half a Century with Sinclair* (Norman, 1954); Gerald Forbes, *Flush Production: The Epic of Oil in the Gulf-Southwest* (Norman, 1942); C. B. Glasscock, *Then Came Oil* (Indianapolis, 1938); Carl C. Rister, *Oil! Titan of the Southwest* (Norman, 1949); Jack T. Conn, *One Man in His Time* (Oklahoma City, 1979); Arrell M. Gibson, *Wilderness Bonanza: The Tri-State District of Missouri, Kansas, and Oklahoma* (Norman, 1972); Donovan L. Hofsommer, *Katy Northwest: The Story of a Branch Line Railroad* (Boulder, Colo., 1976).

Chapter 21

The Image of Oklahoma

What image does "Oklahoma" invoke in the minds of outsiders? For some, Oklahoma is cowboys and Indians, oil wells and boom towns, and high, wide, and handsome politics. For many it is still *The Grapes of Wrath*—worn-out, red soil, erosion-gutted cotton fields, abandoned farmsteads, and caravans of lean, hungry people seeking opportunity farther west. Others look upon Oklahoma as a nursery of athletic prowess. Beginning with the almost legendary feats of Jim Thorpe, the tradition of producing football All-Americans, highly ranked basketball teams, national wrestling champions, and big league baseball greats like Allie Reynolds, Mickey Mantle, and Johnny Bench, is well established.

All of the images have their place in Oklahoma's history; but to persons who have recently visited or settled in the state, Oklahoma is a surging, busy place of growing industry and clean, well-ordered cities, its leaders eager and willing to try the newest in science and technology.

The cowboys and Indians image is a controversial issue locally, and many state leaders would like to suppress it. They claim that it has a negative effect on promoting growth and development and that the frontier fixtures discourage industries from locating here. Champions of the cowboys and Indians image, on the other hand, maintain that state business and political leaders have been too apologetic for the state's western characteristics and that the attempt to erase this vital feature of the Oklahoma heritage could prove harmful to one of the state's key industries, that of tourism. Their position is that the increasingly heavy flow of tourists into Oklahoma reflects the appeal of this image, and they point out that

tourism provides employment for thousands of Oklahomans and ranks among the top four sources of state income. One editor declared that it is "impossible to erase [the cowboys and Indians image] unless you also do away with the great interest of visitors from around the world in seeing such attractions as the American Indian Exposition and Indian City, U.S.A., Hall of Fame for Famous American Indians, and Southern Plains Indian Museum," all at Anadarko, and the National Cowboy Hall of Fame and Western Heritage Center at Oklahoma City. Another advocate wrote that "cowboys and Indians are as much a part of Oklahoma as agriculture, oil, recreation, industry, and politics."

Oklahomans have long been indignant about the *Grapes of Wrath* image. John Steinbeck could have selected any one of a dozen other states where withering drought, erosion, devastating depression, and general ruin set in motion a great exodus of unfortunates. Nevertheless, the fact remains that the author selected Oklahoma as the setting for his best-selling novel and thereby gave the state an image it has lived down only with great difficulty.

Oklahomans are a proud people whose pride stems from frontier values of self-reliance, adaptability, and resourcefulness. Their ability to recover from the dreadful, drought-ridden 1930s and prevent another *Grapes of Wrath* is shown in many ways. Their national leadership in the conservation of soils and minerals and the formation of the Interstate Oil Compact are outstanding examples. Even more dramatic is the record of uninterrupted economic growth and diversification of industry during the past thirty years.

Although Oklahomans take unusual pride in the state's reputation for producing fine athletes, there are matters of much greater significance that lend importance to the state. One is the state's little known but exceedingly significant prehistoric heritage. Representatives of what may well be America's first human family, Clovis man and Folsom man, flourished here. When the analysis of Spiro Mound culture is completed, Oklahoma quite possibly will receive recognition as the locale for the golden age of American prehistory.

Oklahomans also can find satisfaction in that portion of their heritage between 1500 and 1907. As pointed out earlier, the Oklahoma story for this period has a variety, uniqueness, and dramatic quality that few other states can match. Again, perhaps "anomaly" is the best single word to describe the history of these four centuries, for Oklahoma has deviated from the general pattern of state evolution more than any of the other forty-nine states. Unquestionably its fascinating qualities are partly because of its many exceptions to the general pattern of state evolution.

It would not be incorrect to say that Oklahoma has not a culture but a combination of cultures. This is primarily because people came to Oklahoma from all directions, from varying circumstances, and brought with them a conglomeration of social, political, economic, and religious traditions. Constitutional government, schools, newspapers, churches, and other elements of an advanced society did not suddenly begin in 1889 with the coming of the homesteaders or in 1907 with statehood. These were already well-established in Oklahoma in the 1820s under the splendid adaptation of the Five Civilized Tribes.

Southern institutions, including slaveholding—a transplant by the Five Civilized Tribes—are a part of Oklahoma's culture. Oklahoma was a Confederate province during the Civil War, and later underwent a Reconstruction program every bit as vindictive as any experienced by the other components of the Confederacy. This partly accounts for the fact that to this day the southeastern section of the state is known as Little Dixie.

The settlement of the Plains tribes in western Oklahoma after the Civil War added to the

John Rollin Ridge, poet.

cultural complex, for unlike the Five Civilized Tribes, most of these people were at the Stone Age cultural level. Thus in comparing the post–Civil War Indian settlers with the Five Civilized Tribes, one could use the difference between night and day as an analogy.

Aside from military forces, missionaries, and traders, the first large-scale immigration of non-Indian settlers to Oklahoma after the Civil War occurred during the mining boom in the Choctaw Nation in the 1870s. Descendants of these Italian, Slav, Greek, Welsh, Polish, and Russian miners still reside in the old Choctaw Nation and increase the richness of Oklahoma's ethnic community. Add to these the scattered German Mennonite and Czech settlements, many still practicing their Old World customs and holding colorful festivals, and one can readily sense the variety of Oklahoma's cultural elements. At about the same time as the European immigration, cowboys and ranchers came into Oklahoma, as did crews of railroad workers. The greatest influx however, started with the first land rush in 1889, and continued until all the land had been taken. Vigorous, ambitious homesteaders came from all directions, from many states,

Lynn Riggs, playwright.

and from various foreign countries. Differences in customs and traditions are still evident, and only recently has any sort of cultural synthesis taken place.

Another important element of Oklahoma's population are the blacks, who make up about 7 percent of the total. Blacks were among the state's earliest settlers. Most Oklahoma blacks are descendants of slaves belonging to the Five Civilized Tribes, although there was a limited black immigration from the South to Indian Territory immediately after the Civil War. Others came to Oklahoma during the land runs, beginning in 1889.

The blending of these diverse ethnic communities has been rapid in some areas and slow in others. The most resistant groups have been those with folkways steeped in religious ordinance. Thus despite modern technological advances, one still sees the very dignified and determined continuation of old ways by such cultural communities as the Mennonites and certain Indian tribes, notably those of central and western Oklahoma.

Its cultural diversity has produced a kaleidoscope of religions in the Sooner State. The spectrum of Protestantism is represented, with the Southern Baptists and Methodists the most numerous. The Disciples of Christ, Congregationalists, Presbyterians, the Pentecostal groups, Roman and Greek Orthodox Catholics, and Episcopalians are also among the associations of believers. A reflection of the European immigration to the mining camps of the Choctaw Nation is found at Hartshorne, where one of the few Russian Orthodox churches in the entire Trans-Mississippi West is located. The Sooner State's religious scene is further enriched by the persistence of primitive Indian religions. Such historic observances as the Sun Dance and the Ghost Dance have been vital spiritual forces among the tribes of western Oklahoma, and the popular Native American (Peyote) Church is a faith recognized by state charter.

Oklahoma's cultural diversity has generated a vigorous response in the fine arts and humanities, ranging from community theaters and art galleries to writers' clubs and ballet companies. A number of towns and cities support symphony orchestras. The Oklahoma City Symphony, the Tulsa Philharmonic, and the Lawton Symphony are best known. Growth in the number of private teachers of voice, piano, and instrumental music reflects the interest of Oklahomans in providing fine arts opportunities for their youth. Music clinics also are popular among educators and young musicians. The climax of the fine arts year for the youth of Oklahoma is the world-famous Tri-State Music Festival sponsored by Phillips University and held each spring in Enid, where performers gather from all over the nation to show their talents. The fine arts departments at the University of Oklahoma, Oklahoma State University, and other state and private institutions of higher learning have departments offering instruction and courses in music, drama, and art, which provide training for the specialist as well as the general student seeking courses in appreciation.

Several towns feature annual folk plays, operas, festivals, and pageants; one drawing thousands of spectators is the Wichita Mountain Easter Pageant. In 1949 fine arts patrons at Tulsa formed the Tulsa Opera Company to produce light operettas. Four years later it attracted regional and even national interest in its presentation of *Madame Butterfly*.

In the art of ballet, one national critic declared that Oklahoma has unquestioned leadership among the states. Five of the major names in ballet are from Oklahoma and are of Indian descent. Yvonne Chouteau at the age of fourteen was the youngest American ever accepted for the Company of the Ballet Russe de Monte Carlo. She was a member of this famous group for fourteen years, and served eight years as the acclaimed ballerina. Now she is artist in residence at the University of Oklahoma. Other Oklahoma celebrities in the ballet world include Maria Tallchief, former prima ballerina and principal dancer of the New York City Ballet; Maria's sister, Marjorie Tallchief, noted for her career with the Paris Ballet Company; Rozella Hightower of Ardmore, who operates a school of ballet at Cannes, France; and Moscelyne Larkin of Miami, a soloist and later a ballerina of Ballet Russe de Monte Carlo, who at present teaches dance in Tulsa and serves as codirector of the Tulsa Civic Ballet.

Another of the performing arts becoming increasingly popular in Oklahoma is the Indian dance. It provides a modern expression of tribal lore, religious sensitivity, and aesthetic movement. With sixty-seven tribes represented in Oklahoma and many of these holding powwows during the summer and autumn months, much of the dancing has an intimate tribal association and provides a means of fellowship with other tribes. The color, rhythm, movement, and the vivid tableaux of native dancing appeals to non-Indians, too, with the result that the powwows increasingly are attended by outsiders. Annual events such as the Indian Exposition at Anadarko provide outlets for more commercial performances of the Indian dance.

From the earliest frontier days Oklahomans have shown a keen interest in the theater. Guthrie, Kingfisher, and other homesteader towns supported dramatic early-day productions. Even the roistering mining camps of the Choctaw Nation patronized crudely fashioned Shakespearean plays. This theatrical tradition continues into present times, and nearly all junior and senior high school drama classes and clubs present a round of comedy and tragedy each year. Fine arts departments at the various colleges and universities provide training for drama teachers and professional actors, and present a variety of productions for students and townspeople. Little Theater and Community Theater groups receive sustained backing in several cities.

A sign of cultural advance is a sustained, involved interest in art, and many Oklahomans have produced and collected art. In early times, the Sooner State's natural beauty and varied human groups attracted world-famous painters, among them George Catlin, John Mix Stanley, Frederic Remington, and Elbridge Ayer Burbank. In modern times, certain Oklahomans have used their wealth from oil to patronize the arts. Ernest W. Marland's early financial successes and aesthetic tastes account in part for the beauty of Ponca City and made possible his greatest gift to the state, the *Pioneer Woman* statue by Bryant Baker. Thomas Gilcrease devoted his personal fortune to collecting art treasures, including the fabulous Remington and Russell galleries at the Thomas Gilcrease Institute of American History and Art in Tulsa. The Philbrook Art Center, also at Tulsa, is in part the gift of oilman Waite Phillips, and the Woolaroc Museum near Bartlesville, represents the beneficence of Frank Phillips.

Other art collections are situated at the Oklahoma City Art Center; the National Cowboy Hall of Fame and Western Heritage Center, at Oklahoma City; the Oklahoma Museum of Art, Oklahoma City; the University of Oklahoma Art Museum at Norman; and the Saint Gregory's Art Museum, at Shawnee. The Reverend Gregory Gerrer was a pioneer artist and collector who became art director in Saint Gregory's College at Shawnee in 1908. A painter and art authority of international reputation, Father Gerrer brought together a gallery of some two hundred paintings.

The most notable development in the Oklahoma art world was the school of Indian artists developed by Oscar Jacobson at the University of Oklahoma. He encouraged the Indian students to use indigenous themes and a simple form derived from the Indians' historical style in pictorial art. Jacobson's school produced more than thirty native artists from ten different tribes. Among his famous students were five young Kiowas, Stephen Mopope, Monroe Tsa-to-ke, James Auchiah, Jack Hokeah, and

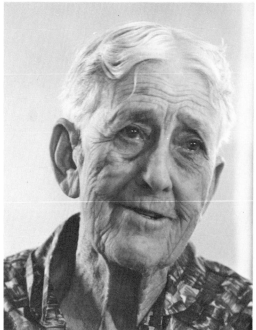

Oklahoma artist Augusta Metcalf.

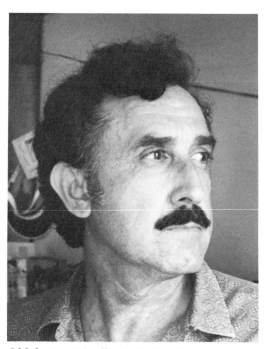

Oklahoma artist Charles Banks Wilson.

Spencer Asah, who came to the Oklahoma University campus in 1928. These and other Indian painters brought renouwn to Jacobson's school through their achievement as painters and muralists.

Other prominent Indian artists have been Acee Blue Eagle, Woodrow Crumbo, Allen Houser, Black Bear Bosin, Archie Blackowl, Jerome Tiger, and Carl Sweezy. One of the most famous of modern Indian artists is Dick West, a Cheyenne. Lee Tsa-to-ke, a Kiowa painter, also is gaining contemporary renown through his skillful use of color and adherence to traditional Indian technique and subject. Willard Stone, a Cherokee, is an exceptionally skilled sculptor in wood. In one-man shows he has attained national fame for the grace and beauty of his unique work.

Non-Indian painters of considerable reputation include John Noble, who after making the Run of 1893 into the Cherokee Outlet, studied art in Paris, Brussels, and London. *The Run* is one of his best-known works. Howell Lewis and Nellie Shepherd used the impressionistic style before 1920 to depict the latent beauty of Oklahoma's hills and prairies. In modern times, Charles Banks Wilson and Augusta

Metcalf rank as the state's most popular artists. Wilson has been honored by the United States Department of State, as well as the International Institute of Arts and Letters in Geneva. His works, mostly southwestern scenes and subjects, have been shown in more than 200 exhibitions in this country and throughout the world. He was the recipient of Oklahoma's first state-commissioned art project, for which he created four large portraits for permanent installation in the state capitol rotunda—life-size figures of Will Rogers, Sequoyah, Robert S. Kerr, and Jim Thorpe—and four huge murals depicting Oklahoma's historical evolution. The late Augusta Metcalf's appeal to the art-loving public is through her perceptive skill in interpreting life in western Oklahoma and her technique of color and attention to detail. Art works of the faculties at the major state institutions of higher learning, as well as the private institutions, are regularly exhibited in Oklahoma, the Southwest, and across the nation.

Architecture as an art form is expressed in great variety in Oklahoma. While most buildings and homes follow conventional period styles, oil fortunes during the 1920s and 1930s produced Italian and Spanish villas, French

Oklahoma architecture: Bizzell Library, University of Oklahoma.

chateaus, colonial homes, and English baronial mansions. Architectural forms in Oklahoma's new industrial and institutional structures especially reflect the influence of Frank Lloyd Wright. One of Wright's most popular designs is the Price Tower at Bartlesville. Ecclesiastical architecture in Oklahoma has shown daring, and many denominations now are departing from the traditional Gothic. The state capitol office buildings in Oklahoma City and the Center for Continuing Education complex on the campus of the University of Oklahoma are other examples of this spirit of progress and change in design.

Oklahoma's strong appreciation for its unique heritage expresses itself further in such activities as establishing museums to preserve the symbols of a colorful and dramatic past. Two in Oklahoma City are the Oklahoma Heritage Center Museum and the Oklahoma Historical Society Museum. Leading museums across the state are the Museum of the Great Plains at Lawton, Gilcrease Institute at Tulsa, Woolaroc Museum near Bartlesville, Stovall Museum at the University of Oklahoma, Black Kettle Museum at Cheyenne, Pioneer Woman Museum at Ponca City, Panhandle Museum at Goodwell, Will Rogers Memorial at Claremore, Museum of the Five Civilized Tribes at Muskogee, and Museum of the Western Prairie at Altus. A museum of national character that includes much of the life and traditions of Oklahoma is the National Cowboy Hall of Fame and Western Heritage Center at Oklahoma City. In addition, an increasing number of small but interesting museums are being developed by various historical organizations throughout the state.

Libraries are symbols of cultural advance, too, and Oklahoma has made substantial progress in developing reading resources for its people. Most towns of any size in the state have public libraries, and improvement of resources is encouraged by the State Library in Oklahoma City through its public service branch and the interest of the state librarian. Among the better-known public libraries are those at Oklahoma City and Tulsa; many smaller communities over the state are served by bookmobiles or traveling libraries.

Oklahoma has a number of famous research collections. These include the Oklahoma Historical Society Library; the Gilcrease Institute Library; the Cherokee Collection at Northeastern State University at Tahlequah; and the Choctaw Collection at Southeastern State University, Durant. The Bizzell Library of the University of Oklahoma has nearly two million volumes and is now the second largest in the Southwest. Its special research collections in the history of science; business history; the Bizzell Bible Collection; and its collections on Indian, Oklahoma, and western history rank with the best in the nation. The Oklahoma State University Library also has received special recognition in such fields as science, tech-

Oklahoma architecture: Church of St. Cecilia, Ardmore.

nology, agricultural economics, and government documents.

As indicated, Oklahoma's cultural diversity has generated a vigorous response in the fine arts and humanities, and nowhere is this more apparent than in literary effort. Writers' clubs, poetry societies, and folklore groups are active across the state, and Oklahoma has a national reputation for producing able writers. Several of Oklahoma's best-known writers have been of Indian blood. These include Alexander Posey (Creek), John Rollin Ridge (Cherokee), John Joseph Mathews (Osage), and Muriel H. Wright (Choctaw). Other prominent Oklahoma writers include Lynn Riggs, Woody Guthrie, and Will Rogers. Woody Guthrie also achieved international renown as a composer. Rigg's *Green Grow the Lilacs* was used as a basis for the well-known Broadway show *Oklahoma*. Will Rogers, Oklahoma's foremost humorist, won international acclaim as an entertainer and also achieved widespread recognition in the field of writing, notably through his autobiography and his syndicated newspaper column.

Oklahoma poets have received wide ac-claim, from the days of the Five Civilized Tribes through the work of John Rollin Ridge and Alexander Posey, to more recent times with Don Blanding, Kenneth Kaufman, and Melvin Tolson.

Publication outlets are vital for writers, and from earliest times Oklahoma authors have had local publishing facilties available. The best-known of the frontier presses was Park Hill. Samuel Austin Worcester, missionary to the Cherokees, established the community of Park Hill in the Cherokee Nation in 1837. In addition to the mission and school, he set up a printing plant, and Park Hill became famous as a center of learning throughout the West. Among other publications, Park Hill Press published the Scriptures in English and Cherokee, the *Cherokee Almanac*, textbooks, and hymnals, and established a tradition for excellence in publishing. This tradition is carried forth and greatly extended in modern times by the world-famous University of Oklahoma Press, which publishes about fifty new books each year. Its most popular books are found in the Civilization of the American Indian Series; regional history and folklore; the Western

Frontier Library Series; the American Exploration and Travel Series; and the Centers of Civilization Series.

Other Oklahoma presses include the Co-operative Publishing Company of Guthrie, which published important historical works, including George Rainey's *Cherokee Strip*; Redlands Press of Stillwater, with such titles as *Chickasaw Rancher* to its credit; and the Harlow Publishing Corporation of Oklahoma City. The Harlow imprint appears on such works as William B. Morrison's *Military Camps and Posts of Oklahoma*. More recently Harlow specialized in state history and geography textbooks and workbooks for classroom use. Western Heritage Press is Oklahoma City's most recently established book firm. The Economy Company of Oklahoma City has long published educational material for a national market.

Several magazines have been published in Oklahoma, each providing a forum for local writers. Three territorial publications were *McMasters' Oklahoma Magazine, Twin-Territories Magazine,* and *Sturm's Oklahoma Magazine*. While the content of each was largely promotional, editors devoted portions to history and lore. The best-known periodical published since statehood is *Harlow's Weekly*, a news magazine rich in political analysis and containing poetry and other works by Oklahoma writers. The principal surviving periodicals are *Chronicles of Oklahoma*, the official publication of the Oklahoma Historical Society; *Great Plains Journal; American Scene; Oklahoma Today; Oklahoma Monthly; Oklahoma Woman;* and *World Literature Today* (formerly *Books Abroad*).

During the 1960s a quickening interest was shown in Oklahoma's aesthetic heritage, and it has continued throughout the 1970s. A tangible manifestation of this was the creation in 1967 of the Oklahoma Arts and Humanities Council. This organization has a statewide outreach, with council members drawn from all walks of life, and includes both laypersons and fine arts professionals. Its purpose is to prepare an inventory of Oklahoma's aesthetic resources, generate public interest in these resources, and encourage widening participation by Oklahomans in art, literature, music,

Oklahoma architecture: Price Tower, Bartlesville.

and other humanistic activity. Oklahoma Arts and Humanities Council projects are funded from private, state, and federal sources.

It is possible that some of Oklahoma's problems, especially those reflected in its politics, are caused in part by the diversity of its ethnic groups and cultures. The viewpoints and attitudes of persons in eastern Oklahoma often differ dramatically from those of persons in western Oklahoma or from the northern and southern quadrants of the state. Thus, it is a challenge to politicians running for office on a statewide basis to know these culture zones and the mind-sets of the people in each. How-ever, these culture zones are not as sharply defined today as they were fifty years ago, or even ten years ago. The infusions of new blood and new ideas and the interactions of people in statewide social, economic, educational, and athletic activities are breaking down local distinctions. Indeed, the process of integration of the various cultures is taking place in Oklahoma at the same rapid pace as it is throughout the nation. It is likely that Oklahomans soon will have little to distinguish them from any other Americans—except geography and cultural heritage.

Notes on Sources, Chapter 21

Published material on Oklahoma's aesthetic character is limited in quantity. Books and articles yielding information on this subject include Walter S. Campbell (Stanley Vestal), *The Book Lover's Southwest: A Guide to Good Reading* (Norman, 1955); Carolyn Foreman, *Oklahoma Imprints, 1835–1937: A History of Printing in Oklahoma from Statehood* (Norman, 1936); Mary Hayes Marable and Elaine Boylan, *A Handbook of Oklahoma Writers* (Norman, 1939); N. Scott Momaday, "The Way to Rainy Mountain," *Reporter* 36 (January 26, 1967): 151–210; W. Terry, "Four Moons: Oklahoma Indian Ballerina Festival," *Saturday Review* 50 (November 18, 1967); Oscar B. Jacobson, *Kiowa Indian Art: Watercolor Paintings by Indians of Oklahoma* (Nice, France, 1929); Green Peyton, *America's Heartland: The Southwest* (Norman, 1948); W. Eugene Hollon, *The Southwest: Old and New* (New York, 1961); John W. Morris, *Ghost Towns of Oklahoma* (Norman, 1977); Angie Debo, *Footloose and Fancy Free* (Norman, 1949); Richard Ketcham, *Will Rogers: His Life and Times* (New York, 1973); and Steve Wilson, *Oklahoma Treasures and Treasure Tales* (Norman, 1976).

Bibliographical Essay

Producing an Oklahoma history is a challenging and provocative task not only because of the drama and depth of the Sooner chronicle but also because of the variety of sources available. In addition, one is impressed with the fact that the history of Oklahoma has attracted wide interest through the years and has engaged a long and distinguished list of investigators and writers. The Oklahoma histories produced thus far fall into two classes, the general history often used as a textbook in elementary and secondary schools or colleges and universities, and the "mug history." The format of the latter is distinguished from the general history in that it usually is multi-volume and in addition to a summary of state history, has the biographies and portraits of subscribers.

"Mug histories" have been produced for towns, counties, and regions of the state, as well as for the entire state. They include C. B. Douglas, *The History of Tulsa,* 3 vols. (Tulsa, 1921); W. F. Kerr and Ina Gainer, *The Story of Oklahoma City,* 3 vols. (Chicago, 1922); John D. Benedict, *History of Muskogee and Northeast Oklahoma,* 3 vols. (Chicago, 1922); Roy J. Johnson, ed., *Oklahoma History South of the Canadian,* 3 vols. (Chicago, 1925); Charles F. Barrett, *Oklahoma After Fifty Years: A History,* 4 vols. (Oklahoma City, 1940); Joseph B. Thoburn, *History of Oklahoma,* 5 vols. (Chicago, 1916); Joseph B. Thoburn and Muriel H. Wright, *Oklahoma: A History of the State and Its People,* 4 vols. (New York, 1929); and Gaston Litton, *History of Oklahoma,* 4 vols. (New York, 1957).

The first general history of Oklahoma was published at Topeka in 1890. Marion Tuttle Rock was the author of this pioneer work, entitled *Illustrated History of Oklahoma: The Land of the Fair God.* Subsequent similar publications have included Joseph B. Thoburn and Isaac M. Holcomb, *A History of Oklahoma* (San Francisco, 1908); L. J. Abbott, *History and Civics of Oklahoma* (Boston, 1910); A. Cantonwine, *Star Forty-Six: Oklahoma* (Oklahoma City, 1911); Joseph B. Thoburn and Isaac M. Holcomb, *Oklahoma History and Government* (Oklahoma City, 1914); Frank S. Wyatt and George Rainey, *Brief History of Oklahoma* (Oklahoma City, 1919); J. F. Hatcher and T. T. Montgomery, *Elementary History of Oklahoma* (Oklahoma City, 1924); James S. Buchanon and Edward E. Dale, *A History of Oklahoma* (Evanston, Ill., 1924); Muriel H. Wright, *The Story of Oklahoma* (Oklahoma City, 1929); Victory E. Harlow, *Oklahoma: Its Origins and Development* (Oklahoma City, 1934); Lerona R. Morris, *Oklahoma Yesterday, Today, Tomorrow* (Guthrie, Okla., 1930); Grant Foreman, *History of Oklahoma* (Norman, 1942); Edward E. Dale and Morris L. Wardell, *History of Oklahoma* (Englewood Cliffs, N.J., 1948); Edward E. Dale, *Oklahoma: The Story of a State* (Evanston, Ill., 1949); Edwin C. McReynolds, *Oklahoma: A History of the Sooner State* (Norman, 1954; rev. ed., 1964); Kaye Teall, *Black History in Oklahoma: A Resource Book* (Oklahoma City, 1971); Arthur L. Tolson, *The Black Oklahoman, A History: 1541–1972* (New Orleans, 1974); Muriel Wright, George Shirk, and Kenny Franks, *Mark of Heritage* (Oklahoma City, 1976); LuCelia Wise, *Oklahoma's Blending of Many Cultures: Illustrated in Oklahoma Art* (Oklahoma City, 1974); Edwin C. McReynolds, Alice Marriott, and Estelle Faulconer, *Oklahoma: The*

Story of Its Past and Present (Norman, rev. ed., 1967; 3rd ed., 1971); and H. Wayne Morgan and Anne Hodges Morgan, *Oklahoma: A Bicentennial History* (New York, 1977).

The extent and diversity of the historical literature that chronicles Oklahoma's evolution from a primitive frontier to a modern community are almost overwhelming at first glance. The most useful bibliographies and guides are Henry H. Evans, *Western Bibliographies* (San Franciso, 1957); Walter S. Campbell (Stanley Vestal), *The Book Lover's Southwest* (Norman, 1955); Jesse L. Rader, *South of Forty, From the Mississippi to the Río Grande: A Bibliography* (Norman, 1947); Ramon F. Adams, *Six-Guns and Saddle Leather: A Bibliography of Books and Pamphlets on Western Outlaws and Gunmen* (Norman, 1954; rev. enl. ed., 1969); Ramon F. Adams, *The Rampaging Herd: A Bibliography of Books and Pamphlets on Men and Events in the Cattle Industry* (Norman, 1959); Oscar O. Winther, *A Classified Bibliography of the Periodical Literature of the Trans-Mississippi West (1811–1957)* (Bloomington, Ind., 1964); Carolyn Foreman, *Oklahoma Imprints, 1835–1907; A History of Printing in Oklahoma Before Statehood* (Norman, 1936); Lester Hargrett, *A Bibliography of the Constitution and Laws of the American Indians* (Cambridge, Mass., 1947); and R. Palmer Howard, "A Historiography of the Five Civilized Tribes," *Chronicles of Oklahoma* 47 (Autumn, 1969):312–31.

Periodical literature is a rich source of information on Sooner State history. *The Reader's Guide to Periodical Literature* indexes articles in national publications pertaining to Oklahoma. During territorial times several magazines were published in Oklahoma, including *Sturm's Oklahoma Magazine, McMaster's Oklahoma Magazine,* and *Twin Territories Magazine,* which are a productive source of historical information.

Harlow's Weekly, published between 1914 and 1942, is the mother lode of information on Oklahoma politics, as well as on the social, economic, and cultural development of that period. A number of contemporary periodicals and journals are published locally and contain useful information. Selected articles from these sources enhance one's knowledge

and appreciation of Oklahoma's unique history. They include the *Chronicles of Oklahoma,* published quarterly by the Oklahoma Historical Society, Oklahoma City; the *American Scene* published quarterly by the Thomas Gilcrease Institute of American History and Art, Tulsa; *Oklahoma Today,* published quarterly by the Oklahoma State Government; the *Great Plains Journal,* published quarterly by the Museum of the Great Plains at Lawton; the *Red River Journal,* published quarterly at Southeastern State University, Durant; and the *Oklahoma Monthly.* The Oklahoma Historical Society Staff has prepared and published a *Cumulative Index for the Chronicles of Oklahoma.*

Tribal publications provide an important source of information on Oklahoma before statehood. These include the *Choctaw Intelligencer,* the *Chickasaw Intelligencer,* the *Cherokee Phoenix,* and the *Cherokee Advocate.* Files of these newspapers are found at the University of Oklahoma Library, Norman; the Oklahoma Historical Society, Oklahoma City; and the Thomas Gilcrease Institute of History and Art, Tulsa. Also, the serious student of Sooner history will find that newspapers published in the border towns during the nineteenth century, notably at Fort Smith and Van Buren, Arkansas; Neosho and Southwest City, Missouri; and Wichita, Kansas, contain interesting and vital information on Indian Territory and Oklahoma Territory affairs, and portray the evolution of the Sooner State.

Files of certain newspapers including the *Oklahoma Journal,* the *Daily Oklahoman* (Oklahoma City), the *Oklahoma City Times,* the *Tulsa World,* and the *Tulsa Tribune* provide information on contemporary affairs. The Oklahoma Historical Society has on file the accumulated files of most newspapers published in the state, and the student will find the society's card subject index useful in finding articles on specific subjects.

Special sources and guides indispensable for a full understanding of Oklahoma history include the *Annual Reports* and *Bulletins* published by the Bureau of American Ethnology; the annual *Reports of the Commissioner of Indian Affairs*; the periodicals and published annual records of missionary groups working among the Indian tribes of Oklahoma, including the *Missionary Herald;* the *Checklist of United State Public Documents, 1789–1909* (Washington, D.C., 1911), for assistance in finding published reports concerning both Indian Territory and Oklahoma Territory; and George Peter Murdock, *Ethnographic Bibliography of North America* (New Haven, Conn., 1960).

Oklahoma subjects have been popular with graduate students in the writing of theses and dissertations at Oklahoma institutions of higher learning and at colleges and universities across the nation. A catalog of theses and dissertations completed at the University of Oklahoma is available to the serious student of Sooner State history. Another helpful guide is Frederick J. Dockstader, *The American Indian in Graduate Studies* (New York, 1957), which lists all theses and dissertations completed on the subject of the American Indian, as well as the college or university library where the student may obtain a particular work on interlibrary loan. See also Vicki Dale Withers, *A Checklist of Theses and Dissertations Relating to Oklahoma History Completed at the University of Oklahoma and Oklahoma State University Through 1973* (M.A. thesis, Stillwater, 1974).

The bedrock material of Oklahoma history —the manuscripts, journals, diaries, and personal papers of prominent men and women— is scattered in libraries and archives across the nation. Many useful collections of manuscript material are in Oklahoma at the Oklahoma Historical Society, Oklahoma City, the Thomas Gilcrease Institute of American History and Art, Tulsa; and University of Oklahoma Library. Guides describing the content of pertinent collections and their locations include the Library of Congress, *National Union Catalog of Manuscript Collections,* 4 vols. (Ann Arbor, Mich. and Hamden, Conn., 1961); *Oklahoma: A Guide to Materials in the National Archives* (Norman, 1951); and Arrell M. Gibson, *A Guide to Regional Manuscript Collections* (Norman, 1960).

Oklahoma's progress in industrialization, urbanization, and general modernization is documented in the *Oklahoma Business Bulletin* and *Oklahoma's Economy,* both produced by the University of Oklahoma Bureau of Business Research. The University of Oklahoma Press has published instructive and helpful books that trace the evolution of the modern Sooner State, including *Oklahoma: A Guide to the Sooner State* (Norman, 1941); and Kent Ruth, ed., *Oklahoma: A Guide to the Sooner State* (Norman, 1957).

Walter Prescott Webb's classic *The Great Plains* (Boston, 1931), describes the climate, plants, and human adaptation to that extensive and distinctive geographic region that includes the western third of Oklahoma, and Carl F. Kraenzel provides a recent interpretation of this region in his *The Great Plains in Transition* (Norman, 1955). The variety of Oklahoma's natural environment is depicted in Charles N. Gould, *Travels Through Oklahoma* (Oklahoma City, 1928), while information on Oklahoma place geography including origins of names for counties, towns, cities, mountains, rivers, and other geographic features is found in Charles N. Gould, *Oklahoma Place Names* (Norman, 1933), and in George Shirk, *Oklahoma Place Names* (Norman, 1965; rev. ed., 1974). Indispensable to the student for map work and place location is John W. Morris, Charles R. Gains, and Edwin C. McReynolds, *Historical Atlas of Oklahoma* new ed. (Norman, 1976).

Oklahoma's rich prehistory has been the subject of extensive writing by archaeologists and anthropologists. Authoritative articles, monographs, and books on this phase of Sooner State development include David A. Barreis, "Preceramic Horizons of Northeastern Oklahoma," University of Michigan, Museum of Anthropology, *Anthropology Papers,* no. 6 (Ann Arbor, 1951); David A. Barreis, "Two New Cultures in Delaware County, Oklahoma," *Oklahoma Prehistorian* 2 (1939): 2–5; Waldo R. Wedel, *Prehistoric Man on the Great Plains* (Norman, 1961); Robert E. Bell, "Recent Archeological Research in Oklahoma, 1946–1948," *Chronicles of Oklahoma* 27 (Autumn, 1949):303–12; Robert E. Bell, "Trade Materials at Spiro Mound as Indicated by Artifacts," *American Antiquity* 12 (1943): 181–84. Henry W. Hamilton, "The Spiro Mound," *Missouri Archeologist* 14 (October, 1952), is the most extensive work in print on this famous Oklahoma archaeological discovery. Despite the title, *Archeology of Eastern United States,* ed. James B. Griffin

(Chicago, 1952), this work contains a section on Oklahoma prehistory by Kenneth G. Orr titled "Survey of Caddoan Area Archeology." See also Robert E. Bell, *Oklahoma Archaeology: An Annotated Bibliography* (Norman, 1969; 2d ed., 1978); and Arrell M. Gibson, "Prehistory of Oklahoma," *Chronicles of Oklahoma* 42 (Spring, 1965).

Vast sources are available on the subject of Oklahoma's Indian heritage. The University of Oklahoma Press alone, in its Civilization of the American Indian Series, has published more than 150 books on the various Indian tribes, many of them now resident in Oklahoma. Two basic sources of information on the tribes generally and on Oklahoma tribes specifically are Frederick W. Hodge, ed., *Handbook of American Indians North of Mexico*, 2 vols. (New York, 1959); Muriel H. Wright, *A Guide to the Indian Tribes of Oklahoma* (Norman, 1951). Angie Debo, *A History of the Indians of the United States* (Norman, 1970); U.S. Bureau of Indian Affairs, *Indians of Oklahoma* (Washington, D.C., 1965); Dale Van Every, *Disinherited: The Lost Birthright of the American Indian* (New York, 1966); Murray L. Wax, *Indian Americans: Unity and Diversity* (Englewood Cliffs, N.J., 1971); and Alvin Josephy, *The Indian Heritage of America* (New York, 1958) are useful survey works on the American Indian.

The effort by various European nations to establish colonial empires in the interior of North America, including Oklahoma, is described in the explorers' journals, traders' accounts, official reports, and government documents. Spanish *entradas* began with Coronado. His journey across western Oklahoma in search of the fabled Gran Quivira is described in Herbert E. Bolton, *Spanish Borderlands* (New Haven, Conn., 1921); Grove A. Day, *Coronado's Quest: The Discovery of the Southwestern States* (Berkeley, Calif., 1940); and *The Coronado Expedition*, ed. George P. Winship (Washington, D.C., 1896). Bolton provided additional information on Coronado in Oklahoma, including Andres do Campo's sojourn, in the very readable *Coronado: Knight of Pueblos and Plains* (New York: 1949).

Historians for years have written that De Soto's peregrinations in the lower Mississippi Valley included Oklahoma. This claim was laid to rest by publication of the definitive *Final Report of the United States De Soto Expedition Commission* (Washington, D.C., 1939), which indicated that this conquistador's party came no farther west than present Little Rock, Arkansas.

Spanish administration and use of its northern borderland, including Oklahoma, is told in Herbert E. Bolton, *Athanase de Mézières and the Louisiana-Texas Frontier,* 2 vols. (Cleveland, Ohio, 1914); Woodbury Lowery, *Spanish Settlements Within the Present Limits of the United States* (New York, 1959); and Alfred B. Thomas, ed., *Forgotten Frontiers: A Study of the Spanish Indian Policy of Don Juan Bautista de Anza, Governor of New Mexico, 1777–1787* (Norman, 1932).

The French period in Oklahoma history is documented by the scarce and out-of-print *Historical Collections of Louisiana,* 5 vols., ed. Benjamin French (New York, 1846–53). Available sources include two articles by Anna Lewis: "French Interests and Activities in Oklahoma, 1718–1719," *Chronicles of Oklahoma* 2 (September, 1924):253–68; and "La Harpe's First Expedition in Oklahoma, 1718–1719," *Chronicles of Oklahoma* 2 (December, 1924):331–49.

A master's thesis by Elizabeth Ann Harper John, "Trade and Diplomacy of the Taovayas Indians on the Northern Frontier of New Spain, 1719–1835" (University of Oklahoma, 1951), is the most detailed and informative work done thus far on the story of the French traders and their Wichita Indian mercenaries in the early economic utilization of Oklahoma resources. See also Elizabeth Ann Harper John, *Storms Brewed in Other Men's Worlds* (College Station, Texas, 1975). For information on military affairs on the Oklahoma border during French times, see Henry E. Allen, "The Parilla Expedition to the Red River in 1759," *Southwestern Historical Quarterly* 18 (July, 1939): 1–71.

Oklahoma as a component of French Louisiana came under United States jurisdiction in 1803. For nearly a quarter of a century the future Sooner State developed much like other frontier regions of the United States—government agents exploring and mapping the area, trappers and traders, the "Long Knives," the harvesting of the natural bounty, and the emerging pioneer settlements—before it was designated as the Indian Territory. One of the most informative general books on this period is Grant Foreman, *Pioneer Days in the Early Southwest* (Cleveland, Ohio, 1926). More detailed information on early explorations is found in *The Expeditions of Zebulon M. Pike*, 3 vols., ed. Elliott Coues (New York, 1895). This book contains the journal of Lieutenant James Wilkinson describing his exploration of northeast Oklahoma in 1806. A highly readable biography of Pike is W. Eugene Hollon, *The Lost Pathfinder: Zebulon Montgomery Pike* (Norman, 1949). See also *The Journals of Zebulon Montgomery Pike,* 2 vols., ed. Donald Jackson (Norman, 1966).

Accounts of the Stephen H. Long and John R. Bell expeditions on the Arkansas and Canadian rivers are found in *Early Western Travels 1748–1865*, ed. Reuben G. Thwaites, vol. 16 (Cleveland, 1905). George Sibley's reconnaissance of Oklahoma's Great Salt Plains is described in "Major Sibley's Diary," *Chronicles of Oklahoma* 5 (June, 1927):196–211. One of the most interesting early Oklahoma adventures is found in Thomas Nuttall, *A Journal of Travels into the Arkansas Territory During the Year 1819,* ed. Savoie Lottinville (Norman, 1980), vol. 66 in the extensive American Exploration and Travel Series published by the University of Oklahoma Press.

The trappers and traders in early Oklahoma are the subject of *The Journal of Jacob Fowler,* ed. Elliott Coues (New York, 1898); and Walter B. Douglas, ed., *Three Years Among the Mexicans and Indians* (Saint Louis, 1916), which chronicles the trading enterprises of General Thomas James in Oklahoma. In Max Moorhead, *Commerce of the Prairies* (Norman, 1954), the reader will find descriptions of the early efforts to blaze a trail along the Canadian River to Santa Fe. On early Oklahoma settlers articles like Grant Foreman, "Nathaniel Pryor," *Chronicles of Oklahoma* 7 (June, 1929):152–63, tell of efforts to settle Oklahoma before it was set aside as the Indian Territory. See also Albert-Alexandre de Pourtalès, *On the Western Tour with Washington Irving: The Journal and Letters of Count De Pourtalès,* ed. George F. Spaulding, trans. Seymour Feiler (Norman, 1968); and Joseph A Stout, Jr., ed., *Frontier Adventurers: American Exploration in Oklahoma* (Oklahoma City, 1976).

Muriel H. Wright, "Early Navigation and Commerce Along the Arkansas and Red Rivers in Oklahoma," *Chronicles of Oklahoma* 8 (March, 1930):65–88, explains the use made of Oklahoma waterways during these early times. See also Wayne Morris, "Auguste Pierre Chouteau: Merchant Prince at Three Forks of the Arkansas," *Chronicles of Oklahoma* 48 (Summer, 1970): 155–63.

The story of the evolution of Oklahoma as a resettlement zone for Indian tribes with the designation of Indian Territory is discussed from a legal viewpoint in Luther B. Hill, *A History of the State of Oklahoma,* vol. 1 (Chicago, 1908). Basic information on Indian culture is found in Frederick W. Hodge, ed., *Handbook of American Indians North of Mexico,* 2 vols. (New York, 1959); Clark Wissler, *The American Indian* (New York, 1938); and James Adair, *The American Indian* (Johnson City, Tenn., 1930).

Muriel H. Wright, *A Guide to the Indian Tribes of Oklahoma* (Norman, 1951), is the most informative work on the sixty-seven tribes presently resident in the Sooner State. John W. Caughey, *McGillivray of the Creeks* (Norman, 1939); Ralph Gabriel, *Elias Boudinot, Cherokee, and His America* (Norman, 1941); and Grant Foreman, *Sequoyah* (Norman, 1938), though primarily biographies of Indian leaders, are especially instructive as studies in acculturation. Accounts of white-Indian relations that produced conflict and removal to Indian Territory include Mary Elizabeth Young, *Redskins, Ruffleshirts, and Rednecks: Indian Allotments in Alabama and Mississippi, 1830–1860* (Norman, 1962); David H. Corkran, *The Cherokee Frontier: Conflict and Survival, 1740–62* (Norman, 1962); and Grant Foreman, *Indians and Pioneers* (New Haven, Conn., 1930).

Oklahoma's indigenous tribes have received the attention of the historian and anthropologist. They are described in John Joseph Mathews, *The Osages: Children of the Middle Waters* (Norman, 1961); Mildred Mayhall, *The Kiowas* (Norman, 1962; 2d ed., 1971); and Ernest Wallace and E. Adamson Hoebel, *The Comanches: Lords of the South Plains* (Norman, 1952). John Methvin wrote widely on the native peoples of western Oklahoma, including *In The Limelight or History of Anadarko* (Anadarko, Okla., 1920).

The agony of removal of the Indian tribes from their ancestral homeland in the East to Indian Territory has appealed to authors from the beginning and continues to be a popular subject for research and writing. While the Five Civilized Tribes have received the most attention in this regard, it should be borne in mind that those tribes north of the Ohio River in the Old Northwest Territory—the Delawares, the Shawnee, the Sacs, the Foxes, the Potawatomies, and the Kickapoos—received identical pressure and harassment and suffered trails of tears of their own. Three books that tell the story of the removal of the tribes from the Old Northwest Territory are Grant Foreman, *The Last Trek of the Indians* (Chicago, 1946); Annie H. Abel, *Indian Consolidation West of the Mississippi,* in the *Report of the American Historical Association for 1906* (Washington, 1906) and Muriel H. Wright, *Guide to the Indian Tribes of Oklahoma* (Norman, 1951).

James Mooney, *Myths of the Cherokees* (Washington, D.C., 1900), describes in vivid detail derived from contemporary accounts the suffering of the Cherokees. On this subject see also Thomas V. Parker, *The Cherokee Indians* (New York, 1907); Marion L. Starkey, *The Cherokee Nation* (New York, 1946); Gary E. Moulton, "Chief John Ross and Cherokee Removal Finances," *Chronicles of Oklahoma* 52 (Fall, 1974):342–59; Gary C. Stein, "Indian Removal as Seen by European Travelers in America," *Chronicles of Oklahoma* 51 (Winter, 1973–74)):399–410; C. W. West, *Fort Gibson: Gateway to the West* (Muskogee, Okla., 1974); Thurman Wilkins, *Cherokee Tragedy: The Story of the Ridge Family and of the Decimation of a People* (New York, 1970); R. Palmer Howard and Virginia E. Allen, "Stress and Death in the Settlement of Indian Territory," *Chronicles of Oklahoma* 54 (Fall, 1976):352–59; Michael Doran, "Population Statistics of Nineteenth Century Indian Territory," *Chronicles of Oklahoma* 53 (Winter, 1976–77):492–515; Arrell M. Gibson, ed., *America's Exiles: Indian Colonization in Oklahoma* (Oklahoma City, 1976); Arthur H. DeRosier, *The Removal of the Choctaw Indians* (Knoxville, Tenn., 1970); Mary Watley Clarke, *Chief Bowles and the Texas Cherokees* (Norman, 1971); Arrell M. Gibson, "America's Exiles," *Chronicles of Oklahoma* 54 (Spring, 1976):3–15; Linda Parker, "Indian Colonization in Northeastern and Central Indian Territory," *Chronicles of Oklahoma* 54 (Spring, 1976):104–29; Tom Holm, "Cherokee Colonization in Oklahoma," *Chronicles of Oklahoma* 54 (Spring, 1976):60–76; Louise Welsh, "Seminole Colonization in Oklahoma," *Chronicles of Oklahoma* 54 (Spring, 1976):77–103; Blue Clark, "Chickasaw Colonization in Oklahoma," *Chronicles of Oklahoma* 54 (Spring, 1976):44–59; H. Glenn Jordan, "Choctaw Colonization in Oklahoma," *Chronicles of Oklahoma* 54 (Spring, 1976): 16–33; Carol Hampton, "Indian Colonization in the Cherokee Outlet and Western Indian Territory," *Chronicles of Oklahoma* 54 (Spring, 1976):130–48; and William W. Savage, Jr., "Creek Colonization in Oklahoma," *Chronicles of Oklahoma* 54 (Spring, 1976): 34–43. Grant Foreman, *Indian Removal: The Emigration of the Five Civilized Tribes of Indians* (Norman, 1932); and Grant Foreman, *The Five Civilized Tribes* (Norman, 1934), provide details on the removal story for all the Five Civilized Tribes. For information on the devastating Seminole War see Charles H. Coe, *Red Patriots: The Story of the Seminoles* (Cincinnati, Ohio, 1898); John K. Mahon, *History of the Second Seminole War, 1835–1842* (Gainesville, Fla., 1974); and John Mahon, ed., *Reminiscences of the Second Seminole War* (Gainesville, Fla., 1966).

The United States treaties that relocated the Cherokees, the Choctaws, the Chickasaws, the Creeks, and the Seminoles in Oklahoma are found in Charles J. Kappler, comp. and ed., *Indian Affairs: Laws and Treaties,* 3 vols. (Washington, D.C., 1904); and Edward E. Dale and Jesse L. Rader, eds., *Readings in Oklahoma History* (Evanston, Ill., 1930). The neglect and cupidity of government removal contractors, which contributed so heavily to the high death rate on the Trail of Tears, are exposed in the published journal of Colonel Ethan Allen Hitchcock, *A Traveler in Indian Territory,* ed. Grant Foreman (Cedar Rapids, Iowa, 1930). Accounts of travel in Oklahoma during this period are found in Washington Irving, *A Tour of the Prairies,* ed. John Francis McDermott (Norman, 1956); Charles Joseph Latrobe, *The Rambler in Oklahoma,* eds.

Muriel H. Wright and George Shirk (Oklahoma City, 1955); and Brad Agnew, "The Dodge, Leavenworth Expedition of 1834," *Chronicles of Oklahoma* 53 (Fall, 1975):376–96.

A work on the removal story, interesting because of its attempt to whitewash Georgia's harassment and persecution of the Cherokees, is Wilson Lumpkin, *Removal of the Cherokee Indians from Georgia,* 2 vols. (New York, 1907).

Until 1866 virtually all of present Oklahoma was divided among the Five Civilized Tribes. The story of the political development of these quasi-independent Indian republics is told in the writings of many historians. The Five Civilized Tribes community has received definitive treatment in such works as Edwin C. McReynolds, *The Seminoles* (Norman, 1957); Grace Steele Woodward, *The Cherokees* (Norman, 1963); Angie Debo, *The Rise and Fall of the Choctaw Republic* (Norman, 1934; 2d ed., 1961); Angie Debo, *The Road to Disappearance: A History of the Creek Indians* (Norman, 1941); and Arrell M. Gibson, *The Chickasaws* (Norman, 1971). See also Grant Foreman, *A History of Oklahoma* (Norman, 1945); James H. Malone, *The Chickasaw Nation* (Louisville, Ky., 1922); Muriel H. Wright, *A Guide to the Indian Tribes of Oklahoma* (Norman, 1951); Grant Foreman, *Indian Removal: The Emigration of the Five Civilized Tribes of Indians* (Norman, 1932); and Grant Foreman, *The Five Civilized Tribes* (Norman, 1934).

The published constitutions and laws of the Five Civilized Tribes are extremely scarce and out of print. They were reproduced in *The Oklahoma Red Book,* 2 vols. (Oklahoma City, 1912). Selected portions are found also in Edward E. Dale and Jesse Rader, eds., *Readings in Oklahoma History* (Evanston, Ill., 1930).

The intellectual development of the Five Civilized Tribes in the period immediately preceding the Civil War is documented in Angie Debo, *The Rise and Fall of the Choctaw Republic* (Norman, 1934; 2d ed., 1961); Grace Steel Woodward, *The Cherokees* (Norman, 1963); Edwin C. McReynolds, *The Seminoles* (Norman, 1957); Arrell M. Gibson, *The Chickasaws* (Norman, 1971); and Angie Debo, *The Road to Disappearance: A History*

of the Creek Indians (Norman, 1941). The most famous of the educators and missionaries working among the Five Civilized Tribes was Samuel Austin Worcester. His life is reported in Althea Bass, *Cherokee Messenger: A Life of Samuel Austin Worcester* (Norman, 1936). Althea Bass, *The Story of Tullahassee* (Oklahoma City, 1960), records educational advancement among the Creeks.

Accounts by missionaries working among the Five Civilized Tribes provide candid and interesting insights into the problems of developing schools and churches on the Oklahoma frontier. These include Henry C. Benson, *Life Among the Choctaw Indians* (Cincinnati, Ohio, 1860); E. B. Cushman, *History of the Choctaw, Chickasaw, and Natchez Indians* (Greenville, Texas, 1899); O. B. Campbell, *Mission to the Cherokees* (Oklahoma City, 1973); Keith L. Bryant, "The Choctaw Nation in 1843: A Missionary View," *Chronicles of Oklahoma* 44 (Autumn, 1966): 319–21; and William G. McLoughlin, "Indian Slaveholders and Presbyterian Missionaries, 1837–1861," *Church History* 42 (December, 1973):535–51.

Work in Indian languages, translations, and publication are told in Carolyn Foreman, *Park Hill* (Muskogee, Okla., 1948); and Ralph Gabriel, *Elias Boudinot, Cherokee, and His America* (Norman, 1941). *Park Hill* records the publication program of Samuel A. Worcester at the famous Park Hill Press. Carolyn T. Foreman, *Oklahoma Imprints, 1835–1907: A History of Printing in Oklahoma Before Statehood* (Norman, 1936), brings to light the pre–Civil War publications produced on presses in the Indian nations. Lester Hargrett, *Bibliography of the Constitutions and Laws of the American Indians* (Cambridge, Mass., 1947), lists and annotates the publications of the Five Civilized Tribes, especially their constitutions and laws. See also Jack Frederick Kilpatrick and Anna Gritts, trans. and eds., *The Shadow of Sequoyah: Social Documents of the Cherokee, 1862–1964* (Norman, 1965); John Philip Reid, *A Law of Blood: The Primitive Law of the Cherokee* (New York, 1970); and Rennard Strickland, *Fire and the Spirits: Cherokee Law from Clan to Court* (Norman, 1975).

Between 1830 and 1861 the citizens of

Oklahoma's five Indian republics showed remarkable initiative and energy in changing this frontier wilderness to settled communities and prosperous farms, ranches, and plantations. The economic advancement of the Five Civilized Tribes is told in Grant Foreman, *Advancing the Frontier, 1830–1860* (Norman, 1933); and Joseph H. Thoburn and Muriel H. Wright, *Oklahoma: A History of the State and Its People*, vols. 1 and 2 (New York, 1929).

Slavery was widely practiced in Oklahoma during this period. The leading works on this institution among the Five Civilized Tribes include Annie H. Abel, *The American Indian as a Slave Holder and Secessionist* (Cleveland, Ohio, 1915); Grant Foreman, *The Five Civilized Tribes* (Norman, 1934); J. B. Davis, "Slavery in the Cherokee Nation," *Chronicles of Oklahoma* 11 (December, 1933):1056–72; and William B. Morrison, "The Choctaw Mission," *Chronicles of Oklahoma* 4 (June, 1926):166–83.

Oklahoma in the antebellum period was tied to the leading economic and political centers of the nation by an extensive system of communications. One of the most heavily traveled arteries in Indian Territory was the Texas Road. See Grant Foreman, *Down the Texas Road* (Norman, 1954), for a description of this famous north–south highway. Thousands of goldseekers crossed Oklahoma along the California Road on their way to Sacramento. Grant Foreman, *Marcy and the Gold Seekers: The Journal of Captain R. B. Marcy with an Account of the Gold Rush over the Southern Route* (Norman, 1939), documents this movement. For exploration and mapping Oklahoma, see W. Eugene Hollon, *Beyond the Cross Timbers: The Travels of Randolph B. Marcy* (Norman, 1955). Muriel H. Wright, "Early Navigation and Commerce Along the Arkansas and Red Rivers of Oklahoma," *Chronicles of Oklahoma* 8 (March, 1930): 65–88, describes commercial traffic on Indian Territory waterways; and the overland mail story is told in Roscoe Conkling, *The Butterfield Overland Mail*, 3 vols. (Glendale, Calif., 1947); and Muriel H. Wright, "The Butterfield Overland Mail One Hundred Years Ago," *Chronicles of Oklahoma* 35 (Spring, 1957): 55–69.

Extended control by the federal government over antebellum Oklahoma produced some peculiar relationships and interesting history. Leading sources on this phase of the Sooner State story include Katharine C. Turner, *Red Men Calling on the Great White Father* (Norman, 1951); Morris L. Wardell, *A Political History of the Cherokee Nation, 1838–1907* (Norman, 1938; reprint, fwd. Rennard Strickland, 1977); Grant Foreman, *Advancing the Frontier 1830–1860* (Norman, 1933); Angie Debo, *The Rise and Fall of the Choctaw Republic* (Norman, 1934; 2d ed., 1961); Grace Steele Woodward, *The Cherokees* (Norman, 1963); Edwin C. McReynolds, *The Seminoles* (Norman, 1957); and Angie Debo, *The Road to Disappearance: A History of the Creek Nation* (Norman, 1941). See also W. David Baird, *Peter Pitchlynn: Chief of the Choctaws* (Norman, 1972); Cheryl Haun Morris, "Choctaw and Chickasaw Indian Agents, 1831–1874," *Chronicles of Oklahoma* 50 (Winter, 1972):415–36; and Kenny Franks, "Political Intrigue in the Cherokee Nation," *Journal of the West* 13 (October, 1974).

Oklahoma's role as a military frontier for the United States is related in William B. Morrison, *Military Posts and Camps in Oklahoma* (Oklahoma City, 1936); Edwin C. Bearss and Arrell M. Gibson *Fort Smith, Little Gibraltar on the Arkansas* (Norman, 1969; 2d ed., 1979); R. Glisan, *Journal of Army Life* (San Francisco, 1874); Grant Foreman, *Fort Gibson* (Norman, 1936); Colonel Ethan Allen Hitchcock, *A Traveler in Indian Territory*, ed. Grant Foreman (Cedar Rapids, Iowa, 1930); and Carol Davis and LeRoy Fischer, "Dragoon Life in Indian Territory," *Chronicles of Oklahoma* 48 (Spring, 1970):2–24. For additional reading on the many military posts in Oklahoma, see *The Cumulative Index to Chronicles of Oklahoma* for articles on specific army installations.

In 1855 the federal government leased the land between the 98th and 100th meridians from the Choctaws and Chickasaws and established the Leased District, a reservation home for the tribes on Oklahoma's western border. Sources on activities in the Leased District include Walter Prescott Webb, *The Texas Rangers* (Cambridge, Mass., 1935); Muriel H. Wright, "A History of Fort Cobb," *Chronicles of Oklahoma* 34 (Spring, 1956):53–71; Nelson Lee, *Three Years Among the Comanches: The Narrative of Nelson Lee, the Texas Ranger* (Norman, 1957); Arrell M. Gibson, *The Kickapoos: Lords of the Middle Border* (Norman, 1963); and Wilbur S. Nye, "The Battle of Wichita Village," *Chronicles of Oklahoma* 15 (June, 1937):226–28.

Military historians have shown their fascination with the story of this struggle in Indian Territory by their prodigious output of articles and books on the subject. Certainly the basic source continues to be the old but unsurpassed work by Annie H. Abel, *The American Indian as a Participant in the Civil War* (Cleveland, Ohio, 1919). Also important are LeRoy Fischer, *The Civil War in Indian Territory* (Los Angeles, 1974); and Muriel H. Wright, *Civil War Sites in Oklahoma* (Oklahoma City, 1967).

Wiley Britton, a Union soldier who spent most of his military service in Indian Territory, has produced three books detailing his experiences: *The Civil War on the Border* (New York, 1899); *The Union Brigade in the Civil War* (Kansas City, Mo., 1922); and *The Aftermath of the Civil War* (Kansas City, Mo., 1924).

Accounts of military operations in Oklahoma are sprinkled throughout the volumes of *The United States Official Records: War of Rebellion*. In this documentary set most of Series One, Volume Three, is devoted to the Civil War in Oklahoma.

Biographies of leading figures of this period include Rachel C. Eaton, *John Ross and the Cherokee Indians* (Menasha, Wis., 1914); Frank Cunningham, *General Stand Watie's Confederate Indians* (Pryor, Okla., 1915). Additional information on Stand Watie, the Confederate Cherokee general, is found in Edward E. Dale and Gaston Litton, eds., *Cherokee Cavaliers: Forty Years of Cherokee History as Told in the Correspondence of the Ridge-Watie-Boudinot Family* (Norman, 1939).

A bizarre phase of the struggle in Indian Territory was its devastatingly destructive guerrilla warfare. Jay Monaghan, *Civil War on the Western Border* (Boston, 1955); and William E. Connelley, *Quantrill and the Border Wars* (Cedar Rapids, Iowa, 1910), are the leading works treating this activity.

The Civil War in Indian Territory has been the subject of many articles in the *Chronicles of Oklahoma*. These include Muriel H. Wright, "Colonel Cooper's Civil War Report on the Battle of Round Mountain, 1861," *Chronicles of Oklahoma* 27 (Summer, 1949): 187–206; LeRoy Fisher and Kenny Franks, "Confederate Victory at Chusto-Talasah," *Chronicles of Oklahoma* 49 (Winter, 1971–72):452–76; Kenny Franks, "The Implementation of the Confederate Treaties With the Five Civilized Tribes," *Chronicles of Oklahoma* 51 (Spring, 1973):21–33; and T. Paul Wilson, "Delegates of the Five Civilized Tribes to the Confederate Congress," *Chronicles of Oklahoma* 53 (Fall, 1975):353–66.

The Reconstruction formula for Oklahoma was set forth by federal commissioners at the Fort Smith Council during September, 1865. The proceedings are described in Annie H. Abel, *The American Indian Under Reconstruction* (Cleveland, Ohio, 1925); and Annie H. Abel, "The Cherokee Question," *Chronicles of Oklahoma* 2 (June, 1924):141–242. The Reconstruction treaties negotiated in 1866 by the federal government with the Five Civilized Tribes are found in Edward E. Dale and Jesse L. Rader, eds., *Readings in Oklahoma History* (Evanston, Ill., 1930). Tribal response to Reconstruction, especially vigilante action, is reported in Joseph B. Thoburn, *History of Oklahoma*, vol. 1 (Chicago, 1916). See also Ohland Morton, "Reconstruction in the Creek Nation," *Chronicles of Oklahoma* 9 (June, 1931):171–79; Hanna Warren, "Reconstruction in the Cherokee Nation," *Chronicles of Oklahoma* 45 (Spring, 1967):180–89; O. H. Platt, "Problems in the Indian Territory," *North American Review* 258 (Winter, 1973): 87–189; Thomas F. Andrews, "Freedmen in Indian Territory: A Post–Civil War Dilemma," *Journal of the West* 4 (July, 1965):367–76; and Lewis Kensall, "Reconstruction in the Choctaw Nation," *Chronicles of Oklahoma* 47 (Summer, 1969):138–53; and Norman Crockett, *Black Towns of Oklahoma* (Lawrence, Kansas, 1979).

Lawlessness in the Indian Territory after the Civil War is described in Burton Rascoe, *Belle Starr: The Bandit Queen* (New York, 1941); Benjamin A. Botkin, *Treasury of Western Folklore* (New York, 1951); and Richard A. Graves,

Oklahoma Outlaws (Oklahoma City, 1915). Isaac C. Parker, the "Hanging Judge" who presided over the federal court at Fort Smith in taming the Indian Territory, has been the subject of many books and articles. These include Glenn Shirley, *Law West of Fort Smith* (New York, 1956); Homer Croy, *He Hanged Them High* (New York, 1952); Fred H. Harrington, *Hanging Judge* (Caldwell, Idaho, 1951); S. W. Harmon, *Hell on the Border* (Fort Smith, Ark., 1898); W. F. Jones, *The Experiences of a Deputy U.S. Marshal in the Indian Territory* (Tulsa, 1937); Bailey C. Hanes, *Bill Doolin: Outlaw O.T.* (Norman, 1968); C. G. McKennon, *Iron Men: A Saga of the Deputy United States Marshals Who Rode the Indian Territory* (Garden City, N.Y., 1967); and Daniel F. Littlefield and Lonnie E. Underhill, "Negro Marshals in the Indian Territory," *Journal of Negro History* 56 (April, 1971):77–87.

The recovery of the Five Civilized Tribes from the ruin of war is told in W. P. Adair, "Indian Territory in 1878," *Chronicles of Oklahoma* 4 (September, 1926):255–74; Angie Debo, "Education in the Choctaw Country after the Civil War," *Chronicles of Oklahoma* 10 (September, 1932):383–91; R. M. Johnson, ed., *Oklahoma South of the Canadian*, vol. 1 (Chicago, 1925); Gaston Litton, *History of Oklahoma*, vol. 1 (New York, 1957); and O. B. Campbell, *Vinita, I.T., The Story of a Frontier Town of the Cherokee Nation, 1871–1907* (Oklahoma City, 1969).

The federal government relocated tribes from Kansas and other western states and territories on land taken from the Five Civilized Tribes by the Reconstruction Treaties of 1866. While many of the immigrant tribes settled peacefully on their new reservation homes in Oklahoma, some had to be subdued by military force. One of the most readable books on the pacification of the western tribes is William H. Leckie, *The Military Conquest of the Southern Plains* (Norman, 1963). Others include Donald J. Berthrong, *The Southern Cheyennes* (Norman, 1963); John H. Seger, *Early Days Among the Cheyenne and Arapaho Indians,* ed. Stanley Vestal (Norman, 1934; rev. ed. 1956; reprint, 1979); Mildred P. Mayhall, *The Kiowas* (Norman, 1962, 2d ed., 1971); Arrell M. Gibson, *The Kickapoos: Lords of the Middle Border* (Norman, 1963); Will-

iam B. Morrison, *Military Posts and Camps in Oklahoma* (Oklahoma City, 1936); Wilbur S. Nye, *Bad Medicine and Good: Tales of the Kiowas* (Norman, 1962); Wilbur S. Nye, *Carbine and Lance: The Story of Old Fort Sill* (Norman, 1937; centennial ed., 1969); Stanley Vestal, *Warpath and Council Fire* (New York, 1948); Alice Marriott, *The Ten Grandmothers* (Norman, 1945); and Ernest Wallace and E. Adamson Hoebel, *The Comanches: Lords of the South Plains* (Norman, 1970); Althea Bass, *The Arapaho Way: A Memoir of an Indian Boyhood* (New York, 1966); Donald J. Berthrong, *The Cheyenne and Arapaho Ordeal: Reservation and Agency Life in Indian Territory, 1875–1907* (Norman, 1976); Berlin B. Chapman, *The Otoes and Missouris: A Study of Indian Removal and the Legal Aftermath* (Oklahoma City, 1965); James H. Howard, *The Ponca Tribe,* Bureau of American Ethnology Bulletin no. 195 (Washington, D.C., 1965); George E. Hyde, *The Pawnee Indians* (Norman, 1974); Virginia Cole Trenholm, *The Arapahoes, Our People* (Norman, 1970); William E. Unrau, *The Kansa Indians: A History of the Wind People, 1673–1873* (Norman, 1971); C. A. Weslager, *The Delaware Indians: A History* (New Brunswick, N.J., 1972); Douglas C. Jones, *The Treaty of Medicine Lodge* (Norman, 1966); Wilbur S. Nye, *Plains Indian Raiders: The Final Phases of Warfare from the Arkansas to the Red River* (Norman, 1968); Robert C. Carriker, *Fort Supply, Indian Territory: Frontier Outpost on the Plains* (Norman, 1970); William H. Leckie, *The Buffalo Soldiers: A Narrative of the Negro Cavalry in the West* (Norman, 1967); Frank Laumer, *Massacre!* (Gainesville, Fla., 1968); Marvin Kroeker, *Great Plains Command: William B. Hazen in the Frontier West* (Norman, 1976); C. Richard King, *Marion T. Brown: Letters from Fort Sill, 1886–1887* (Austin, Tex., 1970); and Robert W. Frazer, *Forts of the West: Military Forts and Presidios and Posts Commonly Called Forts West of the Mississippi River to 1898* (Norman, 1965).

Additional sources on those tribes resettled in Oklahoma after 1865 include William T. Hagan, *The Sac and Fox Indians* (Norman, 1958); John Joseph Mathews, *The Osages: Children of the Middle Waters* (Norman, 1961); Frederick W. Hodge, ed., *Handbook of*

American Indians North of Mexico, 2 vols. (New York, 1959); Thomas Wildcat Alford, *Civilization: And the Story of the Absentee Shawnees* (Norman, 1936); and Muriel H. Wright, *A Guide to the Indian Tribes of Oklahoma* (Norman, 1951).

Two books reporting President Grant's peace policy among the tribes of Oklahoma in the post–Civil War period are Thomas C. Battey, *The Life and Adventures of a Quaker Among the Indians* (Boston, 1875; reprint, Norman, 1968); and Laurie Tatum, *Our Red Brothers* (Philadelphia, 1889). On this same subject see Martha Buntin, "The Quaker Agents," *Chronicles of Oklahoma* 10 (June, 1932):204–18.

Oklahoma's surging economic recovery following the ruin of war and Reconstruction was made possible in large measure by the extension of railroads across the Indian nations. The leading sources on railroad building in this region are V. V. Masterson, *The Katy Railroad and the Last Frontier* (Norman, 1953; reprint, 1978); Grant Foreman, *A History of Oklahoma* (Norman, 1942); Edwin C. McReynolds, *Oklahoma: A History of the Sooner State* (Norman, 1954); James L. Allhands, "Construction of the Frisco Railroad Line in Oklahoma," *Chronicles of Oklahoma* 3 (September, 1925):229–39; John D. Benedict, *History of Muskogee and Northeast Oklahoma*, 3 vols. (Chicago, 1922); Kent Ruth, ed., *Oklahoma: A Guide to the Sooner State* (Norman, 1957); J. F. Holden, "The Story of an Adventure in Railroad Building," *Chronicles of Oklahoma* 11 (March, 1933):637–66; Walter A. Johnson, "Brief History of the Missouri, Kansas-Texas Railroad Lines," *Chronicles of Oklahoma* 24 (September, 1946):340–58; Fred Floyd, "The Struggle for Railroads in the Oklahoma Panhandle," *Chronicles of Oklahoma* 54 (Winter, 1976–77):489–518; and H. Craig Miner, *The Corporation and the Indian: Tribal Sovereignty and Industrial Civilization in Indian Territory, 1865–1907* (Columbia, Mo., 1976).

Mining development in the Indian nations is described in Paul Nesbitt, "J. J. McAlester," *Chronicles of Oklahoma* 11 (June, 1933): 758–64; Frederick L. Ryan, *The Rehabilitation of Oklahoma Coal Mining Communities* (Norman, 1935); Samuel Weidman, *The*

Miami Picher Zinc-Lead District (Norman, 1932); Arrell M. Gibson, "A Social History of the Tri-State District," *Chronicles of Oklahoma* 37 (August, 1959):182–95; and Arrell M. Gibson, "Leasing of Quapaw Mineral Lands," *Chronicles of Oklahoma* 35 (October, 1957):338–47. See also Arrell M. Gibson, *Wilderness Bonanza: The Tri-State District of Missouri, Kansas, and Oklahoma* (Norman, 1972).

Although the big thrust in Oklahoma's petroleum development came after statehood, there were some pioneer efforts in the Indian Territory. These are described in S. B. Bayne, *Derricks of Destiny* (New York, 1924); Wilbur F. Cloud, *Petroleum Production* (Norman, 1937); Muriel H. Wright, "First Oklahoma Oil Was Produced in 1859," *Chronicles of Oklahoma* 4 (December, 1926):322–28; and Angie Debo, *Tulsa: From Creek Town to Oil Capital* (Norman, 1943).

One of Oklahoma's short-lived post–Civil War industries was hide hunting. The destruction of the Great Plains bison herds is told in Wayne Gard, *The Great Buffalo Hunt* (New York, 1959); James H. Cook, *Fifty Years on the Old Frontier: as Cowboy, Hunter, Guide, Scout, and Ranchman* (New Haven, Conn., 1923; reprint, Norman, 1980); Olive K. Dixon, *The Life of Billy Dixon* (Dallas, 1927); and Carl C. Rister, *The Southwestern Frontier* (Cleveland, Ohio, 1928).

Ranching, one of Oklahoma's oldest industries, continues as a leading enterprise in the Sooner State. Its development is told in Wayne Gard, *The Chisholm Trail* (Norman, 1954); Sam P. Ridings, *The Chisholm Trail* (Guthrie, Okla., 1936); Neil Johnson, *The Chickasaw Rancher* (Stillwater, Okla., 1961); Edward E. Dale, *The Range Cattle Industry: Ranching on the Great Plains from 1865 to 1925* (Norman, 1930; new ed., 1960); Edward E. Dale, *Cow Country* (Norman, 1930); and Evan G. Barnard, *A Rider in the Cherokee Strip* (Boston, 1936). Among the many relevant articles on this subject are Ralph H. Records, "Range Riding in Oklahoma," *Chronicles of Oklahoma* 20 (June, 1942):159–71; Edward E. Dale, "Cherokee Strip Live Stock Association," *Chronicles of Oklahoma* 5 (March, 1927): 58–73; Norman A. Graebner, "Cattle Ranching in Eastern Oklahoma," *Chronicles of Oklahoma* 21 (September, 1943):300–11; Arrell

M. Gibson, "The Cowboy in Indian Territory," in Charles W. Harris and Buck Rainey, eds., *The Cowboy: Six-Shooters, Songs, and Sex* (Norman, 1976); R. M. Burrill, "Establishment of Ranching on the Osage Indian Reservation," *Geographical Review* 62 (October, 1972): 542–43; Louis Maynard, *Oklahoma Panhandle: A History and Story of No-Man's Land* (Boise City, Okla., 1972); Charles Francis Colcord, *Autobiography of Charles Francis Colcord* (Tulsa, 1970); and William W. Savage, Jr., *The Cherokee Strip Live Stock Association* (Columbia, Mo., 1973).

It required ten years of Boomer promotion, agitation, and pressure before Congress relented and opened the Indian Territory to the homesteader. Boomer activity is described in Carl C. Rister, *Land Hunger: David L. Payne and the Boomers* (Norman, 1942); Hamilton S. Wicks, "The Opening of Oklahoma," *Chronicles of Oklahoma* 4 (June, 1926):129–42; Dan W. Peery, "Captain David L. Payne," *Chronicles of Oklahoma* 13 (December, 1935):438–56; Dan W. Peery, "Colonel Crocker and the Boomer Movement," *Chronicles of Oklahoma* 13 (September, 1935): 273–96; and George Rainey, *The Cherokee Strip* (Guthrie, Okla., 1933).

For the growth of Oklahoma Territory after the opening of the Unassigned Lands in 1889, see the extensive writings on this subject by Berlin B. Chapman: *The Claim of Texas to Greer County* (Oklahoma City, 1950); *Oklahoma City: From Public Land to Private Property* (Oklahoma City, 1960); *The Founding of Stillwater* (Oklahoma City, 1948); and "Dissolution of the Wichita Reservation," *Chronicles of Oklahoma* 22 (July, 1944): 192–209. Other sources on this subject include Edward E. Dale and Morris L. Wardell, *A History of Oklahoma* (New York, 1948); George Rainey, *No-Man's Land* (Norman, 1948); Emma A. Estill, "The Great Lottery," *Chronicles of Oklahoma* 9 (December, 1931):365–81. Roscoe E. Harper, "Homesteading in Northwestern Oklahoma Territory," *Chronicles of Oklahoma* 16 (September, 1938):326–36; G. E. Lemon, "Reminiscences of Pioneer Days in the Cherokee Strip," *Chronicles of Oklahoma* 22 (December, 1944):435–57; Joe B. Milan, "The Opening of the Cherokee Outlet," *Chronicles of Oklahoma* 9 (September, 1931):268–86, 454–75; Orrin U. Burright, *The Sun Rides High: Pioneering Days in Oklahoma, Kansas, and Missouri* (Wichita Falls, Tex., 1975); Irene Brown Bartel, *No Drums or Thunder* (San Antonio, Texas, 1970); Angie Debo, *Prairie City: The Story of an Amerian Community* (Staten Island, N.Y., 1944); Sidney Thiel, *The Oklahoma Land Rush* (New York, 1973); Guy P. Webb, *History of Grant County, Oklahoma, 1811 to 1970* (North Newton, Kan., 1971); Margaret Withers Teague, *History of Washington County and Surrounding Area* (Bartlesville, Okla., 1967–68); Roy P. Stewart, *Born Grown: An Oklahoma City History* (Oklahoma City, 1974); Robert E. Cunningham, *Stillwater: Where Oklahoma Began* (Stillwater, Okla., 1969); Cecil Chesser, *A History of Jackson County* (Altus, Okla., 1971); Daniel F. Littlefield, Jr., and Lonnie E. Underhill, "Black Dreams and Free Homes: The Oklahoma Territory, 1891–1894," *Phylon* 34 (December, 1973):342–57; W. Eugene Hollon, "Rushing for Land: Oklahoma, 1889," *American West* 3 (Fall, 1966):4–15; Muriel H. Wright, "Captain W. Whipple's Notebook: The Week of the Run into Oklahoma in 1889," *Chronicles of Oklahoma* 48 (Summer, 1970): 146–54; and Doug Hale, "European Immigrants in Oklahoma," *Chronicles of Oklahoma* 53 (Summer, 1975): 179–203.

The rise of political parties and the administration of Oklahoma Territory are reported in Mrs. Thompson B. Ferguson, *They Carried the Torch* (Kansas City, Mo., 1937); Dora Ann Stewart, *Government and Development of Oklahoma Territory* (Oklahoma City, 1933); Dan W. Peery, ed., "Autobiography of Governor A.J. Seay," *Chronicles of Oklahoma* 17 (March, 1939):35–47; Dan W. Peery, "George W. Steele, First Governor of the Territory of Oklahoma," *Chronicles of Oklahoma* 12 (December, 1934):383–92; and John B. Meserve, "The Governors of Oklahoma Territory," *Chronicles of Oklahoma* 20 (September, 1942):218–27. Additional information on this subject is found in John Alley, *City Beginnings in Oklahoma Territory* (Norman, 1939); Edward E. Dale and Jesse L. Rader, eds., *Readings in Oklahoma History* (Evanston, Ill., 1930); Gerald Forbes, *Guthrie: Oklahoma's First Capital* (Norman, 1938); Roy

Gittinger, *Formation of the State of Okla-homa* (Norman, 1939); Charles N. Gould, *Oklahoma Place Names* (Norman, 1933); Terry Paul Wilson, "The Demise of Populism in Oklahoma Territory," *Chronicles of Okla-homa* 43 (Autumn, 1965):265–74; and LeRoy Fischer, ed., *Territorial Governors of Okla-homa* (Oklahoma City, 1975).

Pioneer life on the Oklahoma frontier has attracted several prominent fiction writers. Two of the better-known works in fiction on Oklahoma during territorial times are Edna Ferber, *Cimarron* (New York, 1929); and the excellent *Oklahoma Run*, by Alberta Con-stant (New York, 1955).

Before Oklahoma could be admitted to the Union, the system of landholding in the Indian Territory and certain other changes had to be made. The story of these changes is told in Grant Foreman, *A History of Oklahoma* (Nor-man, 1942); Loren N. Brown, "The Dawes Commission," *Chronicles of Oklahoma* 9 (March, 1931):71–105; Loren N. Brown, "The Establishment of the Dawes Commission for Indian Territory," *Chronicles of Oklahoma* 18 (June, 1940):171–81; Robert L. Williams, "Tams Bixby," *Chronicles of Oklahoma* 19 (September, 1941):205–12; Roy Gittinger, *Formation of the State of Oklahoma* (Nor-man, 1939); Victor E. Harlow, *Oklahoma: Its Origins and Development* (Oklahoma City, 1934); and Norman A. Graebner, "The Public Land Policy of the Five Civilized Tribes," *Chronicles of Oklahoma* 23 (July, 1945): 107–18.

Proposals were made to admit the Twin Territories both as one state and as two sepa-rate states. Details of these plans for admitting Oklahoma Territory and Indian Territory to the Union are found in Amos D. Maxwell, *The Sequoyah Constitutional Convention* (Bos-ton, 1953); C. M. Allen, *The Sequoyah Move-ment* (Oklahoma City, 1925); Thomas H. Doyle, "Single Versus Double Statehood," *Chronicles of Oklahoma* 5 (March, 1927): 18–41, 117–48; and Grant Foreman, "Okla-homa and Indian Territory," *Outlook* 82 (Oc-tober 5, 1907):550–52.

The writing of the Oklahoma constitution and consummation of statehood is best told in Irvin Hurst, *The Forty-sixth Star: A History of Oklahoma's Constitutional Convention and*

Early Statehood (Oklahoma City, 1957); and Gerald Forbes, *Guthrie: Oklahoma's First Capital* (Norman, 1938). See also Albert H. Ellis, *A History of the Constitutional Con-vention of the State of Oklahoma* (Muskogee, Okla., 1923); William H. Murray, "The Consti-tutional Convention," *Chronicles of Okla-homa* 9 (June, 1931):126–38; *Journal of the Oklahoma Constitutional Convention* (Muskogee, Okla., 1907); George O. Carney, "Oklahoma's Territorial Delegates and Prog-ressivism, 1901–1907," *Chronicles of Okla-homa* 52 (Spring, 1974):38–51; James R. Wright, "The Assiduous Wedge: Woman Suf-frage and the Oklahoma Constitutional Con-vention," *Chronicles of Oklahoma* 51 (Winter, 1973–74):421–43; and Blue Clark, "Delegates to the Constitutional Convention," *Chronicles of Oklahoma* 48 (Winter, 1970–71):400–15.

No comprehensive account of Sooner State politics since statehood is available. Several political leaders have been the subjects of published biographical and autobiographical studies, and from these the reader can gain at least a piecemeal look at Oklahoma political action. These studies include Oscar P. Fowler, *The Haskell Regime: The Intimate Life of Charles Nathaniel Haskell* (Oklahoma City, 1933); Gordon Hines, *Alfalfa Bill* (Oklahoma City, 1932); William H. Murray, *The Memoirs of Governor Murray*, 3 vols. (Boston, 1945); Oscar Ameringer, *If You Don't Weaken* (New York, 1940); Edward E. Dale and James D. Morrison, *Pioneer Judge: The Life of Robert L. Williams* (Cedar Rapids, Iowa, 1954); and Keith L. Bryant, Jr., *Alfalfa Bill Murray* (Nor-man, 1968).

Additional sources containing material on early statehood politics are Frederick F. Blachly and Miriam E. Oatman, *The Govern-ment of Oklahoma* (Oklahoma City, 1924); John S. Brooks, *First Administration of Okla-homa* (Oklahoma City, 1908); *Oklahoma Almanac* (Oklahoma City, 1908); and *Direc-tory of the State of Oklahoma*, compiled and published by the State Election Board, con-taining data on national, state, and local elec-tions.

The most productive source of political information for the early statehood period is *Harlow's Weekly* (Oklahoma City). Edward E.

Dale and Jesse L. Rader, eds., *Readings in Oklahoma History* (Evanston, Ill., 1930), contains documentary material on early political administrations. See also Paul Nesbitt, "Haskell Tells of Two Conventions," *Chronicles of Oklahoma* 14 (June, 1936):189–217; and Jimmie L. Franklin, "Prohibition in Oklahoma," *Chronicles of Oklahoma* 43 (June, 1965):19–34. Franklin's article contains an excellent summary of Sooner State prohibition during the Haskell administration. See also Jimmie L. Franklin, *Born Sober: Prohibition in Oklahoma, 1907–1959* (Norman, 1971). Orben Casey, "Governor Lee Cruce and Law Enforcement, 1911–1915," *Chronicles of Oklahoma* 52 (Winter, 1974–75): 456–75, is a superb study of this enigmatic chief executive. Sherry Warrick, "Radical Labor in Oklahoma: The Working Class Union," *Chronicles of Oklahoma* 52 (Summer, 1974):180–95; Howard L. Meredith, "Agrarian Socialism and the Negro in Oklahoma, 1900–1918," *Labor History* 11 (Summer, 1970):277–84; Howard L. Meredith, "The Agrarian Reform Press in Oklahoma, 1889–1922," *Chronicles of Oklahoma* 50 (Spring, 1972):82–94, are outstanding sketches of Sooner radicalism. See also Keith L. Bryant, Jr., "Labor in Politics: The Oklahoma State Federation of Labor During the Age of Reform," *Labor History* 11 (Summer, 1970): 259–76; Keith L. Bryant, Jr., "Kate Barnard, Organized Labor, and Social Justice in Oklahoma During the Progressive Era," *Journal of Southern History* 35 (May, 1969):145–64.

Little-known aspects of Oklahoma race relations are traced in William Bittle and Gilbert Geirs, *The Longest Way Home: Chief Alfred C. Sam's Back-to-Africa Movement* (Detroit, 1964); J. A. Langley, "Chief Sam's African Movement and Race Consciousness in West Africa," *Phylon* 32 (Summer, 1971): 164–78; and R. Halliburton, *The Tulsa Race War of 1921* (San Francisco, 1975).

Biographical studies providing an intimate look at political leaders of the early statehood period are John Joseph Mathews, *Life and Death of an Oil Man: The Career of E. W. Marland* (Norman, 1951); Parker La More, *Pat Hurley, The Story of an American* (New York, 1932); Don Lohbeck, *Patrick J. Hurley* (Chicago, 1956); and Russell D. Buhite, *Pat-*rick J. Hurley and American Foreign Policy* (Ithaca, N.Y., 1973). For additional biographical information on Oklahoma leaders of this period see C. B. Douglas, *The History of Tulsa*, 3 vols. (Tulsa, 1921); W. F. Kerr and Ina Gainer, *The Story of Oklahoma City*, 3 vols. (Chicago, 1922); Joseph B. Thoburn and Muriel H. Wright, *Oklahoma: A History of the State and Its People*, 4 vols. (New York, 1929); Rex Harlow, *Successful Oklahomans* (Oklahoma City, 1927); and Lyle H. Boren, *Who Is Who in Oklahoma* (Guthrie, Okla., 1935). See also Gordon Hines, *Alfalfa Bill* (Oklahoma City, 1932); William H. Murray, *Memoirs of Governor Murray*, 3 vols. (Boston, 1945); and Francis W. Schruben, "The Return of Alfalfa Bill Murray," *Chronicles of Oklahoma* 41 (June, 1963):38–65.

Reactions to Klan activities during the 1920s are described in Ernest T. Bynum, *Personal Recollections of Ex-Governor Walton* (Oklahoma City, 1924); Marion Monteval, *The Klan Inside Out* (Claremore, Okla., 1924); and Howard A. Tucker, *History of Governor Walton's War on the Ku Klux Klan, the Invisible Empire* (Oklahoma City, 1923).

Additional sources on Oklahoma government and politics for this period are Brookings Institution, *Report on a Survey of the Organization and Administration of Oklahoma* (Oklahoma City, 1935); Robert K. Carr, *State Control of Local Finance in Oklahoma* (Norman, 1937); *The Oklahoma Almanac* (Oklahoma City, 1930); *Harlow's Weekly* (Oklahoma City); *The Directory of the State of Oklahoma, 1925–1941* (Oklahoma City); Horace C. Peterson and Gilbert C. Fite, *Opponents of War, 1917–1918* (Madison, Wis., 1957); Gilbert C. Fite, "The Nonpartisan League in Oklahoma," *Chronicles of Oklahoma* 24 (July, 1946):146–57; Rudia Halliburton, Jr., "Statewide Legislation Banning Teaching of Evolution," *Proceedings of the Oklahoma Academy of Science* 43 (1962): 190–98; Rudia Halliburton, Jr., "The Nation's First Anti-Darwin Law: Passage and Repeal," *Southwestern Social Science Quarterly*, 41 (1960):125–29. See also Garin Burbank, *When Farmers Voted Red: The Gospel of Socialism in the Oklahoma Countryside, 1910–1924* (Greenwood, Conn., 1976); Edda Bilger, "The 'Oklahoma Vorwarts': The Voice of German

Americans in Oklahoma During World War I," *Chronicles of Oklahoma* 54 (Summer, 1976):245–60; and Ed Gill, *Oklahoma in the 1920's* (Muskogee, Okla., 1974).

One of the most candid and provocative studies on Oklahoma politics during the 1930s and 1940s is Walter M. Harrison's autobiography, *Me and My Big Mouth* (Oklahoma City, 1954). Additional sources include W. Eugene Hollon, *The Southwest: Old and New* (New York, 1961); H. O. Waldby, *The Patronage System in Oklahoma* (Norman, 1950); Kent Ruth, ed., *Oklahoma: A Guide to the Sooner State* (Norman, 1954); Ross D. Pugmire, *Oklahoma's Children and Their Schools* (Oklahoma City, 1950); H. V. Thornton, *Oklahoma Constitutional Studies* (Guthrie, Okla., 1950); *Directory of the State of Oklahoma, 1961* (Oklahoma City); Walter J. Stein, *California and the Dust Bowl Migration* (Westport, Conn., 1973); Jacqueline G. Sherman, *The Oklahomans in California During the Depression Decade, 1931–1941* (M.A. thesis, University of California, 1970, photocopy, University Microfilms, 1975); and James Ware, "The Sooner NRA: New Deal Recovery in Oklahoma," *Chronicles of Oklahoma* 54 (Fall, 1976):339–51.

In addition to files of the *Oklahoma Journal* (Oklahoma City), *Daily Oklahoman* (Oklahoma City, *Oklahoma City Times, Tulsa Tribune*, and *Tulsa World*, articles on Oklahoma politics during the middle period occur as follows: "Open House in Oklahoma," *Life* 36 (March 26, 1954):181; Johnston Murray, "Oklahoma Is in a Mess," *Saturday Evening Post* 228 (April 30, 1955):20–21; Irving Dillard, "Oklahoma Makes Ready for 1944," *New Republic* 109 (August 9, 1943):194; Robert T. Elson, "If Not Truman, Who?" *Life* 32 (March 24, 1952):118–33; and Marquis W. Childs, "The Big Boom from Oklahoma," *Saturday Evening Post* 221 (April 9, 1949):118–20.

Sources are scarce for the modern period in Oklahoma politics. Race relations occupied center stage for several years, and material on ethnic ferment in the Sooner State is found in Albert Blaustein and Clyde Ferguson, *Desegregation and the Law* (New Brunswick, N.J., 1957); Dan Wakefield, *Revolt in the South* (New York, 1960); Robert P. Warren, *Segregation: The Inner Conflict in the South* (New

York, 1956); Arrell M. Gibson, *The West in the Life of the Nation* (Lexington, Mass., 1976); Gerald D. Nash, *The American West in the Twentieth Century; A Short History of an Urban Oasis* (Englewood Cliffs, N.J., 1973); Cheryl H. Morris, *The Cutting Edge: The Life of John Rogers* (Norman, 1977); Anne Hodges Morgan, *Robert S. Kerr: The Senate Years* (Norman, 1977); Samuel Kirkpatrick, David R. Morgan, and Thomas G. Kielhorn, *The Oklahoma Voter: Politics, Elections, and Political Parties in the Sooner State* (Norman, 1977); David R. Morgan and Samuel Kirkpatrick, eds., *Constitutional Revision: Cases and Commentary* (Norman, 1970); Stephen Jones, *Oklahoma Politics in State and Nation* (Enid, Okla., 1974); David R. Morgan, *Suburban Political Leadership: Profile and Recruitment* (Oklahoma City, 1968); George Lynn Cross, *Blacks in White Colleges: Oklahoma's Landmark Cases* (Norman, 1975); J. T. Hubbell, "Desegregation of the University of Oklahoma, 1946-1950," *Journal of Negro History* 57 (October, 1972):370–84; and J. T. Hubbell, "Some Reactions to the Desegregation of the University of Oklahoma, 1946–1950," *Phylon* 34 (June, 1973):187–96.

Primary reliance for information on Oklahoma politics during the 1960s and 1970s must be on newspaper and periodical files, especially the *Oklahoma Journal* (Oklahoma City), *Daily Oklahoman* (Oklahoma City), *Oklahoma City Times, Tulsa World*, and *Tulsa Tribune*. See also Bureau of Government Research, University of Oklahoma, *Oklahoma Votes, 1907–1962* (Norman, 1964); and, by the same agency, the quarterly *Government Department Newsletter: The Directory of the State of Oklahoma, 1961–1963* (Oklahoma City), which contains election data. National magazine articles concerning Oklahoma politics include Milton MacKaye, "The Oklahoma Kid," *Saturday Evening Post* 231 (May 16, 1959):36–37; Raymond Gary, "I Say Oklahoma's O.K.!" *Saturday Evening Post* 228 (July 9, 1955):27; and Raymond Gary, "The South Can Integrate Its Schools," *Look Magazine* 23 (March 31, 1959):19–21; "Oklahoma: How Wet Is Wet?" *Newsweek* 52 (September 8, 1958):31–32; "Oklahoma's Nugget Head," *Time* 72 (August 4, 1958):16; and "Oklahoma: Life Begins at

Thirty-Seven," *Time* 81 (January 18, 1963): 20.

The most productive sources for information on the Sooner State economy are the business and financial sections of the *Oklahoma Journal, Daily Oklahoman, Tulsa World*, and *Tulsa Tribune*. The writings of Gilbert Hill, business analyst for the *Daily Oklahoman*, are especially instructive. Additional sources include publications of the Bureau of Business Research, University of Oklahoma, *Statistical Abstract of Oklahoma* (Norman, 1957), and *The Oklahoma Business Bulletin*, published monthly.

The bulletins and special reports issued by Oklahoma State University contain information on the role of farming and ranching in the Oklahoma economy. On this subject see also Paul B. Sears, *Deserts on the March* (Norman, 1935; 4th ed., 1980). For works on business and professional leadership, see Clifford Earl Trafzer, *The Judge: The Life of Robert A. Hefner* (Norman, 1975); Mathew P. Bonnifield, *Oklahoma Innovator: The Life of Virgil Browne* (Norman, 1976); Dave R. McKown, *The Dean: The Life of Julien C. Monnet* (Norman, 1973); Mark Reuben Everett, *Medical Education in Oklahoma; The University of Oklahoma School of Medicine and Medical Center, 1900–1931* (Norman, 1972).

Oklahoma's oil industry has attracted more literary attention than any other enterprise. The leading works are Max W. Ball, *This Fascinating Oil Business* (Indianapolis, Ind., 1940); W. L. Connelly, *The Oil Business as I Saw It* (Norman, 1954); Gerald Forbes, *Flush Production: The Epic of Oil in the Gulf-Southwest* (Norman, 1942); C. B. Glasscock, *Then Came Oil* (Indianapolis, Ind., 1938); and Carl C. Rister, *Oil! Titan of the Southwest* (Norman, 1949). On mining see Arrell M. Gibson, *Wilderness Bonanza: The Tri-State District of Missouri, Kansas, and Oklahoma* (Norman, 1972).

Interpretive works on the Southwest and Oklahoma include Angie Debo, *Oklahoma: Footloose and Fancy-Free* (Norman, 1949); Green Peyton, *America's Heartland: The Southwest* (Norman, 1948); W. Eugene Hollon, *The Southwest: Old and New* (New York, 1961); Steve Wilson, *Oklahoma Treasures and Treasure Tales* (Norman, 1976); James M. Smallwood, ed., *And Gladly Teach: Reminiscences of Teachers, Frontier Dugout to Modern Module* (Norman, 1976); Mike McCarville, *OKIE* (Oklahoma City, 1970); Richard Ketcham, *Will Rogers: His Life and Times* (New York, 1973); Kent Ruth, *Oklahoma Travel Handbook* (Norman, 1977); and Ballard M. Barker and William Carl Jameson, *Platt National Park: Environment and Ecology* (Norman, 1975).

On the fine arts in Oklahoma see Oscar B. Jacobson, *Kiowa Indian Art: Watercolor Paintings by Indians of Oklahoma* (Nice, France, 1929); *The American Scene*, a quarterly published by the Thomas Gilcrease Institute of American History and Art, Tulsa; and *Oklahoma Today*, published quarterly by the Oklahoma State Government.

Sources on literature in Oklahoma include Walter S. Campbell (Stanley Vestal), *The Book Lover's Southwest: A Guide to Good Reading* (Norman, 1955); Carolyn Foreman, *Oklahoma Imprints, 1835–1907: A History of Printing in Oklahoma Before Statehood* (Norman, 1936); Mary Hayes Marable and Elaine Boylan, *A Handbook of Oklahoma Writers* (Norman, 1939); Scott Momaday, "The Way to Rainy Mountain," *Reporter* 36 (January 26, 1967):151–210; and W. Terry, "Four Moons; Oklahoma Indian Ballerina Festival," *Saturday Review* 50 (November 18, 1967).

Index